D0888041

CORNELIUS VAN TIL

FOUNDATIONS

OF

CHRISTIAN SCHOLARSHIP

Essays in the Van Til Perspective

Edited by
Gary North

A CHALCEDON STUDY

ROSS HOUSE BOOKS
P.O. Box 67
Vallecito, California 95251

Library of Congress Control Number: 2001117450
ISBN: 1-879998-25-4

Printed in the United States of America

TABLE OF CONTENTS

PREFACE

Chalcedon, Inc., a non-profit educational foundation, is the sponsor of this volume. The goal of the editor and of all the contributors is the spread of the Christian gospel into all realms of life, including the academic. Those readers who find the approach of the book intriguing can contact any of the authors through Chalcedon. If readers should detect errors, omissions, or other facts that should be brought to the attention of the authors, they should contact Chalcedon or the individual author of the essay in question. We hope to revise this study over the years, as Christian scholarship increases our knowledge of God's creation. We would like to be able to include additional chapters dealing with other academic disciplines: literature, archeology, physics, chemistry, anthropology, art, music, and so forth. Scholars who share Van Til's presuppositional approach and who have a chapter which might fit into a new edition of this volume should contact Chalcedon. Furthermore, those interested in receiving additional information about the various programs of Chalcedon, including publications, educational tapes, seminars, and the monthly free newsletter, *Chalcedon Report*, should write to:

CHALCEDON
P.O. Box 158
Vallecito, CA 95251

According to the principle of Protestantism, man's consciousness of self and of objects presuppose for their intelligibility the consciousness of God. In asserting this, we are not thinking of psychological and temporal priority. We are thinking only of the question as to what is the final reference point in interpretation. The Protestant principle finds this in the self-contained ontological Trinity. By His counsel the triune God controls whatsoever comes to pass. If then human consciousness must, in the nature of the case, always be the proximate starting-point, it remains true that God is always the most basic and therefore the ultimate or final reference point in human interpretation.

This is, in the last analysis, the question as to what are one's ultimate presuppositions. When man became a sinner he made of himself instead of God the ultimate or final reference point. And it is precisely this presupposition, as it controls without exception all forms of non-Christian philosophy, that must be brought into question. If this presupposition is left unquestioned in any field all the facts and arguments presented to the unbeliever will be made over by him according to his pattern. The sinner has cemented colored glasses to his eyes which he cannot remove. And all is yellow to the jaundiced eye. There can be no intelligible reasoning unless those' who reason together understand what they mean by their words.

Cornelius Van Til, *The Defense of the Faith* (1963), p. 77

INTRODUCTION

The contents of this book represent an attempt to apply the philosophical teachings of Cornelius Van Til to various academic disciplines. All of the contributors believe with Van Til that the revelation of God to men in the Bible is the authoritative starting point and the final court of intellectual appeal on earth. Each contribution is offered on the assumption that all forms of secular knowledge have been constructed on foundations of epistemological sand. Thus, the articles are intensely critical of modern scholarship. They represent an attempt to avoid the "baptized secularism" of the modern Christian colleges. We offer, hopefully, a thoroughly biblical set of foundations for Christian scholarship.

The authors have attempted to aim their chapters at intelligent laymen, but their primary audience is expected to be upper division college students and graduate students in the universities. If Christians had done their work properly in the field of private Christian education, these essays would be geared for high school seniors, or at the most, college freshmen. But Christian reconstruction is a slow, organic process—the steady conquest of all spheres of life by God's law-order—and the book will therefore scare off the very people who most need it, namely, students who need Van Til's epistemology before they set foot on a college campus.

Professor Van Til's writings are voluminous, and this book can do no more than summarize them and apply a few of them to a selected group of scholarly disciplines. The book is only a small beginning, hopefully setting forth the general direction that Christian scholarship must travel in if it is to be truly successful in challenging the hypothetically autonomous world of secular intellect. We are calling for co-workers in the intellectual division of labor, for we need a legion of serious scholars who will join the task of Christian reconstruction. We have to start somewhere.

Van Til has set forth his case in many forms and in many places. But for the purposes of this volume, we have relied on the basic outline in his great book, *The Defense of the Faith*:

> On the assumptions of the natural man logic is a timeless impersonal principle, and facts are controlled by chance. It is by means of universal timeless principles of logic that the natural man must, on his assumptions, seek to make intelligible assertions about the world of reality or

chance. But this cannot be done without falling into self-contradiction. About chance no manner of assertion can be made. In its very idea it is the irrational. And how are rational assertions to be made about the irrational? If they are to be made then it must be because the irrational is itself wholly reduced to the rational. That is to say if the natural man is to make any intelligible assertions about the world of "reality" or "fact" which, according to him, is what it is for no rational reason at all, then he must make the virtual claim of rationalizing the irrational. To be able to distinguish one fact from another fact he must reduce all time existence, all factuality to immovable timeless being. But when he has done so he has killed all individuality and factuality as conceived of on his basis. Thus the natural man must on the one hand assert that all reality is non-structural in nature and on the other hand that all reality is structural in nature. He must even assert on the one hand that all reality is non-structurable in nature and on the other hand that he himself has virtually structured all of it. Thus all his predication is in the nature of the case self-contradictory.

Realizing this dilemma, many modern philosophers have argued that any intellectual system of interpretation is therefore no more than a perspective. No system, these men assert, should pretend to be more than a system "for us." We have to deal with reality *as if* it will always behave as we have found it behaving in the past. The world of appearance formed by means of the exercise of the intellect must be taken as "somehow" similar to the world of Reality. And thus we seem to have come again upon the idea of mystery, the world of "faith" and of "authority" where prophets and seers may suggest to us the visions they have seen in the night.[1]

Modern thought is shattering as a result of a whole series of irreconcilable intellectual dilemmas, and all of them stem from man's apostate claim of total intellectual autonomy. Man has attempted to elevate himself into God's sovereign position, and the result is intellectual chaos. From the day that Adam tried to act as the "neutral experimenter," testing God's word against Satan's, man's arrogance has led into the paths of destruction. There is no neutral experimental proving ground; there is only the word of God or the cacophonic words of His enemies. Men must face up to the fact that they stand with God and His revelation or else they perish. There is no neutral zone of safety in all the universe. "He that is not with me is against me; and he that gathereth not with me scattereth abroad" (Matt. 12:30).

One of the ways in which scholars attempt to escape from the inherent contradictions in secular thought is to appeal to a rival discipline as the hoped-for ultimate source of meaning and coherence. Scientists appeal to mathematics, theologians appeal to history, historians appeal to philosophy, and philosophers have long ago abandoned any hope of answering such ques-

---

1. Cornelius Van Til, *The Defense of the Faith* (Philadelphia: Presbyterian and Reformed Publishing Co., 1963), pp. 126-27.

tions—although they would affirm that if such questions were worth answering, were valid, and could be answered, only philosophers could answer them. Hopefully, the essays in this book will indicate that each academic discipline is utterly bankrupt epistemologically, and therefore no appeals from one bankrupt discipline to another will be effective. The drifting ships of academia cannot be secured by binding them to each other.

It should be stressed from the outset that Protestantism in the latter third of the twentieth century has virtually ignored the tasks of intellectual reconstruction. The Reformation, by failing to adopt a full-scale commitment to biblical law, and by failing to abandon all traces of Greek philosophy, was not able to shield itself from the impact of Renaissance and Enlightenment thought. Protestant scholasticism bogged down seventeenth-century thought in the quagmire of rationalism, and when this unenlightening mixture was abandoned in the eighteenth century, it was replaced by dualism: internal pietism vs. external Cartesian-Newtonian rationalism. Protestantism has remained dualistic until the present, either baptizing last year's now defunct rationalist fad in the name of "relevant concern," or utterly ignoring such "carnal" intellectual issues in favor of endless quibbling, backbiting, and schisms over prayer, choir meetings, Sunday school curricula, the purchase of a new organ, and the proper mode of baptism. Turning in upon themselves, pietistic churches become disgusted at what they see, so they become pathologically concerned with repairing the leaks of ecclesiastical tradition, while the world is in the process of being flooded.

As one Christian friend of mine once remarked, "Christians are terrified of modern science, viewing it as a roaring lion. Actually, it is a mouse, shivering in the corner." As a trained scientist who once spent his time analyzing hypothetical "war games" in a scientific think-tank, he was well versed with his topic. Yet this analysis should not be limited simply to the natural sciences. One editor, in rejecting the possibility of publishing the present book, explained the policy of the Christian publishing house he was associated with. The organization "has been generally very wary about involving itself in this field. There is no-one of any real competence to get involved in these matters of economics, sociology, etc. [presumably, he means no-one associated with his company], and it would be sticking our neck out with no-one able to answer the charges that might be made. We see the first concern to address ourselves to the prevailing piety in worship, prayer, and preaching. . . ." As he admitted, "This might be seen to be too narrow and too crippling a vision, and part of a vestige of the old Thomistic dichotomy. Not "might be seen," but *must* be seen; and so modern Protestants are culturally impotent. This state of affairs is even more grotesque in the face of the collapsing framework of modern secularism. At precisely the point when the old faith is in the process of dissolution, Protestant Christians—who love to teach young children and new converts that "the Bible has answers for every problem"—are morbidly afraid of commenting on anything beyond a general "God's gonna getcha someday, you nasty atheists." He is indeed, but this in no way absolves Christians for having failed to propose biblical alternatives to the systems constructed by the "nasty atheists."

Why should the critique of modern secularism be left to neo-orthodox theologians like Langdon Gilkey? He points to the obvious historical fact that it was Christianity, with its doctrine of creation, which gave men the necessary confidence to begin modern science. "The optimism and buoyancy of Western culture is more an effect of the idea of the good creation than its cause."[2] It should have been Protestant theologians, scholars, and pastors, rather than Gilkey, who set forth this challenge:

> Now Christianity makes the claim to provide the ultimate basis for a meaningful human existence, and it encourages men to find that meaning within the life of culture rather than outside it. It aims, among other things, to transform and enrich the enterprise of human civilization; it does not seek to overthrow or to flee human community. If, then, philosophy joins science, the fine arts, and the economic and political practices of men as one of the essential ingredients of civilization, it is fully as incumbent upon Christian faith to foster a creative philosophy as it is necessary for it to encourage a sound science and a vital art. Being a Christian in one's ultimate faith does not provide an automatic answer to the question "What is knowledge and how is it gained?" or to the question "What is justice, and what is beauty?" A healthy Christian culture, therefore, must be able to produce Christian philosophers as well as Christian scientists and businessmen if it is to realize, as it claims to do, the potential goodness of human life.[3]

Gilkey, impaled as he is on the ultimately irreconcilable dualism between the Barthian (i.e., neo-Kantian) realm of freedom and realm of scientific necessity, is utterly unable to show how the Bible gives any guidance to man or his society. Like the antinomian neo-Dooyeweerdian "radical Christians"—at last, they have abandoned the word "Reformed"—who are always searching for "Christian attitudes" to problems, Gilkey can offer only the inquiry into "that attitude toward existence characteristic of Christian men."[4] He, like they, is totally opposed to the idea of concrete, revelational, biblical law as an explicit foundation of modern culture and modern legislation. But at least he calls for Christians to do what they say they can do: reform, deepen, and make holy the external culture which their own religious principles helped to establish three centuries ago.

I have heard one pastor in a conservative church call for the congregation

---

2. Langdon Gilkey, *Maker of Heaven and Earth* (Garden City, N. Y.: Doubleday Anchor, [1959] 1965), p. 66.
3. *Ibid.*, p. 138.
4. *Ibid.*, p. 143.

to write letters to the national headquarters of a large retail sales firm to protest Sunday selling, yet in his own denomination—indeed, at the seminary which provides the denomination with the bulk of its ministers—there is an ordained minister who supports abortions-on-demand. Ah, but Sunday selling—there's a true crime! Another pastor at a rapidly growing Southern California fundamentalist church was approached in 1973 by members of the congregation who were concerned about the establishment of nude dancing clubs in the community. They asked him what the church could do to challenge this development. "Nothing," he said. "The church should not get involved in these social action projects." When the salt has lost its savor, it is fit for nothing except to be trodden under foot. It is the suicide of the faith. By retreating from the zones of cultural and intellectual combat, pietism—which accounts for about 95% of the conservative churches—has abandoned the whole world to the devil, and it has done so in the name of a higher, truer religious conviction. Pietists do not have enough courage to face the fact of their own cowardice; like Moses before God's challenge to him to confront the Egyptians, they whine, "O my Lord, I am not eloquent, neither heretofore, nor since thou hast spoken unto thy servant: but I am slow of speech, and of a slow tongue. And the LORD said unto him, Who hath made man's mouth? or who maketh the dumb, or deaf, or the seeing, or the blind? have not I—the LORD? . . . And the anger of the LORD was kindled against Moses . . ." (Ex. 4:11, 12, 14a).

Van Til has called men to consider the claims of God. He has also reminded Christians that they have generally failed to challenge their secular cultures in the name of the God who created all things and promises to restore His elect and their world. Any Christian who thinks he is called to the mission field of higher education and Christian scholarship should sit down with a copy of Van Til's *Survey of Christian Epistemology*, turn to page 195, and absolutely master the next three pages. Until the scope of Van Til's vision is imparted to a generation of intellectuals, the future of scholarship, including pietism's imitation scholarship, is doomed.

GARY NORTH

Part One

EPISTEMOLOGICAL CRITICISM

Are we then to fail to witness for God in the field of science? Is it only because the unbeliever has never been confronted with the full implication of Christianity for the field of science that he tolerates us in his presence still? And are we to have a theory of common grace that prohibits us from setting forth the witness of God before all men everywhere? Is not the Christ to be set forth in His cosmic significance by us after all? Is it not true that there could be no science if the world and all that is therein is controlled by chance? Is it not true that the non-Christian does his work by the common grace of God? A theory of common grace based on a natural theology is destructive of all grace, common or special.

Surely the witness to the God of the Scriptures must be presented everywhere. It must be, to be sure, presented with wisdom and with tact. But it must be presented. It is not presented, however, if we grant that God the Holy Spirit in a general testimony to all men approves of interpretations of this world or of aspects of this world which ignore Him and set Him at naught.

The non-Christian scientist must be told that he is dealing with facts that belong to God. He must be told this, not merely in the interest of religion in the narrower sense of the term. He must be told this in the interest of science too, and of culture in general. He must be told that there would be no facts distinguishable from one another unless God had made them and made them thus. He must be told that no hypothesis would have any relevance or bearing on these same facts, except for the providence of God. He must be told that his own mind, with its principles of order, depends upon his being made in the image of God. And then he must be told that if it were not for God's common grace he would go the full length of the principle of evil within him. He would finish iniquity and produce only war. His very acts of courtesy and kindness, his deeds of generosity, all his moral good is not to be explained, therefore, in terms of himself and the goodness of his nature but from God's enabling him to do these things in spite of his sinful nature. "Will you not then repent in order to serve and worship the Creator more than the creature?"

Van Til, "Common Grace and Witness-Bearing," in *Torch & Trumpet* (Dec. 1954–Jan. 1955).

I

THE EPISTEMOLOGICAL CRISIS
OF AMERICAN UNIVERSITIES

By GARY NORTH

I believe life, human life, all life, is a singular chance. A fluke, which depended on all manner of improbable conditionings happening at the same time, or in the same sequence of time. Between ten and twenty billion years ago there was a big bang, and the universe started. Before that, time did not exist: this is something our minds are not able to comprehend. . . . It has all been a very unlikely process, with many kinds of improbability along the way. . . .

If any asked me on what basis I make these assumptions, I have no answer. Except to affirm that I do. Some will say I am making them because, under all the intellectual qualifications, I am a residual legatee of the Judeo-Christian tradition. I doubt that. I have a nostalgic affection for the Anglican Church in which I was brought up, but for me its theological formulations have no meaning. Nor have any theological formulations of any kind.

—C. P. Snow
"What I Believe"
Britannica Roundtable
Vol. I, No. 3 (1972)

Professional handwringing is the occupational function of intellectuals. It has been thus for approximately as long as men could write. If anything, the better they write, the more vigorous the handwringing. My thoughts on the state of the modern university are not intended to be just another grim cataloguing of the disaster we face. I hope I can gather up a few loose ends and assemble them in terms of a thesis: the crisis of the modern university is a specific instance of a general crisis of faith that the entire world is going through. Modern secularism and technology have shattered the traditional faiths wherever "modernism" has gone. Now, even the faith in secularism and technology is in the process of erosion, and a kind of spiritual and therefore epistemological vacuum has appeared. The visibility of this erosion has been increased since 1964, and therefore I focus my comments on the "new" university of the mid-1960's. The year 1964 began with the visit of the Beatles, and it closed with the Berkeley Free Speech movement. It was the last year in our age of silver —coinage, that is—foreshadowing the age of bronze (well, copper, actually, with phony silver laminate). From an academic point of view, the revolution on the campuses from 1964–70 did not inaugurate an age of gold; instead, we got iron. The Book of Daniel and Hesoid's *Works and Days* could have told us as much.

"All our major institutions, but particularly the university, are afflicted with a threefold sense of loss: loss of community, loss of purpose, and loss of power." So writes Dr. Warren Bennis, president of the University of Cincinnati, in the latter months of 1972.[1] Yet of all modern American institutions, it was the university which was supposed to supply all three: community, purpose, and power. But since 1964 we have seen, unmistakably, what Nisbet calls the degradation of the academic dogma—the idea of knowledge for its own sake is no longer held in high esteem. The quest for power, for government contracts, and for the big time destroyed that most ancient of old Greek dogmas, which had stood at the foundation of Western universities since the twelfth century. The things most necessary for any true community—function, dogma, authority, hierarchy, solidarity, honor or status, and a sense of superiority and distance from the world[2] —were eroded in American universities after 1945, and two decades later the whole system was shaken up (or, in a lot of cases, shaken down) by the student revolution. It may have been a short-lived revolution, but time is less crucial than the damage inflicted on the self-estimation of those who make up a great university. "The greatness that is Harvard and the glory that is Berkeley can perish in but a few years," Nisbet writes.[3] The next few decades will see if he is correct.

I began my college career in the last part of Eisenhower's administration; I ended it in the final year of Nixon's first term as President. From Eisenhower to Nixon: that would not have sounded like much in 1959. For the world of the American university, it was a long, disastrous period. Someone who was not intimately connected with that world (I hesitate to use the word "community") can hardly grasp the turmoil of the late 1960's, and it seems likely that the effects of that turmoil will not soon be healed. The broken windows were easily repaired; all it took was money. Students have calmed down, going back to books, marijuana, and even cheap rotgut wine. Fraternities are making a comeback, although these days they are effectively co-ed. But the scars of the intellectual wars are

---

1. Warren Bennis, "The University Leader," *Saturday Review* (Dec. 9, 1972), p. 44.
2. Robert A. Nisbet, *The Degradation of the Academic Dogma* (New York: Basic Books, 1971), pp. 43-45.
3. *Ibid.*, p. 235.

not yet healed; the battles here are still in progress. What the 1960's brought was a revolution of the mind, or (again quoting Nisbet) "the revolution of epistemological nihilism."[4]

Nihilism, you see, is the son of relativism and brother of intellectual apathy. Relativism fathered them both, and the fact that now the campuses are apathetic should be no more cause for public rejoicing than nihilism was a cause for public hostility. The root problem was, is, and shall continue to be relativism. That is what should have brought on the budget cuts at the private universities and the closing down of the government-financed institutions from kindergarten to graduate school. But relativism has been the official creed of Americans for several generations—the separation not only of church and state but also the separation of religion and state. (Revealed religion, that is, not the religion of humanism.) So when Karl Mannheim heralded the glorious dawn of pure relativism, who was there to speak out against it? Yet it was the philosophy offered by Mannheim which has become the moral and legal foundation of all modern, state-supported schools, as well as their private imitators. Incredibly, Mannheim announced his findings with joy:

> The investigator who undertakes the historical studies suggested above need not be concerned with the problem of what is ultimate truth. Interrelationships have now become evident, both in the present and in history, which formerly could never have been analyzed so thoroughly. The recognition of this fact in all its ramifications gives the modern investigator a tremendous advantage. . . . It is precisely our uncertainty which brings us a good deal closer to reality than was possible in former periods which had faith in the absolute.[5]

Marvelous grace of the neutral void! Now men are freed from the shackles of restraining dogma. Now they are free to marshal their footnotes in more creative ways. We have come at last to intellectual twilight.

> It is imperative in the present transitional period to make use of the intellectual twilight which dominates our epoch and in which all values and points of view appear in their genuine relativity. We must realize once and for all that the meanings which make up our world are simply an historically determined and continuously developing structure in which man develops, and are in no sense absolute.[6]

Take this philosophy, legitimate the modern educational system in terms of it, add multiple billions of dollars worth of federal grants and subsidies, impregnate it with huge doses of "neutral" varieties of contemporary Liberal ideology, diffuse it through the academic world through an exponentially growing body of professional journals—almost 100,000 of them,

---

4. *The New York Times Book Review* (April 5, 1970), p. 36.
5. Karl Mannheim, *Ideology and Utopia* (New York: Harvest, [1936]), p. 84.
6. *Ibid.*, p. 85.

worldwide, by the mid-1960's[7]—bureaucratize it, and present it on campuses of 30,000 and 40,000 teenage students and graduate teaching assistants, and you have an institutional equivalent of a cocked .44 magnum. Katherine Towle pulled the trigger.

Katherine Towle? Who remembers Katherine Towle today? She was the dean of students at the University of California, Berkeley, in the fall of 1964. The Berkeley administration had discovered that a section of Telegraph Avenue, long believed to be a part of the city of Berkeley, was actually a part of the University itself. This meant that rules prohibiting campus political activity—the so-called Kerr Directives of 1960—governed that strip of real estate. For years, students of all political persuasions had used that strip to hand out political literature, raise funds, and recruit new members. On September 14, she sent a letter to all student groups forbidding such activities on this bit of land. Then, literally, all hell broke loose. It did not stop until a group of state militia fired into students at Kent State University in the spring of 1970. From Mario Savio to Mark Rudd to, finally, Mary Ann Vecchio (the 14-year-old runaway who was featured in the famous Kent State tragedy photo: kneeling next to a dead student, hands outspread, screaming): a trigger pulled by a second-level college bureaucrat in a routine decision.[8] It could have happened to anyone on a huge, prestige liberal arts campus. Berkeley was unique only in the visibility of its earlier politicization, not just of students, but of the faculty.[9]

The distance between the spring of 1964 and today is almost unthinkably large, for it was then that William Trombley could write: "The larger campuses, Berkeley especially, are smug in their conviction that they already provide the best university education possible. They believe no important reforms are necessary."[10] Two years later, Herbert Gold wrote in the same magazine: "But Berkeley is surely the leader. It is the most serious and committed to change. Berkeley is, as they say, 'out of sight.' It is the model of the rebellious enclave within the affluence of mid-century America."[11] By 1970, Berkeley's political activists had gone underground, and the Jesus Freaks had taken over the student plaza area, challenged by

---

7. M. King Hubbard, "Are We Retrogressing in Science?" *Geological Society of America Bulletin*, LXXIV (April, 1963), p. 366.

8. "Chronology," in Michael V. Miller and Susan Gilmore (eds.), *Revolution at Berkeley* (New York: Dial Press, 1965).

9. Nisbet, *Dogma*, pp. 152-55. A delightful treatment of Berkeley's years of turmoil, from the pen of a former graduate student, is John Coyne's *The Kumquat Statement* (Chicago: Cowles, 1970).

10. William Trombley, "The Exploding University of California," *Saturday Evening Post* (May 16, 1964), p. 28. By exploding, he meant in size, but the use of the word was almost prophetic.

11. Herbert Gold, "I Am a U. C. Student: Do Not Fold, Bend, or Mutilate," *Sat. Eve. Post* (June 18, 1966), p. 35.

assorted bands of chanting Hare Krishnas. Berkeley, the leader, had finally come back to "normal," with students reading books, joining fraternities, and drinking booze. But we have not come full circle. We have come from optimistic, future-oriented Liberal relativism, then through nihilism, then mysticism, and now grinding apathy. Post-Kantian thought can take many forms, but it is still humanistic at its roots. So are its various social products.

The apathy of the students is not reflected in the academic disciplines themselves. In the departments, everything is up for grabs: presuppositions, methods, conclusions, even tenure. In 1965, Nisbet challenged the idea of tenure, and no one responded.[12] Now the idea is being seriously entertained in educational journals.[13] No received tradition is sacrosanct any longer, with perhaps one major exception: creedal, revealed religion still supposedly has nothing to say in the realm of academics.

Thomas Kuhn's book, *The Structure of Scientific Revolutions,* first published in 1962, is today the handbook of education departments, young sociologists, economists, historians, psychologists, and even physicists (Kuhn, ironically, is a Ph.D in physics, and based his book on the history of natural science, especially physics). Kuhn argues that all scholarship stems from the use of "paradigms"—basic presuppositions that limit the kind of questions asked, means used to answer them, and conclusions reached—and that science advances when scientific revolutions occur, i.e., shifts to new paradigms. Old, established scholars resist these new paradigms, but young professionals and/or skilled amateurs use new paradigms to answer questions that have been forced upon them by new problems. In the field of history, for example, "revisionists" try to rewrite the established inter-pretations. But they are not limited to history departments, as Walter Goodman argues:

> Revisionism was not invented by our current revisionists. There is a natural, and healthy, impulse in every academic field to cry Nay to those who have gone before. It need have nothing to do with politics. There comes a time when any spirited apprentice will turn on his master —to show that he has learned all he can learn, that he is his own man, that the master is the past and he is the future. This healthy impulse must be encouraged, for that way lies progress, does it not? Or at least novelty, which is nearly as desirable.[14]

12. Nisbet, "The Permanent Professors: A Modest Proposal," *The Public Interest* (Fall, 1965), reprinted in *Tradition and Revolt* (New York: Vintage, 1969).
13. Dabney Park, Jr., "A Loyal AAUP Member says: 'Down With Tenure!,'" *Change,* IV (March, 1972). On the economic effects of tenure, see my article, "Subsidizing a Crisis: The Teacher Glut," *An Introduction to Christian Economics* (Nutley, N. J.: Craig Press, 1973). Cf. *U.S. News and World Report* (Dec. 11, 1972), pp. 55-57.
14. Walter Goodman, "Revisionism Revisited," *The New Leader* (March, 1972), p. 12.

Goodman, like all good relativists, is forced to qualify his hope for progress, for we just can't be sure of progress any more, can we? So let us settle for novelty. And novelty is what the many departments are turning out, and if tenure goes, novelty will be just about the only thing turned out, at least until the AFL-CIO organizes the untenured.

All departments in the liberal arts seem to be suffering from the harassment of the Young Turks. New Left historians, sociologists, political scientists, economists, and literature instructors cry out against establishment methods of inquiry, methods of teaching, and methods of faculty promotion. The younger men are busy setting up subdivisions within their departmental turfs, with or without the approval of the faculty zoning commissions. They write for their own journals—just what the academic world needed, more journals—disrupt annual meetings of the disciplines, and of late even participate in the presentation of still more professional papers. The American Economic Association allowed many of the radical economists to deliver their papers, and these were reprinted in the May issue of the *American Economic Review* (1972). The Old Liberals are finally having to listen to the New Leftists, and the New Leftists have agreed to stop shouting so much. The New Left, to use its own phrase, is being co-opted. They have sold their birthright, so to speak, for a mess of footnotes: you read my radical article, and I won't counsel the kids (especially since the kids have stopped coming around for any counseling). Intellectual schizophrenia is rampant.

What happened on the campus after 1964? "Increasingly, as is now very clear," writes Nisbet, "the Old Radicalism found itself on the defensive, more and more the butt of jibes and assaults from the New Radicals. What, after all, had the Old Left to offer except more technology, more political action, more bureaucracy; in short, more of a set of forces that could seem to the New Left fully as repressive of individuality, fully as repressive to the self, to one's sacred identity, as anything that came out of callous capitalism."[15] In the language of Van Til, the nature-freedom scheme once again was at war with itself, as the *science ideal* of pure rationality and total control came into conflict with the *ideal of personality*, i.e., freedom from rational restraints and external (or even internal) controls.

> The student revolution of the 1960's can be seen, I think, as the watershed of current radicalism. In its way it is the reverse of that earlier watershed, the Puritan revolution. What led up to and indeed generated the student revolution in the 1960's was, on the whole, classic, orthodox, and objective. Concern was with such matters as civil rights, ending of the war, welfare, freedom, and participation in power. All of this was familiar and, as we know, aroused the sympathy of the Old Left almost immediately. But what came out of the student revolution

---

15. Nisbet, "Radicalism as Therapy," *Encounter* (March, 1972), pp. 55-56.

was something very different, something that antagonized old radicals, that earned the New Left the relentless hatred of the Old Left. This was the growing, widening, and deepening concern of the young with unalterably subjective matters, with feeling rather than reason, with consciousness rather than visible social structure, and with the whole set of techniques, including drugs and encounter sessions, by which individual consciousness could be affected.

I think it can be said accurately that the Old Left's hatred of the New Left was, and is, based on two fundamental points. The first is obvious enough. It is the New Left's seeming disdain for the nice bureaucratic-humanitarian society the Old-Left had helped build, that had, so to speak, liberalism-and-six-percent as its motto, and that now seemed to be going down the drain as the result of the antics of the New Left. The universities in America, from Harvard across the country to Berkeley, had become cherished, increasingly luxurious homes for Old Radicals, exhilarating settings for the permanent politics to which the Old Left was consecrated. When the New Left turned with such ferocity upon these monasteries of privileged affluence, seeking to destroy them along with Pentagon and General Motors, this was more than the Old Left could bear. An adversary culture was all right so long as it directed itself to the corporation, toward capitalism, toward this or that excrescence of bureaucracy, toward the bourgeoisie (properly defined, of course), but it was something else, something wanton and soul shattering for adversary culture to widen to include the university as a target, for the university, after all, was the source of one's tenure and affluence.

The second point is hardly less fundamental in the Old Left's hatred of the New Left. It lies in the New Left's ever more articulate disdain for the whole rhetoric of rationalism—of objectivism—that for so long had made the Kingdom of Heaven a simple matter of annihilating enough external institutions and pursuing enough ends through the rationalist techniques of politics. From the Old Left's point of view, the increasing references in the New Left to consciousness, to identity, to reflexive states of mind, and to awareness seemed nothing short of a failure of nerve—a recrudescence of the kind of society Gilbert Murray's *Four Phases of Greek Religion* describes in the ancient Athens of the post-Alexandrian period when bizarre beliefs and cults abounded, when the external world seemed nothing more than varied projections of consciousness, when objectivism passed into subjectivism and solipsism.[16]

There were other Bibles of the New Left in the late 1960's. Theodore Roszak's *Making of a Counter Culture* was one of them; Charles Reich's *The Greening of America* was another. Max Weber, the great German sociologist, in the immediate post-World War I years had predicted that modern bureaucratic rationalism would produce various counter movements: a return to the churches, sexual experimentation, and artistic

16. *Ibid.*, p. 56.

expression. Roszak builds his narrative, without mentioning Weber, around these themes. New Leftists, although they may not have read Roderick Seidenberg's *Post-Historic Man*, were convinced that something like his vision of the ant-hill society was in the works of modern bureaucratic civilization, and they wanted none of it. Better the flower children, they said, than men in gray flannel suits.

Best of all,· however, is a fusion of the two. It would seem that the 1970's may bring an attempt at this fusion. The best statement of it was made quite early in the counter culture explosion by the leader of a peculiar San Francisco group, The Psychedelic Rangers. He explained to a *Newsweek* reporter that the group's motto was "the psychedelic baby eats the cybernetic monster." By this, he explained, the psychedelic. euphoria-producing drugs and organic compounds will sweep over modern culture. As in Huxley's *Brave New World*, drugs would bring "life" to an otherwise dead society. What we need, in other words, is a fusion of internal freedom (nonrational) and external controls—noumenal and phenomenal interaction, in Kant's terminology—each providing what the other needs. "We're out to build an electric Tibet."[17]

There is little doubt as to what it was which brought such change to the life of the campus after 1964: the advent of the drug culture and the anti-war movement. These two factors were literally explosive issues. The old arguments of those opposed to marijuana, such as "smoking marijuana generally leads to heroin addiction," were arguments out of the 1930's, when the smoking of marijuana was confined to subcultures—Negro ghettos, the entertainment industry—in which the kind of people who rebelled in this way were more likely to go on to heroin. But marijuana in the hands of a middle-class student, or his parents, was far less likely to become the stepping stone to hard drugs. The real argument against marijuana is that it deliberately distorts God's created reality, and that it involves the deliberate abdication from personal responsibility in subduing that reality for the glory of God. It is the same argument used against the glutton and the drunkard who rebel against family and God (Deut. 21:20). This is why Paul wrote: "And be not drunk with wine, wherein is excess; but be filled with the Spirit" (Eph. 5:18). [An alternative reading of the Greek is "be filled with spirit"; it is not completely clear that this refers to the Holy Spirit.] But this argument is a two-edged sword; it can be used against all forms of drunkenness, and those who write the laws, and who wrote them before 1965, did not want to draw out the argument. It was hypocrisy, and the kids knew it. The only thing that distinguished marijuana from liquor was that investigators found that marijuana is always smoked to get high, while liquor, in small quantities, need not

---

17. *Newsweek* (Feb. 6, 1967), p. 95.

distort perceptions. But as for drunkenness, there was no distinction possible.

There is little doubt that marijuana will be legalized, or at least achieve marginal acceptance, by the late 1970's. The absurdity of the "no highs, pro-drunk" logic has backfired. Even the conservative *National Review* has run an article favoring legalization, and negative replies by the editors were, at best, hedged.[18] The superb study by Kai Erikson, *Wayward Puritans* (1966), indicates what is likely to happen. Legal systems are granted just limited amounts of money to operate. In the United States, the total cost of supporting the police, courts, and prisons was surprisingly small as of 1970: about $10 billion.[19] In an economy of a one trillion dollar Gross National Product (however crude these aggregate estimates may be), that was not a great sum. Spending on all welfare projects—federal, state, and local—was probably $170 billion, triple what it was in 1960.[20] But crime-fighting expenditures, which had also tripled since 1960, remained relatively low. As Erikson shows, societies have definitions of "social deviation." With expenditures at any given level, i.e., with crime-fighting services at any given level, an increase in one form of deviation will draw away revenues from other areas of crime fighting. Thus, a huge increase in one form of deviant behavior cannot be dealt with without significant increases in anti-crime budgets, or reductions elsewhere. Therefore, the new behavior, formerly regarded as significantly deviant, will now be redefined as acceptable. If budgets do not shift, then definitions of deviation must, whenever one form of deviation increases markedly. This was New England's experience in 1651–80. Presumably, it will be ours, with regard to marijuana, in the 1970's. Too many sons and daughters of too many prominent citizens are being "busted." More significant politically, too many middle-class sons and daughters are being arrested. The courts simply cannot handle the inflow of cases. Without a principled, consistently applied definition of "drunken irresponsibility," this overload will force a redefinition of deviation. The marijuana issue will disappear. Until the backlash comes.

The Vietnam issue has also disappeared, at least temporarily. We may see the rise of political movements based on "the stab in the back" or "who lost Vietnam?" but by mid-1973, the issue had faded as an issue at the ballot box. But for epistemology, it was and is a truly revolutionary issue. Establishment Liberalism brought on the war in Vietnam. We were to police the world. We were to extend Wilsonian ideals into every nook and cranny of every tribe on earth. The old progressive optimism was still

---

18. *National Review* (Dec. 8, 1972).
19. *U. S. News and World Report* (June 5, 1972), p. 62.
20. Henry Hazlitt, "Welfarism Gone Wild," *The Freeman* (May, 1972), pp. 266-67.

intact in 1964. American know-how and military might could bring democracy into full bloom everywhere. Democracy—our only national religion—was still the creed of Liberals everywhere. Bruce Kuklick writes: "There are few who would deny the triumph of Wilson's views after World War II, and the intellectual rationale which justified policy decisions became increasingly rich in the postwar period. It is only at this time that it becomes appropriate to speak of a Wilsonian paradigm."[21] Conservatives, who had been staunch isolationists before December 7, 1941, now joined all good Liberal interventionists, as Senator Vandenberg became the symbol of bipartisan foreign policy—a Republican praised greatly by my Liberal professor of foreign policy as late as 1960. The mythology still held.[22]

As the war escalated and the draft calls went up, the intensity of antiwar sentiment increased. The Liberal paradigm in foreign policy began to shift; a Kuhn-like "scientific revolution" took place. The conduct of foreign policy, argues Kuklick, had been conducted after 1945 in terms of a "Munich syndrome."

> Prior to both World Wars, diplomats have believed that the United States attempted to avoid international commitments; it need not or would not act in concert with other powers when an "aggressor" threatened international stability. By 1945 the United States had been "twice burned," and Americans had to alter their behavior. Policymakers acted, so they believed, to avoid the catastrophes of 1917 and 1941; 1941 must not recur as 1917 had. This goal meant specifically that the United States had directly to intervene if it appeared that someone was seriously challenging world peace and order. There were to be no more Munichs. In effect "normal paradigmatic change" took place after World War II as American diplomats "solved" recurring problems by applying this model. Problems were *in fact* problems because they were significant in terms of the paradigm. Indeed, as policy-makers judged the twenty years of diplomacy after World War II in terms of the history that preceded it, they could agree that the Wilsonian disciplinary matrix worked. The horrible wars crucial to the development of the paradigm were avoided. Americans had resolved the crises which gave birth to the new paradigm.[23]

During the Eugene McCarthy campaign, an incredible piece of campaign literature appeared. It was a full-page picture of General Douglas MacArthur, and on the corner of the sheet, this quote from the general appeared: "Anybody who commits the land power of the United States on the Continent of Asia ought to have his head examined." Here was

21. Bruce Kuklick, "History as a Way of Learning," *American Quarterly*, XXII (Fall, 1970), p. 614.
22. For a typical panegyric on Vandenberg, see Cecil V. Crabb, Jr., *American Foreign Policy in the Nuclear Age* (Evanston: Row, Peterson, 1960), pp. 127-30.
23. Kuklick, p. 620.

the ultimate reversal: anti-war radical students were using MacArthur, the nemesis of all good Liberals, to challenge Liberal policies in Vietnam!

Walter Lippmann, probably the most respected of all Liberal commentators, has taken positions favorable to almost anyone's ideology at one stage or another of his career. After 1965, he became a chief intellectual spokesman for "neo-isolationism." Ironically, it had been Lippmann's columns, 1914–17, that had argued that the United States should enter the war in Europe—not to "make the world safe for democracy," but because our national self-interest was involved. What was our national self-interest? World peace through world law, basically—some new form of internationalism. In 1914 he had written: "We do not think the United States should have gone to war. We alone cannot undertake to police the world."[24] Then, in 1916, Lippmann penned one of the most stirring defenses of internationalism ever written:

> Mr. Wilson deserves the gratitude of all decent men for having announced that America is ready to use its force for this civilized end. The whole preparedness agitation, which has been running wild of late by piling jingoism on hysteria, is given a new turn. It becomes our contribution to the world's peace, the only kind of peace in which we can find our own safety. Mr. Wilson has broken with the tradition of American isolation in the only way which offers any hope to men. Not only has he broken with isolation, he has ended the pernicious doctrine of neutrality, and has declared that in the future we cannot be neutral between the aggressor and the victim. That is one of the greatest advances ever made in the development of international morality. His speech means that America is ready to act on the belief that war is no longer a matter between two "sovereign" states, but a common world-problem of law and order in which every nation is immediately concerned. There is something intensely inspiring to Americans in the thought that when they surrender their isolation they do it not to engage in diplomatic intrigue but to internationalize world politics. They will surrender it for that, though they would have resisted bitterly a mere entanglement in the manoeuvers which prepare new wars.[25]

The wave of revulsion after the First World War which swept over the United States in the mid-1920's buried such thoughts as these. The League of Nations idea had torpedoed Wilson's dreams and his political party in 1920; after 1925, a whole series of "revisionist" books appeared, arguing that Germany was not exclusively responsible for the war (S. B. Fay, Harry Elmer Barnes), and that Wilson had maneuvered us into the war (Barnes, Charles C. Tansill, Walter Millis, C. H. Grattan).[26] As Cohen

---

24. Lippmann, "Timid Neutrality," *The New Republic* (Nov. 21, 1914), reprinted in Lippmann, *Early Writings* (New York: Liveright, 1970), p. 15.
25. Lippmann, "Mr. Wilson's Great Utterance," *New Republic* (June 3, 1916), *ibid.*, p. 39.
26. Cf. Warren I. Cohen, *The American Revisionists* (University of Chicago,

shows, after 1939, the Roosevelt foreign policy in favor of intervention in Europe began to lead scholars back into the Wilsonian ideology. Men who had supported revisionist arguments were increasingly suspect in the academic community. Barnes, heretofore a respected scholar, was fired from a teaching job in the obscure Eastern Washington College of Education summer school in June, 1941—a classic case of guild control in Kuhn's analysis.[27] After World War II, sentiments like Lippmann's were once again in the ascendancy, so much so that the 1946 *Annual Report* of the Rockefeller Foundation announced: "The Committee on Studies of the Council on Foreign Relations is concerned that the debunking journalistic campaign following World War I should not be repeated," and it went on to allocate a subsidy of $139,000 for the preparation of more respectable studies of the Second World War (pp. 188-89).[28] Revisionist scholars of the post-WW II period—Charles A. Beard, Tansill, Barnes, George Morgenstern, Frederic Sanborn, Percy Greaves—simply could not get a fair hearing in the academic guilds, and only Beard's great prestige was able to get Yale University Press to publish *President Roosevelt and the Coming of the War* (1948), and it won many enemies for Yale's editor, Eugene Davidson.

In 1953, Robert E. Osgood published what was to become a standard foreign policy study, *Ideals and Self-Interest in American Foreign Relations*, a University of Chicago book that was reprinted in paperback as recently as 1971. It followed Lippmann's lead: America's self-interest is in extending her entangling alliances in the theater of world democracy. My guess is that fewer students will believe this thesis, and fewer professors assign the book (unless they use it for target practice), than was true in 1960. The paradigm has shifted, and with it went much of the prestige of the pre-1965 Liberalism. Neo-isolationism is here, if not to stay, then at least to take a long-term lease.

Even revisionism concerning World War II is having a small flurry of interest. Old Hamilton Fish, Roosevelt's Republican, isolationist critic in the House of Representatives, finds that his speeches on Roosevelt's

---

1967). Cohen's conclusion, written in the tradition of New Deal Liberalism, would have aroused no opposition in 1964; by the time the book was published, had any student read it, he would have rubbed his eyes in disbelief: ". . . a nation not powerful enough to save the world cannot be powerful enough to shield itself from the world" (p. 240). In the context of a critique on the isolationists of the 1930's, this kind of rhetoric was, by the standards of the late 1960's, pure jingoism. I reviewed the book at some length in *Rampart Journal*, III (Winter, 1967). (This is not, by the way, *Ramparts* magazine.)

27. *Ibid.*, p. 231.

28. A critical comment on the CFR's decision can be found in *The Saturday Evening Post* (Oct., 1947), quoted on the dust jacket of Charles C. Tansill, *Back Door to War* (Chicago: Regnery, 1952).

malevolent pre-war maneuvers are receiving far more favorable response from young people than ever before.[29] As Walter Goodman remarks: "Of course, one's timing may be off. The premature revisionists who sought to persuade us before Pearl Harbor that President Roosevelt was bent on drawing the nation into a foreign war could make a plausible case —but they found small welcome. That was not what most of us wanted to hear in 1940."[30] Or in 1960, it should be mentioned.

The crowning blow to the old paradigm, as of 1972, may well be a simple newspaper article in, of all places, *The New York Times* (Jan. 2, 1972, p. 7), "War-Entry Plans Laid to Roosevelt":

> LONDON, Jan. 1 (AP)—Formerly top secret British Government papers made public today said that President Franklin D. Roosevelt told Prime Minister Winston Churchill in August, 1941, that he was looking for an incident to justify opening hostilities against Nazi Germany.
>
> The account of the Roosevelt-Churchill talks was contained in 950 volumes of British War Cabinet papers made public for the first time.
>
> The papers covered the period from January, 1941, to July, 1945, the largest collection of formerly secret British records ever released at one time. . . .
>
> Churchill's account of Roosevelt's attitude toward the war was contained in the minutes of that Cabinet meeting. The minutes, quoting Churchill indirectly, said:
>
> "He [Roosevelt] obviously was determined that they should come in."
>
> "If he were to put the issue of peace and war to Congress, they would debate it for months," the Cabinet minutes added.
>
> "The President had said he would wage war but not declare it and that he would become more and more provocative. If the Germans did not like it, they could attack American forces."

Somehow, I do not believe that the *Times* would have published this

---

29. Reported to me by Richard Hanks, who wrote his Ph.D. dissertation on Fish's Congressional career, in 1971. Fish made the statement to Hanks in late 1970.

30. Goodman, *op. cit.*, pp. 12-13. A number of books were published warning against the impending war with Hitler and Japan, although few modern scholars or graduate students ever hear of them. They were written by anti-New Deal conservative isolationists, socialists, pacifists, and pre-1941 communists. Cf. Mauritz A. Hallgren, *The Tragic Fallacy* (New York: Knopf, 1937); C. Hartley Grattan, *Preface to Chaos* (New York: Dodge, 1936); Porter Sargent, *Getting US Into War* (Boston: Porter Sargent, 1941). Sargent's book is a rare, extremely valuable summary of newspaper clippings, journal literature, books, and other written data. He includes a bibliography on pp. 162-63 of many books on the subject, including Hubert Herring, *And So to War* (Yale University Press, 1939); Larry Nixon (ed.), *When War Comes: What Will Happen and What to Do* (Greystone, 1939); Douglas Reed, *Disgrace Abounding* [on England] (Jonathan Cape, 1939); E. D. Schoonmaker, *Democracy and World Dominion* (Richard Smith, 1939); C. Hartley Grattan, *The Deadly Parallel* (Stackpole, 1939); Boake Carter, *Why Meddle in Europe?* (McBride, 1939). Some enterprising graduate student could produce a useful Ph.D. dissertation using nothing but leads provided in Sargent's book.

story in 1960, let alone 1945. Apparently, once men came to the realization that a President could manipulate the facts in order to encourage military hostilities—which anti-war people believe was the case in President Johnson's Gulf of Tonkin maneuvers—FDR could now be fair game for criticism. I imagine that New Deal Liberals will have to alter their position: before, no decent person could believe such a thing of Roosevelt; now, we must understand that these deceptions were necessary for world order, etc.

Emmet John Hughes, one of the most widely respected Liberal columnists of the 1950's and the 1960's, a speechwriter for President Eisenhower, and now a professor of politics at Rutgers University in New Jersey, granted an interview to newsmen in mid-1973. Some of his remarks were quoted by Robert J. Donovan in a *Los Angeles Times* column (Sept. 27, 1973):

> People like me assumed from the days of F.D.R. on that the Presidency was the unique source of creative and progressive leadership and that the Congress was the resisting, conservative, negative force— the citadel of reaction. This was the typical liberal vision of the Presidency, and it wasn't until the middle of the 1960s that liberals began to question their assumption. As a result, you had this extraordinary reversal of roles. All of a sudden the liberals began to worry about presidential power.

> Senator Fulbright illustrates this shift. In a speech in 1961, even after the Bay of Pigs, he suggested that the President should be given even greater power in foreign affairs than he possessed. ·Ten years later Fulbright made another speech saying that 30 years of war, cold war and crisis have propelled the American political system far along the road to an executive despotism, at least in the conduct of foreign relations and the making of war. . . . It was the whole tragedy of Vietnam rather than the Watergate revelations that forced the liberals to realize that they had terribly underestimated the importance of the restraining power of the Congress and had terribly exaggerated the innate wisdom of the White House.

It is not surprising that Richard Neustadt's *Presidential Power*, once reputed to be John F. Kennedy's Bible, and assigned so enthusiastically by Liberal professors in 1961, is now assigned as a primary source relating to "the mess we are in" today.

This has been a lengthy digression within the framework of my original hypothesis: Kuhn's analysis holds up as well for recent political science or historiography as it does for eighteenth-century science. It took a major disruption of the "facts"—Vietnam—to undermine the old Liberal paradigm concerning America's participation in world diplomacy. Nixon's trips to China and Russia, by attempting to soften the Cold War hostilities, broke with a 1945–70 tradition, and the silence of Congressional conservatives in the face of these trips indicates that the conservative paradigm on the Cold War is weakening. President Johnson operated in terms of a "Munich syndrome," but President Nixon escaped both Munich and the "China, 1949 syndrome." For the present, "no more confrontation" is the rule—except, perhaps, in the case of Israel.

Another sign of the paradigm shift, as of late 1972, was the generally favorable reception of David Halberstam's *The Best and the Brightest.* Halberstam's superb journalistic talents have focused on the utter failure of "can-do technocratic Liberalism" to deal with the Vietnam problem. The great symbol for this technocratic machine, inescapably, is Robert McNamara, the enemy of conservatives in 1963, and the fall-guy of 1967. Halberstam is, quite properly, merciless. Those who had been "greened" by Charles Reich's anti-technocratic tract became ecstatic. So were anti-Communists who resented McNamara's bungling. So were all the disillusioned former New Frontiersmen and Great Society rejects. It is a book which will probably set the climate of opinion for years to come. Robert McNamara, the prophet of the Kantian realm of the phenomenal, i.e., total control and prediction, was upended by a bunch of fellows in black pajamas who were "irrationally" persistent.[31] Halberstam chronicles this ancient Greek process of *hubris*.

But the paradigm shifts were not simply confined to the humanities and social sciences. The physical sciences, especially astrophysics, were in for their share of disturbances. The extent of the changes can only be gleaned from the popular press if one is an amateur scientist, but this is sufficient. The discoveries after 1967 of quasars and pulsars and things that go "zap" in the night have shaken all astrophysical theories about matter, energy, and the origins of the universe. Theories are seriously being offered that suppose the actual existence of dead stars that have collapsed to literal Euclidean points of zero space and infinite density. These so-called "black holes," some have argued, may be somehow related to hypothesized "white holes" out of which the collapsed matter-energy escapes, millions of light-years (or more) away.[32] One article dealing with high-energy physics reports that several of the "promising theories about matter's basic structure now look shaky, and much of the mass of data from the experiments is conflicting. What is needed now, agreed the physicists [at a world-wide conference in Chicago in 1972], is a theory to unify all this data—and this would take an Einstein."[33]

The signs of the shattering of the traditional paradigms in astronomy can

---

31. On McNamara's faith in centralized planning, see his book, *The Essence of Security* (New York: Harper & Row, 1968), pp. 109-10.

32. David Brand, "Where's the Matter?" *Wall Street Journal* (June 16, 1972); Walter Sullivan, "Laws of Universe Put Into Question," *New York Times* (Jan. 27, 1972)—an unreliable essay, one amateur astronomer informs me.

33. *Business Week* (Sept. 16, 1972), p. 62.

best be summarized by the revival of interest among students in the cosmological theories of Immanual Velikovsky. Velikovsky shocked the scholarly world in 1950 with his radically unorthodox theories of the origin of the solar system, which he thinks was completed only in the period of recorded history. Taking as his guide many legends of celestial chaos found in all "primitive" and ancient cultures, he concluded that they did have foundations in actual astronomical events. This was a denial of one of natural science's most cherished presuppositions, the doctrine of uniformitarianism: rates of physical change observed today have been the same throughout history. Velikovsky's catastrophism led to a short-run career catastrophe: his books were literally banned from many campuses. In a sordid tale of academic thought control, professional astronomers, led by the late Harlow Shapley of Harvard, went to Velikovsky's publisher, Macmillan, and threatened reprisals if his best-selling book, *Worlds in Collision*, were not taken out of print. The company buckled under.[34] *Pensée* magazine, in the May, 1972 issue, reproduces part of a letter sent by Dean McLaughlin, professor of astronomy at the University of Michigan, to the president of Macmillan on May 20, 1950. Here, in one classic document, we see the operation of utterly neutral scientific objectivity:

> Can we afford to have "freedom of the press" when it permits such obvious rubbish to be widely advertised as of real importance? . . . Can we afford "freedom of the press" when it can vitiate education, as this book can? Can we preserve democracy when education in true scientific principles . . . can be nullified by the promulgation of such *lies*—yes, lies as are contained in wholesale lots in *Worlds in Collision?* . . . Any astronomer or geologist or physicist could have pronounced it trash of the first order. Its geological errors are so absurd that even I, an astronomer, can identify them at a glance! . . . No, I have not read the book. . . . And I do not intend to waste my time reading it. . . .

A few voices of protest were heard, but not many. Eric Larabee published an essay, "Was Velikovsky Right?" in *Harper's* in 1963; *The*

---

34. Alfred de Grazia (ed.), *The Velikovsky Affair* (New Hyde Park, N. Y.: University Books, 1966). In the huge obituary published on Shapley in the *New York Times* (Oct. 21, 1972), the unsigned author bewails the supposedly terrible persecution suffered by Shapley at the hands of Senator Joe McCarthy, but he does not bother to mention Shapley's notorious bookburning efforts in the Velikovsky affair. What's sauce for unrespected odd-ball scholars is apparently poison for respectable Harvard professors. Neutrality, thou art not the *New York Times*. Cf. Prof. Horace Kallen, "Shapley, Velikovsky, and the Scientific Spirit," *Pensée* (May, 1972). Finally, almost two and a half decades after the publication of *Worlds in Collision*, Velikovsky was invited to speak before the primary organization of the American scientific guild, the American Association for the Advancement of Science. Yet even in late 1973, no faculty member contacted by the science writer of the *Los Angeles Times* would consent to comment on Velikovsky. "That is the last thing in the world I would do," said one unnamed scientist. Another scientist at the Jet Propulsion Laboratory in Pasadena, California, criticized the man's theories, but he also refused to be identified: *L. A. Times* (Oct. 25, 1973).

American Behavioral Scientist produced a series of papers on the Velikovsky affair (and this was reprinted as a book by this title); but *Science* —the ultimate Establishment journal of paradigm control—refused to let his rebuttals appear in their respectable pages. Finally, a student newspaper, *The Daily Princetonian* (Feb., 1964), blew the whistle on the guild. In January, 1965, Dell Books republished *Worlds in Collision*, and his books are now widely read once again. *Pensée* magazine, in spring, 1972, published an entire issue devoted to Velikovsky, and the response in sales was so overwhelming that for the next three years the journal devoted all issues to his ideas. He was invited to speak at Harvard in February of 1972—Shapley's Harvard! The younger students and junior faculty members are no longer listening to their elders, and the elders, with their "neutrality" refuted, their morals questioned, and their theories contradictory, are in no position to outlaw this latest scientific revolution. In short, epistemology counts.

The "UFO flap" has also torpedoed the scientific guild. When Prof. J. Allen Hynek of Northwestern University defected as the quasi-official Air Force apologist—you remember "swamp gas Hynek" and his theory of a 1966 UFO incident?—and called for less biased investigations of the flying saucers, the hole was in the dyke. The book by Saunders and Harkins, *UFOs? Yes: Where the Condon Committee Went Wrong* (1968), demonstrates just how "neutral" the government-hired Ph.D.'s were in this supposedly scientific investigation. Assistant professors are not listening any longer, and if they bide their time (or a flying saucer lands at Harvard), they will probably make it to associate professor.

Most ominous, and possibly most significant of all, is the rise of occultism on the American college campus. I doubt whether this is a universal phenomenon yet, and I doubt that it is as widespread as the press has indicated, but it is certainly more visible than it was in 1965. The fact that a book like Carlos Castaneda's *The Teachings of Don Juan* (1968), the favorable and credulous report of an anthropology graduate student concerning a Yaqui Indian sorcerer, would be published by the University of California Press, is revealing.[35] The advent of a mass market for books on the occult, as indicated by titles in paperback, came in the mid-1960's. Mr. Lyle Stuart, the most successful book publisher in America today in terms of best-sellers per titles published, bought out the relatively stodgy old Mystic Arts Book Club (University Books) at just this point in time. Stuart seldom misses. Occult books, always the backbone of the used book trade, finally became an above-ground phenomenon. Any *Books in Print* guide tells the story.

---

35. The book became a best-seller. By 1975, three best-selling sequels had followed, all published by commercial publishing houses. Castaneda claims that he, too, has become a full sorcerer.

Consider television, the most crucial of mass media. In the late 1960's we had "I Dream of Jeannie" and "Bewitched" as cutesy occult favorites, and we had "The Munsters" and "The Addams Family" as cutesy monsters. These acted as cultural wedges, just as *Playboy* did in the mid-1950's (by today's standards of legal pornography, a 1955 *Playboy* appears mild). Relatively innocent, nothing to get upset about, even charming: this was the beginning. Now we have "The Sixth Sense," in which no pseudo-scientific theories for occult phenomena are offered. We have endless Movies of the Week on occult themes. And, of course, we have Manson's family, one member of which was arrested on attempted murder charges (of President Ford) in 1975. Charming, in every sense of the word.

Is the occult actually in the curricula of colleges? Not generally, but it seems to be coming. Psychologists are paying new respect, for example, to Navajo psychotherapy and shamanism.[36] The Newark College of Engineering is using ESP techniques, and has been since 1962, to determine if there is a relationship between managerial talent and ESP. Technique —Kantian phenomenal technique—is not all there is to it, says Prof. John Mihalasky, especially in top-echelon decisions.[37] Witchcraft studies, like black studies or chicano studies, are possible at UC Berkeley. One thing is certain: it is not 1959 any more. The ridiculous has become, if not sublime, then at least legitimately intriguing for college professors. This, it would seem safe to say, indicates some kind of epistemological disruption.

So much for the social sciences, humanities, and natural sciences. But what about the queen of the sciences? What about theology? Religiously, we have witnessed the same drift from Kantian phenomenalism to Kantian noumenalism. It hit the theologians much earlier, of course, starting in this century with the advent of Barthian neo-orthodoxy, the subject of Van Til's *The New Modernism, Christianity and Barthianism*, and numerous essays. Less significant than Barth, but far more visible in recent years, is the Harvard Divinity School figure, Harvey Cox. Incredible, pathetic Harvey Cox, the man who leaps from fad to fad, is perhaps the most successful of all those who have jumped out of Kant's phenomenal frying pan into Kant's noumenal fire. In 1965, Harvey Cox presented the world with *The Secular City*, a widely read paperback that succeeded in getting Harvard to open its arms to him. It lasted about as long as the "death of God" fad, which is to say about a year and a half. Cox's *City* was the city of man, the new technocratic creation of men who were now freed from the confines of myth and superstition. It was a kind of the theological Bible for the New Frontier, at least for the Protestants;

---

36. *Time* (June 12, 1972), p. 68.
37. *New York Times* (Aug. 31, 1969), sect. III, p. 1.

the Roman Catholics had Teilhard de Chardin. Ah, the wonders of secularism, planning, technique: we could get America rolling again—right into Vietnam, as it turned out. Two years later, Harvey had gone primitive on all of us. He was now the prophet of the noumenal, a return to chaos, the ritual celebration of pure randomness, which is life itself. You have to read the account of his 1970 Easter celebration to believe it.[38] Now he has written *The Feast of Fools,* plus an article on Jesus for *Playboy* (Jan., 1970). As Father Andrew Greeley cogently remarks: "Professor Cox, of course, is well within his rights to change his mind, though some observers would be excused for feeling some reservations about a commentator who so dramatically and completely changes his mind without even pausing to acknowledge the change."[39] Greeley goes on:

> The theologians of play exhort us, "Celebrate!" but they are rather less than clear about the nature of the world view which should lead to celebration. In other words, is the celebration in the play theology a Dionesian escape from reality's ultimate tragic nature or a Jewish and Christian response showing gratitude to a reality that is seen as ultimately benign? From denying that a world view was possible, fashionable theologians have moved to a position where they enthusiastically embrace the sacred without pausing to consider whether one need have a world view, an interpretive scheme, a culture system that underpins an involvement in the sacred. But then it is very difficult to remain a fashionable theologian, and some things are bound to be overlooked.[40]

Greeley may be a liberal theologian, as he maintains, but he seems to have his head screwed on right. The concluding words of his book are superb: "And Professor Harvey Cox has made his pilgrimage from the secular city to his festive city on a mountaintop that sounds rather like Camelot, which, be it noted, was a mythological place both in the time of King Arthur and in the 1960's."[41]

Back in those dear, dead days of 1964, Pelican Books published *Crisis in the Humanities,* edited by England's fine historian, J. H. Plumb. The title of the book, and the insignificance of most of the problems assumed by the contributors to be "crises," creates a silly impression. The epistemological earthquake, not to mention the student rebellions, that took place after 1964 casts these little essays into the limbo reserved

---

38. *Newsweek* (May 11, 1970). Cf. Cox, *The Seduction of the Spirit* (New York: Simon & Schuster, 1973), ch. 6.
39. Andrew Greeley, *Unsecular Man: The Persistence of Religion* (New York: Schocken, 1972), p. 123.
40. *Ibid.,* p. 167.
41. *Ibid.,* p. 264. Garry Wills, once the darling of the conservative Roman Catholic crowd at *National Review,* and now the New Left radical journalist, goes after Cox's *Secular City* with a vengeance, along with McNamara and Teilhard de Chardin: *Bare Ruined Choirs: Doubt, Prophecy, and Radical Religion* (New York: Doubleday, 1972). I reviewed it in the *Wall Street Journal* (Nov. 25, 1972).

for academic prophets who have missed the change of direction in the winds of the climate of opinion.   Donald G. MacRae was only able to muster up the following: "In so far as there *is* a crisis in sociology, it results largely from the fact that sociology is not and should not be the handmaiden of universal virtue, a discipline which exists only to help the public zeal of influential persons and institutions." Now that doesn't sound so bad, does it? And he leaves us with this stirring thought: "Gradually sociology is working out an irreducible technical vocabulary which can be learned. . . . What is more, it is well worth mastering." Yes, sir, with a crisis like this to deal with, I feel certain the sociologists can find a solution or two, if they can get a $6 million government grant. But the real laugher is Alec Vidler's chapter, "The Future of Divinity" (that is, divinity the subject, not *the* Divinity; Vidler does not go into eschatology).

> Theological debates occasionally come in for notice in the Press or on the radio, but that is because it is curious to discover that there are individuals (not necessarily clergymen) who still feel passionately about them, and not because they are a natural or staple element in popular discourse. . . . The questions are not now formulated in theological, or at any rate in traditional terms. . . . The outcome of academic specialization, which was satirized by Ronald Knox in *Let Dons Delight,* has been that, except on a superficial level, experts on one subject can seldom converse with experts in another. Moreover, there is a becoming reluctance in pure academics to express opinions on matters which fall outside their own department of knowledge or fields of research."

Admittedly, the contributors were from English academia, but this last thought is unbelievable. What anthropologist on any Western campus has not commented on Pentagon strategy, what linguist has not offered a full explanation of Vietnam diplomacy? "Thus there appears to be an air of official reticence about the great questions that concern everybody." Somehow, Vidler's "thus" is distinctly a pre-1965 transitional word.

What kind of theological instruction did we need back in 1964? Why, we needed nice, safe, pluralistic, pre-1965 Liberal tolerance, what else? The following is pre-1965 Liberalism at its hard-hitting best:

> It is not for a pluralist university to impose or to endorse a single set of answers, whether Christian or otherwise, to these questions, but it ought publicly to recognize their importance and to see to it that students are given the opportunity to think about them as honestly and openly and deeply as possible. . . . It is evident too that a divinity faculty must plainly cease to be a Christian preserve. Those who teach it should be drawn from the adherents of any creed or none.

Courageous words—in 1850.

Plumb's introduction, however, does throw light on the position of the guild leaders in the days before Vietnam; it also shows how the academic fortress was disrupted so easily by younger members and students.

The Italian Renasissance in the fifteenth century made literary breeding fashionable: a gentleman was expected to be conversant with all knowledge; . . . Alas, the rising tide of scientific and industrial societies combined with the battering of two World Wars, has shattered the confidence of humanists in their capacity to lead or to instruct. Uncertain of their social function their practitioners have taken refuge in two desperate courses—both suicidal. Either they blindly cling to their traditional attitudes and pretend that their function is what it was and that all will be well so long as change is repelled, or they retreat into their own private professional world and deny any social function to their subject.

Two years later they could no longer follow either course easily; their younger colleagues would not permit it, and even they were animated by what they regarded as crises to be opposed in a valid fashion by academic spokesmen. If anything, between 1965 and 1970, academic figures could not seem to be able to shut up, sit down, and stop trying to lead. But this too shall pass. From footnotes to direct political confrontation to encounter groups to . . . ? In any case, relativism has taken its toll. Plumb's pessimism is ultimately well founded (as he argues in his chapter on history): men without faith in progress are lost, and modern men no longer believe in progress. Modern secular men have had their faith challenged, and challenged successfully, in Vietnam's jungles. Modern unsecular man is back to the theologies of eternal return, internal self-transcendence, noumenal escape, and pseudo-mysticism (produced by chemicals, organic products, or the amazing alpha-wave machines[42]). The psychedelic baby eats the cybernetic monster—so long as there is a cheap source of power or organic gardening tools available.

Thus—a 1975 thus—serious Christian scholars have a shot at challenging the minds of the contemporary college generation in a way unimaginable prior to 1965. The epistemological universe of the modern university is now in a state of flux, for the impossibility of keeping Kantian rationalism and Kantian irrationalism in a friendly, workable truce is now more obvious than it was a decade ago. Kant's *Weltanschauung*, to use Richard Kroner's phrase, is a fragmented *Weltanschauung*, as it always was, but the fragmentation is more visible now. Perhaps the modern university is at the end of its road as a major social force. On this point it would appear

---

42. Elanor Links Hoover, "Alpha, The First Step to a New Level of Reality," *Human Behavior* (May/June, 1972). Alpha-wave machines are simplified electroencephalogram devices. The brain produces certain waves, including alpha waves, when the mind is in a state of suspended animation. Zen Buddhist monks and Hindu yogis produce alpha waves during their trances, for example. The machines can translate these waves into a fixed tone, produced in the wearer's earphones, thus enabling him to practice his mysticism. Some people can learn to go into these trances in a few hours of practice. The machines are a sort of symbolic reconciliation of Timothy Leary and B. F. Skinner. Cf. Marvin Karlins and Lewis M. Andrews, *Biofeedback* (New York: Warner, 1973), ch. 3.

that Robert Nisbet and Timothy Leary are in agreement. But in the meantime, Christian students need to be aware of the fact that their position, if consistently biblical and revelational—and especially creedal—should not be an intellectual embarrassment to them. They should not be afraid to make their position known, in whatever discipline they find themselves. (The undergraduate geology major might be wise to stick to crystalography rather than historical geology, however.) They should help to improve that position by applying it in new and promising ways. For too long now we Christians in the academic disciplines have been suffering from a debilitating lack of an intellectual division of labor. There is work to be accomplished and an earth to be subdued. Maybe even a moon, too.

Then further it should be remembered in this connection that because man is a creature of God, it is impossible that he should ever be alienated from God metaphysically. He can never actually become the independent being that he thinks he is. Even the king's heart is in the hand of God as the watercourses. We have seen above that it was exactly because of this fact that man is, as a matter of fact, utterly dependent upon God, that a complete ethical alienation could take place. And it is for the same reason that the ethical alienation can be removed. . . . There is then even in the consciousness of the non-regenerate a *formal power of receptivity*. It is this that enables him to consider the Christian theistic position and see that it stands squarely over against his own, and demands of him the surrender of his own position. . . .

If we thought of the non-regenerate consciousness what it thinks of itself, we should not attempt to reason with it. By that we mean that the non-regenerate consciousness thinks itself to be independent of God metaphysically and ethically. If we thought there was any truth in this we could not argue with it, because with a being metaphysically independent, it would not be possible to come into any intellectual or moral contact at all. We hold, then, that though the ethical miracle of regeneration must occur before argumentation can be really effectual, such an ethical miracle will certainly occur. Not as though we know this with respect to every individual with whom we reason. To hold that would be to deny the free grace of God in connection with the miracle of regeneration. But we do know that it is true, in a general sense, that God will bring sinners to repentance, since the whole work of redemption would fail if he did not. It is thus in *this higher unity of the comprehensive plan and purpose of God* which rests upon his being, that we must seek the solution of the difficulty encountered when we think of the complete ethical alienation of man from God, and the efforts of the redeemed to reason with those who are not redeemed.

Van Til, *A Survey of Christian Epistemology*
(1969), pp. 197-98.

II

THE QUEST FOR COMMON GROUND

By Rousas John Rushdoony

Easy answers are very alluring. They offer a crisis-free solution, as though that were possible. "I am sure," said an arbitrator in a negotiation for a legal dispute, "that you people can get together if you only agree to discuss this calmly and rationally." They did not get together, because more was involved than rational discourse. On one side at least there was a great deal of sin and injustice involved, and a deliberate but legal misuse of the law. Short of surrendering to sin, no easy solution was possible: there was an absence of agreement on a common ground. On the one hand, one group held that an absolute justice is binding on all men, and that laws must be obeyed. On the other, the premise was that whatever you can get away with is legitimate, because there is no law beyond the operative moment. The question thus was beyond the scope of an arbitrator: a philosophical and theological issue was at stake. What constitutes common ground, an absolute and transcendental God and His law, or a relativism in which the existential moment prevails? The mistake of the arbitrator was an error common to our age: he refused to acknowledge that a question even existed. His premise was, indeed, still a third concept of common ground, namely, that all things have a rational solution open to rational discourse. The issue for him was not theological, nor was it existential but rather rational. It was not surprising that no one understood anyone else, since all began on alien premises, and all were convinced that the others were introducing illegitimate and extraneous ideas into the negotiations.

There can be no discourse without common ground. But does common ground exist, and, if it does, what is it? Is the common ground an immanent or a transcendental one? Is it relativistic and existential, or is it an absolute one? In a very real sense, anyone who assumes that a common ground exists, whatever his view thereof, is arguing from within a Christian theistic position, either as an orthodox Christian or as a heretic. If what we have is not a universe but a multiverse, then there is no common order or truth between the varying areas of that multiverse. Each has its own separate source and origin, its own world of developing structure and law, and its own sphere of common ground. Polytheism in antiquity saw the jurisdiction of a particular god, or family of gods, as limited to a particular state and social order. The powers of the gods were likely to end at the borders. Just as the state had to have an imperialistic military adventure in order to extend its power, so the gods could also only extend their powers by conquest. The images and vessels of a conquered temple were always carried to the conqueror's capital and temple because the defeated gods were now the subjects of the conquering god. There was no assurance, however, that the will of the conquering gods would remain in power indefinitely. In a multiverse, imperialism is the only contact between systems, and no system can certainly and/or permanently prevail. History is cyclical, and truth has many faces. Conquest alone establishes a tenuous and fleeting common ground, if it can be called that, in a multiverse. Not surprisingly, a century like the 20th, which holds to a multiverse, has established common ground and discourse by bombs, bayonets, and wars. For its children, truth and common ground spring out of the muzzle of a gun.

To insist on any kind of common ground means that one is a product of a Christian culture. This is no insurance against error. The common ground can be located outside of God and His decree and creation, in which case the *order* of a Biblical world view is sought without its *truth*, and this is too often the case. It is not enough that a man hold to a common ground. It was this fallacy that led many astray in the early church. They found, or thought they found, a common ground principle in Greek philosophy. (This question is not our concern here. Suffice it to say, that what Plato and Aristotle actually said was very different from what Plato and Aristotle were thought to mean when read by Christians who assumed the reality of the creator God and His handiwork, the universe, and then approached the Greek philosophers as though they had pre-supposed a like order. This error is still with us.) The natural man had ostensibly come to a theistic conclusion from his starting point in the autonomous reason of autonomous man. The logical conclusion of this assumption has not been systematically pursued, because it is too obviously in conflict with Scripture. If there is a common ground in man's reason whereby he can, by rational discourse, begin with reason or the natural order and conclude with the God of Scripture, then philosophy offers us an easier plan of salvation than Scripture. Simply insure that all men will be given a thorough grounding by the schools in logical thinking, and reprobation will be eliminated. As simply and as logically as the multiplication tables, all men will see, while they are still children, that their natural reason leads inevitably and inescapably to the God of Scripture.

Then, like the arbitrator in the negotiations for a settlement, we can assume that all men will be Christians if only we can get them to discuss the matter calmly and rationally.

The error in this line of reasoning is the error of Aquinas, who assumed the neutrality of the mind of man. The mind is somehow immune to the fall of man and the taint of sin, so that it examines issues with objectivity and neutrality where properly schooled and trained. The intellect "is like a tablet on which nothing is written."[1] In the process of analyzing the data provided to it by the senses, "the intellect is always true."[2]

It was the assumption of Aquinas that a man is able to reason and to know reality without reference to his ethical status, i.e., whether or not he is a sinner. The problem of knowledge is not a moral question but is rather a question of metaphysics (finitude) or of epistemology (knowledge). Given the proper methodology, and within the bounds of man's metaphysical limitations, the mind of man will assuredly come to the right conclusions.

As against this assumption, the Biblical premise is that a man's knowledge rests on a common ground and premise as his ethical concepts and moral behavior. If man is a covenant-breaker, a sinner at war with God, he will fight that war as a total man. He will at every point be at war with God and will use every instrument of reason to maintain and extend that warfare.

The Thomistic assumption, also the premise of Arminianism, is grounded on a dialectical view of man. Man is a tenuous and unhappy union, supposedly, of two substances, of mind, reason, form, or ideas on the one hand, and of matter on the other. The domain of matter is the domain of the fall, ostensibly, whereas the domain of mind is untouched by the fall and still operative on the same basis as in Eden when properly instructed.

In the Biblical view, man is not made up of two alien elements or substances but is, in all his being, made by God. He is in his totality a created being. He is not two alien substances, mind and body, but "a living soul" (Gen. 2:7), a unity. Man is totally man, totally a creature. He is a unity, and his sin, his rebellion against God, is an act of the total man. In terms of Biblical psychology, it is impossible to assume that the mind of man is immune to the fall. Such a premise belongs to the world of Greek dialectics, which has in its background a multiverse in which mind, all minds, constitute a single universe among the many particulars of the multiverse of being. The presuppositions of the Thomistic and Arminian common ground philosophies are thus implicitly non-biblical and anti-theistic.

---

1. *Summa Theologica*, I, Q 84, A 3.
2. *Ibid.*, I, Q 84, A 6.

For this reason Dr. Cornelius Van Til, in answering Dr. Herman Dooyeweerd, wrote:

> I had for many years rejected the Thomistic-Butler type of approach to apologetics. I had done so because of the unbiblical view of man and the cosmos which underlay this apologetic. I had over and over pointed out that non-Christian schemes of thought, whether ancient or modern, presupposed a view of man as autonomous, of human thought or logic as legislative of what can or cannot exist in reality, and of pure contingency as correlative to such legislative thought. I had for years pointed out that for a Christian to adopt these non-Christian presuppositions about man, together with the dialectical interdependence of legislative logic and brute contingency, and then to join the natural man in asking *whether* God exists and *whether* Christianity is true would be fatal for his enterprise. If we allow that one intelligent word can be spoken about *being* or *knowing* or *acting* as such, without first introducing the Creator-creature distinction, we are sunk. As Christians we must not allow that even such a thing as enumeration or counting can be *accounted for* except upon the presupposition of the truth of what we are told in Scripture about the triune God as the Creator and Redeemer of the world. As a Christian believer I must therefore place myself, for the sake of the argument, upon the position of the non-Christian and show him that on his view of man and the cosmos he and the whole culture is based upon, and will sink into, quicksand. If the unbeliever then points to the fact that non-Christian scientists and philosophers have discovered many actual "states of affairs," I heartily agree with this but I must tell him that they have done so with borrowed capital. They have done so *adventitiously*. The actual state of affairs about the entire cosmos is what the Bible says it is.[3]

One of the objectives of Van Til's philosophy has been to cut out from under man all false doctrines of common ground and to establish man firmly on the only valid ground, namely, that the triune God of Scripture is the creator of all things and that, therefore, all things reveal His handiwork and witness to Him. The common ground is thus that all things are revelational of God, that all men know God and themselves as creatures of God, but that, in terms of St. Paul's declaration, they suppress or hold down the truth in unrighteousness (Rom. 1:18). As Van Til summarized his position,

> I may now add a few words about my view of the nature of facts and of the unbeliever's knowledge of them.
>
> 1. I hold that all the facts of the universe are exhaustively revelational of God.
>   a. This is true of the facts of man's environment in nature and history.

---

3. Cornelius Van Til, "Response," in E. R. Geehan, ed., *Jerusalem and Athens: Critical Discussions on the Theology and Apologetics of Cornelius Van Til* (Nutley, N. J.: Presbyterian and Reformed Publishing Co., 1971), pp. 90 f.

    b. This is also true of man's own constitution as a rational and moral being.

2. In consequence of these two points I hold that all men unavoidably know God and themselves as creatures of God.[4]

All facts, whether in the natural world, in man's constitution or environment, reveal God to man. Sin does not destroy this knowledge. The problem is that man wilfully suppresses it. Not only is created reality revelational of God, but man's ethical reactions to God's revelation, both for and against, are also revelational. According to Van Til,

> At this point a word may be said about the revelation of God through conscience and its relation to Scripture. Conscience is man's consciousness speaking on matters of directly moral import. Every act of man's consciousness is moral in the most comprehensive sense of that term. Yet there is a difference between questions of right and wrong in a restricted sense and general questions of interpretation. Now if man's whole consciousness was originally created perfect, and as such authoritatively expressive of the will of God, that same consciousness is still revelational and authoritative after the entrance of sin to the extent that its voice is still the voice of God. The sinner's efforts, so far as they are done self-consciously from his point of view, seek to destroy or bury the voice of God that comes to him through nature, which includes his own consciousness. But this effort cannot be wholly successful at any point in history. The most depraved of men cannot wholly escape the voice of God. Their greatest wickedness is meaningless except upon the assumption that they have sinned against the authority of God. Thoughts and deeds of utmost perversity are themselves revelational, revelational, that is, in their very abnormality. The natural man accuses or else excuses himself only because his own utterly depraved consciousness continues to point back to the original natural state of affairs. The prodigal son can never forget the father's voice. It is the albatross forever about his neck.[5]

Men want to shift the common ground away from the fact of creation to some inherent and autonomous factor in man or in the universe. To eliminate the common ground as God and His creation of all things as declared in Scripture is also to shift the ultimacy of all things from God to the universe. Another principle of truth and another criterion of judgment has been introduced. The Scriptural position is that man is totally God's creation, and the universe is totally God's creation, so that at no point does man have neutral ground apart from God. At every point man is confronted by the fact of God; all things reveal Him and witness to

---

4. Cornelius Van Til, *A Letter on Common Grace* (Phillipsburg, N. J.: Grotenhuis, 1953), p. 15. Apropos of Van Til's point, a Freudian psychoanalyst wrote a few years ago that he knew of no psychoanalyst who believed in God, nor of one who was not afraid of Him!

5. C. Van Til, "Nature and Scripture," in *The Infallible Word: A Symposium by the Members of the Faculty of Westminster Theological Seminary* (Philadelphia: The Presbyterian Guardian Publishing Corp., 1946), pp. 266 f.

Him, so that man can never find a point of common discourse which does not first and last witness to God.

> The main point is that if man could look anywhere and not be confronted with the revelation of God then he could not sin in the Biblical sense of the term. Sin is the breaking of the law of God. God confronts man everywhere. He cannot in the nature of the case confront man anywhere if he does not confront him everywhere. God is one; the law is one. If man could press one button on the radio of his experience and not hear the voice of God then he would always press that button and not the others. But man cannot even press the button of his own self-consciousness without hearing the requirement of God.[6]

Man begins the course of history, not merely with a capacity for God, but "with *actual* knowledge of God," a knowledge man cannot eradicate, although he works to suppress it.[7] Man the sinner hates God, and his reasoning and his epistemology will reflect this hatred and warfare.[8]

A philosophy which presupposes any other common ground than the God of Scripture and His creation of all things can at best give man an irrelevant and limited God. "If God and man are made interdependent or commonly dependent upon a common universe then there can be no grace of God for man."[9] Man is ready to admit God as a co-worker in building a better universe, but "There must be no God in himself, and no counsel of such a God according to which the course of the world is brought into existence and controlled."[10] Without such a sovereign God who in Himself and of Himself creates and decrees all things and governs and controls them by His own counsel, no Biblical faith is possible, and no truly Christian philosophy can exist. The attempts of men to find a common ground between the unbeliever and the believer in terms of the anti-God premises of man in revolt against God are not only hopeless but are themselves evidences of a departure from God.

Without the presupposition of the God of Scripture, if man is faithful to this presupposition, man can know nothing. When the fallen man has knowledge, it is on borrowed premises. The reason for this is that all reasoning is in terms of and by presupposition. All thinking rests on pre-theoretical and essentially religious presuppositions about reality which either affirm or deny the God of Scripture. The presuppositions determine what the facts are. For the Buddhist, who assumes that nothingness is ultimate, the *facts* of the world have a radically different meaning and are in essence a

---

6. C. Van Til, *A Letter on Common Grace*, pp. 40 f.
7. *Ibid.*, p. 36.
8. C. Van Til, *Common Grace* (Philadelphia: Presbyterian and Reformed Publishing Co., 1947), p. 57.
9. C. Van Til, "Common Grace," in the papers of the *First Annual Institute of the Reformed Faith*, p. 10. Sponsored by the Christ Bible Presbyterian Church, Philadelphia, 1951.
10. *Ibid.*, p. 8.

different set of *facts* than for a Parsee who, as a systematic Zoroastrian, assumes the equal ultimacy of two substances, gods, or beings in the universe and interprets reality in terms of that. Similarly, the presuppositions of Hegel gave him a radically different idea of *facts* than did the presuppositions of Diogenes. Men do not begin with facts, either in the realm of philosophy, of religion, or of the sciences. Kuhn, as a scientist, has called attention to the status of presuppositions in science. Facts in themselves are not available nor workable. The scientist thus approaches them with a theory or paradigm whereby he gives them a workable basis. There is no science without commitment to a paradigm.[11] For Kuhn, paradigms are inescapable; his view of them is relativistic, but he candidly states that science is essentially a series of paradigms rather than facts.[12]

All reasoning is thus circular reasoning. "The starting-point, the method, and the conclusion are always involved in one another."[13] If a man is logical to his presupposition, if he begins with nothingness, after Buddha, he ends with nothingness. But men are rarely logical. To be faithful to the premise of unbelief is to know nothing, and this the sinner will not admit. He insists on knowing nothing only where God is concerned, or where a situation points to God. At all other times, he assumes a universe only God can give while denying the God who made it. By means of a negative apologetics, Van Til systematically cuts the ground out from under the unbelievers. The logic of their presuppositions makes knowledge impossible unless it is exhaustive. If a man claims to begin only with facts, he can know nothing truly unless he knows it exhaustively. If he claims that his paradigm or hypothesis is one drawn from the facts, he is reversing the matter, in that his facts are an aspect of his hypothesis. What Van Til said of history is true in every other area as well: "Back of every appeal to historical facts lies a philosophy of fact."[14] But only the philosophy of fact of Christian theism can account for the facts. Without the God of Scripture, we have only brute factuality, raw, uninterpreted, meaningless and isolated facts, each one a realm to itself. As Van Til points out,

> . . . it is impossible to reason on the basis of brute facts. Every one who reasons about facts comes to those facts with a schematism into which he fits the facts. The real question is, therefore, into whose

---

11. Thomas S. Kuhn, *The Structure of Scientific Revolutions* (Chicago: University of Chicago Press, Phoenix Books, 1964), p. 99. Also issued as vol. II, no. 2, of the *International Encyclopedia of Unified Science* (University of Chicago Press, 1962).

12. See R. J. Rushdoony, *The Mythology of Science* (Nutley, N. J.: The Craig Press, 1967), pp. 85-93.

13. C. Van Til, *The Defense of the Faith* (Philadelphia: Presbyterian and Reformed Publishing Co., 1955), p. 118.

14. C. Van Til, *An Introduction to Theology* (Philadelphia: Westminster Theological Seminary, 1947), vol. II, pp. 139 f.

schematism the facts will fit. As between Christianity and its opponents the question is whether our claim that Christianity is the only schematism into which the facts will fit, is true or not. Christianity claims that unless we presuppose the existence of God, in whom, as the self-sufficient One, schematism and fact, fact and reason apart from and prior to the existence of the world, are coterminous, we face the utterly unintelligible "brute fact."[15]

The brute fact gives us no more than a brute fact. Without the sovereign God of Scripture, no fact has any meaning, and all factuality is then isolated, meaningless, and beyond any interpretation because it is sufficient unto itself. "The only alternative to 'circular reasoning' as engaged in by Christians, no matter on what point they speak, is that of reasoning on the basis of isolated facts and isolated minds, with the result that there is no possibility of reasoning at all."[16]

The Christian can appeal to the facts, in terms of Van Til's statement of the biblical premises, precisely because his appeal is never to brute facts but always to God-interpreted, God-created facts. The test of relevancy for any hypothesis is its "correspondence with God's interpretation of facts. True human interpretation is implication into God's interpretation."[17]

The great advances made by Western man have been made on the basis of the background of Christian thought, in terms of the borrowed capital of biblical theism. As Van Til notes,

> The apparent success of modern science should not blind us to the fact that the whole structure is built upon sand. The success of modern science, we believe, is due to the fact that it really works with borrowed capital. If there really were brute facts there would be no science. There can be no brute facts. All facts are, as a matter of fact, created by God. So too the mind of man is created by God. There are real universals in the world because of the creation of God. Even the mind of sinful man can see something of this in spite of his sin. Hence, though built upon a metaphysic which is basically false, the science of the non-Christian may reveal much of truth. When the prodigal son left home he was generous with his "substance." But it was really his father's substance that he expended.[18]

A prodigal son eventually will come to the end of his substance, and a culture living on borrowed capital will finally expend that capital. Interesting evidence of this is available in the study of a molecular biologist who is not a Christian but who sees the loss of meaning as portending the death of science and of man. The world, says Stent, has looked forward to the

---

15. C. Van Til, *Christian-Theistic Evidences* (Philadelphia: Westminster Theological Seminary, 1947), p. 39.
16. C. Van Til, *Introduction to Theology*, II, 140.
17. *Evidences*, p. 64.
18. *Ibid.*, p. 77.

death of God as its release into a golden age, only to find that it spells instead the death of progress. In a universe in which all things are equally meaningless only a democracy of emptiness and futility exists. We are seeing, Stent holds, the erosion of the reality principle of life in favor of the pleasure principle. Neither the sciences nor man can long endure in a world without truth or meaning. Relativism, however, gives us no other world.[19]

Thus, Van Til's warnings are not lacking in their secular parallels. The unbelieving have at times recognized where their course of action may lead them, but they have not changed their course for all of that. Van Til, however, pushes the unbeliever to the wall as far as his presuppositions are concerned: he does not permit him the luxury of believing on the one hand that his unbelief is a tenable faith, or, on the other, that belief in God is other than inescapable, and that men reject God, not for intellectual reasons but out of an unwillingness to surrender their own sin, their pretension to be as God, determining or knowing good and evil for themselves:

> Either presuppose God and live, or presuppose yourself as ultimate and die. That is the alternative with which the Christian must challenge his fellow man.

> If the Christian thus challenges his fellow man then he may be an instrument of the Spirit of God. The proofs of God then become witnesses of God. The theistic proofs therefore reduce to one proof, the proof which argues that unless *this* God, the God of the Bible, the ultimate being, the Creator, the controller of the universe, be presupposed as the foundation of human experience, this experience operates in a void.[20]

That the world should deny God as the presupposition of its thought, we can understand. In terms of its warfare against God, it naturally seeks to establish the world in terms of man rather than in terms of God. Such men, St. Paul says, have "altered God's truth into falsehood, and revered and served the creature rather than the Creator" (Rom. 1:25, Berkeley Version). But what shall we say of those who profess to uphold the word of God and who still seek to establish philosophy on the husks of the prodigal son? It is not surprising that the church has declined, and that schools and colleges established to propagate the faith have soon become strongholds of the enemy. Even when the school or church continues still to profess faith in the infallible word, its witness in the various areas of life is either syncretistic or simply a baptized paganism, the ideas of humanism lightly sprinkled with holy water.

---

19. Gunther S. Stent, *The Coming of the Golden Age: A View of the End of Progress* (Garden City, N. Y.: The Natural History Press, 1969).
20. Van Til, *A Letter on Common Grace*, p. 61.

Van Til writes, "God is one; the law is one." Precisely. Because God is the sovereign and creator God, all things are subject to Him and derive their life, meaning, and direction from Him. A Christian theistic philosophy, following in the footsteps of Van Til's work, can develop a world and life view which can unfold the law of God for every sphere of being. Philosophy, economics, history, political science, art, agriculture, science, and all things else can be developed in terms of the presupposition of the triune God of Scripture and His law-word.

The mockers within the church ridicule the idea of a Christian historiography, art, political science, or anything else. They deny the possibility of a Biblical economics, or a science premised upon the God of Scripture. They do affirm that these disciplines are tenable in terms of autonomous man and his common ground philosophy. The idea of grounding the arts and sciences on faith is ridiculous to them, because they will not admit that the premise of the autonomy and the autonomous ability of the mind of man is itself a staggering act of faith, and blind faith. Machen insisted that, "far from being contrasted with knowledge, faith is founded upon knowledge."[21] Those who limit the scope of God's sovereignty and of His word and its implications to theology and the church are like the enemies of Israel, who said, "Their gods are gods of the hills; . . . but let us fight against them in the plain, and surely we shall be stronger than they" (I Kings 20:23).[22] But the God of Scripture is the God of the hills and of the plains, of the church and of the sciences as well: He is the only source and ground of interpretation for every realm of life, because all factuality is God-created and God-interpreted.

To begin with the *facts*, we are told, is the only proper scientific method. But men, as we have seen, do not begin with the facts but with a faith concerning the nature of factuality. This faith is disguised, and a facade of objectivity commonly assumed, but it is basic all the same. Van Til insists that the consistent Christian must begin with the fact of God as revealed in Scripture.

> Everybody naturally begins with the "facts," we are told. Would it not be the height of absurdity when the subject under investigation is some form of animal life in the heart of Africa to consult the Bible about information as to that "fact"? Yes, we answer, that would be absurd but that is not what we mean. We are not speaking of getting definite bits of information about certain definite "facts" of biology or physics. But it will be granted at once that whatever "fact" there may be in the heart of Africa or anywhere else is a part of some great realm of "facts" such as those mentioned. The very purpose of scientific knowledge is to

---

21. J. Gresham Machen, *What Is Faith?* (Grand Rapids: Eerdmans, [1925] 1946), p. 46.
22. *Ibid.*, p. 68.

set facts into relation to one another. All the facts of these realms of knowledge have certain qualifications. One characteristic of these facts is that decomposition works among them. Is this a natural something? The Antitheist, we have seen, takes for granted that it is a natural something. But we have also seen that he is not entitled to assume this position. Now it is in Scripture alone that we come to an alternative interpretation of these facts of Africa. It will then be necessary for an investigator in Africa to take into consideration this other interpretation that is given to the fact that he is investigating. The Bible tells him that the interpretation that he by himself gives to that "fact" or any other "fact" is quite wrong. The Bible does not claim to offer a rival theory that may or may not be true. It claims to have the truth about all facts. Consequently if one launches out upon a tour of investigation without his Bible he has already rejected this claim of the Bible and is duty bound to find a solution for the facts that he is about to investigate or make reasonable the claim that no solution can be found. Even to say that a solution may be found in the future without reference to the Bible is to put the Bible aside. Now such "solutions" as scientists have come to of late themselves indicate that the "fact" of knowledge itself remains unaccounted for if Scripture is left out of account. James Jeans, for example, says that science had no pronouncement to make about the nature of reality. He holds that no one can say what the nature of reality is. Such conclusions show that if one begins investigation of any (area) of knowledge without Scripture he will not come to a theistic position in the end. The argument for the necessity of Scripture is accordingly the same in form and in force as the argument for the necessity of thinking of the "facts" as standing in relation to God at the outset of the investigation. Hence if it is unreasonable to start out an investigation by assuming that the "facts" exist in total independence of God it is equally unreasonable to start on an investigation without the Bible.

We conclude then that the fact that "everybody" does take it as such an obvious thing that we must "begin with the facts" is quite innocent because meaningless if we signify by that phrase that the locus of investigation is the African jungles, or that the Bible is not a textbook of science. No one claims that one should go to the Bible *instead* of to Africa. All that we claim is that avowed antitheists should tell us why they do not take their Bibles with them to Africa. We cannot rest satisfied with the mere information that they do not take their Bibles. That is interesting biographically and when analyzed as above has epistemological significance, but it does not justify their procedure.[23]

Let us indeed begin with the facts. And the fact is that a philosophy which does not begin and end with the creator, governor, and interpreter of all factuality, the sovereign and triune God of Scripture, cannot call itself

23. C. Van Til, *Metaphysics of Apologetics* (Philadelphia: Westminster Theological Seminary, 1931), p. 114. This same work was republished in 1969 (Den Dulk Foundation; Presbyterian and Reformed Publishing Co.) as *In Defense of the Faith*, vol. II, *A Survey of Christian Epistemology*, pp. 124 f.

Christian. It has another foundation, it is sand, and its future is an assured collapse (Matt. 7:24-27).

For the unbeliever, "Every fact . . . that has scientific standing is such only if it does not reveal God, but does reveal man as ultimate."[24] The believer must, on the contrary, assume that all factuality is created and controlled by God. That factuality includes himself and the unbeliever, alike the creation of God and revelational of Him. This is their common ground.

---

24. C. Van Til, *A Christian Theory of Knowledge* (Philadelphia: Westminster Theological Seminary, 1954), p. 192.

Part Two

ACADEMIC DISCIPLINES

We will in the first place fearlessly take our concept of God as absolute personality as the standard of human thought. We hold that human thought is analogical of God's thought. Hence we keep the universal and the particular together always. Mankind was created as a unity. The individual experience of one human being could never bring an independent and so-called *native* witness to the nature of religion. No one man ever existed or was meant to exist in total independence of all others. Each human being was meant, to be sure, to show forth something individual and in this way add something to the witness of the whole of humanity as to what God means to man, but this individual should always be thought of in conjunction with the whole race.

Even more important than this, if possible, is the fact that this witness of humanity as a whole must have God as its objective reference and could not exist without this objective reference. God is the presupposition of the very existence of those who give the witness to him; hence their witness is reflective. The human consciousness as a whole cannot be thought of as functioning except upon the presupposition of God and so too the religious consciousness cannot be thought of as functioning apart from God.

It follows from this too that *we will not set the feeling in opposition to the intellect*. God has created man as a harmony. One aspect of man's personality cannot lead us deeper into reality than another aspect can.

Still further it follows that we will seek the solution of our problems as far as possible in the direction of *rationality rather than irrationality*. Individual human beings are not drops afloat upon the sea of the Irrational, but live before the background and in relation to an absolutely self-conscious God.

Van Til, *The Psychology of Religion*
(Syllabus, 1961), pp. 53-54.

PSYCHOLOGY

III

IMPLICATIONS FOR PSYCHOLOGY

By ROUSAS JOHN RUSHDOONY

Clearly, psychology in the twentieth century can be called a "growth industry." How many practising psychologists, psychiatrists and psychoanalysts exist today in the Western world would be hard to say, but they are clearly numerous. Of one of these three classifications, 23,077 were among the 300,000 scientists registered in 1968 by the National Science Foundation. The American Psychological Association has about 30,000 members. Annually, about 25,000 bachelor's degrees, 5,000 master's and 2,000 doctorates are awarded in psychology. There are no shortages of jobs, and more jobs than applicants are in evidence. In 1968, the median salary for psychologists was higher than the median for anthropologists, political scientists, sociologists, biologists, agriculturalists, or mathematicians.[1] The median salary for psychoanalysts and psychiatrists is no doubt much higher than for psychologists.

This eminent position of psychology in the twentieth century is not surprising. Humanism has come into full flower, and the greatest concern of man is with man, himself. In the earlier Middle Ages, theology was the queen of the sciences, because a theological view of man still prevailed; in the twentieth century, psychology is very much resented by other sciences as a newcomer, and its popularity deplored, but, as far as the common man is concerned, psychology is now the queen of the sciences. A book by a biologist, archeologist, or any other scientist can sometimes gain a fairly wide audience, but psychology books are regularly popular with the reading public. More than a few best sellers of the past generation have been works on psychology. In addition, more than a small percentage of the books by biologists, medical doctors, anthropologists, and others have succeeded precisely because they catered to the same hunger, man's interest in man, in man's sexuality, man's "primitive" forms, man's past and future, and so on.

---

1. Richard Ruble, "Psychology in the '70's," in *Journal of the American Scientific Affiliation*, vol. 24, no. 4 (Dec., 1972), p. 129.

We have, however, only scratched the surface. The Bible is no longer a mandatory subject of study in schools and colleges; except for Christian institutions, it largely disappeared quite some time ago. Psychology and related subjects are normally required courses.

It is not, however, necessary to go to school to get a course of instruction in psychology. The churches have seen to that. A few churches have a psychologist on the staff. Almost all preach more psychology than theology from the pulpit. Books in the area of pastoral psychology have long enjoyed a wide audience among the clergy. Since the interest of the laity reflects the humanism of the day, successful pastors have met that need, and their ministry has come to be a form of psychological therapy. This is true in theologically conservative circles also, where the same hunger for psychologically oriented pastorates is as notable as the pious boredom with theology.

"The cure of souls" has always been a concern of the church, and there is a long and important history of the concern of pastors for the personal problems of the flock. This concern, however much clouded by Hellenic rather than Biblical views of man, still had an essentially theological concern. Its concern for peace of mind was theocentric, not man-centered. Its goal was holy living and holy dying.[2]

The modern concern, however, is not only man-centered but also soteriological. The religion of modern man is humanism, the worship of man, and the interest of modern man in psychology is a soteriological interest: man wants salvation by means of psychology. His interest in psychology is thus religious, and it reflects the popular religion of the day.

In psychology, therefore, the Christian Church faces a rival plan of salvation. This does *not* mean that all psychologists are non-Christian; it *does* mean that the modern schools of psychology are not only non-Christian but in essence have a rival doctrine of man and his salvation. We cannot agree, therefore, with Koteskey when he holds that "Behavioral psychology does not conflict with Christianity at the philosophical level as long as it is kept in mind that its assumptions are a set of working assumptions necessary for the pursuit of knowledge by the scientific method."[3] Every assumption has implicit in it a metaphysics and an ethics, and the assumptions of behaviorism are anti-Christian to the core.

Christians are less ready to defend their position because their own assumptions are too often non-Biblical. As Howard has shown, Christian thinkers have usually assumed some form of Hellenistic doctrine concerning man. They have seen man as a union of two substances, body and soul,

---

2. See John J. McNeill, *A History of the Cure of Souls* (New York: Harper, 1951).

3. Ronald L. Koteskey, "Behavioral Psychology in Christian Perspective," in *Journal of American Scientific Affiliation*, vol. 24, no. 4 (Dec., 1972), p. 147.

and, in some cases, of three substances, body, soul, and spirit, or two substances, body and soul, linked by a third factor of some sort, spirit, or by some other combination of these three. The Biblical conception of man is that he is an entity, a living soul, a single personality.[4]

In approaching the subject of psychology, we must, *first* of all, deny that here or anywhere else man can approach the facts without presuppositions or with neutrality. Neutral man does not exist. Man is either a covenant-keeper or a covenant-breaker, either obeying God in faith, or in revolt against God as a would-be god. Calvin, in discussing the healthy person, said of all such, "That we hold God to be the sole governor of our souls, that we hold His law to be the only rule and spiritual directory of our consciences, not serving Him according to the foolish inventions of men" (First letter to the Duke of Somerset, October 22, 1548). Moreover, Calvin wrote to Madame de Crussol (May 8, 1563), "God cannot endure any neutrality."[5] The idea of neutrality is a mask for the total warfare waged by humanistic man (and psychology) against God and His word. To assent in any degree to the concept of neutrality is not only a serious error but also a denial of God as the total lord and creator of all things.

Second, as Van Til has pointed out, the presupposition of humanistic psychologies, whether psychologies of religion or general psychology, is "the assumption of the metaphysical independence of the self-consciousness of man."[6] The idea of neutrality, of course, rests on this premise of man's metaphysical independence from God. The doctrine of creation makes man metaphysically dependent upon God. Man is God's creature, and man and his nature can only be truly understood in terms of man's creation by God and man's revolt against God. The doctrine of creation requires us to understand man, not in terms of a primitive past, an animal ancestry, and the ultimacy of a universal void, but in terms of the sovereign and triune God and man's creation in His image. Man was not born out of the void, and he was created in Adam as a mature man, a fact we shall return to later. Since there is not a fragment of man's being, nor a thought in man's head, which is outside the eternal counsel and decree of God, man has not even the shadow of a degree of metaphysical independence from God.

Third, man's dependence on God is total, which means that not only does man have no metaphysical independence from God but also that man has no moral independence. As Van Til has pointed out, "we cannot as Christians allow the assumption of the ethical independence of the self-

---

4. James Keir Howard, "The Concept of the Soul in Psychology and Religion," in *ibid.*, pp. 147-154.
5. McNeill, *op. cit.*, p. 209.
6. Cornelius Van Til, *Psychology of Religion* (Philadelphia: Westminster Theological Seminary, [1935] 1961), p. 3.

consciousness of man in general and of his religious consciousness in particular. If we are Christians at all we believe in the doctrine of sin, and this makes man ethically alienated from God and yet dependent upon God."[7] The assumption that the human mind is a self-contained entity is a religious assumption: it rests on the humanistic faith in autonomous man. To assume that a belief that man is created in the image of God is unscientific is a conclusion reached on a religious premise, the premise of man the covenant-breaker, whose faith is in himself. As against all such, Van Til observes,

> As Christians, we are quite willing to justify our position on this matter. We do not beg the question and simply begin as though the problem did not exist. That is what our opponents do. We are ready to challenge the starting-point of the psychology of religion school and debate with them on their epistemology and metaphysics. We maintain that their starting-point makes it incumbent upon them to show us that it is reasonable to suppose that human experience, the human consciousness, has sprung out of the void.[8]

It is a myth to believe that man can formulate a psychology which leaves God out of consideration, which does not begin with the fact of creation and the ethical revolt of man in the fall, and yet be in any wise an objective account of man's mind. The statement that man's consciousness has arisen out of the void by means of an evolutionary chance variation of nothing into something is not a matter of observation nor of record but of faith. It is the faith of would-be autonomous man, who insists in terms of the premise of the tempter, that he is independent of God. The word of the tempter was, "Ye shall not surely die" (Gen. 3:4), i.e., God has no eternal decree whereby you are foreordained to begin to die if you disobey Him. The tempter's words imply that there is either no death at all for man, or, at the very worst, no absolute and inescapable decree of death. God, as an earlier product of the void, is the senior citizen of the universe, and He is thus able to push man around to a degree, but there is no necessity for this. By revolting against God's law, the tempter held, man's potential as his own god, determining or knowing good and evil for himself, will be realized (Gen. 3:5).

Problems, of course, have ensued for man, and he does die. Man's real problem, as the reprobate insists on seeing it, are the relics of a God-oriented world-view. As these are eliminated by education, man will be free. Man, as his own god, will overcome death, poverty, war, disease, and all other problems.

The humanistic psychologist insists that all he is doing is to apply "the scientific method" to the problem of human consciousness. Only

---

7. *Ibid.*
8. *Ibid.*, p. 12.

the scientifically validated sources of information can be used, and we are thus strictly limited as to the data which are admissible. But what constitutes admissible data? Koteskey, as we have seen, regards behavioral psychology and Christianity as complementary rather than conflicting when viewed in the proper perspective. He writes,

> Any system must begin with a set of philosophical presuppositions, although these are not often stated explicitly. Kaufman (1968), however, lists the following basic assumptions: (a) The universe is uniform and permanent, (b) the world can be known, (c) the universe is determined, and (d) events do not occur without being caused. The behavioral psychologist builds his structure of laws of behavior with these assumptions as a foundation, and thus, his system of knowledge is only as correct and complete as his initial set of assumptions. That is, if any of these assumptions are incorrect or incomplete, so is the behavioral psychologist's system.[9]

This is a good statement of the case and deserves attention. These assumptions are necessary for some kind of science, but they clearly are assumptions and acts of faith. The scientist's knowledge of the universe is too meager to justify the conclusion of uniformity, and, as far as permanence is concerned, there is no ground for such an assumption. Both assumptions, however, are necessary for a science without God which wants the world of God without a creator. "The world can be known," it is held, a very great act of faith. A product of the void and chance is not amenable to reason: it is utterly lacking in any order, design, or purpose and is impenetrable to reason. Where there is only brute factuality and no connection between fact and fact, there can be no reasoning. To say then that "the universe is determined" is absurd. Where only raw, brute factuality exists, there is no unified determination; every fact is its own god and law, and every fact is its own universe. To add further that "events do not occur without being caused" is to be guilty of a radical anthropomorphism. To project determination and causality on to a universe of raw, brute facts is to insist that human attributes are also the attributes of the universe. The Christian, on the other hand, can insist that determination and causality exist in the universe because the universe is the handiwork of God.

Van Til has repeatedly pointed out that the unbelieving scientist operates on borrowed premises; on his own principle of the ultimacy of chance, there can be no science. Koteskey, in spite of himself, has documented this thesis. Scientists want a universe, not a multiverse of brute factuality, and they ascribe to it all the attributes of mind, purpose, and determination while denying the determiner. This is clearly an amazing and wilful faith, an attempt to have the practical value of God while denying Him. God

---

9. Koteskey, *op. cit.*, p. 144.

is in fact assumed as the guarantor of science and denied vehemently by name. This is not science: it is the same anti-God act of faith that marked the fall, the insistence that God is not ultimate while claiming all the values of God's being and handiwork.

Thus, it will not do to say that science and Christianity both posit that the world can be known, is determined, has causality, and so on, and thereby conclude that they are complementary. On the contrary, humanistic science illogically assumes those things with respect to the universe (and the idea of a universe as against a multiverse is itself a major assumption) only to be better able to dispense with God. If a man has a rich uncle whom he dislikes while liking very much the money he will inherit, he has a problem if he must live with an uncle whose health is better than his own! If he insists on having the money without the uncle, he may murder his uncle. So too theologians proclaim the death of God, and the scientists described by Koteskey have long assumed the death or non-existence of God in order to seize the estate. In assuming that such a relationship is "complementary" rather than murderous, Koteskey comes to a conclusion hardly becoming to a psychologist, whose study is man!

Mowrer is another example of a psychologist who borrows from Christian premises to a degree which makes him attractive to many. Mowrer objects to "the theory that psychoneurosis implies no moral responsibility, no error, no misdeed on the part of the afflicted person."[10] For Mowrer, the theory of mental sickness destroys responsibility and is socially destructive. But Mowrer does not like the idea of sin. However, "And it is here I suggest that, as between the concept of sin (however unsatisfactory it may in some ways be) and that of sickness, sin is indeed the lesser of two evils."[11] Sin for Mowrer is not an offense against God but is humanistically interpreted as irresponsibility between man and man. Irresponsibility in terms of what? By what standard or law is man responsible to his fellow man? To begin within the framework of Mowrer is not tenable, nor can we say his position is complementary to the Biblical position. Pragmatically, Mowrer adopts the idea of sin, but his hostility to God is no less real than that of B. F. Skinner, the behaviorist. Both want a world without God, and their psychologies are expressive of what Van Til calls the Cainitic wish that there be no God. To try to work from Mowrer to Scripture is to establish a humanistic priority in understanding man's psychology. The goal of man in Mowrer is to function effectively, whereas in terms of Scripture, the Catechism tells us, "Man's chief end is to glorify God and to enjoy Him forever."

To understand man, a Biblically grounded psychology will seek to know

---

10. O. Hobart Mowrer, *The Crisis in Psychiatry and Religion* (Princeton, N. J.: Van Nostrand, 1961), p. 40.
11. *Ibid.*, p. 50.

man, not in terms of human relations, but in terms of the image of God. As against this, humanistic psychologies are determined that man be separated from the image of God and understood in terms of the void. As a result, in such psychologies "man wiped out the borderlines that separated man from the beast, and the beast from the inorganic world, thus reducing man to a focus of action and interaction in the sea of ultimate Irrationalism."[12]

Van Til has traced the steps in this process. *First*, the intellect was dethroned, not in the interests of a Christian objection to rationalism, but in the interests of Irrationalism. "Psychology was but following the lead of Schopenhauer and Von Hartman in their ultimate metaphysical voluntarism when it searched in the non-rational for a deeper insight into the nature of the human soul."[13]

Second, psychology reacted, and rightly so, against the dualistic view of man as two separate substances, soul and body. This step could have favored the Biblical point of view, but its purpose was to reduce man to the purely corporeal. The first step laid emphasis on man as emotional and volitional; the second step worked to reduce man to the purely physical, not to a holistic but a reductionistic view of man.

Third, child psychology was progressively stressed, not in terms of doing justice to the individual as God created him, not in terms of purpose, but in terms of the child itself. The child becomes his own standard, an exclusive and isolated personality, growing up in terms of no law but his own. As Van Til notes tellingly on this third step of modern psychology,

> Its *variability* concept by virtue of which it seeks to do justice to childhood is based upon an ultimate activism. Modern psychology thinks of personality as being exclusively a self-accomplishment on the part of man. At this point it is directly opposed to Christianity which holds that personality is created by God. According to the Christian view, then, variability can mean only that man's personality is not fully developed when created but grows into the pattern set for it by God. The activity by which personality realizes itself is, to be sure, very genuine and significant, but it is genuine and significant only because it acts before the background of the plan of God. The integration of personality, that is, the constant readjustment of the particular and the universal within itself, and the constant readjustment of the whole personality as an individual to the universal found in the universe beyond itself, takes place by a more ultimate and constant readjustment of the individual together with his surroundings to God who is the absolute particular and the absolute universal combined in one ultimate personality. The integration of personality, according to the Christian view, is an integration toward and by virtue of an ultimate self-sufficient personality.

---

12. Van Til, *Psychology of Religion*, p. 57.
13. *Ibid.*

In contrast with this the modern concept of the integration of personality is an *integration into the void.* We can best appreciate this if we note that *the concept purpose itself has been completely internalized.*[14]

There is thus a twofold direction in modern psychology. On the one hand, man is abased and reduced from a creature made in the image of God to a creature out of the void, with an animal past. On the other hand, controlling purpose, God's attribute, is taken from God and "completely internalized" by being made the total decision of man.

The *fourth* step cited by Van Til in the descent of man into the irrational in modern psychology is the emphasis upon the unconscious. "The adult is not only to be interpreted in terms of the child, but the child and the adult both are to be interpreted in terms of the subconscious drives."[15]

Sartre has argued against the idea of the unconscious. He adds that "By the distinction between the 'id' and the 'ego,' Freud has cut the psychic whole into two."[16] Sartre's purpose is to keep the door fully open for man's passion to become god, and thus he objects to the limitation imposed by the idea of the unconscious; he is as humanistic, if not more so, than the psychologists.

Van Til has pointed out how the concept of the unconscious has a potential for Calvinism, and how a Christian must hold that, in his creation "in his unconscious as well as in his conscious activity man was directed toward God."[17] In an especially telling passage, Van Til comments:

> It ought to be clear that there are only two positions that are internally consistent on this point. If one begins upon the path of complete activism one cannot stop until one has come to the place where modern psychology has come. If God has not created man, then man has somehow come upon the scene from the realms of chance and one's character has nothing to do with God. Of course it may still be said that one's character is not wholly one's own since each individual is surrounded by cosmic influences of all sorts. But, in any case, God has then been put out of the picture altogether. Hence it is necessary, if the Christian conception is to be defended at all, that it be defended by rejecting modern activism in its entirety. God has created man with intellect, feeling and will. God created man, soul and body. God created the first man as a full-grown person, but has caused later generations to spring up by growth from childhood to maturity. God has related man's self-conscious to his subconscious life; his childhood to his maturity. Every activity of every aspect of the human personality, at any stage of its development, acts as a derivative personality before the background of the absolute personality of God. Man is an

---

14. *Ibid.,* pp. 59 f.
15. *Ibid.,* p. 60.
16. Jean-Paul Sartre, *Being and Nothingness* (New York: Philosophical Library, 1956), p. 50.
17. Van Til., *op. cit.,* p. 61.

analogica. personality. It is this consistently Biblical and Christian-theistic concept alone that can be defended against the activism of modern psychology. Arminianism, here as elsewhere, offers no defense.

If put in this way the issue is taken out of the surface areas in which it is usually discussed. Many Christian apologists use all their ammunition in the fight by contending against modern psychology on the ground that it immerses man in the meshes of drives, etc., over which he has no control. It is said that Christianity insists on the responsibility of man and that it is this that we must seek to defend against modern psychology. Now it is true that Christianity holds man to be responsible. *But to argue in the blue for freedom does not help to establish man's responsibility.* It is true that modern psychology allows for no responsibility but the most basic reason for this is not that it has immersed man's will in the midst of instincts and drives. The real reason why modern psychology has left no room for responsibility is found in the fact that it has taken the whole of the human personality in all its aspects, self-conscious and sub-conscious, and immersed it in an ultimate metaphysical void. Man cannot be responsible to the void. Hence the only way in which we can establish human responsibility is by showing the ultimate irrationalism of all non-theistic thought of which modern psychology is but a particular manifestation. In that way we place man self-consciously and subconsciously in every aspect of his person before the personality of God. Man is responsible in the whole of his personality, but only if he is the creature of God. Man *before God* is the only alternative to man *in the void.*[18]

The *fifth* step into ultimate irrationality taken by modern psychology, Van Til points out, is the study of abnormal psychology. Again, this could be a good thing, but the reason *why* it has been done is significant and an index of the descent. "This reason was the assumption that the normal and the abnormal are both normal in the sense that they are both naturally to be expected in human life. Hence it is said that one can really get as much light on the normal behavior of man by studying his abnormal behavior as one can get on the abnormal behavior of man by studying his normal behavior."[19] The implications of this step are becoming a matter of everyday life. If the normal and abnormal are equally valid, then the claim of the homosexuals today for an equal standing with others has been validated. The insistence of youth that one "life-style" is as good as another is a logical conclusion from the premises of the modern view of man and his psychology. As Van Til stated it,

> Non-Christian thought assumes that evil is as ultimate as the good. It has always assumed this. Now the logical consequence of this position is that men should give up seeking any rational interpretation of life at all. But till recent times men have not been willing to accept the consequences of an ultimate irrationalism, neither yet now are they

---

18. *Ibid.*, pp. 61 f.   19. *Ibid.*, p. 62.

fully willing. Yet it is undeniable that the descent into the irrational has been rapid in modern thought. It could not be otherwise. If there is irrationalism somewhere in the universe, and if it is taken for granted that this irrationalism is as ultimate as rationality itself, it follows that irrationalism must be thought of as never to be overcome. One rotting apple in a bushel will spoil the whole lot in time. One spot of ultimate irrationality will not only spoil rationality in the future but even now makes all talk about complete rationality meaningless.

Christianity with its conception of God as the absolute rationality has taught that man was created wholly rational. That is, though man was not created with the ability to grasp comprehensively the whole of rationality, yet his rationality was sound. Hence irrationality in the mind of man, that is insanity, must be the result of a deflection of man from the source of absolute rationality. Accordingly, the Christian will have to bring in his doctrine of sin when he discusses abnormal psychology.[20]

The *sixth* step into irrationality by modern psychology is the study of "primitive" man and his psychology. As we noted earlier, man was created a mature person in Adam. The normal and the original man is thus not the child, the primitive man, or the animal, but mature and sinless man.[21] Man cannot plead a primitive inheritance as the reason for his ways; he was created a mature man, and his sin was and is a deliberate act. "If Christianity is true the real primitive man was Adam, who came upon the scene of history as a full-grown man. On the other hand, if the teaching of current evolution is true, primitive man is an independent growth out of bare vacuity."[22]

The *seventh* and final step of *the integration of man into the void* is "the elevation of the animal as a principle of explanation for man." As Van Til points out,

> . . . if man is what non-Christian thought says he is, the normal adult stands on no higher level as a principle of interpretation of life as a whole than the child, the abnormal person and the animal. In that case the animal even has a certain priority over the primitive man, the latter over the child and the child over the man on account of the fact that they appeared upon the scene of history first and man was origi- nated from and through them.[23]

What happens now to Koteskey's common ground between humanistic (and behavioral) science and Christianity? Science posits a knowable universe, but, by denying God, admits an ultimate irrationality which negates the possibility of knowledge. Such science insists that the world is determined and is governed by causality, but its denial of the sovereign

---

20. *Ibid.*, p. 63.
21. See R. J. Rushdoony, *Revolt Against Maturity* (forthcoming).
22. Van Til, *op. cit.*, p. 65.
23. *Idem.*

God of Scripture drives it, not to causes and determination but to an irrational and impenetrable surd. Whether humanistic man works in psychology or in any other area of study, when he makes chance and the void man's ultimate environment, he ends up with irrationalism and the surd. Where man recognizes the God of Scripture as his ultimate and determinative environment, then man has a world penetrable by reason and a life and nature integrated into that ultimate plan and purpose. Koteskey's science is not complementary but hostile to Christianity, and at every point it must be challenged. As Van Til has so well stated it, "I believe that unless we press the crown rights of our King in every realm we shall not long retain them in any realm."[24]

---

24. C. Van Til, *The Defense of the Faith* (Philadelphia: Presbyterian and Reformed Publishing Co., 1955), p. 280.

Certainly we may say that [George Burman] Foster seems to see something of the fact that since Christianity claims to be based upon the conception of God who is supra-historical and the Christ who is supra-historical that a method which assumes historical relativism cannot be successful in dealing with these entities unless it has first proved that Christianity's claim to be a supra-historical religion is false. . . . Now it would seem that those who have taken historical relativism as their starting-point ought to be consistent and say that there is no such thing as the essence of Christianity or for that matter of anything. . . . In the first place, no merely historical series can in and by itself raise any problems because there is in a mere historical series no relation of elements to one another. This is the primary metaphysical difficulty in which all non-theistic thought is involved. In the second place, granted that one were able to think of an historical series as having meaning in and for itself, all the facts of this historical series should be considered as of equal value. There is never any excuse for any one historical being in and of himself to lord it over other historical beings and say to them that their religion is not valuable. No standard of judgment could be evolved from a mere historical series. . . . One has to go back of the "facts" of history to a discussion of the meaning of history. That is, one has to give an intellectual interpretation to the whole of history, for the meaning of history as a whole cannot be discussed except in intellectual terms.

Van Til, *The Psychology of Religion*
(Syllabus, 1961), pp. 35, 36, 73.

HISTORY

IV

THE PROBLEM OF HISTORICAL INTERPRETATION

By C. GREGG SINGER

Some five years ago at an annual meeting of the American Historical Association the writer had the occasion to meet informally with a group of the more famous historians in attendance at that conference. The subject under discussion was the meaning and purpose of history. These half dozen scholars were of the opinion that history lacks any decisive meaning and any discernible purpose. The writer then posed to this group of distinguished scholars one question: If this be the case, then why do we teach history? The scholars looked at him with surprise and even disgust, but no answer was forthcoming from any one of them. The group broke up as each went to his own particular luncheon group and discussion of various phases of a subject which they could not really justify as part of a college curriculum and yet which they continue to teach as if the knowledge of it had some inherent value.

This incident is by no means unique. The professional historians in this country and in Europe have come to the place where they have little faith in the subject to which they have devoted their lives. Historians with increasing and distressing frequency are openly admitting that history has no meaning and shows little or no purpose or goals. But neither is this anti-intellectual attitude peculiar to the professional historians. The existentialist and positivistic philosophies have entered into the thinking of most areas of human thought and activity with devastating results. In conjunction with the Freudian school in psychology, they have made irrationalism and anti-intellectualism fashionable and have virtually removed the concepts of purpose and meaning from the thinking of many historians and those who proclaim themselves to be "social scientists."

It is no wonder that, under the impact of these currents of thought, historians and political scientists have abandoned the search for ultimate meaning in these areas and have therefore surrendered the traditional approach to these branches of knowledge, contenting themselves with a descriptive approach to history and to the study of governmental activity.

The negation of Christian theism has brought in its wake an intellectual sterility which has now penetrated nearly every segment of Western culture. But this sterility does not merely discourage meaningful intellectual activity. It virtually denies that such activity is possible.

This intellectual paralysis which has contemporary scholarship in its grip is not a sudden development. It is not the product of existentialism, nor even of the immediate antecedents of the existentialist philosophy, although it has certainly contributed to the demoralization of the Western mind. The irrationalism which has undermined the basic assumptions of the historians of the nineteenth and twentieth centuries has its roots in the rationalism of the Renaissance. Although these historians produced their masterpieces with a calm assurance and sense of certainty that they were presenting historical truth in a manner that could withstand any possible onslaughts which later scholarship might hurl against them, the very philosophical presuppositions which Von Ranke, the positivists, and the Hegelian writers used have not only been severely scrutinized by their twentieth-century successors, but, for the most part, have also been rejected by these critics. Even during the nineteenth century the currents of irrationalism were eating away the foundations of the mansions of scholarship. Kantian idealism laid the foundations for a pervasive skepticism which would ultimately bring into serious question the possibility of any knowledge. The Kantian reaction to Locke and Hume became the tool by which an all-out offensive was launched against those basic assumptions which historians of the nineteenth century assumed would yield that same degree of certainty in the study of history as the application of the scientific methodology was assumed to yield in the study of physics, chemistry, and the other physical and natural sciences.

However, these disturbing manifestations of the trend toward irrationalism in Western thought did not have their origin in either Kant or Locke. Rather do we find that this irrationalism was deeply imbedded in the humanistic philosophy of the Renaissance. As Van Til has observed with his usual amazing insight, the irrationalism of our day is nothing more than the logical conclusion of the rationalism inherent in Renaissance thought.[1] The frustrations of contemporary historiography are the result of some five hundred years of the development of irrationalism from the womb of Renaissance Humanism.

The very strength of the Reformation in many parts of Europe so shook the political prestige of the Roman Church that the forces of unbelief which had formerly been restrained by the heavy hand of the Inquisition now made themselves felt in the development of European philosophy. Al-

---

1. For an interesting corroboration of this insight into the nature of Humanism by secular historians, see W. Coates, H. V. White, and J. Salwyn Schapiro, *The Emergence of Modern Humanism* (New York, 1960).

though Descartes made a strong profession of loyalty to the Church, nevertheless in his dualism he took a giant stride in proclaiming the freedom of philosophy from any kind of subservience to Roman Catholic dogma or Christian theism. The rationalism of Liebniz was likewise a declaration on the part of a Protestant scholar that philosophy is sufficient unto itself and need not hearken to the Scriptures in its affirmations. In a somewhat different manner Locke and the other English empiricists issued a similar declaration, and the irrationalism of the empiricists was a further step in the revolt against the Christian view of life inherent in the theology of the Reformers.

These philosophical developments ultimately had an important impact on the writing of history in the eighteenth century. No longer did historians view the history of man from the vantage point of Reformation theology. The old conviction that history ultimately derives its meaning and purpose from God was gone. As a result, historians like Gibbon, Robertson, Voltaire, Vico, and others of the eighteenth century were forced to seek the meaning of history elsewhere, and they turned to the doctrines of natural law as formulated by Newton to explain history. The doctrine of natural law, with its concept of mechanical causation, replaced not only the biblical view but the rationalistic concept of history as well. But this Newtonian world and life view itself came under increasing attack, and in the philosophy of David Hume the theory of causation as it was held by the Natural Law School was virtually destroyed with a resounding crash that brought Kant to the rescue of all philosophical endeavor.

This Kantian attempt to rescue philosophy from the irrationalism of eighteenth-century empiricism was equally doomed to failure. It too was essentially irrational, as Van Til has so eloquently demonstrated in so many of his writings. It would be needless repetition in this particular chapter to deal at length with Van Til's masterful exposition of the fallacies in Kantian and post-Kantian thought. It is necessary only to point out that the Kantian dualism deeply affected historical thought in the nineteenth century through Kant's own interpretation of history, and even more sweepingly through Hegel's dialectical approach to the problem of meaning and purpose in the historical process. To attempt to trace this influence in detail would be far outside the scope of this chapter. However, in Hegel and other idealists there was a very grave danger that the importance of ascertaining factual data as an inescapable part of sound historiography would be forgotten by those historians who were enamored by the various ramifications and possibilities of the Idealistic approach which Kant and Hegel had given to them. The ultimate product of this was a school of history which put more emphasis on what historians thought about past events than on the facts of history themselves. Comparative historiography replaced history in this school.

This development in turn invited the emergence of a school which placed all the emphasis on the facts themselves. The positivists adopted the principle, "Let the facts speak for themselves." Apparently oblivious to the difficulties inherent in their underlying assumptions, the positivists proceeded to apply to the study of history the methodology which they derived from the physical and natural sciences, on the assumption that man can and should be viewed as an animal in his various relationships and history. The positivists' approach to historiography brought confusion and a sense of futility to those historians who still believed that somehow it is the task of the historian to ascertain the facts and then draw meaningful and valid conclusions which could be regarded as historical truth.

The frustrations of twentieth-century scholarship are really the continuation of the confusion of the nineteenth, and it called forth the efforts of Collingwood and Croce in Europe, and Beard, Becker, and others in this country, to find a new basis of historical scholarship which would avoid the errors inherent in the nineteenth-century philosophies of history. The attempts of the positivists to find meaning and purpose in a purely objective approach to the data of history, and the attempts of the idealists to find them in a pure realistic approach, had ended in the confusion of irrationalism and the denial that either meaning or purpose could be detected in the historical process. Collingwood and Croce had attacked the problem as philosophers, while Beard and Becker wrote as historians. But neither approach was satisfactory. The confusion remains with us today, not only in history as such, but in the other disciplines frequently called social sciences: economics, political science, and sociology. They have retreated to behavioralism as the psychological framework for their interpretations of the economic and political activities of man as an animal and for man as social animal. The debacle occasioned by these nineteenth-century philosophies is not confined to history and its related spheres of interest, but has spread to nearly every area of human thought today.

This bankruptcy of historical scholarship is quite evident in the philosophies of R. G. Collingwood in England and Carl Becker and Charles A. Beard in this country. In order to understand Van Til's refutation of their irrationalistic approaches to the study of the meaning of history, we must now turn to a brief exposition of the philosophies of these men. R. G. Collingwood, the Oxford philosopher, is an important figure in twentieth-century English thought. Defending history as an autonomous branch of human knowledge, he also argued for its acceptance and respectability in philosophical circles. But for this recognition he forced historical scholarship to pay a heavy price. The price was actually nothing less than the claim to intellectual respectability which he thought he had gained for it. In his essay, "The Historical Imagination," first published in 1935 and then later included in his *The Idea of History*, Collingwood repudiated not only the positivist approach to history, but all those schools of interpretation which insist that facts have an objectivity of their own apart from the mind of the historians, and that historians can recapture past events in some way by recourse to the scientific methodology. He discussed the common-sense approach to history, which bases the possibility of a knowledge of past events on memory and authority, declaring it to be bankrupt.

Collingwood insisted that the historian must come to the realization that he is his own authority and that his own thought is both autonomous and self-authorizing. The criterion of historical truth cannot be the fact that some statement is made by an authority, simply because it is the truthfulness and information of the so-called authority which are in question. The historian must answer the question for himself on his own authority.[2] Even if the historian accepts what the authorities say, he does so not because they say it, but because what they say satisfies his own criterion of historical truth.

This brings Collingwood to a consideration of the vital question, "What is this criterion of historical truth?" If it is not to be found in an agreement of authorities and the sources, where is the historian to turn for historical certainty? Collingwood found the criterion of historical truth in what he called the web of imagination, by which he meant the historian's own *a priori* imagination. This *a priori* imagination furnishes the historian with a picture of the past, which in turn justifies the sources which the historian uses in its construction. The historian thus gives credence to the sources only because they are justified in this manner. This *a priori* imagination enables the historian to judge whether the picture of the past to which the evidence leads is a coherent and continuous picture—in short, whether it makes sense or not.

Collingwood thus assigned to this *a priori* imagination the role of criticizing the data which it also uses at the same time in constructing its picture of the past. But in such a system what constitutes historical evidence? Collingwood denied that evidence in itself is really historical knowledge "to be swallowed and regurgitated by the historian." In sweeping terms he insisted that everything is evidence which the historian can use as evidence. The whole perceptible world is potentially and in principle the evidence which the historian may use. But it becomes actual evidence only in so far as he can use it. To use it he must come to it with the right kind of historical knowledge. Evidence is evidence only when someone contemplates it historically. Otherwise it is only perceived fact and "historically dumb."

Collingwood concluded that historical knowledge can come only from

---

2. R. G. Collingwood, *The Idea of History* (Oxford, 1959), pp. 236-238.

historical knowledge. But if this is the case, how does it begin at all? As an answer to this dilemma he declared that historical thinking is an original and fundamental activity of the human mind, by which he seems to mean that the idea of the past is a kind of innate idea. Thus, historical thinking is that activity of the imagination by which we seek to provide this innate idea with a detailed content. And we do this by using the present as evidence for its own past. Collingwood insists that every present has a past of its own. Thus any imaginative reconstruction of the past aims at reconstructing the past of this present. But the perceptible present can never be perceived or interpreted in its entirety. Thus, in the writing of history no achievement, no interpretation is final. This is true in all areas of human endeavor.

Every new generation must rewrite history in its own way. New historians must not be content with giving new answers to old questions. They must actually revise the questions. The reason for this mandate lies in Collingwood's conception of history as a river into which no man can step twice. Aware that such a definition of the historical process must lead to skepticism, Collingwood quickly repudiated such a possibility by insisting that what appears to be an inherent skepticism is only "the discovery of a second dimension of historical thought, the history of history: the discovery that the historian himself, together with the here-and-now which forms the total body of evidence available to him, is a part of the process he is studying, has his own place in that process, and can see it only from the point of view which at this present moment he occupies within it."[3]

If this argument against skepticism seems less than conclusive, Collingwood's conclusion is even less adequate. He reaffirmed that the criterion of history itself must be the idea of an imaginary picture of the past. This idea is both innate and *a priori*. It is an idea which every man possesses as a part of the furniture of his mind. It is also one to which no fact of experience exactly corresponds. Thus, in spite of all his careful study, the historian can never say that his picture of the past is at any point adequate to his idea of what it ought to be.

It is quite understandable and hardly surprising that Collingwood had little to say about the meaning or purpose of history. Since every historian interprets history according to his own frame of reference or furnishing of his own mind, an objective and discernible meaning and purpose cannot be logically predicated of the historical process. At best every historian and each new generation is free to assign to history that meaning or purpose which fits the needs of the moment.

The relativism of Collingwood was echoed to a degree in this country

---

3. *Ibid.*, p. 84.

by the eminent and influential Carl Becker (1873–1945), who very clearly and concisely stated his philosophy of history in several important and frequently quoted essays, the most important of which are his "What Are Historical Facts"[4] and "Everyman His Own Historian."[5] Like Collingwood, Becker was very critical of the positivist insistence that the historian must let the facts speak for themselves, for he saw quite clearly that facts simply cannot speak for themselves. He denied the contention that the simple historical fact is a hard, cold something with a clear outline and measurable. Becker rightly contended that it is utterly impossible for the facts of history to speak through the historian, and this is because of the nature of historical facts. They do not lend themselves to this kind of treatment by the historian. Becker insisted that the historian does not and cannot deal with historical events themselves, but only with statements which affirm the fact that the event did occur. The historian can only deal with the affirmation of the fact that something is true. At this point Becker made what he felt was a very important distinction between the ephemeral events which disappear and the affirmation about the events which persist. Thus the historical fact is not the past event, but a symbol which enables the historian to recreate it imaginatively. It is dangerous to maintain that a symbol is either false or true. The most that a historian should claim for a symbol is that it is more or less appropriate. But appropriate for what? Becker fails to answer this important question.

In keeping with his discussion thus far, Becker then went on to discuss the location of these historical facts or symbols. With more than a touch of dogmatism, Becker insisted that historical facts must be in someone's mind or they are nowhere. To illustrate his meaning at this point, Becker distinguished between the actual event and the historical fact. Lincoln was assassinated on April 14, 1865; this was an actual event. But we now speak of that event as a historical fact. "The event was, but is no longer. It is only the affirmed fact about the event that now is, that persists and will persist until we discover that our affirmation is wrong or inadequate."[6]

This distinction brought Becker to the admission that there are two histories: the actual series of events, on the one hand, and the ideal series, on the other, which we affirm and hold in memory. The first is

4. *Western Political Quarterly*, VIII, No. 3 (1955), pp. 327-40; reprinted in Hans Meyerhoff, ed., *The Philosophy of History in Our Time* (New York, 1959), pp. 120-37.

5. Presidential address delivered to the American Historical Association, December 29, 1931, in a book by the same name (New York, 1935). For an introduction to the impact which Becker had on the historical profession, see John C. Rule and Ralph D. Handen, "Bibliography of Works on Carl Lotus Becker and Charles Austin Beard, 1945–1963," *History and Theory*, V, No. 3 (1966), pp. 302-14.

6. *Everyman His Own Historian*, p. 234.

absolute and unchanging, while the second is relative and always changing in response to the increase or refinement of historical knowledge. But, according to Becker, these two series generally correspond, and it is the duty of the historian to strive to make them correspond as much as possible. Yet the actual series of events exists only for the historian in terms of the ideal series which he affirms and holds in memory. Thus, Becker was forced to acknowledge that history is our knowledge of events rather than the actual events themselves. History, then, is the *memory of events* which have occurred in the past.

Having located the historical fact in the mind or memory of the historian rather than in the world of objective reality, Becker went on to discuss the question: When is the historical fact? Here his subjectivism and relativism become even more pronounced. He insisted that if the historical fact is present imaginatively in someone's mind, then it must be a part of the present. But what is the present? Here another serious dilemma confronted Becker. Since the present is a very slippery thing, and an indefinable point in time, the image or the idea which the historian has present in his mind slips instantly into the past.

Becker then concluded his discussion of the nature of historical facts with a confession which reveals the bankruptcy and futility of his position: "In truth the actual past is gone, and the world of history is an intangible world recreated imaginatively and present in our minds." This admission brought with it the logical conclusion that this living history—the ideal series of events which the historian holds in memory—is in a state of flux. It cannot be precisely the same for all historians at any given time or the same for one generation as for another. Thus, every generation rewrites the story of its own past to suit its own needs. Inescapably the history fashioned by historians is a convenient blend of fact and fancy. Becker closed his essay, "Everyman His Own Historian," with the observation that however accurately we may determine the facts of history, "the facts themselves and our interpretation of them and our interpretation of our interpretations, will be seen in a different perspective or a less vivid light as mankind moves into the unknown future."[7]

The whole tenor of Becker's philosophy of history militates against any possibility of an objective meaning and purpose being discernible, and yet for the greater part of his professional career Becker was somehow able to synthesize this relativism with a conviction that the triumph of democracy was the key to human history and the hope of the future. Not until the last few years of his life did he surrender his allegiance to the eventual triumph of democracy and yield to the pessimism inherent in his view of the nature of the historical process and his denial that history

---

7. *Ibid.,* pp. 254-55.

has objectivity. His frustration and even despair are quite obvious in his last major work on modern democracy.

The same irrationalism which undermined the brilliant historical achievements of Carl Becker also haunted the equally scholarly efforts of Charles A. Beard (1876-1948), Becker's great contemporary who is generally regarded as one of the most influential, if not the most influential, American historians of the first half of the twentieth century. Although Beard won his fame because of the economic interpretation of American history as he set it forth in his *Economic Interpretation of the Constitution of the United States* (1913) and his *Economic Origins of Jeffersonian Democracy* (1915), his basic philosophy was quite similar to that held by Carl Becker. It is found in his famous presidential address, "Written History as an Act of Faith," delivered at the meeting of the American Historical Society 'r December, 1933.[8] In his discussion of the nature of history and the proper historical methodology, Beard reaffirmed the view of Croce that history is essentially contemporary thought about the past. To be sure, in one sense history as past actuality includes all that has been done, said, felt and thought by human beings on this planet since humanity began its long career. But when we use the term history we mean *history as thought,* not as actuality, record, or specific knowledge. History is thought about past actuality, constructed and delimited by history as record and knowledge.

Beard, in his attack on the use of the scientific method in historical scholarship, insisted that every historian is a product of his age and that his work must necessarily reflect the spirit of the times, of a nation, or a race, group, class or section. Neither a Gibbon nor a Bancroft could be duplicated today. All historians reflect their own predilections in their choice of fields for investigation and in the facts which they will include in their work.

Fundamental in Beard's approach to the problems of contemporary historiography was his insistent injunction that the historian must cast off his servitude to the assumptions of natural science and the dead hand of Leopold Von Ranke. Beard clearly saw that the intellectual formula which historians have borrowed from both the physical and biological sciences have cramped and distorted the operations of history. He indicted the historians for borrowing from the methodology of the physical sciences the concept or assumption of causation. Under the hypothesis that it is necessary to imitate the natural sciences, historians have been arranging events in neat little chains of causation which explain, to their satisfaction, why succeeding events happen.[9] But Beard was equally caustic in his comments on those historians like Spengler who, suspicious of the methods

---

8. In *American Historical Review,* XXXIX, No. 2 (January, 1934), pp. 219-29; reprinted in Meyerhoff, pp. 140-51.
9. Meyerhoff, p. 144.

of the physical sciences, turned to Darwin and conceived of history as a succession of cultural organisms rising, growing, competing and declining. He rightly described the fallacies involved in any attempt to find an analogy between cause and effect in history and the conception of cause and effect as it is used in the scientific method. But the realization of the futility of trying to interpret history by means of a methodology adapted from the methodology of the natural sciences immediately posed a serious dilemma which Beard was quick to recognize. The dangers lay in the fact that, having broken the tyranny of physics and biology, historiography was in great danger of declaring that all written history is merely relative to time and circumstances and therefore a passing shadow or an illusion. Accordingly he offered a remedy. When absolutes in history are rejected, the absolutism of relativity must also be rejected. Thus, argued Beard, "as the actuality moves forward into the future, the concept of relativity will also pass as previous conceptions and interpretations of events have passed." Therefore, Beard urged the happy possibility that, according to the doctrine of relativity, the skepticism of relativity will also disappear in due time. One is tempted to interject a question at this point in the argument. How can Beard argue that the conception of relativity will pass on? Is this not a subtle reintroduction of the idea of the absolute or an unconscious reliance on Darwin, a reliance which he had originally repudiated as an integral part of historical methodology? Beard again is aware of the dilemma confronting him. When the historian accepts none of the assumptions of theology, philosophy, physics, or biology, "when he passes out from under the fleeting shadow of relativity, he confronts the absolute in his field—the absolute totality of all historical occurrences past, present, and becoming to the end of all things."[10]

When the historian arrives at this place he has three choices: to accept the idea that history as a total actuality is chaos; that history as actuality is a part of some order of nature and revolves in cycles eternally; or that history is moving in some direction away from the low level of primitive beginnings on an upward gradient toward a more ideal order. Beard admitted that much evidence can be found for all three possible approaches to the solution of the riddle of history, but he insisted that "all the available evidence will not fit any one of them." But if the historian has only these three possible choices and the available evidence does not support any one of them, what is there left to him?

Beard's answer to this query only reveals the abyss of hopelessness inherent in his position. He voiced his hope for historiography in the idea that written history is an act of faith. What Beard means by this is the conviction that something true can be known about the movement of

---

10. *Ibid.*, p. 148.

history. But this conviction is a subjective decision, not a purely objective discovery. Beard did not, and apparently could not, be totally content with a solution that was totally subjective and lacking in any objective validity. He could not quite come to the point where he was willing to dismiss casually the scientific method as of no value. So he wrote, "Nor is the empirical or scientific method to be abandoned. It is the only method that can be employed in obtaining accurate knowledge of historical facts, personalities, situations and movements. It alone can disclose conditions that made possible what happened. It has a value in itself—a value high in the hierarchy of values indispensable to the life of a democracy." Beard dismissed the scientific method in history only to bring it in again through the back door. But he could not find a place for it in his final conclusion concerning the meaning of history. His confusion and hopelessness are born of this contradiction in his philosophy, if we may call it that. After affirming his conviction that in some mysterious way history is moving forward to the emergence of a collectivist democracy, he then offered his final testimony. "History is chaos and every attempt to interpret it otherwise is an illusion. History moves around in a kind of cycle. History moves in a line, straight or spiral, and in some direction. The historian may seek to escape these issues by silence or by a confession of avoidance or he may face them boldly, aware of the intellectual and moral perils inherent in any decision—in his act of faith."[11]

Beard's final achievement in historical scholarship, *President Roosevelt and the Coming of War* (Yale University Press, 1948), brought him face to face with the destruction of his own faith in the triumph of democracy as the ultimate goal of a chaotic history. Like Carl Becker before him, Beard came to the realization that democracy, the only god he worshiped, had betrayed him—the tragedy of most historians today. Their very greatness as historians only serves to emphasize the bankruptcy of contemporary historiography. Historians continue to write their monographs and textbooks and to teach their students with no sense of purpose in their teaching and no conviction that the history they present is worth teaching or learning. This attitude stands in sharp contrast to the professional attitude of a great scholar of the old school who on the first day of class addresses his graduate students with this "young gentlemen, the roots of the present lie deeply buried in the past. Start digging!"

I have dealt at some length with the philosophies of history found in the works of R. G. Collingwood, Carl Becker, and Charles A. Beard, not only because their positions are quite similar, but because in revealing the basic irrationalism inherent in all non-Christian thought they lead us to a deeper understanding of Van Til's incisive and devastating criticism of

---

11. *Ibid.*, p. 151.

modern historiography and a greater appreciation of the grandeur of his own biblical apologetic.

Although it is not within the scope of this chapter to deal at any length with Van Til's basic theology or apologetics in detail, a brief survey of some of their basic postulates is necessary. Without such understanding as a foundation, much of Van Til's analysis will escape the reader.

Van Til is a dedicated and convinced Calvinist and perhaps more than any other living biblical scholar he has sought to create a system of apologetics for the Christian faith which is faithful to all aspects of biblical revelation. In his discussion of the meaning of history, he rejects every effort to formulate an explanation of historical events derived from philosophical methodology. Thus, for Van Til there can be no philosophy of history, but only a theology of history. No philosophy can offer any true interpretation of history, for the mind of man cannot confer meaning on human existence. Neither can history supply the clue to its own meaning. History is neither self-originating nor self-sustaining. Neither can time exist in and of itself. The great questions which man asks concerning his life on earth can be answered only by the Scriptures.

The doctrine of creation assumes a major role in Van Til's interpretation of history and in his analysis of the historians previously discussed in this chapter. History can and must be interpreted only in terms of that ultimate meaning which God conferred upon it in the act of creation. Thus, the subsequent history of man on earth derives its meaning from this original act of creation.

For Van Til the doctrine of creation does not stand apart from the doctrine of God revealed in Scripture. The God of creation is a sovereign Being who governs His creation and who entered into a covenantal relationship with man whom he made in His own image. Man therefore bears the divine image and enjoys this covenantal relationship with the Sovereign. Man was endowed with the ability and duty to find both the meaning of human life and his own purpose on earth within the will of God.

Starting at the apex of creation, man, the image of God, was by virtue of this fact capable of knowing Him and doing His will. But this knowledge which man has of God, of himself, and of his world is "analogical." Van Til, with Augustine and Calvin, places great emphasis on the fact that man can know himself only by that same act by which he knows God.

Man is, therefore, a steward of God, a vice-regent under Him in his intellectual life, and as such, he is fully responsible to Him not only for discovering God's purpose for human life through revelation, but also the meaning and purpose of the world in which he lives. This is the very essence of that covenantal relationship which man has with God through creation. Man is under a mandate to investigate the meaning of both nature and history, not in the light of the presuppositions and methodology he would construct for himself, but in the light of those presuppositions revealed to him by God.

Equally important in Van Til's evaluation of the irrationalism of modern historiography is the biblical doctrine of sin. This emphasis, an integral part of his approach to history, immediately and irrevocably separates Van Til from most contemporary historians. When mankind through Adam fell into sin, men became covenant breakers. But Van Til is rightfully insistent that the fall of man into sin in no way destroyed or lessened the covenantal responsibility which man owes to the God who created him, although it rendered him totally incapable of fulfilling the conditions of his stewardship at all points. Van Til gives a well-balanced and biblical emphasis to the noetic as well as to the moral effects of the fall. ·

By grace the elect are regenerated through faith in Jesus Christ, and they are thus to a degree enabled to resume their role as stewards in a manner acceptable to God. Only then by grace do they begin to recover to some degree their spiritual insight derived from the Scripture by the power of the Holy Spirit into that meaning which God assigned to both nature and human history.

Van Til constantly insists that all philosophical and theological systems which deny the biblical doctrines of the sovereignty of God, creation ex nihilo, the special creation of man in God's image, the fall, and man's redemption through sovereign grace by faith in Christ, are basically committed to irrationalism. Here a note of caution should be inserted. In stating that all non-Christian thought bears the marks of irrationalism, Van Til does not mean that the unbeliever is incapable of logical thought or of achieving certain scientific and practical truths in the area of common grace. Rather is he quite insistent that unbelievers do have a natural ability to produce great literature, great music, and great art, and to make momentous discoveries in the areas of theoretical science and medicine. The natural man does have an aptitude for cultural achievement because, although he is a covenant breaker and in rebellion against God, he still bears the image of God metaphysically. By the fall he did not cease to be man. But as a sinner, as a covenant breaker, he can no longer think God's thoughts after Him. He can no longer discover the meaning of nature or of history in terms of those presuppositions which he in his rebellion substitutes for those revealed to him in the Scriptures. Van Til uses irrationalism in this latter sense and it is a vitally important element in his criticisms of modern historiography. It becomes one of the basic elements in his indictment of the historians and philosophers of history who have adopted either positivism or various forms of subjectivism in their attempts to find meaning for the data of history and purpose for the totality of events which we call human history.

For Van Til, irrationalism is an inescapable characteristic of all non-

Christian thought, whether it be that of Plato, Aristotle, Zeno, Descartes, Leibniz, Locke, Hume, Kant, Hegel, or their various disciples. All systems of thought which rest on the humanistic assumption that the mind of man is capable of achieving all truth and that man is sovereign, possessing the inherent and inalienable right to decide the truth, or even deciding if truth exists, must bear the stigma of irrationalism.

With this understanding of Van Til's basic theology and the world and life view or *Weltanschauung* which he derived from it, we are now ready to examine his critical treatment of the contemporary historians. Van Til rightly indicts Collingwood for his insistence that the theological or biblical view of history carries with it the doctrine of determinism and that in theological history humanity is not an agent, but partly an instrument and partly a patient, of the acts recorded.[12] The root of Collingwood's dilemma at this point lies in his refusal to think of man as made in the image of God and therefore as an analogue of God. This refusal enables Collingwood to insist that man's thought must be absolutely his own. Man must be his own interpreter. At this point Van Til raises the supremely important question: What happens to the objective facts of history, given this point of view? The answer is that they gradually disappear into the subject who interprets them. But lying beneath this subjectivism is Collingwood's reliance on the Kantian view of freedom. Collingwood's defiant assertion of human supremacy is starkly asserted in his frank statement that Kant succeeded in justifying history.

> Kant has thus achieved the remarkable feat of showing why there should be such a thing as history—because man is a rational being, and his full development therefrom requires a historical process.

Van Til rightly sees that in this assertion we have reached an important milestone in the development of the modern view of history. According to Collingwood's position, he quite correctly points out that without the biblical view of things, Collingwood cannot explain why there should be any history at all.

Kant and Collingwood dismissed the biblical view as completely inadequate because it denies human freedom. They therefore replaced it with a concept of human freedom in the sense of its right and ability to make its own laws for human nature. Van Til continues his analysis of this approach: "Thus man has reached an inward teleology. And it is this inward teleology in terms of which the idea of history as a whole as well as the significance of each of its phases and each of its figures must be viewed."[13] Teleology in history is inward. Human freedom as an autonomous entity creates its own subjective teleology.

---

12. Collingwood, *The Idea of History*, p. 15. For Van Til's comments see *Christianity in Conflict*, Part 1 (1962 syllabus), p. 10.
13. *Christianity in Conflict*, Part 1 (1962), p. 12.

But this Kantian influence on Collingwood had a disastrous effect on the facts of history in his philosophy. The conception of reality as the life of the mind, as history, meant for Collingwood that "the facts of history are present facts and the historical past is only the world of ideas which the present evidence creates in the present. The paradoxical result is that the historical past is not a past at all; it is present. It is not a past surviving into the present; it must *be* the present."[14] The world of objective history has been dissolved in the grip of this Kantian dualism. Perhaps Van Til's most devastating criticism of Collingwood's subjectivism and consequent relativism is his brilliant application of it to the New Testament and the words of the Christ who speaks through it and to the records of those who were the apostles of Jesus of Nazareth. Van Til now raises the question: What would Collingwood do with these records? He then coins a possible answer from *The Idea of History* and attributes to Collingwood the following:

> The Biblical records cannot be considered from the point of view of whether they are true or not.

Truth is an irrelevant question. The historian cannot take the statements in the New Testament by or about Jesus of Nazareth as directly indicating the state of affairs about which they speak. The historian must not follow a "scissors and paste" method of historical research. When Jesus Christ says that He is the Son of God and has existed from eternity with the Father, but now has become incarnate in order that He might save people from their sins, the scientific historian (as Collingwood uses the term) must not take this statement at face value. If he should, he would disqualify himself as a scientific historian. And why must he refuse to accept this statement? Because it lacks proper support. If the scientific historian should accept it, he would surrender his own autonomy. The irrationalism inherent in Collingwood's and Kant's basic assumptions has destroyed the possibility of history as a meaningful and purposeful account of the life of man on earth. The objective facts on which such an account must rest have been dissolved in a Kantian subjectivity erected to make secure his view of human autonomy. Van Til disposes of Wilhelm Dilthey's irrational historicism in much the same way as he treated Collingwood. Contending that in his *A Critique of Historical Thought* Dilthey sought to do for history what he thought Kant did for science, Van Til quickly concludes that in these "desperate" efforts he was no more successful than Kant. The reason for failure is the same in both cases. Dilthey, following Kant, assumed the intelligibility of the historical subject to itself even though the environment in which it depends for its meaning is irrational. Van Til correctly points out that the type of historical rela-

---

14. *Ibid.*

tivism represented by Dilthey gave way to the existentialist movement, particularly in the *Sein und Zeit* of Martin Heidegger, who tried to combine "pure thought and pure sensibility." For Heidegger, both of these must be conceived as the modes of the transcendental imagination which is essence in time and self-hood. But Heidegger merely succeeded in dissolving man into the morass of the unrelated.

Van Til concludes his discussion of this idealistic school of historical interpretation with an observation which has too often been overlooked, even at times by those who claim to be within the evangelical tradition.

> The main outlook of recent philosophy of history is that of a general process-philosophy. And this fact itself shows clearly that the conflict between those who believe in historic Christianity and of those who do not cannot be carried by a discussion of "facts" without at the same time discussing the philosophy of fact.[15]

Very few philosophers, theologians, or historians have stated this basic question of the nature of fact so forcefully as it applies to problems of the meaning of facts themselves. Thus far in this essay we have analyzed in detail idealism and its inherent irrationalism which so emphasizes the subjectivity of the historical processes that facts cease to have any objective reality or propositional meaning discernible to anyone but the interpreting historian.

On the other hand, Van Til was no less aware of the dangers to the Christian position inherent in the positivism of August Comte and his successors, nor was he any less aware of the fatal end to which positivism would lead those historians who attempted to find a working analogy between the scientific method used in the natural or physical sciences and that scientific method which the historian should apply to his own craft. For Van Til, the dictum, "Let the facts speak for themselves," was no less fatal to a sound historiography than was the idealism inherent in the philosophies of Collingwood and Dilthey.

Although Van Til paid much less formal attention to Comte and posivitism in general than he paid to Collingwood, this does not mean that his apologetical system has not offered an equally strong biblical refutation of this other form of nineteenth-century irrationalism. Quite the contrary.

The positivistic approach to history is irrational for the same reason as the idealistic. Positivism, like idealism, builds its system of thought on the assumption of the ultimacy of human experience. It takes the facts of man's own existence and the facts of man's environment to be intelligible in and of themselves without the light of Scripture. It is on this basis that positivist historians assumed and even insisted that facts can speak and historians must be the mouthpieces for the cold, hard facts of history.

---

15. *Ibid.*, p. 17.

Van Til's insight into the implications of the doctrines of creation in general and of man as the image bearer of God provides the basis for the theistic answer to the challenge of positivism in all its forms. In his discussion of Dooyeweerd's concept of categories, Van Til offers a convincing refutation of the basic assumptions of positivism.[16] His argument is essentially this: It is because of the light of Scripture that a Christian philosopher knows all things in the world to be created and that the world is redeemed by Christ. The unbelieving historian cannot at any point know the mind of Christ as to the meaning of this world and the facts of history. God reveals himself to man in history, but the unregenerate man cannot correctly read the meaning of this revelation. By the very fact that the world and man were created by God for His own glory—by this act of creation—the world and the facts of human history received their meaning from God. But these facts cannot and do not speak for themselves, automatically, through the mouths of "neutral" historians.

As a knowing mind in a knowable world, it was man's great prerogative and duty to interpret correctly the data supplied by the world and history. But by the fact of the plunge into sin man was no longer able to carry out this divine mandate. As the covenant breaker, he lost that ability to perform the terms of the covenant. He could no longer know as once he knew.

In saying this Van Til is not in any way taking the position that either the world or history expresses the essence of God exhaustively. But the fact that history (or the world) does not express or reveal God exhaustively does not imply that it does not reveal God clearly. But this revelation can be correctly interpreted only by those who have the mind of Christ—by those whose noetic processes have been made captive to the Word of God by the Holy Spirit. Facts of nature and of history are to be known by believing minds, not exhaustively but correctly.

Positivism reverses this, the proper order for the interpretation of historical data. It insists that cold hard facts speak for themselves and convey their own meaning through the activities of historians whose only duty it is to collect and present them. By implication, in interpreting this data every reader must ultimately become his own historian by assigning to the data that meaning which most closely reflects his own philosophical frame of reference. The assumption of the positivists, namely, that all historians would interpret the facts in the same way, is an utter impossibility. No historian is neutral. No historian can passively allow the cold facts to speak through him. At every point in his historical investigations the scholar betrays his own frame of reference in choosing the area of history in which he does his research and in the facts he will ultimately use out

---

16. See his *Biblical Dimensionalism*, Part 3, pp. 40 et sq.

of the mass of data he has collected and in the meaning he assigns to those facts. Such neutrality is impossible because man is a thinking being, and as a thinking being he is under compulsion to find meaning and purpose in all that he does. To refuse to do so is to repudiate the divine mandate upon him as an image-bearer, and this is sin.

Thus the neutrality demanded by positivism is impossible because the historian is either a covenant breaker and therefore at enmity with God or through the new birth he is a new creation in Christ Jesus, possessing the mind of Christ as he engages in his historical research. Thus, he views the data of history either as a covenant breaker and sinner or as a Christian. There is no other position possible for the historian to hold. Neutrality is impossible.

In his theistic approach to problems raised by non-Christian historical scholarship, Van Til provides the only possible answer to one of the most persistently baffling problems which historians face and with which they must deal. This is the problem of causation.

It is quite obvious that the approaches of Collingwood, Beard, and Becker destroy any meaningful theory of causation. The complete subjectivity and relativism of their basic philosophy precludes any meaningful concept of causation. Neither Beard nor Becker seemed to be aware of this fact, and they tried to find causal factors in their treatment of history. But their efforts were in contradiction to their whole conception of the nature of historical facts. The most glaring contradiction between fact and theory is evident in Beard's attempt to find the causes of both the writing of the Constitution and the rise of Jeffersonian democracy in economic factors. Although Beard shifted from his economic determinism in later works, and turned to other causal factors in history, he never seemed to be aware of the inherent contradiction between his theory and his practice. This same contradiction is an insurmountable obstacle and nemesis for all contemporary historians who interpret history in the light of idealism, positivism, or existentialism. The inherent irrationalism in all of these approaches precludes a satisfactory solution to the pressing problem of causation in the historical process.

While Van Til does not discuss the problem of causation in any detail or in any of his writings, his apologetical system offers a sound biblical solution to what must otherwise remain an insoluble problem. The solution as offered by Van Til lies in his doctrine of the sovereignty of God over nature and history. Not only positivists but many other scholars belonging to various schools of historical interpretation have generally assumed a theory of causation based on the assumption that event A causes event B, B causes C, and so on. To put it in a somewhat different form, they have taught great movements in history are the result of many antecedent causes which somehow or other have produced the given result. Indeed, this has become the standard approach to explain all the great movements in history from the fall of Rome to World War II.

They have tacitly accepted an Aristotelian or Thomistic concept of causation with little or no questioning of its validity. The positivist application of the methodology of the natural sciences to the problem of causation only further increased the confusion. For if facts speak for themselves then it is ridiculous to believe that a fact can inform us that it is *either* the result of fact A or the cause of fact B. Yet this is what positivism would have us believe. It is evident that the whole idea of causal relations must be a subjective concept in the mind of the positivist historian and not the product of any objective affirmation on the part of the facts themselves. On the other hand, the answers furnished by the idealist approach of the Hegelians or Collingwood, Beard, and Becker are just as unsatisfactory, for they are completely subjective and also bear the stigma of irrationalism.

Once again we must look to the insights furnished by Van Til for a rationally satisfying answer to the problem of causality in history. And the answer is in the doctrine of the sovereignty of God, the sovereign Lord who governs and controls His creatures and all their actions for His own honor and glory. God foreordains all that comes to pass in the stream of history. Thus the usual concepts of causation held by unbelievers do not and cannot explain this vexing historical problem. In fact, any theory of causation which insists that prior events are the cause of those which follow must also be deficient, because such theories fail to take into account the doctrine of foreordination, which tells us that God sees the end of history from the beginning and the ultimate cause of historical events is to be found in the eschatological goal of history. Thus, according to this view, events which have not yet taken place are an important cause of those which have taken place already, since both past and future events have a role in God's plan. This is not only a distinctly Christian solution to the problem of causation, but it is likewise uniquely found in a Calvinistic world and life view which places all of history under the dominion of the sovereign God.

Conclusions

By this time it certainly must have occurred to the reader that the philosophy, or better, the theology of history set forth by Van Til is unique in the world of modern historical scholarship. (Every historian writes with a conscious dedication to some particular approach.) Unfortunately, many historians who are within the evangelical camp do not write under the influence of a biblical world and life view and unwittingly accept some secular interpretation of history. And it is impossible for those who do consciously seek to apply theistic principles to the interpretation of history to give adequate coverage to all areas of history where such an interpretation is desperately needed today.

In bringing this chapter to a conclusion the writer would like to make a few suggestions as to where Christians could and should concentrate their efforts in order to write their histories for the glory of God. Perhaps one of the most needy fields is the area of church history itself, with special emphasis upon the continuing infiltration of Greek thought into the theology of the medieval church. We need to restudy both the Renaissance and the Reformation from this point of view, as well as the intellectual history of Europe from the close of the Reformation to the present day. Christian historians need to apply the insights furnished by Van Til to the influence of Kant and Hegel on nineteenth-century historical scholarship, particularly that dealing with the causes, course of, and results of the French Revolution. The very nature of this movement has been grossly misinterpreted; in turn, this misinterpretation has led to an equally fatal misunderstanding of the results of the revolution as they unfolded in European history after 1815.

In the field of American history these same insights need to be applied to Puritanism and the intellectual development of the colonies in the seventeenth and eighteenth centuries. A great challenge confronts Christian theistic historians in the study of the causes and meaning of the American Revolution and the writing of the Constitution, as they seek to answer the approaches of Jensen, Beard, Becker, and A. M. Schlesinger, and as they re-examine the basic theses of such scholars as A. C. McLaughlin and C. M. Andrews.

Nineteenth-century American history will also offer a tremendous challenge for the historian who consciously seeks to apply the principle of theism to such issues as western expansion, the rise of slavery and its defense, the rise of Transcendentalism, and the reform movements of the period from 1825 to 1861. Of particular significance is the period of Reconstruction and rise of Social Darwinism after 1865. Christian historians have neglected one of the most fertile of all fields of investigation in their failure to explore the relationship between post-war radicalism and Darwinism, and the relationship between American reform movements after 1890 and Social Darwinism. But perhaps the greatest challenge of all for the Christian historian is twentieth-century America, particularly the theological radicalism which lay behind the architects of the New Deal and all subsequent popular movements which have emphasized democracy as the key to American history. In fact, Christian scholarship must frankly and soberly attempt to trace the development of the democratic dogma in American history and its close relationship to unbelief, ranging from the deism of the American Revolution to the relationship between democracy and communism after 1850. Sooner or later Christian scholarship is going to have to come to grips with the continuing conflict between the humanism of the Renaissance on one hand, and the theology of the Reformation on the other, as this conflict is reflected in the pattern of modern history of the West in general, and as it is reflected more particularly in the continuing conflict between democracy and constitutionalism in this country. While we must sternly reject any temptation to simplify the complex nature of history, we must also be alert to the basic issues around which history revolves.

I say, therefore, to those who ask about the Christian system somewhat as follows: "You, my friends, state and defend or reject what you call *systems* of reality and knowledge. Well, I too have a 'system,' but it is a different kind of system. It is neither a deductive nor an inductive system, in your sense of the term. Nor is it a combination of these two. My 'system' is not that of empiricism, of rationalism, of criticism, or of any of the other 'systems' you may read about in the ordinary texts on philosophy. Nor is my 'system' a synthesis between one of your systems with that of the Bible. My 'system' is attained by thinking upon all the aspects of reality in the light of the Christ of Scripture. I try to think God's thoughts after him. That is to say, I try as a redeemed covenant-creature of the triune God to attain as much coherence as I, being finite and sinful, can between the facts of the universe. God's revelation is clear, but it is clear just because it is *God's* revelation and God is self-contained light. My 'system' is therefore an analogical reinterpretation of the truth that God has revealed about himself and his relation to man through Christ in Scripture. I construct my 'system' by means of a variety of gifts that God has created within me. Among these gifts is that of concept-formation."

Van Til, "Response" to
Herman Dooyeweerd, in
E. R. Geehan (ed.),
Jerusalem and Athens (1971), p. 126.

ECONOMICS

V

ECONOMICS: FROM REASON TO INTUITION

By GARY NORTH

> This, then, is a further sense in which Economics can be truly said to as-
> sume rationality in human society. It makes no pretence, as has been alleged
> so often, that action is necessarily rational in the sense that ends pursued
> are not mutually inconsistent. There is nothing in its generalisations which
> necessarily implies reflective deliberation in ultimate valuation. It rests
> upon no assumption that individuals will always act rationally. But it does
> depend for its practical *raison d'etre* upon the assumption that it is desirable
> that they should do so. It does assume that, within the bounds of necessity,
> it is desirable to choose ends which can be achieved harmoniously.
>
> LIONEL ROBBINS[1]

Modern economics as a discipline suffers from the same crucial limitations found in all other post-Kantian fields of scholarship. Ultimately
resting on a foundation of pure contingency and chaos, the economics
profession affirms rationality as its *raison d'etre*. Yet economists cannot
escape the fundamental rational antinomies of Kantian thought: unity vs.
plurality, structure vs. change, law vs. freedom, deduction vs. induction,
theory vs. brute factuality, definition vs. application. When pushed to the
limits of exposition, every economist finally rests his case on "intuition" or
"experience" to bridge the unbridgeable gap between mind and matter.
Reason collapses into mystery at the heart of the economist's task.

What is the economist's task? That's a little hard for the economists to
say exactly. James Buchanan cites two classic definitions:

Jacob Viner: "Economics is what economists do."

Frank Knight: "And economists are those who do economics."[2]

The problem, to use Van Til's phrase, is that for the most part, economists
are not epistemologically self-conscious. Two decades ago, Fritz Machlup,
while acting as chairman of an American Economic Association workshop
in methodology, remarked: "Usually only a small minority of American
economists have professed interest in methodology. The large majority

---

1. Lionel Robbins, *An Essay on the Nature and Significance of Economic
Science* (2nd ed.; London: Macmillan, [1935] 1962), p. 157.
2. James Buchanan, "What Should Economists Do?" *Southern Economic Journal*,
XXX (Jan., 1964), p. 213.

used to disclaim any interest in such issues."[3] Things have only become worse since then. The total triumph of mathematical economics has created a new, highly specialized economic technician who is buried in an esoteric universe of his own. "A methodological addict, he shows singular unconcern with the world as it exists. His standard of success—his pay-off matrix—is to impress the tastemakers of an ever-narrowing professional specialty. He is more and more cut off from specialists in other fields, and finds it increasingly difficult to communicate to the lay world. The result is a sort of apartheid: economists are no longer able to see the real world, and the world no longer can understand what economists are saying."[4] The quality of scholarship is increasingly Alexandrian: endless unreadable articles which have a half-life of six years or less, falling into oblivion with rare exception almost immediately.[5] Yet the basis of personal and departmental advancement is in the publication of such articles in a handful of specialized journals.[6]

This trend has no. gone unchallenged in recent years. The advent of the New Left economists, whether Marxian, extreme Galbraithian, or whatever, has forced the establishment economists to re-examine their calling, but nothing changes. Still, there has been far more interest—critical interest—in epistemology since 1965 than could have been reasonably predicted in 1963. As Bronfenbrenner has commented, in 1964 he could not find any indication of radical economics in America. "Only five years later, in late 1969, the end of ideology had itself ended."[7] Walter Weisskopf could fight the good Galbraithian battle against methodological neutrality and sterility with his lively and unread Alienation and Economics (Dutton, 1971). But criticisms against irrelevance are, for the profession, annual rituals that have zero effect. The fact of the matter is, as Bronfenbrenner states it: "The general economist may be travelling the way of the Dodo or Passenger Pigeon Highway to extinction. He survives—as I am a survivor—as dilettante, journalist, or elementary [principles] teacher, or as an exotic variety of multiple-specialist whose several specialisms fall in more than one of our ordinary classification boxes."[8] And it does not help the situation

---

3. Fritz Machlup, "Introductory Remarks," American Economic Review, Papers and Proceedings, XLII (May, 1952), p. 34.

4. Walter Adams, "Economic Science, Public Policy, and Public Understanding," Diogenes (Fall, 1969), p. 24.

5. A. W. Coats, "The Role of Scholarly Journals in the History of Economics: An Essay," Journal of Economic Literature, IX (1971), p. 42.

6. John J. Siegfried, "The Publishing of Economic Papers and Its Impact on Graduate Faculty Ratings," J. Econ. Lit., X (1972), pp. 31-49.

7. Martin Bronfenbrenner, "Radical Economics in America: A 1970 Survey," J. Econ. Lit., VIII (1970), p. 747. Cf. Wall Street Journal (Feb. 11, 1972); Business Week (March 18, 1972).

8. Bronfenbrenner, "Trends, Cycles, and Fads in Economic Writing," Am. Ec. Rev., Papers & Proceedings, LVI (May, 1966), p. 539.

to read Joseph Schumpeter's remark that "Economists in particular, much to the detriment of their field, have attached unreasonable importance to being understood by the general public. . . ."[9] Yet he was eminently readable and a generalist; two decades later he would have found less reason to bother with writing that sentence. But the evil had already been accomplished; he got his wish!

One thing seems certain, however. Since 1965 we have not heard speeches like the one John Kennedy delivered at Yale University in 1962. It was one of those typical "end of ideology" performances by the consummate pragmatist of the era:

> Today these old sweeping issues have largely disappeared. The central domestic problems of our time are more subtle and less simple. They relate not to basic clashes of philosophy or ideology, but to ways and means of reaching common goals—to research for sophisticated solutions to complex and obstinate ideas. . . . What is at stake in our economic decisions today is not some grand warfare of rival ideologies which will sweep the country with passion, but the practical management of modern economy. What we need are not labels and cliches but more basic discussion of the sophisticated and technical questions involved in keeping a great economic machinery moving ahead. I am suggesting that the problems of fiscal and monetary policy in the Sixties as opposed to the kinds of problems we faced in the Thirties demand subtle challenges for which technical answers—not political answers—must be provided.[10]

Well, as it turned out, "can do" Liberalism couldn't, and we bogged down in a fruitless war in Vietnam and saw the nation blow apart. Anyone wishing to read a post-mortem on JFK's faith in technocratic solutions can go through David Halberstam's *The Best and the Brightest*. The naivete of this kind of world view is officially dead, if not yet operationally defunct (due to tenure and other forms of guild control) in the economics profession. The established men may believe in technocratic wisdom, but they are at least more humble today.

What is Economics?

There have been a number of influential economists over the years who have outspokenly denied the validity of the question. Vilfredo Pareto, the late-nineteenth-century social scientist, Gunnar Myrdal, and T. W. Hutchison are among these.[11] Schumpeter, whose *History of Economic Analysis* is a classic, is another.[12] Others, most notably Lionel Robbins,

---

9. Joseph A. Schumpeter, *A History of Economic Analysis* (New York: Oxford University Press, 1954), p. 10.

10. John F. Kennedy, quoted by Theodore Roszak, *The Making of a Counter Culture* (Garden City, N. Y.: Doubleday Anchor, 1969), p. 11.

11. Israel Kirzner, *The Economic Point of View* (Princeton: Van Nostrand, 1960), p. 7.

12. Schumpeter, *History*, p. 10.

vigorously deny this form of skepticism. When open disagreement can exist on so fundamental a point as the definition of what constitutes a science, the extent of the intellectual confusion is indicated. Drawing hermetically sealed definitional boundaries is not possible, given the nature of human thought and the inescapable fact of unity and diversity in all created structures, but men need operational definitions for their work. Buchanan's warning is significant: "Economics, as a well-defined subject of scholarship, seems to be disintegrating . . . and realistic appraisal suggests that this inexorable process will not be stopped."[13]

Israel Kirzner's very fine study of *The Economic Point of View* (1960) surveys several definitions of economics that have been employed by members of the profession since the seventeenth century: the study of trade, of wealth and welfare, of greed, of getting the most from the least, of money and measurement, of economic choice in a scarce world, of human action. But there is one common feature that stands out over three centuries, and William Letwin calls attention to it forcefully: "Nevertheless there can be no doubt that economic theory owes its present development to the fact that some men, in thinking of economic phenomena, forcefully suspended all judgments of theology, morality, and justice, were willing to consider the economy as nothing more than an intricate mechanism, refraining for the while from asking whether the mechanism worked for good or evil. That separation was made during the seventeenth century."[14] The autonomy of economics as a science from "metaphysics," namely any revelation from God, is the hallmark of all contemporary economic practice. Perhaps the strongest statement on behalf of the total autonomy of economics comes from Ludwig von Mises, who equates liberalism and free market economics:

> Liberalism is based upon a purely rational and scientific theory of social cooperation. The policies it recommends are the application of a system of knowledge which does not refer in any way to sentiments, intuitive creeds for which no logically sufficient proof can be provided, mystical experiences, and the personal awareness of superhuman phenomena. . . . They [the policies] are radically opposed to all systems of theocracy. But they are entirely neutral with regard to religious beliefs which do not pretend to interfere with the conduct of social, political, and economic affairs.[15]

The most widely respected work in the area of modern economic epistemology is Lionel Robbins' *An Essay on the Nature and Significance of Economic Science* (2nd ed., 1935). "The economist studies the disposal of scarce means," he writes. "Economics is the science which

---

13. Buchanan, p. 222.
14. William Letwin, *The Origins of Scientific Economics* (Garden City, N. Y.: Doubleday Anchor, 1965), pp. 158-59.
15. Ludwig von Mises, *Human Action* (3rd ed.; Chicago: Regnery, 1966), p. 155.

studies human behaviour as a relationship between ends and scarce means which have alternative uses."[16] Biblically, we would say that he accepts the existence of the effects of Genesis 3:17-19, which separates him from the utopians, Marx, and many of the New Left economists. Economics is a science of human choice among scarce alternative resources.

So far, so good, but it does not stop here. Everyone who claims to be a modern scientist wants his colleagues to regard him as utterly neutral and objective. Of course, he admits in theory that this is ultimately impossible, citing Heisenberg, Kuhn, and so forth to show he is epistemologically literate, but at least all good scientists are neutral and objective with respect to revelational religion. Robbins is no less a part of this tradition of neutrality. "The economist is not concerned with ends as such. He is concerned with the way in which the attainment of ends is limited. The ends may be noble or they may be base. They may be 'material' or 'immaterial'—if ends can so be described. But if the attainment of one set of ends involves the sacrifice of others, then it has an economic aspect."[17] Ultimate ends are economically irrelevant. The economist is primarily—perhaps entirely—a technician. Robbins believes that in sealing off economics from questions of ultimate ends he has accomplished a necessary task, but in fact he has opened up an overwhelming problem for epistemology, one which almost no economist has had the courage to face publicly. Frank Knight is an exception:

> The "scientific" view assumes that changes in man can be completely accounted for in terms of external and prior natural conditions. A theory which recognizes ends and allows man real initiative in changing himself or his environment is in contradiction with a scientific conception of human nature and transfers the discussion to a different realm of discourse. In the writer's opinion the contradiction is insurmountable in the present stage of intellectual development. Philosophy and experience have not taught us concepts which enable us to think comfortably in the terms of what experience and common sense force us to recognize as real and valid.[18]

This may be the reason that Armen Alchian, a leading economist and formerly chairman of the department at U.C.L.A., refused to use the word "choice" in front of a colloquium of graduate students and scholars in 1969. He hedged by using "demonstrated preference" or similar terms. The concept of choice implies an unscientific, methodologically unverifiable concept of human freedom.

There is nothing in Robbins' work to indicate that he understands the

16. Robbins, *Nature*, p. 16.
17. *Ibid.*, p. 25. Cf. Mises, *Human Action*, pp. 95-96.
18. Frank H. Knight, *On the History and Method of Economics* (University of Chicago, 1956), p. 194 n.

issue he is raising. He simply goes on: "Economics is neutral as between ends. Economics cannot pronounce on the validity of ultimate judgments of value."[19] "Applied economics consists of propositions of the form, 'If you want to do this, then you must do that.' "[20] The economist may only advise men in terms of their stated ends. I suppose the economist in Nazi Germany or the Soviet Union in the 1930's would not have questioned the national ends of liquidation or mass imprisonment; he only would have examined the technical questions concerning the least expensive means of accomplishing these ends. Economics is pure technique, and therefore value-free, you see. Economists promise not to tell moralists what to think in the realm of ends, and by this treaty they gain autonomy for their own technical activities. Moralists are supposed to agree not to influence the form or content of economics. As Milton Friedman puts it: "Positive economics is in principle independent of any particular ethical position or normative judgment."[21] Economics is therefore rational, as contrasted to moralistic or value-laden.

Why this religious quest for neutrality, for a value-free science? George Stigler, Friedman's colleague, has offered one straightforward explanation: "The reason for assigning such an austere role to economics is this: it is the fundamental tenet of those who believe in free discussion that matters of fact and of logic can (eventually) be agreed upon by competent men of good will, that matters of taste cannot be reconciled by free discussion. Assuming this to be true, it is apparent that if value judgments were mixed with logic and observation, a science would make but little progress."[22] F. A. Hayek has announced a similar faith in human reason. Speaking of those who favor socialistic solutions, he writes: "Yet if we have not convinced them, the reason must be that our arguments are not yet quite good enough, that we have not yet made explicit some of the foundations on which our conclusions rest."[23] It is more than a little ironic that Hayek and Stigler, the proponents of faith in reason, both supporters of free market ideas, both friends, cannot agree on the whole question of reason in the social sciences. Stigler is an inductionist, while Hayek's *Counter-Revolution of Science* is one of the most eloquent pleas for a deductivist approach. When groups of "Chicago School" economists and "Austrian School" economists get together, they have to avoid the whole issue of epistemology if the conference is not to break down entirely. So much for

19. Robbins, p. 147.
20. *Ibid.*, p. 149.
21. Milton Friedman, *Essays in Positive Economics* (University of Chicago, 1953), p. 4.
22. George Stigler, *The Theory of Competitive Price* (New York: Macmillan, 1942), pp. 15-16.
23. F. A. Hayek, in *What's Past Is Prologue* (Irvington-on-Hudson, N. Y.: Foundation for Economic Education, 1968), p. 41.

the efficacy of (supposedly) screening out value judgments for the sake of sweet reason and ultimate intellectual accord.

Reason: Inductive

The vast bulk of economists regard themselves as essentially empirically oriented inductivists. They are men who rely, ultimately, on "the facts." They are not empiricists in the old German Historical School mold, however. That late-nineteenth-century group of Prussian academic socialists, led primarily by Gustav Schmoller, was initially committed to the premise that economic theory is always relative to time and place, and that only by exhaustive monographic studies of cultural history could scholars come to judgments about economic theory.[24] The approach of this school was holistic and organic: all of human life had to be studied, not simply an "isolated segment" known as economic life. This approach was so utterly fruitless in the production of economic theorems that it was abandoned by the turn of the century. There were just too many data to handle coherently; the unsophisticated positivism of the German Historical School could not sustain itself against the demands of intellectual specialization. In order to examine human history, the investigator has to have an idea of what he is looking for, which in the area of economic history means that he needs some basic economic theory. "Facts" did not speak for themselves, and "laws" did not leap off of the pages of historical data.

Today's empiricist is committed to the idea of economic theory. His model is generally that of the natural sciences. Friedman's description of positive economics is standard: "Its task is to provide a system of generalizations that can be used to make correct predictions about the consequences of any change in circumstances. Its performance is to be judged by the precision, scope, and conformity with experience of the predictions it yields."[25] He goes on to state that the decisive test "is whether the hypothesis works for the phenomena it purports to explain."[26] The test is therefore factual: "Only factual evidence can show whether it [theory] is 'right' or 'wrong' or, better, tentatively 'accepted' as valid or 'rejected.' "[27] Economics is empirical, inductive, *a posteriori*, fact-oriented. Facts cannot prove a theory, but they may fail to disprove some theories.[28] The process is: . . . facts . . . theory . . . facts . . . theory— endlessly, always in a refining process.[29] If you can find a better theory (at no extra cost), choose it.

Friedman then confronts a basic post-Kantian antinomy, the problem of defining "theory," "fact," and explaining the interrelationship of each to each and both to the human mind.

---

24. Schumpeter, *History*, pp. 807 ff.
25. Friedman, *Essays*, p. 4.
26. *Ibid.*, p. 30.
27. *Ibid.*, p. 8.
28. *Ibid.*, p. 9.
29. *Ibid.*, p. 13.

More generally, a hypothesis or theory consists of an assertion that certain forces are, and by implication others are not, important for a particular class of phenomena and a specification of the manner of action of the forces it asserts to be important. We can regard the hypothesis as consisting of two parts: first, a conceptual world or abstract model simpler than the "real world" and containing only the forces that the hypothesis asserts to be important [Weber's "ideal type"—G.N.]; second, a set of rules defining the class of phenomena for which the "model" can be taken to be an adequate representation of the "real world" and specifying the correspondence between the variables or entities in the model and observable phenomena.

These two parts are very different in character. The model is abstract and complete; it is an "algebra" or "logic." Mathematics and formal logic come into their own in checking its consistency and completeness and exploring its implications. There is no place in the model for, and no function to be served by, vagueness, maybe's, or approximations. The air pressure is zero, not "small," for a vacuum; the demand curve for the product of a competitive producer is horizontal (has a slope of zero), not "almost horizontal."

The rules for using the model, on the other hand, cannot possibly be abstract and complete. They must be concrete and in consequence incomplete—completeness is possible only in a conceptual world, not in the "real world," however it may be interpreted. . . . In seeking to make a science as "objective" as possible, our aim should be to formulate the rules explicitly in so far as possible and continually to widen the range of phenomena for which it is possible to do so. But, no matter how successful we may be in this attempt, there inevitably will remain room for judgment in applying the rules. Each occurrence has some features peculiarly its own, not covered by the explicit rules. The capacity to judge that these are or are not to be disregarded, that they should or should not affect what observable phenomena are to be identified with what entities in the model, is something that cannot be taught; it can be learned but only by experience and exposure to the "right" scientific atmosphere, not by rote. It is at this point that the "amateur" is separated from the "professional" in all sciences and that the thin line is drawn which distinguishes the "crackpot" from the scientist.[30]

First, just how coherent is the model? Friedman asserts that it can be consistent and complete. I suspect that he is here giving more credit to a rival discipline—mathematics—than the discipline's best minds ever claim for it. The essay in this volume by Vern Poythress indicates the epistemological problems of mathematics. It might be mentioned that Gödel's hypothesis denies that a mathematical proposition can be simultaneously consistent and complete, which is precisely what Friedman naively asserts as an ideal for the logic of the economic model.

Second, how do the rules for using the model actually connect it with

---

30. *Ibid.*, pp. 24-25.

the data? Why is such a contact possible? Eugene Wigner, the Nobel Prize winner in physics, has called attention to this very anomaly: it is an unreasonably effective correspondence which secular scientists simply cannot explain.[31] If the rules are incomplete, how can they be fitted with the "complete" model?

Third, the "real world" which Friedman is careful to put in quotation marks is really the product of our senses, as interpreted by our minds. In Kantian language, concepts without percepts are empty, while percepts without concepts are blind. So the data are never raw; there is no operational brute factuality. The data are already interpreted as we receive them. How do we know, for example, when a perceived trade cycle is nothing more than the product of our own ingenuity? The great mathematical economist, Ragnar Frisch, once demonstrated the existence of a particular economic cycle before a group of professional colleagues—a regularity where none had been perceived before by any of them. Harlan McCracken describes the finale: "When the group was thrilled and almost dumfounded by the results, they were mildly informed that the omega operations had been performed on a relief map of Europe."[32]

Finally, what of Friedman's appeal to "the capacity to judge" and "experience"? Here we have an appeal, ultimately, to some form of intuition as the means of bridging the gap between the model and the perceived historical data (that may or may not be in conformity to the economic world "out there"). There is no strict one-to-one application of the abstract mental model and perceived reality, for then the model would be as complex as reality itself, swallowed up in the immensity of brute factuality. Yet it is believed to be in conformity to the basic outline of the already perceived facts. But how do we know? How can we have such faith in the coherence of our minds, the orderliness of nature, and the intuitive ability of our minds (or whatever it is) to bridge the gap? We have faith—a remarkable quantity of faith. Without it, there could be no economics. So our neutral, rationalistic practitioners simply put this statement of faith in the back of their minds and forget it. Epistemology, at the truly crucial points, is not a popular topic among secularists.

Ultimately, Friedman asserts, "The construction of hypotheses is a creative act of inspiration, intuition, and invention; its essence is the vision

31. Eugene P. Wigner, "The Unreasonable Effectiveness of Mathematics in the Natural Sciences," *Communications on Pure and Applied Mathematics*, XIII (1960), pp. 1-14.

32. McCracken, "Comments," *Am. Ec. Rev., Papers & Proceedings*, XLIII (May, 1953), p. 277. Cf. Gunther Stent, *The Coming of the Golden Age: A View of the End of Progress* (Garden City, N. Y.: Natural History Press, 1969), pp. 115 ff.; Benoit Mandelbrot, "New Methods in Statistical Economics," *Journal of Political Economy*, LXXI (1963), pp. 421 ff.

of something new in familiar material."[33] He is quite correct, of course, but this does not answer the question. How is man so endowed, for what purpose does he have the gift? How, in fact, are we sure on rational grounds that he does have it? We need a theory to explain the phenomenon, and intuition, being nonrational at bottom, cannot be made to fit any rationalistic theory. We think we perceive men in the activity of linking theories and facts, but can they, really, and if so, how? In effect, the secularist repies, "he just can, that's all!" Faith, faith, wonderful faith!

Is there some accepted, fairly stable body of acceptable theory? Probably not, says Friedman. "Observed facts are necessarily finite in number; possible hypotheses, infinite" [I do not understand this—G.N.][34] Furthermore, "Any theory is necessarily provisional and subject to change with the advance of knowledge."[35] In short, all we can say, somehow, in faith, is that "some parts of economic theory clearly deserve more confidence than others."[36] (Try and find one that all economists agree on!) You can check these statements by comparing them with "facts." But which facts? Facts selected by which theorist? Not all facts, since our knowledge can never be exhaustive.[37] Remember, "we cannot perceive 'facts' without a theory."[38] Yet within the shifting sands of knowledge, there is somehow structure enough to establish an academic discipline. Or at least maybe there is.

Van Til, as usual, has put the problem into a starkly penetrating analysis:

> If man is made the final reference point in predication, knowledge cannot get under way, and if it could get under way it could not move forward. That is to say, in all non-Christian forms of epistemology there is first the idea that to be understood a fact must be understood exhaustively. It must be reducible to a part of a system of timeless logic. But man himself and the facts of his experience are subject to change. How is he ever to find within himself an a priori resting point? He himself is on the move. . . . If we do not with Calvin presuppose the self-contained God back of the self-conscious act of the knowing mind of man, we are doomed to be lost in an endless and bottomless flux.[39]

Is there a coherent world out there, out beyond the powers of our perception? Does it, or some part of it, conform to the logical structure of our minds? Is there some means by which we can discover such order? How do we find the rules that might allow us to make deductions from our theories and predictions about the facts? The facts are like beads for the secularist, says Van Til, and the theories are like string. But on the premises of the

---

33. Friedman, *Essays*, p. 13.
34. *Ibid.*, p. 9.
35. *Ibid.*, p. 41.
36. *Ibid.*
37. *Ibid.*, p. 32.
38. *Ibid.*, p. 34.
39. Cornelius Van Til, *An Introduction to Systematic Theology* (Syllabus, Westminster Theological Seminary, 1961), p. 167.

secularist, the beads have no holes in them and the string is infinitely long. Furthermore, there may be more than one string! The only way to string them is unknown, and this the secularist calls "intuition." Friedman is no different from epistemologists in other academic disciplines. Either the theory is swallowed up in the facts, or the facts are swallowed up by the theory, or else theory remains wholly removed from all facts. Van Til's words are inescapable:

> The point we are now concerned to stress is the atomistic character of the non-Christian methodology. The idea of system is for it merely a limiting notion. It is merely ideal. What is more, it must forever remain but an ideal. To become reality this ideal would have to destroy science itself. It would have to demolish the individuality of each fact as it came to know it. But if it did this, it would no longer be knowledge of a fact that is different from any other fact. The method of non-Christian science then requires that to be known facts must be known as part of a system. And since the Christian idea of a system as due to the counsel of God is by definition excluded, it is man himself that must know this system. But to know the system he must know it intuitively. He cannot know it discursively because discursive thought, if it is to be in contact with reality at all, must partake of the piecemeal character of non-rational being. Each individual concept that pretends to be a concept with respect to things that have their existence in the world of time must partake of the *de facto* character of these facts themselves.[40]

Intuitive knowledge is all that is left for man, and intuitive knowledge, not being discursive, participates in the chaos of random factuality, i.e., is not rational knowledge. Friedman, ending as he does with intuition, destroys the logical character of hypothetically rational inductive economic science. At the heart of "rational" inductive thought is a gaping bedrock of irrationalism. Without a doctrine of divine creation, the inductive rationalist builds his foundation on the sand of pure chance, and whirl does not give up his kingdom.

I have not singled out Friedman as a stick man. He is an eloquent defender of modern economic science, and his chapter on methodology is standard in the profession. Other expositions echo his. Gregor Sebba, a mathematical economist, has raised similar issues. He writes that "Classical economics made the tremendous discovery that the quantifiable features of a modern economy can be represented by a general mechanistic model capable of mathematization and presumably prediction."[41] Positive economics, officially neutral with respect to values, can predict the future.

---

40. Van Til, *Apologetics* (Syllabus, Westminster Theological Seminary, 1959), pp. 76-77.

41. Gregor Sebba, "The Development of the Concepts of Mechanism and Model in Physical Science and Economic Thought," *Am. Ec. Rev., Papers & Proceedings,* XLIII (May, 1953), p. 261.

But with prediction comes control, Sebba argues. New forms of macro-economic planning are possible through the use of input-output techniques developed by both Soviet and Western economists. "Here the distinction between 'technical' and 'economic' problems obviously no longer applies."[42] But then a problem appears which had been held back by the hypothetical value neutrality of positive economic theory:

> Unlike classical theory, it is not confined to the question what the terminal state of the economic system will be, given its initial state and its laws of operation; normative economics can simultaneously consider the initial and the terminal state and select the minimum path from one to another. The theory of allocations has the markings of a rigorous, predictive, general theory of planning.[43]

And as Hayek has shown so eloquently in his *Road to Serfdom*, central planning can never be neutral; it is based on the value preferences of the central planners.

Positive economics, because it involves knowledge, necessarily involves power. And power is never neutrally applied. Sebba sees this clearly, and he drives home his point:

> Control then consists of prediction offered as purely technical, neutral, powerless advice. The sons of Adam Smith fear control of man over man. And rightly so, for such control implies the dehumanization of the human realm. The ethos of classical economics revolts against this consequence. But its epistemology works towards it. So long as the theory is unpredictive, the conflict can remain unresolved and even undetected. But should the theory become predictive, it may yet turn against its origins and become instrumental in subverting economic freedom.[44]

The nature-freedom antinomy of all modern thought reasserts itself once again. On the one hand, knowledge of the world is seen as giving men power and therefore freedom from an impersonal, capricious universe. Yet with the advent of power, man falls under the sway of his own creation, like Dr. Frankenstein and his monster. Man, defined as being no more than a natural creature, becomes as subject to his own laws as nature is. Secular law eats away at the foundations of secular freedom.[45] Classical economics destroys itself in an orgy of planning. The attempt at being epistemologically neutral to God and all values becomes dust in the mouth; values, never truly banished from science's closed universe, reappear in power.

---

42. *Ibid.*, p. 263.
43. *Ibid.*, p. 264.

44. *Ibid.*, p. 266.

45. It seems to me to be quite likely that input-output analysis will prove to be premature, and that Mises' argument that without a free market and private ownership, no rational planning is possible, will reassert itself. But to the extent that modern economists believe that they have predictive power due to any economic tool, there is a tendency for that tool to become a means of economic planning and external control.

Reason: Deductive

For at least half a century, deductive reasoning in the social sciences has been out of favor. Its defenders are limited almost exclusively in economics to the followers of Ludwig von Mises. Inductive reason, supposedly the characteristic of the natural sciences, has been adopted by most modern economists. Now, however, the perception on the part of some social scientists of the implications of Thomas Kuhn's *The Structure of Scientific Revolutions* (1962) has begun to shake their faith in the paradigm of purely inductive research. It has become more and more obvious to the readers of Kuhn's book that there is no scholarship apart from intellectual presuppositions. Academic guilds form around an accepted body of these premises, and they in turn become the foundation of "normal science"—the drudge-like repetitive science of the vast majority of men in any given era or discipline. Thus, research is guild-oriented and essentially *a priori*: the questions asked, the ways in which the questions are to be answered, the form of presentation of the answer are all determined by the prevailing definition of the particular discipline as set forth by the academic guild. Thus, Kuhn's analysis argues, science is never purely inductive, objective, or neutral. It is governed by presuppositions that are thought to be "rational" and "inescapable." From time to time younger members of the guild do escape them, overturning the accepted paradigm; this constitutes a scientific revolution.

The writings of Ludwig von Mises constitute the strongest case for pure deductive rationalism. He takes seriously the second half of Kant's slogan, "percepts without concepts are blind." There is no scientific investigation by the social scientist that is not in terms of fixed intellectual categories. His is the consistent Kantian world of humanism. Man is the starting point. "*Panta rei*, everything is in ceaseless flux, says Heraclitus; there is no permanent being; all is change and becoming. . . . For epistemology, the theory of human knowledge, there is certainly something that it cannot help considering as permanent, viz., the logical and praxeological [science of human action] structure of the human mind, on the one hand, and the power of the human senses, on the other hand."[46] Mises brings back the old debate between Parmenides and Heraclitus. Parmenides held, in Van Til's words, "that only that can exist which is fully subject to the laws of human logic. In other words Parmenides assumes that the reach of human logic is the limit of possible existence."[47] But Heraclitus countered that the essence of the world is flux, beyond the static categories of universal human reason. So Mises, like all post-Kantians, holds to both positions:

46. Mises, *The Ultimate Foundation of Economic Science* (Princeton: Van Nostrand, 1962), p. 1. Mises died in 1973.
47. Van Til, *A Christian Theory of Knowledge* (Nutley, N. J.: Presbyterian and Reformed Publishing Co., 1969), p. 171.

logic is static and can understand some things "out there," but there is some aspect of flux and chaos in the universe, and it is here that man finds his freedom from totalitarian humanistic law. In other words, as far as human nature is concerned, "epistemology must look upon it as unchanging."

Man needs an unchanging point of reference, Mises believes, if he is to be able to say anything about anything. The unchanging point of reference is the human mind.

> Kant, awakened by Hume from his "dogmatic slumbers," put the rationalistic doctrine upon a new basis. Experience, he taught, provides only the raw material out of which the mind forms what is called knowledge. All knowledge is conditioned by the categories that precede any data of experience both in time and in logic. The categories are a priori; they are the mental equipment of the individual that enables him to think and—we may add—to act. As all reasoning presupposes the a priori categories, it is vain to embark upon attempts to prove or disprove them.[48]

What are these categories? They are independent of biological evolution. Evolution is continuous, while the catagories appeared in man discontinuously.[49] They are not innate ideas. "They are the necessary mental tool to arrange sense data in a systematic way, and transform them into facts of experience. . . ."[50] They are *pragmatic*: "Only those groups could survive whose numbers acted in accordance with the right categories, i.e., with those that were in conformity with reality and therefore—to use the concept of pragmatism—worked."[51] Apparently, had the world been a different kind of world, those using the categories would not have survived, and the categories would have disappeared—not, somehow, evolving into something else. Where categories are concerned, life is one huge crap shoot; you either got them or you ain't. Or, paraphrasing one scholar, "when you're hot, you're hot, and when you're not, you're not."

The reason that the categories function is that the universe is orderly, in part. "No thinking and no acting would be possible to man if the universe were chaotic, i.c., if there were no regularity whatever in the succession and concatenation of events. In such a world of unlimited contingency nothing could be perceived but ceaseless kaleidoscopic change. There would be no possibility for man to expect anything."[52] Therefore, he concludes, "Reasoning is necessarily always deductive. . . . All human knowledge concerning the universe presupposes and rests upon the cognition of the regularity in the succession and concatenation of observable events. It would be vain to search for a rule if there were no regularity."[53]

---

48. Mises, *Ultimate Foundation*, p. 12.
49. *Ibid.*, pp. 8, 14.
50. *Ibid.*, p. 16.
51. *Ibid.*, p. 15.

52. *Ibid.*, p. 19.
53. *Ibid.*, pp. 21-22.

This is empiricism's Achilles heel: it rejects the category of regularity in the microscopic sphere, looking instead for statistical laws of probability in aggregate events. Empiricists fail to search for explanations in terms of individual human action.[54] It is a misuse of the methodology of the natural sciences, on the assumption that people are not acting beings. Empiricism postulates pure randomness of individual events.[55]

Mises comes to the heart of the epistemological problem:

> Following in the wake of Kant's analysis, philosophers raised the question: How can the human mind, by aprioristic thinking, deal with the reality of the external world? As far as praxeology [the science of human action] is concerned, the answer is obvious. Both, a priori thinking and reasoning on the one hand and human action on the other, are manifestations of the human mind. The logical structure of the human mind creates the reality of the action. Reason and action are congeneric and homogeneous, two aspects of the same phenomenon.[56]

Mises is far more epistemologically self-conscious than most contemporary economists. He has read his Kant, he knows the ground on which all modern secularists must stand if they are to defend the idea of modern science from total chaos, and so he affirms, as Kant did, the creative ordering power of the human mind. This, as Van Til has argued throughout his career, is the heart of modern Kantian thought. Mises acknowledges it and builds upon it.

The historical sciences, however, are different from praxeology and its most developed subdivision, economics. History is concerned with the flux of human life, not regularities. "What distinguishes the descriptions of history from those of the natural sciences is that they are not interpreted in the light of the category of regularity."[57] Men must look to history for *meaning*; unlike natural events, men act in terms of final causes. The interpreter searches for meaning in the minds of the participants: what did it mean for them? "The autonomy of history or, as we may say, of the various historical disciplines consists of their dedication to the study of meaning."[58] The goal, of course, is radical autonomy: "History is man-centered; it has nothing to do with any point of view of God or some quasi-God. . . ."[59] Man provides the meaning. God's knowledge is not available to man.[60] However, the mind is bounded by the limits of understanding:

---

54. *Ibid.*, p. 23.
55. *Ibid.*, pp. 27-28. Cf. the exchange on this point between Gary S. Becker, an empiricist of the Chicago School, and Israel Kirzner, a follower of Mises: Becker, "Irrational Action and Economic Theory," *Journal of Political Economy*, LXX (Feb. 1962); Kirzner, "Rational Action and Economic Theory," *JPE*, LXX (Aug., 1962); "Reply" and "Rejoinder," *JPE*, LXXI (Feb., 1963).
56. *Ibid.*, p. 42.
57. *Ibid.*, p. 43.   59. *Ibid.*, p. 44.
58. *Ibid.*   60. *Ibid.*, pp. 37, 64.

the "meaning of the whole" is beyond us.[61] There are no general laws in history; historical events are entirely unique.[62] But somehow historiography is "objective."[63] Yet it cannot be a complete reproduction of the infinite facts of the past. The historian must select, yet be neutral.

The rock-bottom data that resist classification in terms of the categories of the social sciences are those that are historically unique. Here, the historian must use "sympathy" or "understanding" in order to make these data intelligible. However, such understanding must not contradict the teachings of neutral social science. No matter how many historical documents testify to the existence of a devil, "no appeal to understanding could justify a historian's attempt to maintain that the devil really existed otherwise than in the visions of an excited human brain."[64] The same, of course, is true of any relationship between witches and the devil.[65] One wonders if, in some future time, the same may be said of Ludwig von Mises, who has far fewer historical documents testifying of his existence. Indeed, in some future socialistic state, it may be more dangerous to the authorities to have people believe in Mises than in witches. Socialist "understanding" will erase the possibility of Mises from real life, although socialist historians may admit that people once believed that they had seen Mises or even read a book by him. Naturally, they were deranged. There could never be such a creature as Mises!

How objectivity is to be guaranteed, or even thought to be possible, in the historical sciences is never explained. How does the historian know that his sympathetic understanding of the motives or hopes of past individuals has any relationship with the past? How can he be certain that his understanding links up with theirs? There can never be such assurance. Furthermore, how can the bedrock data of history be related to any system of general understanding? How is it possible to make sense out of the infinite data of history? Mises assumes too much for the historical disciplines. He gives too much credit to the ability of the irrationalist powers of the Kantian noumenal "understanding" to make intelligible judgments and statements about Kant's phenomenal realm.

How do we link the a priori categories of the mind with the external reality of the social sciences? Mises, at least, is honest:

> Science, which is dependent both on discursive reasoning and on experience, does not present us with a unified picture of the world.

---

61. Mises, *Epistemological Problems of Economics* (Princeton: Van Nostrand, 1960), p. 48.
62. Mises, *Theory and History* (New Rochelle, N. Y.: Arlington House, [1957] 1969), p. 212.
63. Mises, *Human Action*, p. 47.
64. *Ibid.*, p. 51.
65. Mises, *Epistemological Problems*, p. 100.

It reduces phenomena to a number of concepts and propositions that we must accept as ultimate, without being able to establish a connection between them. It proves incapable of closing the gap that exists between the system of the science of human thought and action and the system of the sciences of physical nature. It does not know how to find a bridge between sentience and motion or between consciousness and matter. What life and death are elude its grasp.[66]

There is an inescapable dualism in Mises' Kantian universe, and Mises is perfectly willing to admit its existence:

But as long as we do not know how external (physical and physiological) facts produce in a human "soul" definite thoughts and volitions resulting in concrete acts, we have to face an insurmountable dualism. In the present state of our knowledge, the fundamental statements of positivism and monism are mere metaphysical postulates devoid of any scientific foundation. Reason and experience show us two separate realms: the external world of physical and physiological events and the internal world of thought, feeling, and purposeful action. No bridge connects—as far as we can see today—these two spheres. Identical external events result sometimes in different human responses, and different external events produce sometimes the same human response. We do not know why.[67]

But if a gap exists from external event to the human will, then the will is totally separated from the external world. This is the most fundamental of all Kantian dualisms. Action, argues Mises, "is the outcome of a man's will. Of course, we do not know what will is. We simply call *will* man's faculty to choose between different states of affairs. . . ."[68] It seems to be the equivalent of Friedman's *intuition*. It is the mysterious bridge between thought and action, stimulus and response (and secularists can never be sure whether this relationship is *active*—thought leading to action—or *passive*—response to a stimulus).

How do we know if our *a priori* mental concepts correspond with the facts of the external world? "The question whether or not the real conditions of the external world correspond to these assumptions is to be answered by experience."[69] *Experience*: we are back to Friedman's intuitional, experiential link. We are back to testing once again—testing on the assumption that there is the mind-matter link. Mises acts in faith that this mystical link exists, although he denies any mysticism in such an affirmation. "Science is sobriety and clarity of conception, not intoxicated vision."[70] But what is experience? How does it relate mind and external

---

66. *Ibid.*, p. 44.
67. Mises, "The Treatment of 'Irrationality' in the Social Sciences," *Philosophy and Phenomenological Research*, IV (June, 1944). I am using a mimeographed reprint of the article published by the Foundation for Economic Education, p. 8.
68. *Ibid.*, p. 4.
69. Mises, *Ultimate Foundation*, p. 44.
70. Mises, *Epistemological Problems*, p. 46.

matter? Is it the same as will? Is it the same as intuition? How sure are we of the correspondence of the two realms? Not very. "But if the answer is affirmative, all the conclusions drawn by logically correct praxeological reasoning strictly describe what is going on in reality."[71] *If the answer is in the affirmative,* our *a priori* mental concepts correspond with data—some data, i.e., the relevant data—of the external world. Here is a huge "if clause" in Mises' epistemology. It is, in fact, a statement of faith, incapable of proof, as he admits, and yet the very intellectual foundation of his *a priori* rationalism.

Our ignorance of the nature of this link between mind and matter is the source of our personal freedom. On the other hand, our faith in its existence is the source of our knowledge and power. Here is the Kantian nature-freedom antinomy in its sharpest form. We need power to escape the chaos of nature—to gain freedom as men in nature—yet this power destroys our freedom, or threatens to:

> We do not know how out of the encounter of a human individuality, i.e., a man as he has been formed by all he has inherited and by all he has experienced, and a new experience definite ideas result and determine the individual's conduct. We do not even have and surmise how such knowledge could be acquired. More than that, we realize that if such knowledge were attainable for men, and if, consequently, the formation of ideas and thereby the will could be manipulated in the way machines are operated by the engineer, human conditions would be essentially altered. There would yawn a wide gulf between those who manipulate other people's ideas and will and those whose ideas and will are manipulated by others.[72]

Here is the heart of the dilemma sketched by C. S. Lewis in his *Abolition of Man* and *That Hideous Strength.* It is an inescapable contradiction in all post-Kantian thought. Secularists must affirm the existence of the mind-matter link, yet they dare not affirm it.

Within the framework of this antinomy, man's ignorance of the nature of this link—indeterminacy—protects him from manipulation by other men. Yet it is the determinacy of the link that allows him to control nature (of which man is said to be a part). Thus, we are said to be able to rationalize only a few segments of reality. "Reason and science deal only with isolated fragments detached from the living whole and thereby killed."[73] Mises then retreats into Kantian mysticism in order to preserve man's freedom and living humanity:

> This personal experience of wholeness, unity, and infinity is the loftiest peak of human existence. It is the awakening to a higher humanity. It alone transforms everyday living into true living. It is not vouchsafed

---

71. Mises, *Ultimate Foundation,* p. 45.
72. *Ibid.,* p. 58.
73. Mises, *Epistemological Problems,* p. 44.

to us daily or at all places. The occasions on which we are brought closer to the world spirit must await a propitious hour.[74]

To recapitulate, the foundation of economic reasoning is the existence of universal, timeless categories of human logic.[75] All facts require theories to interpret them; there can be no uninterpreted factuality for men to deal with intellectually. Thus, facts cannot refute accurate theories, since they have existence only in terms of theories. The theories are autonomous. "They are not subject to verification or falsification on the ground of experience or facts."[76] Unfortunately, Mises has been forced to appeal to experience in answering the question concerning the existence of the mind-matter link.[77] Thus, he both affirms and denies experience as a means of checking the validity of his theorems' applicability. Experience in some necessarily unstated way links theory to fact, yet it cannot criticize theory. But it can somehow *warn* theory: "If the facts do not confirm the theory, the cause perhaps may lie in the imperfection of the theory. The disagreement between the theory and the facts of experience consequently forces us to think through the problems of the theory again. But so long as re-examination of the theory uncovers no errors in our thinking, we are not entitled to doubt its truth."[78] And experience *can* criticize *bad* theory: "Precisely because the phenomena of historical experience are complex, the inadequacies of an erroneous theory are less effectively revealed when experience contradicts it than when it is assessed in the light of correct theory."[79] But these inadequacies are, apparently, revealed in part, though less effectively than by theory, through the contradictions of experience. It is impossible to give a precise definition of "experience" as found in Mises' writings.

On the one hand, we are asked to believe that science is value-free, since "no standard of value of any kind is contained in the system of economic or sociological theory or in the teachings of liberalism, which constitute the practical application of this theory to action in society."[80] On the other hand, we are not supposed to regard as in any way value-laden the following statement: "Every individual desires life, health, and well-being for himself and his friends and close relations."[81] Conclusion:

> To the man who adopts the scientific method in reflecting upon the problems of human action, liberalism must appear as the only policy that can lead to lasting well-being for himself, his friends, and his loved ones, and, indeed, for all others as well. Only one who does not want to achieve such ends as life, health, and prosperity for himself, his friends, and those he loves, only one who prefers sickness, misery, and suffering

---

74. *Ibid.*, p. 45.
75. *Ibid.*, p. 27; cf. pp. 198, 204.
76. Mises, *Human Action*, p. 32.
77. Mises, *Ultimate Foundation*, p. 44.
78. Mises, *Epistemological Problems*, p. 30.

79. *Ibid.*, p. 29.
80. *Ibid.*, p. 40.
81. *Ibid.*, p. 38.

may reject the reasoning of liberalism on the ground that it is not neutral with regard to value judgments.[82]

But, the Bible states explicitly, "But he that sinneth against me wrongeth his own soul: all they that hate me love death" (Prov. 8:36). Even if all men were to agree about the true nature of health, joy, and the good life, it does not follow that all men truly want these things.

Mises' hypothetical neutrality is uncritically naive. He holds to a value-free science that in turn presupposes agreement among all men concerning "the good life." What he assumes is the universal validity of the goals of Western civilization (which is in itself an overwhelming mental abstraction[83]):

> Of course, the objections the economists advanced to the plans of the socialists and interventionists carry no weight with those who do not approve of the ends which the peoples of Western civilization take for granted. Those who prefer penury and slavery to material well-being and all that can only develop where there is material well-being may deem all these objections irrelevant. But the economists have repeatedly emphasized that they deal with socialism and interventionism from the point of view of the generally accepted values of Western civilization.[84]

While Western civilization may have been the product of a world-view based on the idea of the sovereignty of the God of the Bible (a fact Mises conveniently ignores), today our universe is, by definition, closed to God. "It is not to be denied that the loftiest theme that human thought can set for itself is reflection on absolute questions. Whether such reflection can accomplish anything is doubtful."[85]

> Our own thinking is utterly powerless to discover anything whatever about what such a superhuman or divine being would think. But within the cosmos in which our action is effective and in which our thinking paves the way for action, the findings of our scientific reasoning are so securely established as to render meaningless the statement that, in a broader setting or in a deeper sense, they would have to lose their validity and yield to some other cognition.[86]

God and His revelation are therefore irrelevant for the content of economic science, since "whatever firmly withstands the logical scrutiny of our reason can in no way be refuted by the assertions of metaphysics."[87] In short, "We may leave aside the genuine dogmas such as Creation, Incarnation, the Trinity, as they have no direct bearing on the problems of interhuman

82. *Ibid.*, p. 39.
83. Robert A. Nisbet, *Social Change and History* (New York: Oxford University Press, 1969), pp. 245-46.
84. Mises, *Theory and History*, p. 33.
85. Mises, *Epistemological Problems*, p. 49.
86. *Ibid.*, p. 50.
87. *Ibid.*

relations."[88] We can say nothing about God at all. However, God is "wholly other,"[89] and He is incapable of action (being perfect),[90] and He is socially irrelevant.[91] The only universals for man are the universal categories of his own mind.[92] Without these, men could not think or act, so these *have* to exist.[93]

Man's dignity stems from his freedom. Yet he lives in a determinate universe in which universal laws rule. Still, "The main fact about human action is that in regard to it there is no such regularity in the conjunction of phenomena. It is not a shortcoming of the sciences of human action that they have not succeeded in discovering determinate stimulus-response patterns. What does not exist cannot be discovered."[94] Except that such patterns may exist:

> . . . in the present state of human science it is impossible to reduce the emergence and the transformation of ideas to physical, chemical, or biological factors. It is this impossibility that constitutes the autonomy of the sciences of human action. Perhaps natural science will one day be in a position to describe the physical, chemical, and biological events in which the body of the man Newton necessarily and inevitably produced the theory of gravitation. . . . The sciences of human action by no means reject determinism. The objective of history is to bring out in full relief the factors that were operative in producing a definite event. History is entirely guided by the category of cause and event. In retrospect, there is no question of contingency. The notion of contingency as employed in dealing with human action always refers to man's uncertainty about the future and the limitations of the specific historical understanding of future events.[95]

In principle, there is no contingency, all is determined, and natural science may fuse with human science to produce the society of total planning. It is only a question of gaining adequate knowledge.

There is a dualism between determinism and indeterminism. Man needs to preserve both his power and his freedom. "Free will means that man can aim at definite ends because he is familiar with some of the laws determining the flux of world affairs. There is a sphere within which each man can choose alternatives. He is not, like other animals, inevitably and irremediably subject to the operation of blind fate. He can, within definite limits, divert events from the course they would take if left alone."[96] Man is therefore morally responsible. "Comparing himself with all other beings, man sees his own dignity and superiority in his will."[97] But Mises has

88. Mises, *Theory and History*, p. 46.
89. Mises, *Ultimate Foundation*, p. 37.
90. *Ibid.*, p. 3.
91. Mises, *Epistemological Problems*, pp. 24, 57, 150.
92. *Ibid.*, pp. 91, 204.
93. *Ibid.*, p. 98.
94. Mises, *Theory and History*, p. 9.

95. *Ibid.*, p. 93.
96. *Ibid.*, p. 179.
97. *Ibid.*

already admitted that we do not know what the will is. It fills the gap between external causality and the rational categories of human thought. And man loses his freedom once that bridge is erected; men can control the responses of others once we know how the link is to be made. So free will therefore means simultaneously that we cannot bridge that gap, that we cannot be controlled. Our so-called free will requires a determinate universe to hold off nature's blind fate, and it needs an indeterminate universe to hold off the controllers. Mises, as all post-Kantians, is impaled on the horns of the nature-freedom dilemma.

Mises has no consistent theory of law, no link between mind and reality, other than "experience" and "will," both left undefined. Yet in his humanistic confidence he says of the natural sciences: "They provide the only mental tool that can be used in the ceaseless struggle for life. They have proved their practical worth. And no other way of knowledge is open to man, no alternative is left to him."[98] No alternatives, by *a priori* dictum— and this cannot be refuted by theology or facts. This is the closed universe of nineteenth-century neo-Kantian rationalism. It is overconfident even in its all-encompassing contradictions.

Living With Dualism

Unlike Mises, Prof. Frank H. Knight (d. 1972) had a sense of the intellectual dualisms of secular thought. He was also a neo-Kantian. He separated the natural sciences from the human sciences in terms of epistemology, something that Paul Samuelson refuses to do.[99] Social science must "strive to tell the whole truth, to recognize all the facts" in its quest for exhaustive knowledge.[100] Yet we are involved in an intellectual antinomy: the science ideal vs. the ideal of free human personality. "As far as science is concerned, free will, which is the only real dynamism, is either an illusion or simply a methodological limitation."[101] Free will is of very limited scope in life, in spite of the fact that it is "infinitely important." Here is the basic dilemma of all attempts at explaining social causation:

> There is equal insistence that causality is an *active* principle, and, on the other hand, upon concrete methods of problem-solving which are "scientific" in the sense of natural science as purely empirical, phenomenalistic, and positivistic. The main criticism of the book [R. M.

98. *Ibid.*, p. 304.
99. Knight, *History and Method*, p. 121. Cf. Paul Samuelson, "Economic Theory and Mathematics—An Appraisal," *Am. Ec. Rev., Papers & Proceedings*, XLII (May, 1952): "There are no separate methodological problems that face the social scientist different in kind from those that face any other scientist" (p. 61). This is the modern, post-Heisenberg viewpoint; Mises and Knight are clinging to Newtonian concepts of natural science.
100. Knight, p. 131.
101. *Ibid.*, pp. 140-41.

MacIver's *Social Causation*] is that the author sees both horns of this intellectual dilemma but fails to recognize it and to see that it has no real solution.[102]

How do we link mind and external reality? Again, Knight admits, there is no secular, rational solution:

> With regard to the relation between deduction and observation, or intelligence and the senses, in our knowledge of nature, there is not much that should need to be said. Surely anyone who has made any progress at all in the study of philosophy, or even in private reflection about its problems, can be assumed to know that any simple antithesis between observation and inference is utterly untenable, if not downright foolish. The question as to the primary or immediate data of consciousness is perhaps the main perennial, unsolved and probably unsolvable problem of the theory of knowledge as a whole.[103]

Thus, since it cannot be solved, it is "downright foolish" to bring it up any longer, at least if the proposed antithesis is "simple." We must live with our inescapable intellectual contradictions.

Then how do we know the "facts" of economic scarcity or the idea of a "best" apportionment of scarce resources? We know "by living in the world 'with' other intelligent beings; we neither know them *a priori* nor by one-sided deduction from data and sense observation."[104] We know by "living." What kind of knowledge is economic knowledge? "Methodologically considered, economics is a highly abstract 'concrete deductive' science, similar to geometry or to mathematical mechanics; but in addition its data are intuitive in a far higher or purer sense than is true of mathematics itself."[105] We are back, once again, to *intuition*. We are always back to intuition.

What then becomes of Friedman's categories of prediction? Not much, answers Knight. "A more fundamental weakness of inductive prediction in economics is that empirical (i.e., statistical) data never present anything like an exhaustive analysis of phenomenal sequences down to really elementary components, and the correlation of and extrapolation from composite magnitudes or series never can be very reliable."[106]

Theory or fact: where do we start? How do we string together the infinite number of hole-less beads with our infinitely long string of theory? Schumpeter simply concludes that we have to push very, very hard on the string: "It stands to reason that these two activities are not independent of one another but there must be an incessant give and take between them."[107] In short, "there is not and there cannot be any fundamental opposition between 'theory' and 'fact finding,' let alone between deduction and in-

---

102. *Ibid.*, p. 137.
103. *Ibid.*, p. 159.
104. *Ibid.*, p. 164.

105. *Ibid.*, p. 168.
106. *Ibid.*, p. 176 n.
107. Schumpeter, *History*, p. 45.

duction."[108] Then why the endless battles between inductivists and deductivists? And how can you solve the problem of fitting facts with the proper theories if you deny that the problem even exists?

Alfred Marshall, the great nineteenth-century Cambridge economist, wrote that an economist "needs the three great intellectual faculties, perception, imagination and reason: and most of all he needs imagination."[109] He is echoed by Kenneth Boulding: "Decision making by instinct, gossip, visceral feeling, and political savvy may stand pretty low on the scale of total rationality, but it may have the virtue of being able to take in very large systems in a crude and vague way, whereas the rationalized processes can only take subsystems in their more exact fashion, and being rational about subsystems may be worse than being not very rational about the system as a whole."[110] Finally, we have the testimony of Michael Arbib:

> Any science that supposedly captures reality in two or three equations is inadequate to describe the systems formed by both brain and society —systems with billions of variables. Thus it would seem that, given the incomplete state of our formal theories, we must complement them with our everyday knowledge as members of society. In short, our rational analysis of society must strike a balance between precise description of certain subsystems and, quite frankly, intuition and feeling about other problems.[111]

Modern man has no epistemology. He wants to stand on balanced ground, but where is balance to be found? What are the criteria of true balance? How does one apply these criteria to the data of the external world? How does one go about proving the existence of such criteria of balance? The whole epistemology of modern man collapses into intuition, feeling, and endless measurement of increasingly useless minute data.

Knight argues that one thing scientists need is a sense of corporate honor. "Without a sense of honor (as well as special competence) among scientists—if, say, they were all charlatans—there could be no science."[112] To support the superstructure of rational science we have to have honesty— indeed, honor, an essentially feudal, military concept. Science rests on ethics. Can ethics be neutral? If not, value-free science rests on value-laden assumptions about man, honesty, and fairness. Economic science is not and cannot be autonomous. It is not and cannot be rational. It is intuitional and ethics-oriented. Its secular neutrality is a sham.

---

108. *Ibid.*
109. Alfred Marshall, quoted by Vincent W. Bladen, "John Stuart Mill's *Principles:* A Centenary Estimate," *Am. Ec. Rev., Papers & Proceedings*, XXXIX (May, 1949), pp. 4-5.
110. Kenneth Boulding, "The Economics of Knowledge and the Knowledge of Economics," *Am. Ec. Rev., Papers & Proceedings*, LVI (May, 1966), p. 11.
111. Michael Arbib, "Complex Systems: The Case for a Marriage of Science and Intuition," *The American Scholar*, XLII (Winter, 1972–73), p. 53. Arbib is a professor of computer science at the Massachusetts Institute of Technology.
112. Knight, p. 157.

Epistemologically, there is simply no legitimate way open for post-Kantian economists to defend their affirmation of neutrality. Neutrality implies a fixed, straightforward, universally recognized link between the external world and the logic of the human mind. But it is this link that is both affirmed and denied by modern philosophers of the social sciences. By appealing to intuition again and again in order to fill the gap between mind and matter, the modern social scientist must abandon his confidence in neutrality. The noumenal realm of will, feeling, intuition, or experience is nonrational, by definition. Kantians can say nothing about its operations. What goes on in the noumenal realm is closed to pure reason, that is, the logical and mathematical reasoning of phenomenal science. All is mystery in Kant's noumenal realm, as Richard Kroner has shown so well in his book, *Kant's Weltanschauung*. Logical neutrality implies a fixity of reference, and the noumenal realm is a zone of pure contingency—total chaos, as far as logic can determine. It is the realm of Kant's God, Kant's ethics, and Kant's "things in themselves." Once washed in the chaos of intuition, neutrality emerges as a myth. The determinacy of logic erodes in the acid sea of chance.

There is absolutely no likelihood that the *a priori* approach of Prof. Mises and the *a posteriori* approach of Prof. Friedman will ever be reconciled, in spite of the fact that each approach ultimately appeals to the irrational and the intuitive in the crucial task of uniting the laws of thought and the world beyond. From Parmenides and Heraclitus to Mises and Friedman, the basic opposition has in no meaningful way been bridged, despite the stupendous effort of intellectuals to overcome it. Nevertheless, on the most fundamental of all issues, Parmenides and Heraclitus could join hands, just as Mises and Friedman do: the issue of human autonomy. Van Til has put it quite well:

> It is not the differences between them but that fact that all of them, whatever their differences, have in common the assumption of human autonomy that is basic to an understanding even of their internal differences. I do not speak of the *autonomy of theoretical thought* but of the *pretended* autonomy of apostate *man*. It is this and, as it appears to me, basically *only* this which all schools of apostate thought have in common. Assuming this autonomy apostate man gives a rebellious covenant-breaking response to the revelational challenge that he meets at every turn. The face of the triune God of Scripture confronts him everywhere and all the time. He spends the entire energy of his whole personality in order to escape seeing this face of God.[113]

Conclusion

The Bible tells us what mankind is apart from grace: blind, rebellious,

---

113. Van Til, "Response" to Herman Dooyeweerd, in E. R. Geehan (ed.), *Jerusalem and Athens* (Nutley, N. J.: Presbyterian & Reformed, 1971), pp. 96-97.

in need of salvation, perverse. Every man requires limits on his thought processes—balance, to use Arbib's concept—and this means authoritative revelation. He is unable to find such a balance on his own. He needs biblical law to help him construct social and economic institutions, each with its proper legitimate sphere of authority. Men are not autonomous, and by claiming full autonomy they hurl themselves into the intellectual void of intuition. The faith of the secular economist in the full autonomy of the discipline is a shaky faith indeed.

This should not give comfort to the pietist or the Barthian who is antinomian to the core anyway. There are far too many of both groups—in the South, waiting for the rapture, or in Grand Rapids or Toronto, waiting for Christian labor unions—who are unwilling to discover the common grace (or restraining grace) of secular economists like Mises, Friedman, or Knight. Brushing off their scholarship with a brief comment like the following gets us nowhere: "They're just secularists, so they have nothing to teach us, so we can adopt guild socialism that is neither intelligent nor revealed in the Bible, but we like it because it sounds radically Christian!" There is no social hope in an antinomian retreat into the vague socialism of the German Historical School or other anti-theoretical economics systems. Where Mises and Friedman say things that are in conformity to the Bible, we should take their careful expositions seriously. We have the responsibility of recognizing what is and what is not in conformity to the Bible's concrete revelation whenever we read the works of secular economists. Abandoning reason in the name of vague "Christian feelings of charity" is no substitute for prayerful scholarship into the implications of our acts. Christian reconstruction will not be the result of pietistic singing about the joy, joy, joy, joy down in the heart, nor will it be the result of endless affirmations of empty Dooyeweerdian spheres. It will be the result of the concrete application of biblical law in the external spheres of life and the application of sovereign grace in the hearts of men. Antinomianism, whatever its form, leads to cultural impotence. Because the secular economist has no epistemological cloak does not, in and of itself, clothe the Christian in robes of purple. The Christian has to make his own clothing.[114]

In order to make myself perfectly clear, as President Nixon used to say, let me spell out precisely what I mean. The slogan of too many Christians has been "no creed but the Bible, no law but love." Another is the familiar "we're under grace, not law." This is pure antinomianism. It makes Christianity utterly impotent to challenge the scholarship of the secularists. It makes it impossible to construct intellectual or institutional

---

114. I have attempted to sketch a few areas where the logic of modern free market economists agrees with biblical principles in my book, *An Introduction to Christian Economics* (Nutley, N. J.: Craig Press, 1973).

alternatives to the various secular systems. We are not under the curse of law, but we are under its limitations for our external conduct, including social conduct. The *progressive sanctification* of the Christian—fighting the good fight, pressing on to the mark for the prize of God's high calling (Phil. 3:14)—is in terms of law. If a Christian is an economist, then his own progressive sanctification must be in terms of the Bible's revelation concerning both the theory and facts of economic thought. The "mind-matter" link is there because he is made in the image of God, and God comprehends His own creation. The rebellion of Adam made God's verbal revelation necessary in order to restrain man's apostate thought, including economic thought. Without the Bible and its concrete economic instruction, the "mind-matter" link will inevitably be warped; the theories of economics, as well as the facts selected in terms of these theories, will be in error, sooner or later. In this century, probably sooner.

Less influential numerically than antinomian pietism, but increasingly influential on many Christian college campuses, is the neo-Dooyeweerdian movement. These followers of the Dutch scholar, Herman Dooyeweerd, have adopted all of their master's errors (especially his faulty view of Scripture) and few of his assets. Dooyeweerd's criticisms of the pretended autonomy of secular thought are quite valuable; his theory of the spheres of human thought and action might be valuable if he were willing to allow the concrete revelation of the Bible to inform him of the content of each sphere. This he and his followers are unwilling to allow. Thus, they are as antinomian as the pietistic fundamentalists they always criticize.[115] Dooyeweerd's view of Scripture is Barthian and basically heretical; his followers are far, far worse.[116] Most of them are guild socialists—or worse.

---

115. See my remarks on Prof. Troost's socialism in "Social Antinomianism," *International Reformed Bulletin* (Oct., 1967); reprinted in my book, *An Introduction to Christian Economics*, ch. 30. On the implications of pietism's antinomianism, see R. J. Rushdoony, "The Heresy of the Faithful," also reprinted in *An Introduction to Christian Economics*, ch. 32.

116. An early criticism of some of the aspects of neo-Dooyeweerdianism was made by R. J. Rushdoony in *Westminster Theological Review* XXX (Nov., 1967), pp. 101-03. See especially Norman Shepherd, "The Doctrine of Scripture in the Dooyeweerdian Philosophy of the Cosmonomic Idea," *The Christian Reformed Outlook* XXI, 2, 3 (Feb., March, 1971). See also John M. Frame and Leonard J. Coppes, *The Amsterdam Philosophy: A Preliminary Critique* (R.D. 2, Phillipsburg, N. J.: Harmony Press, n.d.; available from Westminster Theological Seminary Book Store, Philadelphia 19118); Gordon Clark, "How to Let the Bible Confuse You," *Episcopal Recorder* (Feb., 1972), a critical review of the appalling Dooyeweerdian book by Degraaff and Seerveld, *Understanding the Scripture*; Shepherd, "God's Word of Power," *International Reformed Bulletin* XII (July, 1969).

In the first place, Christian theism maintains that the subject of knowledge owes its existence to God. Accordingly, all its interpretative powers are from God and must therefore be reinterpretative powers. In the second place, when the subject of knowledge is to come into contact with the object of knowledge, the connection is possible only because God has laid it there. In other words, the subject-object relation has its validity via God. Theologically expressed, we say that the validity of human knowledge in general rests upon the *testimonium Spiritus Sancti.* In addition to this, Christian theism maintains that since sin has come into the world, no subject of knowledge can really come into contact with any object of knowledge, in the sense of interpreting it properly, unless the Scripture give the required light and unless the regeneration by the Spirit give a new power of sight.

In opposition to this, the antitheist holds it to be self-evident that the subject of knowledge exists in its own right and can interpret truly without any reference to God. The "natural man" claims to be able to interpret nature and history properly without the need of any reference to God, to Scripture, or to regeneration.

It follows from this clear-cut difference, a difference that goes to the bottom so that not a single "fact" or "law" is left for neutral territory, that the one group must naturally regard the other as being blind. Accordingly, it is when the question of the subject-subject relation comes up, that the problem as to what one group thinks of the other group, becomes acute. The reason why Christians have not always been alive to this difficulty is that they have not always been consistent in drawing the distinction between the Christian theistic and the antitheistic system of epistemology clearly and fully. All too often they have allowed a hazy fringe to remain when it came to the question of whether unbelievers really know material facts aright. Christianity has all too often been interpreted in a narrowly soteriological [salvational] fashion.

> Van Til, *A Survey of Christian Epistemology*
> (1969), pp. 184-85.

EDUCATION

IX

VAN TIL'S VISION FOR EDUCATION

By WILLIAM N. BLAKE

Proverbs warns and promises: "Where there is no vision, the people perish [cast off restraint]: but he that keepeth the law, happy is he."[1] The rootlessness of both individuals and societies demonstrates the lack of vision prevalent in our world today. This Scripture teaches that a culture without direction casts off the discipline of an ordered life, thus anticipating its ultimate downfall. Witness on every side the suicidal tendencies of contemporary life. Doomsday prophets abound. God's word, we hear, provides the antidote. Evangelists and liberal ecumenists alike agree that the Bible has the answer, yet their zealous efforts during this century have failed to lead us out of the fog and night of our current humanistic bumblings. Why have these visionaries led us only further into the abyss of confusion? The answer is simply that their trumpets have put forth an uncertain and unclear call to the people of this land. We need the clear and uncompromising directives boldly set forth by Cornelius Van Til.

Van Til presses men to take God's Word for what it is and what it says. His numerous studies bring to light compromises with Adam's fallen race that have led only to weakness and to a muddled, ineffective stance. Van Til is simply saying that our Lord is a jealous God requiring strict adherence to His holy gospel and law. Sin can never reward— only obedience to God affords the good life: "Take my yoke upon you, and learn of me; for I am meek and lowly in heart: and ye shall find rest unto your souls. For my yoke is easy, and my burden is light."[2]

Both private and state schools act without rudder and direction. Today, the whirlwinds of their humanistic proclivities hasten the demise of learning. Only renewed vision can turn the tide and restore to education its once honored role among men of noble purpose.

My intention in this discourse is to show the relevance and urgency of Van Til's outlook for education at this time. In particular, my study

1. Proverbs 29:18.
2. Matthew 11:29, 30.

shall grapple with those philosophical directives prerequisite to good teaching and learning.

Universal or common education marks those nations having roots in Christian culture. One of the compelling forces of the Christian outlook is the notion of progress. Schools under Christian direction aim to subdue further the world for God's glory. The schools accordingly provide an important springboard for men to build a better way of life. "Thy kingdom come" motivates the Christian. Culture and education are thus never stagnant or aimed at preserving the past for its own sake no matter how rich and good it might have been. The future guides the Christian and that future is as bright as the promises of God.

Van Til restores anew to God's people a clear vision of the Christian way of life. The ineffectiveness of many Christian schools today is attributable to their lack of compelling directives. With the Van Til perspective, men once again come face to face with God and confront His truth and the consequent blessings for their lives.

How does this position in particular do more than other Christian views? This philosophical outlook begins more forthrightly with the Bible as the absolutely authoritative source of truth for interpreting all of life.[3] Christian philosophy made great strides in our culture in so far as it moved closer to this stance. Whenever it compromised with humanistic thinking, it stumbled and faltered. Van Til is on the forefront of Christian philosophical development because he brings us closer to the enriching voice of God. Christian polemic founded in "thus saith the Lord" propelled our Christian culture ahead in the past and is our only hope for the future! Education impregnated with the voice of God contributes to this advance. Such a vision moves men out of their status quo, and education becomes viewed as a significant vehicle to move people ahead. A reckoning of educational costs to fulfil this task proves itself worthwhile because the benefits clearly outweigh the costs.

Van Til sharpens our vision of divine revelation by holding firmly to the Biblical idea of the Bible.[4] The Scripture adequately informs us about itself and its teachings. Neither man, church, council, nor state are needed to identify the Scriptures for what they are and what they teach.[5] Van Til ably demonstrates the weakness of various eclectic Christian understandings of the Bible in which human logic attempts to stand over the Bible as its judge and light.[6] The Bible, however, ought to be our judge and light. The extent to which Christians consistently submit themselves to the authority of Scripture, to this extent they acknowledge God as the

---

3. Cornelius Van Til, *A Christian Theory of Knowledge* (Philadelphia: Presbyterian and Reformed Publishing Co., 1969), p. 291.
4. *Ibid.*, pp. 25-40.
5. *Ibid.*, p. 156.   6. *Ibid.*, pp. 195-212.

center of their lives. To manipulate or to support the Scripture by human reason is to detract from its authority and centrality.

Van Til argues that only by taking the Bible as absolutely authoritative can God be made central in education.[7] Every domain of education must come under the scrutiny and influence of the Bible. The importance of this position can be seen when we consider the impact education has upon the individual and his culture. Basic to education is its ministry for reasoning and for vocation which it affords the immature. That education serves men best which sheds itself of myth and fantasy and operates on principles of truth. In view of the proclivity of Adam's fallen race to believe lies and to suppress the truth,[8] the daily and lifelong discipline of taking the Bible as the source of truth is mankind's only hope for deliverance from the ravages of self-deceit and self-destruction.

The question likely arises as to why God should be preeminently important for education. Other than by using a heavy dosage of Christian terminology, can Van Til demonstrate the real necessity of God's centrality in education? This concern deserves attention, since Christian education frequently in the experience of modern man has demonstrated more rhetoric than something substantial and compelling.

Crucial to education is the availability of universally valid knowledge. Modern educators understood this and accordingly boasted much of the exponential growth of knowledge. This explosion of knowledge enhanced their importance to society. Educators anxiously concerned themselves with methods of retrieval and assimilation of this great boon to mankind. This was a short-lived glory, however. As this storehouse of learning increased other scholars questioned the objective validity of this knowledge. Robert Nisbet in particular takes notice of this regrettable turn of events. He deplores this almost unbelievable phenomenon, "the very recently begun, fast accumulating nihilistic repudiation in the social sciences of the ancient Western ideal of dispassionate reason, of objective inquiry, in the study of man and society."[9] This avant-garde of current thought contends that "objectivity of inquiry is not even a proper end of social sciences," and furthermore they believe "what can only be called *the necessary ethnic root of science.* . . . There is a black science and a white science, and the twain shall never meet."[10] The implications are obvious. Objective knowledge vanishes with nothing of universal value to teach. Fragmentation of this order obviously strips the schools of that which

---

7. Van Til, *The Dilemma of Education* (Philadelphia: Presbyterian and Reformed Publishing Co., 1956), pp. 30, 31.

8. Romans 1:18. Cf. John Murray, *The Epistle to the Romans* (Grand Rapids: Wm. B. Eerdmans Publishing Co., 1959), Vol. I, pp. 36, 37.

9. Robert Nisbet, "Subjective Sí! Objective No!," *The New York Times Book Review*, April 5, 1970, p. 1.

10. *Ibid.*, pp. 1, 2.

gave them high purpose and viability. Nisbet deplores the growth of this disastrous attitude toward science as much as he bemoans efforts of students and professors "who would seek to destroy the university in a matter of days."[11] Nisbet offers no positive solution to this predicament, apart from a return to the original "academic dogma": the idea that the pursuit of knowledge, in and of itself, is a self-justifying task—to be financed by state taxation, if necessary.[12]

An extremely subjective approach to the social sciences promises to make wreckage of these disciplines. What would schools be without the study of history, doubtless the most significant social science?[13] Without a sense of history Western civilization cannot survive. For example, Christians alone have confessed their faith for centuries in terms of the Apostles Creed, which is largely phrased in terms of historical events rather than ideas. Knowledge itself advances by arguing for a place in the history of the development of ideas. What compelling kind of arguments would scholars henceforth advance to show the significance of their discoveries? New learning traditionally took its place by showing the weakness of the older ideas and the significance of the new. But this is a historical argument and would accordingly become taboo to this new movement. It is a wonder that men so quickly overthrow this discipline so vital to our way of life. The explanation for this lamentable state of contemporary scholarship is found in Van Til's perspective. Men lose all ground for intelligible predication when they operate on non-Christian principles of individuation and unification. Van Til argues "that identification of any fact or truth in the phenomenal realm is possible to man in history only because all things in history are controlled by God back of history. . . . Only if the authority of God's self-identification and of his self-authenticated revelation to man in history is assumed can there be any intelligible predication by man."[14] The present trend which so disturbs Nisbet is but the necessary development of the humanist captivity of these sciences. It is the logical outcome of Karl Mannheim's joyful affirmation of total relativism in the social sciences—a joy which is rooted in despair:

> Only when we are thoroughly aware of the limited scope of every point of view are we on the road to the sought-for comprehension of the

11. *Ibid.*, p. 1.
12. Robert Nisbet, *The Degradation of the Academic Dogma* (New York: Basic Books, 1971).
13. The term "social science" denotes efforts to discover God's ordering of the social life of man: and the modern concept of social science in which man aims at total control over life is rejected. See R. J. Rushdony, *The Biblical Philosophy of History* (Nutley, N. J.: Presbyterian and Reformed Publishing Co., 1969), pp. 18-27.
14. Van Til, *A Christian Theory of Knowledge*, p. 202. The author furnishes throughout his writings abundant and thorough analyses of humanistic thought to demonstrate the validity of this claim.

whole. The crisis in thought is not a crisis affecting merely a single intellectual position, but a crisis of a whole world which has reached a certain stage in its intellectual development. To see more clearly the confusion into which our social and intellectual life has fallen represents an enrichment rather than a loss. That reason can penetrate more profoundly into its own structure is not a sign of intellectual bankruptcy.[15]

The restoration of objectively valid knowledge in history and the social sciences consists in a return to Biblical standards of identification as outlined by Van Til.

The irony of the present dilemma in the sciences is that they owe any previous progress to the fact of God which they have sought to suppress. Building on the Van Til perspective, Rushdoony argues that "God, clearly, is an inescapable premise of human thought. Man either faces a world of total chance and brute factuality, a world in which no fact has meaning and no fact has relationship to any other fact, or else he accepts the world of God's creation and sovereign law."[16] Nisbet's contemporaries have faced this plight of humanistic thought, and instead of accepting the truth of God they have abandoned objective knowledge. Intellectual suicide appeals to them more than submission to the authority of Scripture. The Van Til assertion remains valid that "science is absolutely impossible on the non-Christian principle."[17]

> It will then appear that Christian theism, which was at first rejected because of its supposed authoritarian character, is the only position which gives human reason a field for successful operation and a true method of true progress in knowledge.[18]

The flourishing of the sciences does not depend upon thwarting Nisbet's enemies of science, but rather in a return to Biblical standards. These standards can flourish only in Christian schools, for only they are prepared and legally able to build on the foundations of truth set forth by Van Til. The very survival and progress of science rests upon renewed growth of Christian education.

Van Til's epistemology offers basic instruction for teachers who must understand the nature and structure of knowledge if effective teaching is to mark their efforts. Given the availability of knowledge, how is this wealth of learning most effectively transmitted to the young? The end of all knowledge-getting should be the attainment of an understanding of life as it is. Knowledge consists of knowing who God is, who man is, and what the external world is. All learning thus can generally be subsumed

---

15. Karl Mannheim, *Ideology and Utopia* (New York: Harcourt, Brace and World, Inc., 1936), p. 105.

16. Rousas John Rushdoony, *The Mythology of Science* (Nutley, N. J.: The Craig Press, 1967), p. 42.

17. Van Til, *The Dilemma of Education*, p. 285.

18. *Ibid.*, p. 119.

under these three categories. The important question is how does man come to know God, the world, and himself? Does one begin with the external world and from there move to God and man? Can priority be ascribed to one avenue of approach over another in this most fundamental educational concern? What entrance does one make into the field of learning? Van Til asserts that God is the completely original and exclusively original personality which serves as the foundation for the meaning of all human predication.[19] Only on this Biblical premise can a pupil know himself or the world he lives in. This is the basic attitude to which teachers must ascribe importance if pupils are to end up knowing anything. Any other approach destroys the Creator-creature distinction which is absolutely fundamental to one's thinking.[20]

This kind of thinking, Van Til shows, is analogical in nature. It means that man must think God's thoughts after Him if he is to know anything. How does one know whether he is thinking God's thoughts? To the extent that God's thoughts are revealed to us in Scripture, to this extent can we think His thoughts after Him. The Bible is our criterion: "all of man's interpretations in any field are subject to the Scriptures given him."[21] This perspective sets the same tone for the classroom as Adam experienced when he was first taught by God in Paradise. Adam thought and acted under the direct revelation of God in all the interpretations that he would make of his environment. Sin severed this direct teacher-pupil relationship. The grace of Christ restored it. There is thus no textbook more important in all the curriculum than the Bible. It is not merely a text alongside other texts, but it contains the interpretive principles to determine the content and structure of all texts. It is the Light of all lights. Christian education has frequently failed to situate the self-attesting Scriptures at the center of the curriculum. The Bible as the voice of God must be the central orientating principle around which all knowledge becomes knowledge and becomes knowable. When this is done the teacher makes God the final reference point in all predication. God becomes knowable; man becomes knowable and so does the world he lives in.

Analogical thinking further informs teachers how to treat the relation of theory and facts or the problem of unity and plurality in human understanding. Man thinks in terms of the one and the many because he was created in the image of God, who is one being and at the same time three persons. Thus Van Til asserts, "Unity in God is no more fundamental than diversity, and diversity in God is no more fundamental than unity."[22] Man reflects this unity and plurality in the very constitution of his being

---

19. Van Til, *A Christian Theory of Knowledge*, p. 209.
20. *Ibid.*, p. 296.
21. *Ibid.*, p. 16.
22. Van Til, *The Dilemma of Education*, p. 42.

and thought. No science or learning proceeds without expressing its discoveries in terms of universals and particulars. It does so because men and all things represent God, who made them. None can rid himself of his metaphysical status. What Adam's fallen race will not accept is the ontological Trinity as the unifying principle for all their thinking. In vain men seek to establish systems of knowledge based on the presupposition that man is capable through his own rationality to unify science. Man hereby situates himself as the final reference point in human predication, but every effort of man to do this only ends in failure. Humanism leads ultimately to skepticism and uncertainty, for men end up in either "an ocean of pure contingency or abstract possibility."[23]

One of the gravest sins a science teacher can possibly commit in a modern school is to suggest that faith in God has something to do with the reliability of knowledge. As in the days of the Greeks, the teacher can take two general approaches to his subject matter. First, he can be a logical *a priorist*. All external factuality must be interpreted in terms of universal axioms of the autonomous human mind. All scientific reasoning must therefore be deductive. It is impossible to interpret particular facts apart from universal principles of the mind.[24] Where does the mind obtain these axioms? They are the "givens" of human nature. The deductive process is autonomous, however. To bring in God is to distort this process. Opposed to the *a priorist* is the modern empiricist. He believes that one must begin with the facts of this world as they "really are." In the beginning of this process no universal supposedly exists. Inductive method is therefore the accepted method of investigation. This is the official, if not the operating, foundation of all positivism, and today it dominates both the social sciences and the natural sciences. No principle can exist, universally, uninfluenced by changes in geography, time, and culture.[25] It is a sign of intellectual weakness to accept a universal without its being validated by the facts. On only one point can the empiricist fully agree with the *a priorist*: To bring God in is to distort this process. The radical empiricist sees the particulars as the foundation of all human science; the *a priorist* sees the unity of the autonomous mind as the foundation of all human science. Take your pick: Worship the creation or the creature.

Van Til escapes the false problematics of humanistic thought by showing the intimate relation of universal and fact.

We believe the facts of the universe are unaccounted for except upon

23. Van Til, *A Christian Theory of Knowledge*, p. 47.
24. Cf. Ludwig von Mises, *Human Action* (Chicago: Henry Regnery Co., 1966), ch. 2; *Epistemological Problems of Economics* (Princeton, N. J.: D. Van Nostrand, 1960).
25. Mannheim, *op. cit.*, p. 82.

the Christian-theistic basis. In other words, facts and interpretations of facts cannot be separated. It is impossible even to discuss any particular fact except in relation to some principle of interpretation. The real question about facts is, therefore, what kind of universal can give the best account of the facts. Or rather, the real question is which universal can state or give meaning to any fact.[26]

Van Til's outlook sees no inherent conflict between universals and particulars in the temporal order of things because temporality represents the ontological Trinity in which unity and plurality exist with equal ultimacy. Conflicts between universals and facts cannot be resolved in humanistic systems of knowledge because autonomous man attempts to unify his system (give meaning to it) by ascribing ultimacy to some aspect of the temporal order. Humanists shift from one ultimate to another because each is shown in time to be untenable. Van Til's elucidation of the analogical nature of human thought, on the other hand, prevents the teacher and student from following countless blind alleys. The task of building God's kingdom can thus be greatly enhanced by presenting in our classrooms the actual nature of human thought.

A more contemporary philosophy of science, advanced by the physicist Thomas S. Kuhn, gives ultimacy to the universals or "paradigms" of science. This view looks at the other side of the coin by asserting that only those facts come to light which the paradigm or model permits. Kuhn argues that "scientists work from models."[27] Scientists thus do not begin, as they usually claim, with brute factuality, but with universals. A fact is what it is by virtue of the paradigm. This reversal of the traditional explanation of the understanding and teaching of science recognizes something of Van Til's emphasis. It gives credence to the importance of universals in science, but Kuhn accomplishes this at the expense of situating universals as original and particulars as derivative. Van Til's model for determining the legitimate role of universals and particulars in the temporal order is found in the ontological Trinity, where unity and plurality are equally ultimate.

> In God's being there are no particulars not related to the universal and there is nothing universal that is not fully expressed in the particular.
> It goes without saying that if we hold to the eternal one and many in the manner explained above we must hold the temporal one and many to be *created* by God.[28]

. . . .

26. Van Til, *Christian Theistic Evidences* (Philadelphia: Westminster Theological Seminary, 1961), p. i.

27. Thomas Kuhn, *The Structure of Scientific Revolutions* (Chicago: University of Chicago Press, 1970), 2nd ed., p. 46.

28. Van Til, *The Defense of the Faith* (Philadelphia: Presbyterian and Reformed Publishing Co., 1955), p. 43.

All aspects being equally created, no one aspect of reality may be regarded as more ultimate than another. Thus the created *one and many* may in this respect be said to be equal to one another; they are equally derived and equally dependent upon God who sustains them both. The particulars or facts of the universe do and must act in accord with universals and laws. Thus there is order in the created universe. On the other hand, the laws may not and can never reduce the particulars to abstract particulars or reduce their individuality in any manner.[29]

With God as the ultimate standard, Van Til can set forth the appropriate understanding of universals and particulars. Kuhn argues against the self-proclaimed official ideology of traditional science by giving ultimacy to the universals—aspects of the temporal order. Autonomous man refuses to acknowledge the Creator and accordingly must choose some aspect of the temporal order as determinative. Kuhn's viewpoint is welcomed as a necessary break with the traditional view of science, but it fails to do full justice to all aspects of the created order. His paradigms are purely pragmatic; he can acknowledge no universally valid paradigm in science.

A teacher treats both universals and particulars at every turn in education. Van Til's position affords a basis for developing the proper treatment of these in the classroom. The teacher accordingly will not emphasize universals at the expense of facts, nor facts at the expense of universals. Both will be viewed for their importance in God's created order. A teacher who concentrates on facts at the expense of universals will likely concentrate on the regurgitation of these facts at the expense of understanding them. They will be quickly forgotten, not being tied to any universal organizing principles. On the other hand, stress on the universals will seem irrelevant to pupils.[30] Study will not be truly "now!" as they say. Van Til furthermore furnishes a powerful tool to the teacher for assessment of non-Christian or semi-Christian literatures. The steady application of these insights at the classroom level promises much toward the advance and propagation of knowledge in coming generations.

Pedagogy and consequently the teaching profession have been under steady attack since John Dewey's philosophy seized the attention and loyalty of the teaching profession. The dismal morass into which this kind of thinking has led the profession offers no hope for the restoration of learning and of the consequent respect for teachers. Pedagogy is the teacher's method of operating in his chosen profession. A teacher practices teaching just as a medical doctor practices medicine or a lawyer practices law. The success of any profession depends to a large extent upon the

---

29. *Ibid.*, p. 44.
30. The scope of this study does not allow detailed demonstrations of such educational experiences, but a showing is imperative if teachers are to perceive what they are actually doing and ought to be doing in the classroom.

effectiveness of its methodology. Professional schools for the training of teachers are as essential for the advancement of this vocation as they are for medicine, law, or theology. Pedagogy can be revitalized with the resultant upgrading of the profession. What formulas will produce this desired effect? It is my view that a consistent and empirically tested application of the vision and methodology enunciated by Van Til will indeed yield a productive pedagogy. The basic tenets are stated in these words:

> It is the notion of the ontological Trinity that ultimately controls a truly Christian methodology. . . . Christian methodology is therefore based upon presuppositions that are quite the opposite of those of the non-Christian. It is claimed to be of the very essence of any non-Christian form of methodology that it cannot be determined in advance to what conclusions it must lead.[31]

> Whatever is in accord with Scripture is educative; whatever is not in accord with it is miseducative. Difficult as it may be for both the teacher and the pupil to make out in individual instances how to apply this criterion, the criterion is plain and simple enough.[32]

This viewpoint provides the vision and motivation necessary for the reconstruction of education. It is for others to forge out the details of this pedagogy in schools that prove their worth to men and to God.[33] There is a great future for Christian schools which make God central in all facets of their efforts. One can easily say that if learning is to survive in this land, it will do so only in schools governed by the Holy Scriptures.

The theory of evolution largely governs educational methodology today. According to this view the mind and personality of the child are determined by his environment because man originally developed through successive environmental changes and undergoes similar growth now. Man's creator is thus nature, not God. Man is accordingly passive toward his creator, i.e., his environment. Part of this environment is his community and state. Is it any wonder that increasing numbers of people view themselves in a passive role over against the government, hereby overthrowing the Christian position that government is the responsibility of people? On the other hand, a minority of activist students—often very bright—want to take control of the reins of power in order to reshape their environment, thereby reshaping mankind. They become technological experts, managers of society, planners; or they become revolutionaries who in some way are motivated by Marx's words: "The philosophers have only *interpreted* the world, in various ways; the point, however, is to *change*

---

31. Van Til, *Apologetics* (Philadelphia: Westminster Theological Seminary, 1963), p. 59.
32. Van Til, *The Dilemma of Education*, p. 33.
33. Men are reconstructing education along consistently Biblical lines. See Benson, Reed & Robert Lee, "How to Stop Heir Pollution," *The Review of the News*, July 8, 1970, pp. 21-32. This article reports the efforts of R. L. Thoburn at developing a Christian school and shows some of the unique features of this adventure. Notice

it."[34] In either case, the result of such unbridled humanism—men playing God—is the end of human freedom. Academically, the result tends to be the production of dull, academic drones or lawless student revolutionaries. Here, too, the alternatives spell the death of education.[35] Van Til shows the dangers of not making "the Creator-creature distinction absolutely fundamental"[36] in one's thinking. Christian educators have the foundation for a methodology that will produce stalwart men. In the Christian methodology, the human being is seen as master of his environment, precisely because he is under the sovereignty of a Creator God.[37] Any psychology of methodology in education that fails to establish itself squarely on the doctrine of creation strips man of his dignity and is accordingly illiberal.

Should schools be primarily concerned with the training of the mind? What role does vocational education have in the common schools? Christian education traditionally chose to develop the intellect in the common schools and leave vocational concerns to industry or specialized schools. John Dewey's strong polemic favoring the practical as an intrinsic aspect of education changed this long-standing tradition, but Dewey's schools depreciated the value of the intellectual such that students became increasingly incapable of becoming effective workmen in society. The change in em-

---

must be given to Baptists who vigorously promote Christian education and have in a short time realized remarkable gains. Claiming to be the largest independent Christian school in this country, the Pensacola Christian School, 125 St. John's Street, Pensacola, Florida, holds leadership conferences during the school year to promote the advance of Christian education. Another Baptist school, which developed under the inspiration of the Rev. Jack Hyles of Hammond, Indiana, deserves mention. In his book, *A Guide to the Christian School* (Hammond, Ind.: Hyles Publications), Dr. Robert J. Billings sets forth those features contributing to the success of this school. A little-noticed educator at this time is Dr. George Cormack of Edmonton, Alberta, Canada. He is likely the greatest living pedagogue today. The key to his success is a return to the well springs of education in Western civilization with a keen eye to modern advances. The new Woodbridge Christian School of 1600 Horner Road, Woodbridge, Virginia, patterns its pedagogy after the remarkable advances made by this humble servant of God. A very outstanding school is the St. Thomas School at Houston, Texas. The Rev. T. Robert Ingram gives inspiration and leadership in the development of this school. His attempt has been to direct education according to implications derived from the truth of creation. Building on the premise of a sovereign Creator, Ingram has established a school of promise. No doubt other worthwhile examples deserve public attention. A detailed survey of growth is much needed.

34. Karl Marx, "Theses on Feuerbach" (1845), in *Marx-Engels Selected Works* (Moscow: Foreign Languages Publishing House, 1962), II, 405.

35. Cf. Gary North, "Statist Bureaucracy in the Modern Economy," *An Introduction to Christian Economics* (Nutley, N. J.: The Craig Press, 1973), reprinted from *The Freeman*, January, 1970.

36. Van Til, *A Christian Theory of Knowledge*, p. 296.

37. John C. Raines, "From Passive to Active Man: Reflections of the Revolution in Consciousness of Modern Man," in John C. Raines and Thomas Dean, eds., *Marxism and Radical Religion* (Philadelphia: Temple University Press, 1970), pp. 112-115. Cf. Rushdoony, *The Biblical Philosophy of History*, pp. 12, 13.

phasis produced some good in terms of bringing education in line with
the realism and demands of a technological society, but it was unable to
wed together successfully training of the mind with training for vocation.

Van Til links the theoretical and the practical by viewing knowledge as
a means to accomplish man's God-given task on earth. Discussing the goal
of education, Van Til says:

> The nature or essence of every created fact lies in its function in the
> process of divine self-revelation to man. . . . His historical task was,
> as God's image-bearer, to show forth the glory of God.
>
> It is in this connection that we must refer to the original supernatural
> revelation that was given Adam. Through it man was actually told
> about his future task. He was to increase in the self-conscious manipu-
> lation of the facts of the universe to the glory of God. He was thus
> to build the kingdom of God.[38]

Learning and doing are thus intimately linked by Van Til. Learning is
never for learning's sake alone, but at every point it aims to fulfill the divine task given to man. The ivory tower image of university training is
thus inconsistent with Christian theism. Academic education and vocational
education are not antithetical or even supplementary but necessarily coexist.
Learning is never in the abstract, whether it is academic with no task or
vocationalism with no purpose. Learning is doing something in this
world—it goes somewhere. Vocation is no less possible without adequate
training of the mind, for by development of the intellect man obtains the
necessary tool to know God's revealed will and the world he is under
command to subdue as God's vicegerent:

> The most important aspect of this program is surely that man should
> *realize himself as God's vicegerent in history.* Man was created God's
> vicegerent and he must realize himself God's vicegerent. There is no
> contradiction between these two statements. Man was created a charac-
> ter and yet he had to make himself even more of a character. And so
> we may say that man was created a king in order that he might become
> more of a king than he was.[39]

Therefore, "man's project is to build the kingdom of God."[40] Doing and
learning are accordingly inseparable if man is to stand before God as a
fully developed human. Van Til's perception lays the foundation for a
more Biblical approach to combining knowing and doing in our schools.

The school's ministry, then, deals with two inseparable aspects of education, namely, meaning and calling.[41] With this perspective knowledge-

38. Van Til, *The Dilemma of Education*, pp. 31, 32.
39. Van Til, *Christian Theistic Ethics* (Philadelphia: Westminster Theological
Seminary, 1964), p. 38.
40. Van Til, *The Dilemma of Education*, p. 32.
41. See Rushdoony, *The Messianic Character of American Education* (Nutley,
N. J.: The Craig Press, 1963), pp. 2 ff. Rushdoony, influenced by Van Til, develops
this notion more thoroughly.

getting will always be relevant to the times and to the cultural setting.

Christian schools are enabled to accept the realism of the day because "God controls whatsoever comes to pass."[42] The Christian's duty is to subdue the world God has given him. This indeed involves building on godly foundations, but it requires cultural house cleaning as Van Til declares: "The destruction of all evil everywhere is the negative but unavoidable task of every member of the kingdom of God."[43] On the other hand, beneficial attainments of one's given epoch must be recognized as products of God's domain: "God has one unified plan. It is within this plan that men engage in their cultural pursuits. This is the positive basis for the unity of human culture."[44] Failure to appreciate the accomplishments of all men, including the non-Christian, is failure to recognize the kingship of our Lord Jesus Christ. Christian schools thus have the strongest reason to be relevant to the times in a way that is an honor to both God and man.

The church, the state, or independent groups of citizens have dominated schools in our Western civilization. The truly independent school has been more the exception than the rule. Why should education be collectivized by either church, state, or private associations? Does God's government of the world imply the subordination of one sphere of human concern to the other in order to achieve social harmony and good? Has not our experience with the totalitarian claims of the church during the Middle Ages and those of the state in our day adequately demonstrated the havoc such arrangements have wrought upon education? Van Til touches upon God's order in this world: "All aspects being equally created, no one aspect of reality may be regarded as more ultimate than another."[45] Van Til acknowledges that Vollenhoven and Dooyeweerd have developed more thoroughly the notion of Christian dimensionalism.[46] Fundamental to all these theorists is that God has established an order, and it is our duty to discover it and operate in terms of this law structure. "It requires the intellect of man to *find* the dimensions of created reality, without *legislating* for it."[47] What schools have largely faced in the past is church, state, and associations legislating for education. The Van Til position points in the direction of discovering God's order for these respective spheres.

Education that functions directly under the tutelage of Scripture and independent of other institutions promises the greatest benefit to mankind. Quality education will be the result of operating schools in harmony with

---

42. Van Til, *A Christian Theory of Knowledge*, p. 224.
43. Van Til, *Christian Theistic Evidences*, p. 71.
44. Van Til, *The Dilemma of Education*, p. 36.
45. Van Til, *The Defense of the Faith*, p. 44.
46. Van Til, *A Christian Theory of Knowledge*, pp. 50, 51.
47. *Ibid.*, p. 51.

God's law-order as excellence in any human endeavor depends upon obedience to created law. There is much rhetoric today about quality of education, but the proposals only offer further examples of man's vain attempt to legislate rather than to discover God's order of education. Christian educators, on the other hand, have a fruitful vocation opened before them by following closely the notion of God's order for education.

Education reconstructed along Biblical lines produces stalwart and sensitive professionals. They become stalwart by independently owning school properties and developing solid educational programs in accordance with the dictates of Scripture and the needs of the people. They become sensitive because their opportunity to own property and to manage an educational program depends upon the quality of service rendered. The freedom of parents in education is likewise guaranteed under this arrangement, for their effective control of education comes from their right to patronize or to boycott a given school. This system of checks and balances reckons squarely with the reality of man's total depravity.

Cornelius Van Til, in summary, offers new vistas of inspiration and endeavor for Christian education. To the extent that he assists the teaching profession to hear the clarion call of God in education, to this extent his perspective opens the door for the revitalization of education in our land. Education today, along with our culture, is adrift in foreboding waters. People who have cast off the restraints of an ordered life under God's law perish. People who seek and love the law of God shall prosper. Let us by the grace of God reorder education according to this Biblical vision and enjoy again the benefits that shall surely follow.

From these considerations it ought to be evident that one cannot take the possibility of neutrality for granted. To be philosophically fair, the antitheist is bound first of all to establish this possibility critically before he proceeds to build upon it. If there is an absolute God, neutrality is out of the question, because in that case every creature is derived from God and is therefore directly responsible to him. And such a God would not feel very kindly disposed to those who ignore him. . . . It follows then that the attempt to be neutral is part of the attempt to be antitheistic. For this reason we have constantly used the term antitheistic instead of *nontheistic*. To be nontheistic is to be antitheistic. The narrative of the fall of man may illustrate this point. Adam and Eve were true theists at the first. They took God's interpretation of themselves and of the animals for granted as the true interpretation. Then came the tempter. He presented to Eve another, that is, an antitheistic theory of reality, and asked her to be the judge as to which was the more reasonable for her to accept. And the acceptance of this position of judge constituted the fall of man. That acceptance put the mind of man on an equality with the mind of God. That acceptance also put the mind of the devil on an equality with God. Before Eve could listen to the tempter she had to take for granted that the devil was perhaps a person who knew as much about reality as God knew about it. Before Eve could listen to the tempter, she had to take it for granted that she herself might be such an one as to make it reasonable for her to make a final decision between claims and counter-claims that involved the entire future of her existence. That is, Eve was obliged to postulate an ultimate epistemological pluralism and contingency before she could even proceed to consider the proposition made to her by the devil. Or, otherwise expressed, Eve was compelled to assume the equal ultimacy of the minds of God, of the devil, and of herself. ·And surely this excluded the exclusive ultimacy of God. This therefore was a denial of God's absoluteness epistemologically. *Thus neutrality was based upon negation. Neutrality is negation.*

Van Til, *A Survey of Christian Epistemology* (1969), pp. 20-21.

POLITICAL SCIENCE

VII

THE POLITICS OF PRAGMATISM:
THREAT TO FREEDOM

By LAWRENCE D. PRATT

For one who has worked in education and politics, it is easy to see that liberals and other statists have a "ground of being" other than the God of the Bible. It is not as easy to accommodate the fact that conservatives who proclaim the cause of freedom are not often any better grounded than their opponents.

The confusion in the ranks of conservatives, and their gradual acceptance at least in part of the "inevitability" of collectivism and appeasement of communist expansion, appears to be rooted in essentially the same fundamental errors made by the opponents of freedom.

Conservatives, even those who profess to be Christians, all too often have accepted the secularist argument that their religious doctrines do not apply to worldly affairs. Family life and other personal, social relationships are deemed to be a subjective matter where one might choose to apply a religious ethic, whereas one's actions in economic, political, or educational endeavors are to be governed by a different moral code. For some time men in the West have tended to believe that an individual man should behave according to Christian moral precepts, or some secular derivate, whereas a man as a thinker, a politician, or a worker should behave by precepts uniquely suitable to those types of activity.

More recently, proponents of the widely heralded "new morality" have been increasingly successful in injecting the "old immorality" into the zones of personal affairs. The earlier dictum of *real politique*, that states have only permanent interests not permanent friends, has now tended to be accepted not only as applying to foreign affairs, but in marriage as well. Behavior intended to gratify "needs" (read: desires) has replaced behavior intended to glorify God.

Even pagans have recognized that conclusions are the result of their premises; it was Seneca who remarked that "As a man speaks, so is he." The late Richard Weaver's *The Ethics of Rhetoric* was devoted to examining precisely this proposition:

The rhetorical content of the major premise which the speaker habitually uses is the key to his primary view of existence; that no man escapes being branded by the premise that he regards as most efficacious in an argument.[1]

No matter how close to the surface of an argument may be the actual major premise of a contemporary American politician or academician, pragmatism is the rationale most often offered. "In view of the situation what else are you going to do?" is a kind of proposition characteristic of the pragmatic argument (or the argument from circumstance, as Weaver labelled it).

Instead of clearly setting forth the major premise (which must usually be ferreted out from between the lines), vague words capable of being construed in a wide variety of ways are employed. Weaver called these charismatic terms. "Needs" and "social justice" are examples of frequently employed charismatic terms capable of providing an emotionally laden moralistic cover for any number of schemes designed to curry favor for a proposition.

Orwell, in observing the rhetoric used to justify the operation of the totalitarian regimes of the twentieth century, observed that abstract words employed as charismatic terms become so free from any concrete references, that nobody blinks when these regimes claim that "Slavery is Freedom."

The nineteenth-century classical liberal view of freedom, confident in its faith in man's autonomous rationality and will, argued that freedom should be understood in terms of the absence of coercion and fraud. As modern autonomous man began to realize his estrangement from other men and the universe about him,[2] freedom came to be understood in terms of the power needed to control a lawless universe. Without power to protect himself in a universe of chance, men increasingly felt desperate and meaningless.

The evolution of the classical liberal's laissez-faire doctrine into the contemporary liberal's programs for statist compulsion that have increasingly claimed sovereignty over all aspects of an individual's life is but a record of the dialectical tension inherent in the presuppositions of the claims of autonomous man. And this record is but a recent chapter in the long history of man's usurpation of God's sovereignty. As Van Til has pointed out in *A Survey of Christian Epistemology*, the first chapter of this usurpation is recorded in the Genesis account of Eve's assumption of "the equal ultimacy of God, the devil and man."[3] The eating of the for-

---

1. Richard Weaver, *The Ethics of Rhetoric* (Chicago: Regnery), p. 55.
2. Albert Camus's *The Stranger* vividly portrays this stark awareness.
3. Cornelius Van Til, *A Survey of Christian Epistemology* (Nutley, N. J.: Presbyterian and Reformed Publishing Co., 1969), p. 29.

bidden fruit was but the inevitable conclusion of her major premise.

Plato, without the agonizing of Eve, made the same assumption that the mind of man and the mind of God are on the same plane, that they are equally ultimate. To presuppose this requires that both God and man exist within a universe which neither can know fully and control, and therefore both are forced to contend with the vagaries of chance. To claim that man's cognitive powers are ultimate—that even one fact can be known apart from its relation to God—is also to claim a neutrality for man's knowledge. This neutrality is precisely what the pragmatist assumes when he asserts that he will judge each situation on an *ad hoc* basis apart from the relation of eternal principles of right and wrong.

The consequences of men claiming to organize governments independent of God's law have followed the same pattern of oscillation between individualism and statism as has occurred in the case of liberalism over the course of a century. To assume that man's mind is as ultimate as God's, and therefore to conceive of the universe as a world of chance, requires one to posit the locus of sovereignty apart from God somewhere else in a universe that is greater than both man and God. As it happens, men have posited two basic possibilities for the source of sovereignty apart from God: the individual or the state.[4]

The cause of the defense of freedom has suffered because conservatives have been unwilling to face the true nature of the threat of tyranny. The attempts to formulate a system of nontyrannical government most often employed by conservatives have been either the warm cocoon of an organic tradition or the brave adventurousness of the rugged individualist. In either case, sovereignty has not been recognized to be God's alone. As a result, the conservative has based his defense of freedom on the same presuppositions as those used by tyrants and outlaws to justify their actions.

The more systematic is the libertarian conservative's positing of sovereignty in the individual, the more clearly does his view of man resemble Rousseau's or that portrayed in Marx's post-withering-of-the-state utopia. This is necessarily so because the thoroughgoing libertarian has presupposed that all values are relative and only apply to each individual. To assume that all that is required for harmony in the relations among normless men is the removal of force where its monopoly has been ordained by God is to assume that man is so well-intentioned that he needs no general law.

The more systematic is the traditionalist conservative's positing of sov-

---

4. This is but an aspect of the more general problem of the one and the many which Van Til treats in several places, including *A Survey of Christian Epistemology*. R. J. Rushdoony has explored this through the history of Western political thought in *The One and the Many*.

ereignty in existing institutions and the organic, unruptured development of institutions, the more clearly does he share the pharaonic view that there are only two classes of men—the rulers and the ruled: or the similar Bolshevik view of the enlightened vanguard in whose hands History has placed the fate of the rest of mankind. Justifying institutions because they function stably (the Soviet Union, for one) hardly provides the basis for condemning an established tyranny. Much of the history of mankind is the long history of stable despotisms.

The question that the libertarian must answer is "Why should men choose to cooperate in a non-coercive environment?" The answer usually put forward is "Each man is more productive when society is organized this way," or "Each man is freer." But the question is still begged unless the libertarian is prepared to defend productivity, or a maximum of personal freedom, as the highest goal of man and the central presupposition of his beliefs. But why should others agree with the libertarian rather than with Franco or with Atilla the Hun?

The same problem faces the traditionalist. Are institutions as institutions to be the cornerstone of life? Or perhaps, stable institutions? But again, why institutions, why stability? Why not war and circuses?

It has only been the systematic theists, i.e., Biblical Christians, who have clearly set forth the basis of society in terms of a straightforward exposition of their presuppositions. The dialectical shiftings of the "neutral" reason of autonomous man can provide no protection against the demagogic promises of the statist. This is so even when attempts are made to rise above pragmatism since man's ultimate concerns are not made dependent on God. Only the revealed law of the Bible can protect man's freedom from the usurpations of the state that claims total allegiance as the sovereign source of all law in exchange for its putative protection of alienated men afloat in a sea of randomness.

Conservative opposition to statist tyranny is not usually articulated in systematically libertarian or traditionalist terms outside a small number of classrooms, periodicals, and books. In the political arena, even conservatives who have shown a familiarity with libertarian and traditionalist conservative thought do not consistently translate these philosophies into political action. It goes without saying that virtually no politician can be accused of pursuing policies that could be called Biblical.

The irony of this is that even conservative politicians who have at one time or another warned against creeping socialism find themselves contributing to the very menace they have warned against. In practice, this means that a policy put forth by statists or those who would appease the external threat of communists is accepted by many conservatives as a limiting factor for their own formulation of policies. Rather than oppose a dangerous policy on principle, the tendency is increasingly for conservatives to offer but a more moderate program than one advanced by demagogues. Pragmatism is preferred to the unpleasantness of a principled position.

American conservatives usually agree that government has over-extended itself in this century (if not a good deal earlier). The most obvious political solution to ill-conceived programs is first to stop further increases in government spending, and then to go on to reduce the spending to proper levels. No spending, no programs.

But when revenue sharing was proposed, the conservative insight into the problem of big government disappeared as a dream upon awakening. Revenue sharing was ballyhooed as a return to local solutions to local problems because the national government would be turning over tax money to local governments. Part of the problem reflected a conservative confusion about the relative danger of national as opposed to local government intervention in the lives of the citizenry. Unfortunately, the problem is not usually stated in these terms. There is rather a mystique about the desirability of local governments doing things that are considered to be undesirable when the national government does the same things. The mystique obscures the point that American government at all levels has overstepped the bounds of the administration of law and order and providing for the common defense.

This mystique contributed to another conservative blind spot. Too few conservatives objected to the proposition that whatever the merits of local governments carrying out this or that program, the proposition that local politicians should be spending money they did not themselves directly tax from the electorate is highly irresponsible. The best the conservative "opposition" could come up with to the growing takeover by government of the lives of the citizenry was to insist that the revenue "shared" by the national government should not contribute to an even larger expenditure from the national treasury. Instead, the conservative critics called for revenue sharing to be accomplished at the expense of already existing national governmental programs. Almost no conservative politicians objected that this "special" revenue sharing would only contribute to the already monumental irresponsibility of local politicians operating programs that were no more the business of government at the local level than at the national level.

Many politicians of diverse orientations have objected to the forced busing of school children for the purpose of achieving some vague and arbitrary definition of racial balance. Critics of this kind of busing correctly observe that government has no business compelling people to conform to the precepts of a faddish sociological theory that has nothing to do with the role of government as a keeper of law and order.

Very few busing critics, however, have pointed out that the same reasoning should also oppose the establishment of compulsory public education on the grounds that the state has no business in this area of primary parental responsibility. True, Americans still have the expensive option of providing a non-public education for their children. But the principle that allows the state to establish public schools and set forth the curricula of these schools also by logical extension allows the state to compel busing for racial balance under the rubric of necessary for the "proper" education of children. Indeed, there is no logical reason to believe that by the same principle the government could not prohibit all non-public options on whatever "scientific" grounds that catered to the democratic ethos of the moment.

Busing is even harder to oppose when one recognizes that the financing of extravagant school systems has been passed up to higher levels of government in an effort by local officials to avoid the unpleasantness of themselves calling for the ever-heavy burden of taxation required to pay for the public schools. And once the financing has passed to the state and the national levels, then the control of the local public schools has also fallen into the hands of public officials at those levels of government. Parenthetically, here is another credibility gap in the revenue sharing proposition. With the example of the leverage higher levels of government have used to force unwanted programs on local school districts, are we really to believe that other revenue sharing schemes would fare any differently?

That the hedonistic attitudes fostered by socialism ramify in a country's foreign policies was observed in Britain by C. Northcoate Parkinson in his book *Left Luggage*. As the something-for-nothing lusts of the citizenry are whetted by statist programs, public opinion in a democratic country increasingly militates against defense expenditures of even the most obvious sort. By the end of 1971, the United States had allowed its level of military preparedness to decline to an alarming level vis-a-vis the Soviet Union. On several occasions conservatives even raised their voices against this folly. Yet the majority of them, because they happened to be in the same party as the President, were unwilling to call for the defeat, if necessary, of a party leader-President who had failed almost totally to exert the leadership required to protect the very safety of the country.

The reasoning of conservatives reluctant to call for the political retirement or defeat of their party leader who happened to be President was justified by an appalling moral pragmatism. They seemed to argue that their leader was only doing reluctantly what he regarded as the inevitable. Therefore better to have him than one who actually approved of the "inevitable." This same illogic was applied not only in foreign affairs, but domestic as well.

Politically, this would seem to be about the end of the road of conjoining pragmatism and the defense of freedom. Pragmatism claims the same epistemological neutrality as did Eve. The pragmatist may often be heard to argue against the obvious excesses of the openly diabolical, but the pragmatist himself has accepted the same presuppositions as has the open champion of tyranny. "As a man speaks, so is he."

It is unfortunately only a matter of time before the pragmatist is forced to yield his temperamental defenses against the excesses of tyranny in the face of the logic of tyranny. Neither the pragmatist nor the statist advocate of tyranny accepts the sovereignty of God as the foundation for all government, so neither the pragmatist nor the statist can put forth a viable defense of freedom.

Only when conservatives are willing to defend freedom in clearly theistic, biblical terms will they be able to do the job they claim they have set out to do.

The self-authenticating man appears, at first glance, to be very modest. Has he not limited reason in order to make room for faith? Does he not disclaim all territorial ambition beyond the world of phenomena? Has he not even given up his own youthful ambition of controlling all reality by logic? Is he not restricting the use of the law of contradiction to the merely negative function of protecting his own borders?

The answer to such questions as these must be that the self-authenticating man cannot be modest. His vision is always the same. In this vision, he sees himself as God. He sees himself as alone able to determine what can be and what cannot be. He is, according to his vision, the source of all possibility. Even when, speaking through Kant, he limits reason to make room for faith, he first makes sure that the object of his faith *cannot* be the Christian story. Kant keeps the God of Christianity out of his *noumenal* as well as out of his *phenomenal* realm. Actually he could not do the one without at the same time doing the other. To make room for his own faith, the self-authenticating man must remove the Christian faith.

Thus, the "reason" of the self-authenticating man is the willing servant of the faith of the self-authenticating man. So far as he sincerely thinks that he is open-minded and therefore ready to follow the facts wheresoever they may lead him, he is self-deceived. He assumes that pure contingency or change is the matrix of all the material of all possible knowledge. He takes for granted that the facts to which he is about to apply his hypotheses cannot have been created by God and cannot be controlled by God. He thinks that the very possibility of progress in scientific knowledge requires the exclusion by assumption of the whole Christian story. The self-authenticating man assumes that only in terms of his totality-vision can law and fact come into fruitful union with one another.

Van Til, *The Case for Calvinism*
(1964), pp. 136-37.

SOCIOLOGY

VIII

MAX WEBER: RATIONALISM, IRRATIONALISM, AND THE BUREAUCRATIC CAGE

By GARY NORTH

The technical superiority of the bureaucratic mechanism stands unshaken, as does the technical superiority of the machine over the handworker. . . . Imagine the consequences of that comprehensive bureaucratization and rationalization which already to-day we see approaching. . . . Take as an extreme example the authoritative power of the State or of the municipality in a monarchical constitution: it is strikingly reminiscent of the ancient kingdom of Egypt, in which the system of the "minor official" prevailed at all levels. To this day there has never existed a bureaucracy which could compare with that of Egypt. This is known to everyone who knows the social history of ancient times; and it is equally apparent that to-day we are proceeding towards an evolution which resembles that system in every detail, except that it is built on other foundations, on technically more perfect, more rationalized, and therefore more mechanized foundations. The problem which besets us now is not: how can this evolution be changed?—for that is impossible, but: what will come of it? . . .

This passion for bureaucracy, . . . is enough to drive one to despair. It is as if in politics the spectre of timidity—which has in any case always been rather a good standby for the German—were to stand alone at the helm; as if we were deliberately to become men who need "order" and nothing but order, who become nervous and cowardly if for one moment this order wavers, and helpless if .they are torn away from their total incorporation in it. That the world should know no men but these: it is in such an evolution that we are already caught up, and the great question is therefore not how we can promote and hasten it, but what can we oppose to this machinery in order to keep a portion of mankind free from this parcelling-out of the soul, from this supreme mastery of the bureaucratic way of life.

—Max Weber
Speech to the *Verein für
Sozialpolitik*, 1909

—Reprinted in J. P. Mayer
Max Weber and German Politics
(London: Faber & Faber, 1956),
pp. 126-28
Used by permission

Introduction: Philosophical Precedents

The history of Western philosophy can be traced in terms of several basic intellectual antinomies that have confronted philosophers, theologians, and social thinkers. One obvious theme is the conflict between the one (unity) and the many (diversity). How can we classify discrete objects under some overarching general category without destroying either the uniqueness of the objects or the universality of the category?[1] This problem is related to another recurring antinomy, that of rationalism versus irrationalism. Are all phenomena subject to absolute laws, especially mathematical laws, in all times and places? Can such phenomena be investigated in terms of general patterns of configuration that are accessible to human reason? In other words, can these general patterns be said to correspond to—"do justice to"—the various empirical data? If such a relationship does exist, how can we account for such a remarkable occurrence?[2] Are these general laws self-sustaining in some fashion, or do they rely on a chance universe to undergird them? Do they have metaphysical validity, or are they merely the products of human thought? In short, what is the relationship which exists between a hypothetical rationality and the world of multitudinous phenomena?

The issue was set forth by two pre-Socratic philosophers, Heraclitus and Parmenides. Parmenides saw all reality as static; only that which can be conceptualized by a universal, unchanging human logic has ultimate validity. Everything else is mere illusion.[3] Heraclitus represents the other half of the antimony. He pointed to the ceaseless flux of all existence, arguing that all reality is nonstructural at bottom. All factuality is brute factuality; it is formless, endlessly changing, and ultimate. Chance governs all things.[4] The categories of human thought have not been able to escape the terms and implications of this great intellectual conflict, and Weber found himself confronted inescapably with the issue. The "form-matter" dualism of the ancient world has remained with all subsequent secular systems of thought, however modified the original terminology has become in modern applications: law versus chance, theory versus factuality, metaphysical form versus recalcitrant matter.

Charles N. Cochrane, in a remarkable work of intellectual history, treats the breakdown of the Greco-Roman world as a function of the collapse of these antinomies into a fragmented, intellectual chaos. The Roman Empire had as its foundation the universalistic assertion of a natural reason

---

1. Rousas J. Rushdoony, *The One and the Many* (Nutley, N. J.: Craig Press, 1971), surveys the history of this philosophical issue at considerable length.
2. Cf. Eugene P. Wigner, "The Unreasonable Effectiveness of Mathematics in the Natural Sciences," *Communications on Pure and Applied Mathematics*, XIII (1960), 1-14. Wigner is a Nobel Prize winner in physics.
3. R. G. Collingwood, *The Idea of Nature* (New York: Oxford University Press, [1945] 1961), 68-69.
4. Charles Norris Cochrane, *Christianity and Classical Culture* (New York: Oxford University Press, [1939] 1957), 459-60.

which knows no geographical or cultural boundaries. This assertion was unique in the pre-Christian era.[5] When the idea broke down under the weight of its internal contradictions, Cochrane argues, so did the Empire: "The fall of Rome was the fall of an idea, or rather a system of life based upon a complex of ideas which may be described broadly as those of Classicism; and the deficiencies of Classicism, already exposed in the third century, were destined sooner or later to involve the system in ruin."[6] For the masses of men, the problem manifested itself in less strictly philosophical, but no less fundamental, terms. Men felt that they were being ripped apart by the conflict of pure chance (luck) against pure determinism (fate). The rise of astrology as a popular movement showed the nature of the crisis. Men were being reduced in their own minds to mere automata.

> The acceptance of such beliefs involved a picture of nature in terms of either sheer fortuity or (alternatively) of inexorable fate. By so doing, it helped to provoke an increasingly frantic passion for some means of escape. This passion was to find expression in various types of supernaturalism, in which East and West joined hands to produce the most grotesque cosmologies as a basis for ethical systems no less grotesque.[7]

Cochrane's central thesis is that Christianity came into a culture rent by a series of inescapable dualisms, and as such, the new faith restored the lost unity of the Western world. Appropriately, he ends his study with a chapter on Augustine, precisely the place where William C. Bark begins his *Origins of the Medieval World* (1961). Augustine stands as the central figure between the two civilizations.

The medieval world incorporated much of the earlier philosophy into its own categories of thought; a new synthesis of Classical philosophy and Christian theology was constructed. The "form-matter" dualism was transformed into the medieval variant, the "nature-grace" schema. Natural philosophy or natural reason—Platonic before the twelfth century and increasingly Aristotelian after—was given full autonomy in the area of "common ground." Both believers and unbelievers can use this hypothetically neutral reasoning faculty to discover identical truths in the realm of nature. Grace, the realm of faith, was alone closed to the reasoning powers of the pagan world. Revelation was needed to provide men with full knowledge of faith, the sacraments, and the Church. Even some knowledge of God was said to be available to the pagan, through the use of logical proofs of God's existence. A fundamental unity was ascribed to the two kinds of thought. Thomistic philosophy rested on the supposition that truths derived from natural philosophy are not in opposition to those derived from revelation, since God's creation is not self-contradictory. Inevitably, the basic dualisms of the ancients were incorporated into

---

5. *Ibid.*, 73.   6. *Ibid.*, 355.   7. *Ibid.*, 159.

medieval thought because the basic presupposition of the Classical thinkers was retained for the "natural" sphere: the autonomy and neutrality of the rational mind. And these antinomies were compounded with those which arose from ultimately irreconcilable conflicts between biblical revelation and theology in opposition to propositions derived from Classical presuppositions.

The coming of nominalism, best represented by William of Ockham (*ca.* 1325) and especially his followers, shattered the proposed medieval synthesis of faith and reason. By denying the "realist" position, nominalism undercut the Classical foundations from the position which the Church had always maintained, namely, that the universal forms of thought correspond to metaphysical entities, since these forms are projections of the mind of God. If, as Ockham argued, the forms have no metaphysical existence, but are merely abstract creations of the human intellect, then the unity provided by the forms is destroyed. A radical individualism then threatens the whole structure of thought, and ultimately a radical relativism. Ockham asserted that the forms or universals—those entities which Classical thought demanded in order to provide coherence in a world constantly challenged by the processes of total flux and diversity—are merely symbols that stand for individual, concrete entities. The nominalists abandoned any synthesis laid down on the lines proposed by Aquinas or Scotus; they rejected scholastic reasoning as a misguided effort.[8]

The fourteenth century brought with it far more than a challenge to the intellectual foundations of the medieval culture. It brought famine in the disastrous years of horror, 1315–17.[9] Land hunger, as a result of a rising population, put many peasants in a marginal economic position; any crisis of agricultural production would reflect itself in mass starvation. Then, in 1348–50, the first wave of the bubonic plague struck Europe, and estimates of the death toll have ranged as high as one-third overall, and possibly half of the urban populations.[10] This meant that perhaps as many

---

8. Distinctions can of course be drawn between Aquinas and Scotus, but both were moderate realists, since both asserted the objective reality of the universals, but both denied their independent existence apart from the individual objects in which they dwelt. Cf. Arthur Cushman McGiffert, *A History of Christian Thought* (New York: Scribner's, 1933), I, 306. McGiffert contrasts Aquinas and Scotus with Ockham; ch. 13.

9. H. S. Lucas, "The Great European Famine of 1315, 1316, and 1317," *Speculum*, V (1930), 343-77.

10. Warren S. Thompson, *Population Problems* (4th ed.; New York: McGraw-Hill, 1953), 57. Philip Ziegler's comprehensive study of the secondary sources, *The Black Death* (New York: John Day, 1969), estimates the overall death toll in Europe due to the plague at about 30%. An important revisionist work written by a professor of bacteriology, J. F. D. Shrewsbury, *A History of Bubonic Plague in the British Isles* (New York: Cambridge University Press, 1970), presents the case that from a medical standpoint, the mortality could not have been over 5% for the

as 25 million people perished. Succeeding outbreaks of the plague continued for well over a century; the last significant occurrence took place in Marseilles as late as 1720.[11] An incipient Cochrane thesis lies ready and waiting for any scholar who would like to argue that the collapse of values caused, or at least paralleled, the crises of the fourteenth century. The famous razor of Ockham had shaved away the theological side of the "nature-grace" synthesis, while simultaneously calling into question the "form" side of the "form-matter" dualism of the Classical philosophers. Men could ignore the search for metaphysical universals; they could also ignore all efforts to rationalize the realm of grace. Ockham did not personally carry his system to such lengths, but his followers did, and the rationalists of the Enlightenment and Renaissance did. Gordon Leff describes the results of the shattering of the scholastic synthesis: the realm of absolute faith broke away from the realm of sovereign human reason. Bradwardine, the best representative of the revelationists, could no longer communicate with Ockhamite nominalists:

> The importance of the disputes between Bradwardine and his opponents lies in the change wrought upon scholasticism. Each side, in starting from either faith or reason to the exclusion of the other, made them virtually separate pursuits. Since Ockham and his followers refused to see the supernatural through the natural, they put faith beyond reason's bounds. Because Bradwardine allowed reason no autonomy it lost any validity, and faith became the only law. This meant that, on the one hand, reason, philosophy and science tended to become autonomous disciplines without reference to theology; while, on the other, faith and theology became increasingly a regime for worship, independent of ratiocination.[12]

The dualism between rationalism and irrationalism was now put into a new formulation. No longer did rationalists regard the universals as possessing metaphysical existence. The emphasis now shifted to the rationalizing capacity of the autonomous human mind and to mathematical relationships, discoverable by autonomous reason, that govern the affairs of the cosmos. Descartes is the representative of the deductive, aprioristic reasoning process, while Bacon stands as the representative of the inductive

---

population as a whole, with a maximum of one-third in the seaport cities. Even if this figure is correct, it does not upset the thrust of my thesis, namely, that the intellectual and moral effects of the plague indicate a shaking of medieval culture. As Shrewsbury wrote to me (27 August, 1970): "What I have stated in my history—and I thought I had emphasized, although only one reviewer among more than 30 has so far noted it—is that the panic terror created by 'The Great Pestilence' in the British Isles had a much greater and more persistent effect upon the national mind than its mortality." The same would certainly be true for Europe as a whole.

11. Jean-Noel Biraben, "Certain Demographic Characteristics of the Plague Epidemic in France, 1720–1722," *Daedalus* (Spring, 1968), 536-45.

12. Gordon Leff, *Bradwardine and the Pelagians* (Cambridge University Press, 1957), 19.

approach which seeks for patterns in the data themselves. The fusion of the two approaches comes with the Newtonian revolution: laws deduced by means of human reason—mathematical laws especially—are used to describe relations which exist externally to the rational observer.[13] The goal of these early rationalists was to conquer an external world of nature which on the surface seemed to be irrational and capricious. Men were now to escape from the caprices of an irrational, unpredictable, uncontrollable nature. Only in this way could they attain true freedom. The total flux of nature could be curbed by man and his reason. Newton's discoveries seemed to confirm this new faith. Hobbes asserted as a goal for social scientists that which Newton had achieved for the astronomical scientists: the discovery of mathematical laws governing the world of politics. This idea was widely popular among Enlightenment thinkers, as Louis Bredvold's book, *Brave New World of the Enlightenment* (1961), demonstrates so forcefully.[14]

The dualism of the modern world has become a dichotomy along lines that are supposedly non-metaphysical: the "nature-freedom" antinomy.[15] In the early stages of this rationalistic impulse, men hoped to achieve freedom through the exercise of reason and power. The post-Kantian focus has reversed this goal: freedom is now seen in terms of an escape from the very rationalized power which man has created for his universe and his fellow men.[16]

David Hume's speculations called into question the presuppositions of the Newtonian faith. He argued that the universe could not be shown to obey any universal laws of causality. The mind of man only concludes out of force of habit that certain regularities do, in fact, exist. Such regularities cannot be proven; they are only assumed for the sake of convenience. Kant labored under Hume's shadow throughout his life. It was his desire to support the validity of human reason. He believed that he had accomplished his goal by limiting the realm in which scientific logic can operate. The realm of the phenomenal is ordered by the universal categories of human thought. We cannot know the raw data—the "brute

---

13. Wigner, *op. cit.*

14. Bredvold's position is hostile to the Enlightenment. He favors a return to the more conservative principle of Natural Law. Cf. E. A. Burtt, *The Metaphysical Foundations of Modern Science* (Garden City, N. Y.: Doubleday Anchor, [1924] 1954).

15. Cf. Herman Dooyeweerd, *In the Twilight of Western Thought* (1959) and *A New Critique of Theoretical Thought* (4 vols., 1955), both published by the Presbyterian and Reformed Publishing Co., Philadelphia.

16. C. S. Lewis, *The Abolition of Man* (New York: Macmillan, [1947] 1965), ch. 3. Weber categorizes this shift in perspective as the Renaissance's hope in the possibility of discovering Nature through the art of science, and today's attempt to discover Nature by escaping science. Weber, "Science as a Vocation," (1919) in H. H. Gerth and C. Wright Mills (eds.), *From Max Weber: Essays in Sociology* (New York: Oxford University Press, 1947), 141-42.

facts"—apart from our own mental constructs. "Concepts without percepts are empty; percepts without concepts are blind": here is the basic premise of Kantian epistemology. Weber's writings are the direct outcome of this methodological perspective. This is the modern reconciliation of the "theory-fact" dualism. The unity is provided by the process of reason itself; facts as such, i.e., things in themselves, are unknowable.

Scientific knowledge concerns itself only with the phenomenal realm. Material elements of the universe are subject to observation through scientific ordering. The noumenal realm is the realm of the spiritual and/or the unknown. It is not subject to the rationalizing process of conceptual, cognitive reasoning. It is, in short, a non-rational realm. It is the sphere of ethical judgment and human freedom, in contrast to the deterministic realm of rigorous scientific knowledge.[17] Thus, modern, post-Kantian thought is simultaneously rational and irrational, just as it was in the medieval nature-grace synthesis and the form-matter schema of the Classical world. Rationalism and irrationalism are epistemological corollaries of each other. A sea of infinite, unknowable chance is the corollary of total law and an absolutely supreme (in its proper realm) scientific reason. Human freedom is now seen in the non-rational realm of the noumenal, outside the jurisdiction of scientifically rationalized human power, i.e., the phenomenal realm. Van Til therefore asserts:

> Thus the ocean of facts has no bottom and no shore. It is this conception of the ultimacy of time and of pure factuality on which modern philosophy, particularly since the days of Kant, has laid such great stress. And it is because of the general recognition of the ultimacy of chance that rationalism of the sort that Descartes, Spinoza and Leibniz represented, is out of date. It has become customary to speak of post-Kantian philosophy as irrationalistic.[18]

Van Til's summary of the epistemological dualism of modern philosophy is rather lengthy, but it is worth reproducing here. It establishes the framework under which Weber operated, and it presents the fundamental

---

17. Richard Kroner, *Kant's Weltanschauung* (University of Chicago Press, [1914] 1956). Kroner writes: "Kant deals in the *Critique of Practical Reason* with man as an empirical individual being endowed with desire and inclination, pursuing practical interests and purposes, making decisions and carrying them into effect. All this is done by empirical practical reason, whereas pure practical reason disciplines the will morally, sets up moral standards of doing and judging motives and actions. Practical reason is empirical and hence can be criticized; pure practical reason, on the contrary, commands the empirical will and makes moral character and moral life possible. Practical reason falsifies morality, if it pretends to be a source of ethical principles. . . . Theoretical knowledge has to be restricted and finite in order to allow room for practical volition and action, and eventually for practical faith and hope." *Speculation and Revelation in Modern Philosophy* (Philadelphia: Westminster Press, 1959), 217.

18. Cornelius Van Til, *Apologetics* (Syllabus, Westminster Theological Seminary, 1959), 80.

intellectual problem Weber confronted when he treated the whole question of rationalization, bureaucratization, and human freedom.

> In the second place modern irrationalism has not in the least encroached upon the domain of the intellect as the natural man thinks of it. Irrationalism has merely taken possession of that which the intellect, by its own admission, cannot in any case control. Irrationalism has a secret treaty with rationalism by which the former cedes to the latter so much of its territory as the latter can at any given time find the forces to control. Kant's realm of the noumenal has, as it were, agreed to yield so much of its area to the phenomenal as the intellect by its newest weapons can manage to keep in control. Moreover, by the same treaty irrationalism has promised to keep out of its own territory any form of authority that might be objectionable to the autonomous intellect. The very idea of pure factuality or chance is the best guarantee that no true authority, such as that of God the Creator and Judge of men, will ever confront man. If we compare the realm of the phenomenal as it has been ordered by the autonomous intellect to a clearing in a large forest we may compare the realm of the noumenal to that part of the same forest which has not yet been laid under contribution by the intellect. The realm of mystery is on this basis simply the realm of that which is not yet known.[19]

It was Max Weber's vision of the impending advent of a totally rationalized world which indicates the speed at which the forces of the phenomenal today seem to be extending the scope of the clearing. The clearing, because it is subject to the rule of impersonal law and rationalized control by specialized experts, has now become a cage. What Descartes would have hailed as a newly won freedom, and what Enlightenment rationalists of the eighteenth century would have welcomed as the triumph of man's liberating reason, Weber recognized as the "polar night of icy darkness and hardness" which is encompassing increasingly large chunks of human existence. Weber, as I hope to show, was unable to escape the antinomies of the nature-freedom dualism: the fine balance of rationalism and irrationalism, law and freedom, would slip first to one side and then to the other. Weber the scientist constantly came into conflict with Weber the humanist; the echoes of the crashing which resulted can still be heard.

Rationalism versus Irrationalism: The Problem of Freedom

Weber saw human freedom in terms of both irrationalism and scientific rationalism. This dualistic tension remained throughout his writings. In one case he denied the validity of any argument which would equate human freedom with a retreat from the realm of law, i.e., a retreat into irrationalism:

---

19. *Ibid.*, p. 81. Cf. statement by John Walsh, "Creationists and Evolutionists: Confrontation in California," *Science* (17 Nov., 1972): "Since the time of Voltaire, most religious creeds have learned to coexist with science by waiving rights to any territory claimed by science. This is why the National Academy of Sciences could pass a resolution last month stating that 'Religion and science . . . are separate and mutually exclusive realms of human thought' " (p. 728).

The error in the assumption that any freedom of the will—however it is understood—is identical with the "irrationality" of action, or that the latter is conditioned by the former, is quite obvious. The characteristic of "incalculability," equally great but not greater than that of "blind forces of nature," is the privilege of—the insane. On the other hand, we associate the highest measure of an empirical "feeling of freedom" with those actions which we are conscious of performing rationally— i.e., *in the absence of physical and psychic "coercion," emotional "affects" and "accidental" disturbances of the clarity of judgment,* in which we pursue a clearly perceived end by "means" which are the most adequate in accordance with the extent of our knowledge, i.e., in accordance with empirical *rules*.[20]

Weber seems to be hedging somewhat when he appeals to a "feeling of freedom." He is aware of the intellectual problem he is facing. It is precisely this scientific spirit which is bringing total rationalism into existence within modern industrial civilization. "Scientific progress is a fraction, the most important fraction, of the process of intellectualization which we have been undergoing for thousands of years. . . ."[21] This does not mean, however, that we understand our environment better than a savage understands his. In practice, the American Indian knows more about his tools than we know about ours. What rationalistic knowledge means is something different. It sets before us the ideal of *exhaustive knowledge*, i.e., "the knowledge or belief that if one but wished one *could* learn it at any time. Hence, it means that principally there are no mysterious incalculable forces that come into play, but rather that one can, in principle, master all things by calculation." Technical means have been substituted for magical manipulation of the universe. "This means that the world is disenchanted. . . . This above all is what intellectualization means."[22]

While Weber argues that the "feeling of freedom"—or perhaps more accurately, the feeling of power—can be increased through the use of rational calculation and planning, he nevertheless realizes that as the noumenal realm of man's ethical life is eroded away by the inroads made by phenomenalistic science, man's freedom is slipping away. He poses the question quite well:

The question is: how are freedom and democracy in the long run at all possible under the domination of highly developed capitalism?

20. E. A. Shills and H. A. Finch (eds.), *Max Weber on the Methodology of the Social Sciences* (Glencoe, Ill.: Free Press, 1949), 124-25. Wolfgang Mommsen writes: "To put Weber's view more succinctly, the personality needs rational orientation in order to become 'itself,' to become 'free.'" Mommsen, "Max Weber's Political Sociology and His Philosophy of World History," *International Social Science Journal* (Unesco), XVII (1965), 29.

21. Weber, "Science as a Vocation," in Gerth and Mills, *op. cit.*, 138. This lecture was first delivered to students of Munich University.

22. *Ibid.*, 139.

Freedom and democracy are only possible where the resolute will of a nation not to allow itself to be ruled like sheep is permanently alive. We are 'individualists' and partisans of 'democratic' institutions 'against the stream' of material constellations. He who wishes to be the weathercock of an evolutionary trend should give up these old-fashioned ideals as soon as possible. The historical origin of modern freedom has had certain unique preconditions which will never repeat themselves.[23]

It is not capitalism as such which has destroyed freedom; it is the scientific, technological and bureaucratic ideology, coupled with institutions based on rational calculation and production for a mass market, which have brought forth industrial society. Socialism would be, if anything, even more systematic in its reduction of the sphere of freedom, since a centralized state planning apparatus would control all production and distribution.[24] Weber's line of reasoning is straightforward:

A progressive elimination of private capitalism is theoretically conceivable, although it is surely not so easy as imagined in the dreams of some literati who do not know what it is all about; its elimination will certainly not be a consequence of this war. But let us assume that some time in the future it will be done away with. What would be the practical result? The destruction of the steel frame of modern industrial work? No! The abolition of private capitalism would simply mean that also the *top management* of the nationalized or socialized enterprises would become bureaucratic. Are the daily working conditions of the salaried employees and the workers in the state-owned Prussian mines and railroads really perceptibly different from those in big business enterprises? It is true that there is even less freedom, since every power struggle with a state bureaucracy is hopeless and since there is no appeal to an agency which as a matter of principle would be interested in limiting the employer's power, such as there is in the case of a private enterprise. *That* would be the whole difference.

State bureaucracy would rule *alone* if private capitalism were eliminated. The private and public bureaucracies, which now work next to, and potentially against, each other and hence check one another to a degree, would be merged into a single hierarchy. This would be similar to the situation in ancient Egypt, but it would occur in a much more rational—and hence unbreakable—form.[25]

---

23. Quoted by Gerth and Mills, 71. Mommsen's analysis is perceptive: "The principle of individuality and the principle of rationality were in Weber's mind dialectical quantities. They belonged together: a rational, methodical way of life was in his opinion an essential feature of the personality. Nevertheless, Weber repeatedly stressed the fundamental antagonism between the ideal of personality and the products of rationalization, with particular reference to the modern disciplined working world and its bureaucracies. The conflict between the two principles was in his view the great theme of world history." Mommsen, *op. cit.,* 45.

24. Robert Nisbet, *The Sociological Tradition* (New York: Basic Books, 1966), 145.

25. Weber, "Parliament and Government in a Reconstructed Germany," Appendix #2 of Weber's *Economy and Society: An Outline of Interpretive Sociology*, edited by Guenther Roth and Claus Wittich (New York: Bedminster Press, 1968), 1401-02. This is the official translation of Weber's *Wirtschaft und Gesellschaft*, although the essay cited first appeared as a series of pieces for the German press, and

Gerth and Mills, in their introductory remarks to their collection of Weber's essays, capture the essence of the antinomy: "For Weber, capitalism is the embodiment of rational impersonality; the quest for freedom is identified with irrational sentiment and privacy. [This, of course, is the Weberian equivalent to the Kantian realm of the noumenal—G.N.] Freedom is at best a tarrying for loving companionship and for the cathartic experience of art as a this-worldly escape from institutional routines. It is the privilege of the propertied and the educated: it is a freedom without equality."[26] For the elite—the new caste members—the escape from the world of hyper-bureaucratization would be through eroticism and artistic expression on the one hand, or through mystical, religious flight on the other.[27] The key essay in this regard is his study, "Religious Rejections of the World and their Directions," published during the First World War in 1915.

> The total being of man has now been alienated from the organic cycle of peasant life; life has been increasingly enriched in cultural content, whether this content is evaluated as intellectually or otherwise supra-individual. All this has worked, through the estrangement of life-value from that which is naturally given, toward a further enhancement of the special position of eroticism. Eroticism was raised into the sphere of conscious enjoyment (in the most sublime sense of the term). Nevertheless, indeed because of this elevation, eroticism appeared to be like a gate into the most irrational and thereby real kernel of life, as compared with the mechanisms of rationalization.[28]

With this as his framework, he traces the development of eroticism in the Occident from the medieval troubadour tradition, through the Enlightenment's salon culture, and into the mechanized present. Eroticism has become intensified, Weber argues, paralleling the intensification of rationalization, for irrational, animalistic eroticism has been infused with power:

> As the knowing love of the mature man stands to the passionate enthusiasm of the youth, so stands the deadly earnestness of this eroticism of intellectualism to chivalrous love. In contrast to chivalrous love, this mature love of intellectualism reaffirms the natural quality of the sexual sphere, but it does so consciously, as an embodied creative power.[29]

Artistic expression has taken on the character of a religion, given the

---

is included in *Gesammelte Politische Schriften* (Tübingen: Mohr, 1958). On the highly centralized but extremely fragile bureaucracy of ancient Egypt, see Lewis Mumford, "The First Megamachine," *Diogenes*, #55 (1966), 1-15. For a contrast between socialism's bureaucratic administrative structure and capitalism's profit-seeking firm, see Ludwig von Mises, *Bureaucracy* (New Rochelle, N. Y.: Arlington House, [1944] 1969).

26. Gerth and Mills, 73.

27. Weber, *The Sociology of Religion*, trans., Ephraim Fischoff (Boston: Beacon Press, 1964), 236. [*Economy and Society* (hereinafter cited as *E&S*), 601.]

28. "Religious Rejections of the World and Their Directions," (1915); Gerth and Mills, 344-45.

29. *Ibid.*, 347.

"development of intellectualism and the rationalization of life": "Art takes over the function of a this-worldly salvation, no matter how this may be interpreted. It provides a *salvation* from the routines of everyday life, and especially from the increasing pressures of theoretical and practical rationalism."[30] Although Weber did not expand on this topic, it would not be difficult to extend his analysis to account for the increasingly formless and irrationalistic types of artistic expression that have appeared since his era.[31]

The essay which is one of the best known of all Weber's shorter works, "Science as a Vocation," delivered before students at the University of Munich in 1918, presents his most pessimistic evaluation of modern life in a rationalized, bureaucratized world. The goal of Western science has contributed to the bleak picture that confronts us, he says. Its goal and underlying presupposition is that man's knowledge can become exhaustive. Yet this guarantees that every scientist (unlike the artist) is certain to see his life's work superseded, if not refuted, in ten, twenty, or fifty years. "Every scientific 'fulfilment' raises new 'questions'; it *asks* to be 'surpassed' and outdated."[32] Men pursue a goal which never comes in reality. There is always another step possible in the march of scientific progress. Modern man, on the treadmill of scientific and cultural progress, grows tired of life; he knows that he can never experience more than a tiny fraction of life, if life is progressive, linear, and irreversible.

> He catches only the most minute part of what the life of the spirit brings forth ever anew, and what he seizes is always something provisional and not definitive, and therefore death for him is a meaningless occurrence. And because death is meaningless, civilized life as such is meaningless; by its very "progressiveness" it gives death the imprint of meaninglessness.[33]

Science therefore tells us nothing of the meaning of either life or death. With such a bleak picture of the modern human condition, it is not surprising that Weber could conclude his parallel lecture, "Politics as a Vocation," with this assessment of what the future holds:

> Not summer's bloom lies ahead of us, but rather a polar night of icy

30. *Ibid.*, 342.
31. Matthew Josephson, *Life Among the Surrealists* (New York: Holt, Rinehart and Winston, 1962), explores the professed irrationalism of the leading French Dadaists in the 1920's; ch. 7. On the irrational aspects of contemporary "underground" art, see Barry Farrell, "The Other Culture," *Life* (Feb. 17, 1967). Cf. Gunther S. Stent, *The Coming of the Golden Age: A View of the End of Progress* (Garden City, N. Y.: Natural History Press, 1969), ch. 6. Stent argues that irrational musical and art forms cannot "progress" simply because they possess no rational structures from which progression can be measured. Irrationalism is the end of the artistic road. This would seem to substantiate some of the material on contemporary art that is presented by Francis Schaeffer in his book, *The God Who Is There* (InterVarsity Press, 1969).
32. Gerth and Mills, 138.
33. *Ibid.*, 140.

darkness and hardness, no matter which group may triumph externally now. Where there is nothing, not only the Kaiser but also the proletarian has lost his rights. When this night shall have slowly receded, who of those for whom spring apparently has bloomed so luxuriously will be alive? And what will have become of all of you by then? Will you be bitter or banalistic? Will you simply and dully accept world and occupation? Or will the third and by no means the least frequent possibility be your lot: mystic flight from reality for those who are gifted for it, or—as is both frequent and unpleasant—for those who belabor themselves to follow this fashion?[34]

Weber, it should be pointed out, did not regard such a flight into the irrational as something to be scorned automatically in all cases, although he regarded the attempt to invent new religions apart from "genuine prophecy" as a futile endeavor.[35] "To the person who cannot bear the fate of the times like a man, one must say: may he rather return silently, without the usual publicity build-up of renegades, but simply and plainly. The arms of the old churches are opened widely and compassionately for him." But the retreat from the phenomenal realm of rational thought is an inescapable concomitant of this particular avenue of escape. "One way or another he has to bring his 'intellectual sacrifice'—that is inevitable. If he can really do it, we shall not rebuke him."[36]

Why is this sacrifice really mandatory? As he admits, "All theology represents an intellectual *rationalization* of the possession of sacred values."[37] But modern rationalism is changing this. "Every increase of rationalism in empirical science increasingly pushes religion from the rational into the irrational realm; but only today does religion become *the* irrational or anti-rational supra-human power."[38] Thus, Weber's Kantian dualism brought him to a strikingly Barthian theological position at least three years prior to the publication of Barth's enormously influential *Commentary on the Epistle to the Romans* (1918):

> Salvation religion, however, viewed from its own position, is to be blamed for equally inconsistent trespasses as soon as it surrenders the unassailable incommunicability of mystic experiences. If it is consistent, such religion can only have the means of bringing mystic experiences about as *events*; it has no means of adequately communicating and demonstrating them. Every attempt to influence the world must entice mystical religion to run this danger, as soon as the attempt assumes the character of propaganda. The same holds for every attempt to interpret the meaning of the universe rationally, but nevertheless the attempt has been made again and again.[39]

34. "Politics as a Vocation," (1919); *ibid.*, 128.
35. "Science," *ibid.*, 155.
36. *Ibid.*
37. *Ibid.*, 153.
38. "Religious Rejections," *ibid.*, 351. Cf. "The Social Psychology of World Religions," (1915); *ibid.*, 281.
39. "Religious Rejections," *ibid.*, 353.

(As an aside, the reader should grasp the importance of Weber's use of such phrases as "salvation history" and "events." For decades, Van Til has insisted that Barth's use of such terminology as "Christ-event" and "salvation history"—*Heilgeschicte*—demonstrates that Barth's theology is essentially neo-Kantian and in no sense orthodox. He has been ridiculed by followers of Barth for claiming such a supposedly preposterous theory. But Weber's far clearer and far more-honest exposition of the implications of the neo-Kantian antinomy between phenomena and noumena should indicate how right Van Til has been all along. Such a vision makes religion impotent and irrelevant to the affairs of the cognitive: "Every attempt to influence the world must entice mystical religion to run this danger," i.e., the danger of trying to communicate anything to the realm of logical thought. The growing disillusionment of modern radical clerics with the old Barthian mysticism—all dressed up in its orthodox Sunday finery—is finally coming home to roost. A consistent Barthian is as impotent to speak to the affairs of life as the consistent Zen Buddhist. Any attempt to do so assumes, in Weber's words, "the character of propaganda." For almost half a century, we have been subjected to an unending stream of just such Barthian propaganda: the social gospel baptized in the name of a noncognitive, neo-Kantian "Christ-event.")

Rationalism, when added to mysticism, creates propaganda. This equation is crucial for Weber's social analysis. As he says, "the attempt has been made again and again." The tide of rationalization makes continual inroads into the forest of the irrational. Those who systematically proclaim the irrational as a solution to mankind's loss of external freedom may well find their programs self-defeating in the long run:

> And finally, science as a way "to God"? Science, this specifically irreligious power? That science today is irreligious no one will doubt in his innermost being, even if he will not admit it to himself. Redemption from the rationalism and intellectualism of science is the fundamental presupposition of living in union with the divine. This, or something similar in meaning, is one of the fundamental watchwords one hears among German youth, whose feelings are attuned to religion or who crave religious experiences. They crave not only religious experience, but experience as such. The only thing that is strange is the method that is now followed: the spheres of the irrational, the only spheres that intellectualism has not yet touched, are now raised into consciousness and put under its lens. For in practice this is where the modern intellectualist form of romantic irrationalism leads. This method of emancipation from intellectualism may well bring about the very opposite of what those who take to it conceive as its goal.[40]

Modern life is split: it seems to lead men simultaneously into the realms of the rational and the irrational. Rationalism results in the quest

---

40. "Science," *ibid.*, pp. 142-143.

for power, and mysticism, to the extent that it is rationalized, becomes propaganda. Freedom is achieved both as a direct function of law and knowledge and at the same time achieved only through an escape into the internal realm of the mystical or the "lawless" activities of artistic expression and eroticism. Society is impinged on the horns of a radical, and increasingly burdensome, dilemma.

Rationalism: Formal vs. Substantive

Weber's analysis of modern life goes beyond any simple "rationalism-irrationalism" antinomy of post-Kantian thought. One of his recurring themes is the internal conflict of rationalism itself—not merely the old debate between *a priori* deduction and *a posteriori* induction, but rather the continual conflict between formal rationalism and substantive rationalism. It occurs in the areas of politics, economics, and legal thought; it is inescapable.

Max Rheinstein's introduction to Weber's *On Law in Economy and Society* (an extract of *Wirtschaft und Gesellschaft*) presents a remarkable summary of Weber's typology of legal systems. There are the irrational systems, i.e., systems not guided by general rules. *Formal irrationalism* is guided by rigidly binding rules which are beyond the control of reason: ordeal, oracle, etc. *Substantive irrationalism* is guided by the reaction of the judge to the individual case and is purely arbitrary. Rational law, on the other hand, is guided by general rules. *Substantive legal rationalism* is guided by principles of an ideological system other than the law itself: ethics, religion, power politics, etc. Finally, there is *formal legal rationalism*, which in turn is divided into two forms: extrinsically, which ascribes significance to external acts observable by the senses (contracts, oaths, signature, symbolic acts); logically, which expresses its rules by the use of abstract concepts created by legal thought itself and conceived of as constituting a complete system.[41] These last two elements are in competition. Weber writes: "This process of 'logical rationality' diminishes the significance of extrinsic elements and thus softens the rigidity of concrete formalism."[42]

Formally rational law is the most perfect expression of legality in Weber's perspective:

> According to present modes of thought it represents an integration of all analytically derived legal propositions in such a way that they constitute a logically clear, internally consistent, and, at least in theory, gapless system of rules, under which, it is implied, all conceivable fact situations must be capable of being logically subsumed lest their order lack an effective guaranty.[43]

41. Max Rheinstein, "Introduction," *Max Weber on Law in Economy and Society* (New York: Simon & Schuster Clarion, 1967), xlii.
42. *Ibid.*, 63. [*E&S*, 657.]
43. *Ibid.*, 62. [*E&S*, 656.]

In short, "the peculiarly professional, legalistic, and abstract approach to law in the modern sense is possible only in the measure that the law is formal in character."[44] The Decalogue is therefore superseded.

Substantive law is preferred by monarchs, theocratic rulers, and proponents of regimes run in terms of ideological or ethical principles. Formal law interferes with the ability of such rulers to decide specific cases in the light of the ultimate values to which the rulers are committed. On the other hand, to the extent that rulers desire an efficient legal mechanism, substantive principles interfere with this goal. "Juridical formalism enables the legal system to operate like a technically rational machine." The danger to the monarch from legal formalism is obvious: "Thus it guarantees to individuals and groups within the system a relative maximum of freedom, and greatly increases for them the possibility of predicting the legal consequences of their actions." The system is based on inviolable "rules of the game."[45] Without this legal framework, bureaucratic agencies and capitalist entrepreneurs find it more difficult to plan rationally for the future. In a crucially important passage, Weber sketches the nature of the conflict:

> Formal justice guarantees the maximum freedom for the interested parties to represent their formal legal interests. But because of the unequal distribution of economic power, which the system of formal justice legalizes, this very freedom must time and again produce consequences which are contrary to the substantive postulates of religious ethics or of political expediency. Formal justice is thus repugnant to all authoritarian powers, theocratic as well as patriarchic, because it diminishes the dependency of the individual upon the grace and power of the authorities. To democracy, however, it has been repugnant because it decreases the dependency of the legal practice and therewith of the individuals upon the decisions of their fellow citizens. Furthermore, the development of the trial into a peaceful contest of conflicting interests can contribute to the further concentration of economic and social power. In all these cases formal justice, due to its necessarily abstract character, infringes upon the ideals of substantive justice.[46]

Weber concludes that the bourgeois state has tended to favor formally rational law.[47] Capitalism in its modern form has nevertheless flourished under the various legal systems of Western Europe, so Weber is careful to add this disclaimer: "We may thus conclude that capitalism has not been a decisive factor in the promotion of that form of rationalization of the law which has been peculiar to the continental West ever since the rise of

---

44. *Ibid.*, 64. [*E&S*, 657.]
45. *Ibid.*, 226-27. [*E&S*, 811.]
46. *Ibid.*, 228 [*E&S*, 812-13.]
47. *Ibid.*, 231. [*E&S*, 814.] Cf. F. A. Hayek, *The Constitution of Liberty* (University of Chicago Press, 1960). Hayek is one of the most eloquent defenders of the idea of formal legality as the foundation of the free market and the free society.

Romanist studies in the medieval universities."[48] English capitalism has been under a less formalistic system without suffering.

In referring to the development of the modern welfare state from its origins in the institutions of the eighteenth century's enlightened despots to the present, Weber stresses the conflict between formal and substantive law.[49] It was the advent of capitalist production techniques which brought the most fully rationalized economic system into being that the world has yet experienced. "It is only in the modern Western World that rational capitalistic enterprises with fixed capital, free labour, the rational specialization and combination of functions, and the allocation of productive functions on the basis of capitalistic enterprises, bound together in a market economy, are to be found."[50] Other aspects of this economic system are such things as flexible market prices based on a stable currency, free entry into business, private property, and a rational judicial system. These are the formal freedoms of society. Production is aimed at profitability, and a whole new method of cost accounting has been developed to calculate better the extent of profit and loss. The whole system is formally rational.

Capitalism, however, is not substantively rational, Weber argues. It is efficient technically in production matters, but the distribution of its goods and services is not based upon ethically—substantively—justified standards. Here he raises the issue of "human rights vs. property rights," although he never uses the phrase. Some persons or groups are hurt by this emphasis on calculated efficiency. Substantive questions, on the other hand, involve ideas of "social justice"—of merit. Those scholars who tend to see the greatest human benefits as products of the unhampered market economy inevitably discount questions concerning individual "merit" that are not directly connected with profitable productivity. For example, F. A. Hayek, perhaps the most eloquent defender of the free market in recent years, argues that questions of merit inevitably involve the decisions of central planners of the economy as to what kinds of merit are to receive rewards. Men are paid in terms of their productivity on the impersonal market, or else they are paid in terms of the value-preferences of the central authorities.[51] This, both Hayek and Weber believe, will necessarily lead to results that are irrational economically. It is this which the socialist —at least the socialist who has not yet gained power—is willing to accept in the name of a higher rationalism, i.e., substantive rationalism. The same held true, Weber says, in the decisions of medieval theologians; they

---

48. *Ibid.*, 318; cf. 315. [*E&S*, 892; cf. 890.]
49. Weber comments on the welfare state aspects of enlightened despotism, *ibid.*, 279. [*E&S*, 856.]
50. *The Theory of Social and Economic Organization*, edited by Talcott Parsons (New York: Free Press, 1964), 279. [*E&S*, 165.]
51. Hayek, *Constitution*, ch. 8.

resisted the inroads of an impersonal, economically rational, and ethically irrational market system.[52]

Socialism cannot achieve a formal rationality comparable to capitalism's. Both Weber and Ludwig von Mises came to this conclusion at the same time.[53] Both base their arguments on this fact: without the existence of a free market based upon flexible prices and the private ownership of the means of production, it is impossible to impute the economic value of either the output of the economy or the tools which make possible that output. Rational, economical planning must be based on a price system which reflects supply and demand, and pure socialism has no such mechanism, since it of necessity operates in terms of a substantively rational plan drawn up by a group of central planners. In short, pure socialism is formally irrational.[54] Weber spells this out in no uncertain terms:

> Where a planned economy is radically carried out, it must further accept the inevitable reduction in formal rationality of calculation which would result from the elimination of money and capital accounting. This is merely an example of the fact that substantive and formal rationality are inevitably largely opposed. This fundamental and, in the last analysis, unavoidable element of irrationality in economic systems is one of the important sources of all the problems of social polity, above all, the problems of socialism.[55]

The problem, ultimately, is the problem of the conflict among a multiplicity of goals. Rational means of carrying out one set of goals will interfere with—"be irrational" in terms of—another set of goals. "Socialistic and communistic standards which, though by no means unambiguous in themselves, always involve elements of social justice and equality, form only one group among the indefinite plurality of possible points of view."[56] One man's reasonable proposal is another man's irrationality, however consistent internally the proposals may be. The

---

52. *Sociology of Religion*, 215 ff. [*E&S*, 583 ff.] Cf. "The Market: Its Impersonality and Ethic (Fragment)," *E&S*, 635-40.

53. Weber was familiar with Mises' essay on socialist economic calculation, which was published during the time Weber's essay was at the printers, a few months before Weber's death. *Theory*, 211n. [*E&S*, 107.] Mises has informed me (Nov. 4, 1971) that he had discussed this matter with Weber at some length.

54. *Theory*, 203-10. [*E&S*, 100-07.] Cf. Gary North, *Marx's Religion of Revolution* (Nutley, N. J.: Craig Press, 1968), for a summary of the literature on socialist economic calculation, Appendix A; F. A. Hayek (ed.), *Collectivist Economic Planning* (London: Routledge & Kegan Paul, 1935); Oskar Lange, *On the Economic Theory of Socialism* (New York: McGraw-Hill, 1964); T. J. B. Hoff, *Economic Calculation in the Socialist Society* (London: Hodge, 1949), are the basic sources on this debate.

55. *Theory*, 214-15; cf. 212, 339. [*E&S*, 111; cf. 108, 224-25.]

56. *Ibid.*, 185. [*E&S*, 86. The translation here is slightly different: "There is an infinite number of possible value scales for this type of rationality, of which the socialistic and communistic standards constitute only one group." He was referring, of course, to substantive rationality.]

division between formal rationality and substantive rationality is therefore comparable to the distinction Weber makes between "value-rational" and "purpose-rational" systems:

> We have to remind ourselves in advance that "rationalism" may mean very different things. It means one thing if we think of the kind of rationalization the systematic thinker performs on the image of the world: an increasing theoretical mastery of reality by means of increasing precise and abstract concepts. Rationalism means another thing if we think of the methodical attainment of a definitely given and practical end by means of an increasingly precise calculation of adequate means. These types of rationalism are very different, in spite of the fact that ultimately they belong inseparably together.[57]

For the Christian sociologist, Weber's admission and coherent exposition are vitally important. There is no single form of "rationalism." The secularist who dismisses the idea that biblical revelation can serve as a guide to academic inquiry invariably complains that such a revelational approach is not truly rational. But the implicit assumption lying behind such casual comments is that there is, in fact, a single form of reason. It is precisely the lack of such a unified reason that is driving the academic world into chaos. The dualism between Kant's practical reason (the noumenal ideal of personality) and Kant's pure reason (the phenomenal ideal of science) appears whenever modern secularists begin to formulate their "rational" approaches to any academic discipline. Weber devoted years of study to the development of Western rationalization, but he was careful to point to the latent ambiguities of such rationalization. Modern thought has been incapable of resolving the dualism of the two reasons. Weber only confirms what Van Til has been arguing throughout his career: the hypothetically autonomous mind of man is unable to come to grips with itself or with the hypothetically autonomous world outside the mind. Weber admitted this when he called attention to the inescapable tension between formal rationalism and substantive rationalism. He never believed that either could fully eliminate the other, although he did expect formal, bureaucratic rationalism to expand constantly its control over substantive residuals in society. But this division cannot be ignored by any scholar claiming to be wholly rational. Weber's assertion of a fundamental dualism is not some peripheral issue to be dismissed casually.

In religious terms, the division stands between what Weber calls the "ethic of ultimate ends" and the "ethic of responsibility." The former asserts that the good intent of the actor, if in conformity with some higher standard of righteousness, is justification of his actions, even if they should result in bad results. The evil is blamed on the world, or the stupidity of

---

57. "Social Psychology of World Religions," Gerth and Mills, 293. Weber cites as one example of this distinction the differences between English physics and Continental physics.

others. The ethic of responsibility is concerned with the question of means and the influence of means on the outcome of action.[58] In politics, he says, the truly great man is he who can somehow fuse the two; in this sense, "an ethic of ultimate ends and an ethic of responsibility are not absolute contrasts but rather supplements, which only in unison can constitute a genuine man—a man who *can* have the 'calling for politics.' "[59]

At this point, Weber sounds optimistic. But another fusion of substantive and formal rationality is possible, and it is this one which fascinated Weber. In his discussion of Weber's typology of law, David Rothstein makes this fundamental point:

> It is at this point that we can see most clearly the fundamental conflict between substantive and formal law. It is the conflict between universalism and particularism, personal and impersonal or in traditional sociological terms organic and mechanical, *Gemeinschaft* and *Gesellschaft*. On the one hand there is an orientation or commitment to what is regarded as an absolute value and on the other an orientation or commitment to self-interest. . . . As long as there is a conflict between substantive and formal law there will be areas of ambiguity in which individuals may move, there will always be an appeal to a higher, independent, substantive authority. But when substantive law adopts as its absolute value the concept of rationality and the achievement of the objectives of purposive rational action, i.e., self-interested goals, the conflict will cease to exist and men will be dominated in a total sense. Orwell saw this possibility in *1984*; likewise did Huxley in *Brave New World*. It is at this point that a dispassionate, value-free consideration becomes almost impossible. When we speak of substantive law becoming the servant of formal law, we are speaking of totalitarian rule and its possibility for our own society.[60]

Weber's vision of the increasingly bureaucratic, rationalized society hinged on the very real probability of such a subordination of substantive law to formal law. That, in fact, is what characterizes the development of Western capitalism and its techniques of mass production and rational calculation. Weber saw this process as inescapable and irreversible. He hated what he saw, but he saw no escape. Bureaucracy, whether socialistic or capitalistic, is here.

---

58. "Politics as a Vocation," *ibid.*, 120 ff.

59. *Ibid.*, 127. Guenther Roth writes concerning Weber's idea of political leadership: "He was convinced that responsible political leadership cannot afford to adhere to moralistic, legalistic or any other kind of ideological absolutism, since these are inherently self-defeating. His sociological ethic was thus a latter-day version of Stoic philosophy in that virtuous conduct was more important than any notion of ultimate salvation in a this-worldly or other-worldly millennium—and only in this sense was Weber a Machiavellian." Roth, "Political Critiques of Weber: Some Implications for Political Sociology," *American Sociological Review*, XXX (1965), 215. Cf. Mommsen, *op. cit.*, 39 ff., who emphasizes the Nietzschian "will to power" aspect of Weber's concept of charismatic political leadership.

60. David Rothstein, *Weber's Typology of Law and Some Aspects of the Conflict Between Formal and Substantive Law* (1968), unpublished ms., 12-13.

Social Change

Weber regarded conflict and competition as the primary stimuli for social change. Those individuals or groups which, for reasons of skill or accident, can survive the rigors of conflict will emerge as the victors. This process of selection is inescapable: biological evolution is a fact of life.

> Not every process of social selection is, in the present sense, a case of conflict. . . . It is only in the sense of "selection" that it seems, according to our experience, that conflict is empirically inevitable, and it is furthermore only in the sense of *biological* selection that it is inevitable in principle. Selection is inevitable because apparently no way can be worked out of eliminating it completely. It is possible even for the most strictly pacific order to eliminate means of conflict and the objects of and impulses to conflict only in that it deals with each type individually. But this means that other modes of conflict would come to the fore, possibly in processes of open competition. But even on the utopian assumption that all competition were completely eliminated, conditions would still lead to a latent process of selection, biological or social, which would favour the types best adapted to the conditions, whether their relevant qualities were mainly determined by heredity or by environment.[61]

Modern capitalism, the world's most rational and efficient economic form, emerged as the product of centuries of conflict. A long struggle took place between the older, traditional economic order of feudalism-manorialism and capitalistic entrepreneurs. "The decisive impetus toward capitalism could come only from one source, namely a mass market demand, which again could arise only in a small proportion of the luxury industries through the democratization of demand, especially along the line of production substitutes for the luxury goods of the upper classes."[62] The distinguishing characteristics of this economic system are, first, the rational organization of labor on a hitherto unprecedented scale, and second, the removal of the traditional barrier between the ethics of trade within a clan or religious group and the ethics determining trade with outsiders.[63]

It is only in the Occident, Weber asserts, that we find a rationalized system of law, a state grounded upon the existence of professional, highly specialized administrators, the specifically urban concept of "citizen," and modern science. "Finally, western civilization is further distinguished from every other by the presence of men with a rational ethic for the conduct of life."[64] This last factor was the object of Weber's intensive comparative studies of religion. In the study of Weber's which is perhaps

---

61. *Theory*, 134. [*E&S*, 39.]
62. Weber, *General Economic History*, trans., Frank H. Knight (New York: Collier, [1927] 1961), 230. This book is a compilation of the lecture notes from Weber's last completed course, given in the winter of 1919–20.
63. *Ibid.*, 232.
64. *Ibid.*, 233.

his most famous, *The Protestant Ethic and the Spirit of Capitalism* (1904–05), Weber presented his argument that the inner-worldly asceticism of Protestantism, and especially the Quaker and Puritan forms of Protestantism, constituted a major force favoring the development of rational calculation and systematic labor. The kingdom of God is to be brought into this world through godly labor—the calling—and the apostate world is to be subdued for the glory of God.[65]

Weber did not rest his case merely on the influence of religion. He was far too wise a scholar to rely on any monocausational theory, as the final paragraph of the *Protestant Ethic* indicates. Religion has been only one factor among many in the process of Western rationalization. Today it is probably a minor factor; it is no longer needed to sustain the process. Rationalization is now self-sustaining:

> Since asceticism undertook to remodel the world and to work out its ideals in the world, material goods have gained an increasing and finally an inexorable power over the lives of men as at no previous period in history. To-day the spirit of religious asceticism—whether finally, who knows?—has escaped from the cage. But victorious capitalism, since it rests on mechanical foundations, needs its support no longer. The rosy blush of its laughing heir, the Enlightenment, seems also to be irretrievably fading, and the idea of duty in one's calling prowls about in our lives like the ghost of dead religious beliefs. . . . No one knows who will live in this cage in the future, or whether at the end of this tremendous development entirely new prophets will arise, or there will be a great rebirth of old ideas and ideals, or, if neither, mechanized petrification, embellished with a sort of convulsive self-importance. For of the last stage of this cultural development, it might well be truly said: "Specialists without spirit, sensualists without heart; this nullity imagines that it has attained a level of civilization never before achieved."[66]

Exogenous factors may be present, either stimulating or retarding this rationalization of life, but there seems to be no force that possesses sufficient power to reverse the basic course of events. The risk-bearing entrepreneur is being replaced by the technocratic bureaucrat. The manager replaces the older owner-entrepreneur. The economy is less and less characterized by economic profits that are based on the process of economic

---

65. *Ibid.*, 267 ff. Cf. Weber, *The Protestant Ethic and the Spirit of Capitalism*, trans., Talcott Parsons (New York: Scribner's, 1958); Talcott Parsons, *The Structure of Social Action* (New York: Free Press, [1937] 1968), II, chs. 14 and 15. For an introduction to the debate over Weber's famous thesis, see Robert W. Green (ed.), *Protestantism and Capitalism* (Boston: D. C. Heath, 1959); S. N. Eisenstadt (ed.), *The Protestant Ethic and Modernization* (New York: Basic Books, 1968). Two of the most prominent of the anti-Weber critiques are Kurt Samuelsson, *Religion and Economic Action* (New York: Harper Torchbook, [1957] 1964) and H. R. Trevor-Roper, "Religion, the Reformation and Social Change," published in his book, *The Crisis of the Seventeenth Century* (New York: Harper & Row, 1968).

66. *Protestant Ethic*, 181-82.

innovation and the accurate forecasting of the unknown. Rent is replacing entrepreneurship in the increasingly bureaucratized processes of production. Rent is the more automatic return on capital; there is less uncertainty involved, as any good medieval baron could have understood.[67] The result is a new caste system. In a sense, the forces which tended toward formal freedom and individual initiative—forces which shattered the more personalistic medieval economy and social system—have turned in upon themselves:

> . . . everywhere the house is ready-made for a new servitude. It only waits for the tempo of technical economic "progress" to slow down and for rent to triumph over profit. The latter victory, joined with the exhaustion of the remaining free soil and free market, will make the masses "docile." Then man will move into the house of servitude. At the same time, the increasing complexity of the economy, the partial governmentalization of economic activities, the territorial expansion of the population—these processes create ever-new work for the clerks, an ever-new specialization of functions, and expert vocational training and administration. All this means caste.[68]

Weber appears to have returned to a vision of the economy similar to that held as ideal types by Adam Smith and David Ricardo: specialized, productive, and essentially stationary. This static economy would be the outcome of the forces of change, as a balance of population, land, and output is achieved. The tempo of economic progress will eventually slow down, and rent will replace profit. The realm of chance will be reduced by rationalistic calculation, and the range of profit and loss will consequently be narrowed. This almost apocalyptic vision has been extended by Jacques Ellul in his book, *The Technological Society* (1964), and by Roderick Seidenberg's promise of the advent of a static "ant-hill society."[69]

---

67. On entrepreneurial forecasting and innovation, see Joseph A. Schumpeter, *The Theory of Economic Development* (New York: Oxford University Press, [1911] 1963), ch. 4; Frank H. Knight, *Risk, Uncertainty and Profit* (New York: Harper Torchbook, [1921] 1965), esp. chs. 8 and 9; Ludwig von Mises, *Human Action* (New Haven: Yale University Press, 1949), 286-97. Weber held to this basic perspective: *Theory*, 204. [*E&S*, 101-02.] He did not develop the idea extensively, however.

68. Quoted by Gerth and Mills, 71. It is this vision which lies behind Schumpeter's belief that modern capitalism is atrophying: *Capitalism, Socialism and Democracy* (3rd ed.; New York: Harper Torchbook, [1950] 1962), chs. 11-14. A unique criticism of Schumpeter's hypothesis, and, by implication, of Weber's, is provided by Henry Manne, *Insider Trading and the Stock Market* (New York: Free Press, 1966), chs. 8 and 9. Manne argues that the entrepreneur will be financially motivated to perform efficiently if he is permitted to trade his inside information without government interference (assuming the information he exchanges is not fraudulent). Without this freedom, Manne believes, the Schumpeter-Weber prophecy may come true. Manne asserts that in the modern corporation, financial returns from the sale of inside information is the chief form of compensation for entrepreneurial forecasting.

69. Roderick Seidenberg, *Post-Historic Man: An Inquiry* (1950) and *Anatomy of the Future* (1961), both published by the University of North Carolina Press, Chapel Hill.

Unlike Seidenberg, who welcomes the exchange of freedom for total economic productivity, Weber and Ellul have not welcomed such a society, but both are pessimistic about the possibility of alternative systems to compete with the technological juggernaut.

What are the possibilities for social change in the future? Did Weber really believe in a time when "the polar night of icy darkness and hardness" will somehow "have slowly receded," a time when spring will bloom "so luxuriously"? Weber, in his characteristically cautious manner, produced passages that would seem to lead in opposite directions. Guenther Roth, certainly one of the best informed Weber scholars, writes: "Despite his fulminations, he did not consider the oppressive dominance of bureaucracy politically inescapable."[70] Yet the passage he cites as evidence is highly ambiguous, and at best admits only the impossibility of making any *a priori* judgments in this regard. "In general," Weber writes on the page Roth cites, "only the following can be said here: The power position of a fully developed bureaucracy is always great, under normal conditions overtowering."[71] Weber goes on to show how administrative secrecy and the ruler's dependence on his bureaucracy tend to undermine all countervailing powers. "The political 'master' always finds himself, vis-à-vis the trained official, in the position of the dilettante facing the expert."[72] Roth, in this very same essay, cites a passage in which we read: "It is very likely that the bureaucratization of society will one day subdue capitalism just as it did in antiquity. Then the 'anarchy of production' will be replaced by that 'order' which, in a very similar way, characterized the late Roman Empire and, even more, the New Kingdom and the rule of the Ptolemies in Egypt."[73]

Irrationalism, however, can never be totally absent from any social arrangement. This is a basic premise of Weber's analysis. What are the possibilities for some form of irrational behavior escaping from the noumenal into the phenomenal realm? Could a force appear which would overturn or at least retard the impersonal machine of bureaucracy? Could some charismatic figure assemble a political party and thwart the operation of the process of total rationalization? Did Weber foresee something like the Nazi movement?

---

70. Guenther Roth, "Introduction," *Economy and Society*, LXIII.

71. *Ibid.*, 991.

72. *Ibid.* Cf. Gary North, "Combatting Bureaucracy: Let a Hundred Otepkas Bloom," *Reason*, V (Oct., 1973).

73. *Ibid.*, LII. Weber's reference to the "anarchy of production" and "order" would appear to be a means of gently chiding the hope of Marx and Engels that socialism would in some way solve the problem of the loss of human freedom under capitalist techniques of mass production and the "anarchy" of free market distribution. In opposition to this, Weber argues that any system of rationalized labor will fall under the domination of bureaucracy. On Marx and Engels' position, see North, *Marx's Religion*, 60-61, 113-17.

Scholars do not agree at this point. Talcott Parsons writes that "considering the blindness of most of his contemporaries, Weber on the whole saw the nature of the crisis, and the general direction of change very clearly. He did not predict Hitler, but he quite clearly saw that a large-scale charismatic movement in reaction against modern 'liberal' institutions but with certain democratic elements was a very real possibility."[74] Parsons even goes beyond this:

> Any situation where an established institutional order has to a considerable extent become disorganized, where established routines, expectations, and symbols are broken up or are under attack is a favourable situation for such a movement. This creates widespread psychological insecurity which in turn is susceptible of reintegration in terms of attachment to a charismatic movement. . . . There is reason to believe that a social order of which a system of rational-legal authority is an important part is considerably more subject to this kind of disorganization than is a highly traditionalized society.[75]

This may very well be true, but it would be hard to draw such an assessment of rational-legal authority directly from anything Weber actually wrote. Reason is a dynamic force in Weber's system, as Parsons argues, but it was Weber's assertion that reason creates a bureaucratic cage from which escape is almost impossible. It was another of his paradoxes: a dynamic force turns upon itself, even as the traditional Protestantism of inner-worldly asceticism helped to unleash the dynamic force of rationalization.

In partial contrast to Parson's position, Reinhard Bendix declares flatly, "Weber did not at all foresee the development of totalitarian government."[76] Bendix does think that Weber's analysis can account for such a possibility, however. Totalitarians would gain power by substituting substantive principles in order to thwart formal law. Arbitrary rule can then reassert itself. A dual chain of authority can be established, the Party and the State, thus destroying the unity of bureaucratic command which was a fundamental part of Weber's perspective. But Bendix shows that this will lead to the destruction of stable operating norms; bureaucrats will therefore fight back by withholding information or in other ways hindering the imposition of what are "irrational" demands from the bureaucratic point of view.

Weber no doubt would have been willing to admit that substantive totalitarian leadership, like any charismatic force, would act as a barrier to the triumph of formally rational law, economics, and politics. What he

---

74. Parsons, "Introduction," *Theory*, 85.
75. *Ibid.*, 71.
76. Bendix, *Max Weber: An Intellectual Portrait* (Garden City, N. Y.: Anchor, 1962), 466.

would not accept is the premise that such opposition is more than temporary. Political charisma is constantly subjected to the process of routinization by professional bosses. "Emotional revolutionism is followed by the traditionalist routine of everyday life; the crusading leader and the faith itself fade away, or, what is even more effective, the faith becomes part of the conventional phraseology of political Philistines and banausic technicians."[77] The result is clear: "After coming to power the following of a crusader usually degenerates very easily into a quite common stratum of spoilsmen."[78]

At best, Weber was unsure of what was to come in the way of political leadership: "Therefore, today, one cannot yet see in any way how the management of politics as a 'vocation' will shape itself. Even less can one see along what avenue opportunities are opening to which political talents can be put for satisfactory political tasks."[79] One thing does seem certain, however: Weber did not regard the modern legal-rational system of authority as unstable. This may very well constitute a major flaw in his analysis—that, at least, is my own belief. For example, he was only too aware of the enthusiasm that war had generated in the early months of 1914. He knew that war serves men as a substitute for the loss of *Gemeinschaft*: "As the consummated threat of violence among modern polities, war creates a pathos and a sentiment of community. War thereby makes for an unconditionally devoted and sacrificial community among the combatants and releases an active mass compassion and love for those who are in need."[80] War creates in the army on the field "a community unto death." It allows men to believe once again that their deaths have some meaning: ". . . in war, and in this massiveness *only* in war, the individual can *believe* that he knows he is dying 'for' something."[81] The same passion and the same sense of community, Weber might have concluded, is present in the thirst for revolutionary action. Given Weber's realization of modern man's frantic rush into personalized, internal, or irrational outlets as ways of escaping the iron cage of rationalization, he should have been more alert to the possibility of the popularity of a doctrine which could proclaim that "War alone brings all human energies to their highest tension and sets a seal of nobility on the peoples who have the virtue to face it."[82] Roger Caillois' *Man and the Sacred* pinpoints the problem: contemporary

77. "Politics as a Vocation," Gerth and Mills, 125.
78. *Ibid.* Cf. Mommsen: "In the endless struggle between creative charisma and rational bureaucracy the latter, in Weber's opinion, was bound to win, if only because it had every material condition on its side." Mommsen, *op. cit.*, 38.
79. *Ibid.*, 114.
80. "Religious Rejections of the World," *ibid.*, 335.
81. *Ibid.*
82. Benito Mussolini, "The Doctrine of Fascism," in *Readings on Fascism and National Socialism* (Denver: Alan Swallow, n.d.), 15. This is a translation of his article for the *Enciclopedia Italiana*, vol. XIV.

rationalized culture has stifled the operation of ritualistic chaos as an emotional outlet; the result has been the rechanneling of this urge to destruction into avenues of technological, systematic chaos, i.e., the advent of total war.[83] Or, one could add, of total revolution.

Weber was too skilled a historian to be completely beguiled by the metaphor of growth. He would never have argued that "society" in some way "develops"—as some biological entity develops—irrespective of historical events. He did not see societies as concrete entities that follow a predetermined pattern of growth that, in Robert Nisbet's summary, is continuous, directional, immanent, irreversible, and uniformitarian.[84] Yet many passages can be gleaned from his writings that indicate that he believed in just such an analysis of modern Occidental rationalization. One wonders if he ever took seriously the possibility that the bureaucratic machine might break down, that it might not be a self-sustaining process. Rationalization as a continuing process may not be inevitable in a world of total—and even totalitarian—specialization. Men who have lost any vision of life's meaning—who have substituted methodology for meaning, to use Weber's characterization—may not be equipped to keep the machine running smoothly.[85]

If Cochrane is correct in his thesis that Rome fell as a result of the collapse of its own intellectual presuppositions, then a new Cochrane thesis may yet be applied to the twentieth century. The antinomy of the rational and the irrational was basic to Weber's treatment of society, and he did not believe that any society could ever overcome that tension completely. In an age which finds itself increasingly bound in a cage of

---

83. Roger Caillois, *Man and the Sacred* (Glencoe, Ill.: Free Press, 1959), esp. ch. 4.

84. Robert A. Nisbet, *Social Change and History* (New York: Oxford University Press, 1969), traces the impact of the metaphor of growth on the history of Western social philosophy and social science. For a brief introduction to the book, see my review in *Modern Age* (Fall, 1969). On Weber's rejection of the use of "cultural stages" as anything more than useful classification devices, see the passage cited by Roth, "Introduction," *Economy and Society*, xxxviii.

85. A thought-provoking discussion of the inner antinomy of Western rationalized culture is offered by Walter A. Weisskopf in his book, *Alienation and Economics* (New York: Dutton, 1971), ch. 2. He argues that all societies require some forms of repression, especially inner discipline, and that for a century, "technical rationalism [has] undermined *all* belief systems which could have supported any kind of repression, even the one inherent in social, technical, organizational, bureaucratic rationalism itself. . . . However, one should not even call science and technology ideologies or rationalizations because, being value-empty means, they are not able to support, legitimize, rationalize, justify their own existence. . . . They have no justification in any superordained, all-embracing value system" (pp. 51-52). Recent expressions of discontent by intellectuals and young people in the Soviet Union indicate that even the Marxist religion of materialism is not without its heretical opponents. An important study, based on the Soviet underground literature—the *Samizdat* (self-published) typewritten and photocopied literature—is Cornelia Gerstenmaier's *The Voices of the Silent* (New York: Hart, 1972).

technological specialization, threatened by irrational outbursts of both a systematic and unsystematic kind, the antinomies are compounded. Since the technological cage no longer rests on the old Puritan asceticism, it has appropriated other fundamentally religious presuppositions to serve as a foundation: increased economic output is desireable in itself; progress through technology is likely (if, indeed, it is not irresistible); democracy is a self-evident good; the Lord helps those who help themselves (Ben Franklin's legacy).[86] When these depart—and some of our contemporary ecological activists are challenging several of them—what then? The modern ecological prophets are now echoing the words of the Hebrew prophets of the eighth century, B.C.: beware of the sword, the pestilence, and the famine.

Weber believed that certain forces are, once begun, autonomous and self-sustaining. Human reason is one of them; Western rationalization is another. He accepted this on faith. The result was a blind spot in his concept of social change. Social statics are by no means that certain to those who must live in the 1970's.[87] The age of the charismatic prophet—the gifted individual who serves in Weber's system as the primary motivating factor in social change[88]—may not yet be abolished.

Conclusion

Weber's importance to modern sociological theory cannot be over-estimated. Indeed, he is the foremost social theorist of this century, although he has been dead half a century. He took the philosophical presuppositions of post-Kantian rationalism, and he applied a devastating critique to a society built on those same presuppositions. This is why his work is so important in the final third of the twentieth century. The writings of Theodore Roszak and Charles Reich will not be understood apart from an awareness of Weber's far superior intellectual contributions. His critique will survive when Reich and Roszak are long forgotten (and they will be forgotten soon enough).[89] If the defender of modern post-

---

86. Gary North, "The Theology of the Exponential Curve," *The Freeman*, XX (May, 1970), included as a chapter in *An Introduction to Christian Economics* (Nutley, N. J.: Craig Press, 1973).

87. Gary North, "Statist Bureaucracy in the Modern Economy," *The Freeman*, XX (Jan., 1970), reprinted in *ibid*. On the problems of over-bureaucratized industries, see Robert Townsend's irreverent and humorous *Up the Organization* (New York: Knopf, 1970). Cf. "America the Inefficient," *Time* (March 23, 1970). A number of case studies of corporate crises can be found in Richard Austin Smith's *Corporations in Crisis* (Garden City, N. Y.: Doubleday, 1963). It is not surprising that the companies he selects as examples are those generally associated with government contracts and those companies that were tempted to overexpand during times of state-inaugurated monetary expansion, only to be "whipsawed" when the government's central bank temporarily halted the increase of new money coming into the economy.

88. This is the thesis, which I accept, offered by Wolfgang Mommsen, *op. cit.*, 33 ff.

89. Theodore Roszak, *The Making of a Counter Culture* (Garden City, N. Y.:

Kantian civilization is to convince his audience of the validity of that civilization, he must come to grips with Weber's writings. Weber looked deeply into the very heart of modern society, and he constructed a terrifying vision of where it would inescapably lead.

The Christian does not need to accept the rational-irrational dichotomy of modern thought. He therefore can criticize both Weber and modern culture from a standpoint removed from both. But at the same time, he can use Weber as a means of gaining insight into the workings of modern bureaucratic organization. Weber has offered the Christian critic an introduction to the crisis of our age. The Christian can better see where a society grounded on the rational control of life by self-proclaimed autonomous man is going. If a man like Weber could see no way out, given the presuppositions of modern life and thought, then the Christian is informed of the crucial nature of his task of intellectual and social reconstruction. "Where there is no vision, the people perish: but he that keepeth the law, happy is he" (Prov. 29:18).

Admittedly, Weber underestimated the extreme forms that irrationalism might take in this century. He overestimated the irresistable nature of the processes of rationalization. But if the alternatives to his bureaucratic cage consist of irrationalism, or the rise of totalitarian parties, or the collapse of industrial production, the secularist has not made his commitment to modern autonomous man very convincing. If Weber was correct, then the bureaucratic cage is waiting; if he was wrong through a failure to see the possibilities of social cataclysm, then another kind of terror faces modern man. In either case, the culture built on the foundations of Kantian autonomy promises destruction of the idea of free, responsible man. That is why the Christian needs to take Weber seriously. He needs to be reassured that the onions of Egypt are not worth the slavery needed to produce them (Num. 11:4-6). If Christians should be forced to leave the cage at some point, they should be forewarned that escape is worth the sacrifice. Weber stands as the prophet of the world to be lost, and he reminds us that the loss will be a mighty blessing. The task of Christian reconstruction will thereby seem more mandatory and less foreboding.

Avenues for Christian Sociology

Weber's distinction between formal rationalism and substantive rationalism could easily serve as a watershed. It revives that ancient distinction be-

---

Doubleday, 1969); Charles Reich, *The Greening of America* (New York: Random House, 1970). The latter book, incredibly, was a runaway best-seller. A devastating review of it was made by the English journalist, Henry Fairlie, "The Practice of the Puffers," *Encounter* (Aug. 1971). Cf. Philip Nobile (ed.), *The CON III Controversy: The Critics Look at the Greening of America* (New York: Pocket Books, 1971).

tween the letter and spirit of the law. Any number of crucial questions can be asked by serious Christian investigators. How can we preserve human freedom in institutions that are heavily substantive in their legal structure? How can the arbitrariness of human decisions be restricted? How can the letter of the law be imposed to force judges, both civil and ecclesiastical, from deviating from the spirit of the law? But we must also face the alternate question: how can we preserve the spirit of the law from bureaucratic formalism, in which the appearance of legality is present, but the judge uses formal standards of litigation to impose his own will? How can legal technique be restrained in its apparently irreversible thirst for ever more technical jurisprudence? How can church courts be preserved from this same blight, where the body of Christ is institutionally impotent to reach simple decisions? Men are not saved by *Robert's Rules of Order*.

The answer seems to lie in the investigation of the one and the many. We need a truly biblical pluralism, in which local institutions, voluntary as well as compulsory, provide communal bonds and dispense substantive justice. The constant expansion of central power along bureaucratic lines must be reversed; the central government must limit itself to a smaller set of rules and regulations. Similarly, local congregations must increase their sovereignty. Local ownership of church property is only a minimal step in the right direction. The face-to-face situation which permits personal decisions by more patriarchal leaders—analogous to the father's rule in the family—needs to replace the distant, more abstract rule of the administrative bureaucracy. The many must not be permitted to be swallowed up by the political one. Christian sociologists must be guided by biblical law in this search for proper boundaries of legitimate sovereignty; they must use God's revelation to discover the middle excluded by anarchism and totalitarianism. Between formal law and substantive arbitrariness, Christians must find the proper applications of biblical law; autonomous human reason has been pushed as far as it can go, as Weber's writings demonstrate, and it has led to despair, confusion, and continual tension. Christian institutions dare not imitate secular counterparts. Christians need to return to the one thing which sets them apart intellectually from secular scholarship: the revelation of the Bible, as interpreted by a living Spirit. Without this alternative, we are as doomed as Weber and his intellectual heirs.

The incentive to rethink the social institutions of modern life is not simply an intellectual exercise. Weber assumed that the development of technology is irreversible, but if it is not—if it should turn back upon itself, self-destruct on masses of computerized data (much of it erroneous)— Christians will not be immune to the social effects. Roberto Vacca's chilling prophecy in *The Coming Dark Age* (Doubleday, 1973) of a breakdown in computer technology should be warning enough of the possibility that there are limits to technological advance. The message of Deuteronomy 8 and 28, that blessings follow the obedient culture and destruction follows an apostate culture, should not be dismissed automatically. When Gunther Stent predicts a society in which few people take knowledge seriously, since all meaning has disappeared from the various academic callings, Christians should reconsider their own confidence in a culture which is both apostate and productive. Either the culture's faith must change, or else the endless progress will be shown to be all too finite.

If a nuclear war or a major economic, technological, or social disruption should occur in our lifetimes, we should understand that there are no social and political vacuums in life. If the push toward total centralization should continue, thus producing a breakdown first at the local level, followed by the ultimate loss of central authority, other groups will try to step in and fill the local vacuum. Christians must be psychologically prepared and intellectually ready to assume authority (and therefore responsibility) in local situations. If Christians retreat from this responsibility, other groups, possibly occult or criminal in nature, will do so. Christians must not miss this opportunity for social reconstruction.

The gift of logical reason was given by God to man in order that he might order the revelation of God for himself. It was not given him that he might by means of it legislate as to what is possible and what is actual. When man makes a "system" for himself of the content of revelation given him in Scripture, this system is subject to, not independent of, Scripture. Thus the idea of system employed by the Christian is quite different from the idea of system as employed in modern philosophy.

It is therefore pointless for Christians to tell non-Christians that Christianity is "in accord with the law of contradiction" unless they explain what they mean by this. For the non-Christian will take this statement to mean something entirely different from what the Christian ought to mean by it. The non-Christian does not believe in creation. Therefore, for him the law of contradiction is, like all other laws, something that does not find its ultimate source in the creative activity of God. Accordingly the non-Christian will seek to do by means of the law of contradiction what the Christian has had done for him by God. For the Christian, God legislates as to what is possible and what is impossible for man. For the non-Christian, man determines this for himself. Either positively or negatively the non-Christian will determine the field of possibility and therewith the stream of history by means of the law of contradiction.

Van Til, *An Introduction to Systematic Theology* (Syllabus, 1961), p. 256.

MATHEMATICS

IX

A BIBLICAL VIEW OF MATHEMATICS

By VERN S. POYTHRESS

CONTENTS

1. Introduction

In their world-views, Christian and non-Christian differ at fundamental points. Granted. But surely that doesn't affect mathematics. Here, finally, is a neutral area, where Christian and non-Christian can agree. Both know that $2 + 2 = 4$. How could religious differences ever affect it?

In our culture, such is the usual reaction to a mention of "Christian" mathematics. Incredulity. Yet the irony appears in the fact that this very incredulity exposes at several levels its own *non-neutrality*, its own dogmatically anti-Biblical stance.[1]

I. *The dogmatism of "neutrality"*

Let's look more closely at the "neutrality postulate." This postulate says that the knowledge and structure of a science—for example, mathematics—is not influenced by religious belief.[1a] Or at least science *ought* not to be influenced by religious belief. To put it more baldly, true scientific knowledge remains the same whether or not God exists. We intend to criticize this postulate both in terms of its fit with the actual phenomena of mathematics, and in terms of its internal self-inconsistency.

A. *The neutrality postulate not borne out by the phenomena of mathematics*

The neutrality postulate holds special attractiveness as applied to mathematics, because of the apparent widespread agreement about mathematical truths. "Everybody knows that $2 + 2 = 4$." If religious beliefs really have an influence, why is there such widespread agreement, cutting across religious lines? We intend to answer this question on several levels: (1) by showing that the agreement in mathematics is not so widespread, nor so uncorrelated with religious beliefs, as the textbooks would have you believe (§§2-7); (2) by showing that non-Christian philosophy of mathematics is involved in deep-set cleavages and antinomies in its understanding of even so simple a truth as $2 + 2 = 4$ (§§11-18); (3) by showing that only on a thoroughgoing Biblical basis can one genuinely understand and affirm the real *agreement* about mathematical truths (§25).

So, first of all, what differences have arisen in mathematics in connection with religious belief? Differences have arisen over arithmetical truth, over standards for proof, over number-theoretic truth, over geometric truth, over truths of analysis, over mathematical existence—not to mention the long-standing epistemological disputes over the source of mathematical truth. Let's consider these areas one at a time.

---

1. The anti-Biblical presuppositions of innocent-looking agnostic statements have long been a target for Van Til's penetrating criticism. See, for example, Cornelius Van Til, *A Survey of Christian Epistemology*, Volume II of the series *In Defense of Biblical Christianity* (Philadelphia: den Dulk Christian Foundation, 1969), pp. 212-213.

1a. Over against the neutrality postulate, we are by *no* means advocating a "relativity of truth" which would say that what is really true depends on the observer. On the contrary, the truth is (by definition) what God knows, and hence completely fixed from the beginning. That much we presuppose. However, in Parts I and II, and especially in Part I, we want to focus on what *people* believe and know about mathematical truth. *Which* truths they know, and what they do with them, depend on their religious convictions.

2. Arithmetical truth

It may surprise the reader to learn that not *everyone* agrees that '2 + 2 — 4' is true. But, on second thought, it must be apparent that no radical monist can remain satisfied with '2 + 2 = 4.' If with Parmenides[2] one thinks that all is one, if with Vedantic Hinduism[3] he thinks that all plurality is illusion, '2 + 2 — 4' is an illusory statement. On the most ultimate level of being, 1 + 1 — 1.[4]

What does this imply? Even the simplest arithmetical truths can be sustained only in a world-view which acknowledges an ultimate metaphysical plurality in the world—whether Trinitarian, polytheistic, or chance-produced plurality. At the same time, the simplest arithmetical truths also presuppose ultimate metaphysical *unity* for the world—at least sufficient unity to guard the continued existence of "sames." Two apples *remain* apples while I am counting them; the symbol '2' is in some sense the *same* symbol at different times, standing for the *same* number.

So, at the very beginning of arithmetic, we are already plunged into the metaphysical problem of unity and plurality, of the one and the many. As Van Til and Rushdoony have pointed out, this problem finds its solution only in the doctrine of the ontological Trinity.[5] For the moment, we shall not dwell on the thorny metaphysical arguments, but note only that without *some* real unity and plurality, '2 + 2 = 4' falls into limbo. The "agreement" over mathematical truth is achieved partly by the process, described so elegantly by Thomas Kuhn and Michael Polanyi, of excluding from the scientific community people of differing convictions.[6] Radical monists, for example, are not invited to contribute to mathematical symposia.

---

2. William K. C. Guthrie, *A History of Greek Philosophy*, Vol. II (Cambridge: at the University Press, 1967), p. 30.

3. "In thought should it be heeded, / Here is no plurality anywhere; / By death is he bound fast to death / Who here contemplates plurality." Paul Deussen, *The Philosophy of the Upanishads*, trans. by A. S. Geden (Edinburgh: T. & T. Clark, 1906), p. 232, quoted from Brih (adâranyaka) 4.4.19. ". . . there is no plurality and no change. Nature which presents the appearance of plurality and change is a mere illusion (mâyâ)" (*ibid.*, p. 237).

4. "There is however in the whole universe, alike in heaven and on earth, nothing besides the atman:—'There is no second outside of him, no other distinct from him.' " *ibid.*, p. 157, quote from Brih (adâranyaka) 4.3.23-30. Cf. also Sravepalli Radhakrishnan, *Indian Philosophy*, Vol. 2 (London: George Allen & Unwin Ltd., 1927), p. 535.

5. Cornelius Van Til, *The Defense of the Faith*, revised and abridged (Philadelphia: Presbyterian and Reformed Publishing Co., 1963), pp. 25-26; *A Survey of Christian Epistemology*, p. 96; and Rousas J. Rushdoony, *The One and the Many: Studies in the Philosophy of Order and Ultimacy* (Nutley, N. J.: Craig Press, 1971).

6. Thomas S. Kuhn, *The Structure of Scientific Revolutions*, 2nd ed. (Chicago: University of Chicago Press, 1970), p. 168; and Michael Polanyi, *Personal Knowledge: Towards a Post-Critical Philosophy* (London: Routledge & Kegan Paul, 1958), pp. 160-167.

3. Standards for proof

Mathematicians do not always agree about which proofs are valid. Intuitionists like L. E. J. Brouwer and Arend Heyting do not accept the law of excluded middle or the proof by *reductio ad absurdum* (proof of an assertion by deducting a contradiction from its negation).[7] Hence they will not accept some proofs that others will accept. The differences between intuitionists and the others have religious roots in the fact that these intuitionists will not accept as meaningful an appeal to the fact that God knows the truth about the matter, whether or not we do.[8] For them, in some sense truth has its ultimate locus in the *human* mind. Mathematics is "only concerned with *mental* constructions" (italics mine).[9]

4. Number-theoretic truth

The intuitionists also provide the most convenient example of how religious differences can lead to disagreement over number-theoretic truth. Consider the statements

A: Somewhere in the decimal expansion of pi there occurs a sequence of seven consecutive 7's.

B: There are infinitely many primes p such that p + 2 is prime.

In 1975, no man knows whether either A or B is true. Nor is there any known procedure by which, in a finite amount of time, we could be assured of obtaining a definite yes-or-no answer. For the intuitionists, this means that A and B should not be considered as *either* true or false.[10] It makes no sense to *talk* about truth or falsehood so long as we have no way of checking. On the other hand, the Christian, on the basis of I John 3:20 ("God is greater than our hearts, and he knows everything"), Psalm 147:5, and other passages, is likely to feel that at least *God* knows perfectly definitely whether A or B is true. Our own limitations set no limits to His knowledge (§24) (cf. Isa. 55:8-9; Ps. 139:6, 12, 17-18).

5. Geometrical truth

Immanuel Kant's philosophical commitments led him to the conviction

---

7. Arend Heyting, "Disputation," in Paul Benacerraf and Hilary Putnam, eds., *Philosophy of Mathematics: Selected Readings* (Englewood Cliffs, N. J.: Prentice-Hall, Inc., 1964), p. 61.

8. "The . . . point of view that there are no *non-experienced* truths and that logic is not an absolutely reliable instrument to discover truths, has found acceptance with regard to mathematics much later than with regard to practical life and to science" (italics mine). Luitzen E. J. Brouwer, "Consciousness, Philosophy, and Mathematics," in *Philosophy of Mathematics*, p. 78. Note the correlation that Brouwer makes between "life" and "science" on the one hand (expressing a religious world-view) and mathematics on the other. Elsewhere he acknowledges his philosophical debt to Kant, "Intuitionism and Formalism," in *ibid.*, p. 69.

9. Arend Heyting, "Disputation," in *Philosophy of Mathematics*, p. 61.

10. Cf. Luitzen E. J. Brouwer, "Intuitionism and Formalism," in *ibid.*, p. 77, and Arend Heyting, "Disputation," in *ibid.*, p. 56, for intuitionistic discussion of questions similar to A and B.

that we know *a priori* the truths of Euclidean geometry. However, with the advent of the non-Euclidean geometries of Bolyai-Lobatchewsky and Riemann,[11] and then the general relativity of Einstein, the "truth" of Euclidean geometry was put in question.[12] Even the question of what it *means* for a geometry to be "true to" the world is now in dispute.[13] And the deep-going philosophical differences between operationalism and realism, positivism and Platonism heavily influence one's conclusions.

One might object that purely axiomatic geometry (as opposed to applied geometry) is at least free from these difficulties. Everyone can agree when a geometrical theorem is proved. But once again the intuitionists object to *reductio ad absurdum* proofs. Not only that, but one finds that a rigorous adherence to the demands of axiomatic geometry in the modern set-theoretic style requires the use of uncountable sets of points and uncountable sets of congruence transformations, thereby introducing the philosophical problematics of infinity (see §7 below).

6. *Truths of analysis*

Disagreements also arise over the truths of analysis. One of the primary reasons for this is that only a countable number of the real numbers are definable in the sense of being computable by a Turing machine. By Cantor's theorem, the vast "majority" of reals are thus undefinable! Are we to treat these undefinable reals on the same plane as computable reals? Our answer to this question will depend heavily on our prior philosophical convictions.

If we have the Platonist philosophical disposition which supposes that real numbers are "there" whether or not we can define them, we are predisposed toward classical analysis. If, on the other hand, we have a more anthropocentric world-view which regards man as the measure of all things,[14] we are likely to prefer constructive analysis such as de-

---

11. For an evaluation of non-Euclidean geometry from a Christian viewpoint, cf. the discussion in Dirk H. Th. Vollenhoven, *De Wijsbegeerte der Wiskunde van Theïstisch Standpunt* (Amsterdam: Wed. G. Van Soest, 1918), pp. 140-147.

12. Cf., for example, the discussion in John J. C. Smart, ed., *Problems of Space and Time* (New York: The Macmillan Company, 1964).

13. "Are we, following Poincaré, to attribute these findings [of physical experiment] to the influence of an external force postulated for the purpose? Or are we to take our findings at face value, and accept the geometry to which we are led as a natural geometry for physical science? The answer to this methodological question will depend largely on the *universality* of the geometry thus found—whether the geometry found in one situation or field of physical discourse may consistently be extended to others—and in the end partly on the predilection of the individual or of his colleagues or of his times." Howard P. Robertson, "Geometry as a Branch of Physics," in Paul A. Schilpp, ed., *Albert Einstein: Philosopher-Scientist* (Evanston, Ill.: The Library of Living Philosophers, Inc., 1949), p. 325.

14. Compare the discussion in §3.

veloped by Errett Bishop.[15] Finally, if we are committed to a more conventionist view of mathematics (see §14), or, like Leibniz, to the reality of infinitesimals, we are likely to be favorably disposed toward the nonstandard analysis of Robinson.[16] Thus three different world-views, if they do not absolutely determine, yet decisively influence one's attitude toward alternative constructions of analysis.

Since the undergraduate is usually exposed only to the classical version of analysis, he gets the impression that this version is the unchallengeable gospel truth. Yet the theorems of different versions of analysis are sometimes in radical conflict. In classical analysis, the set of real numbers

$$\{X \in R: \text{ there exists an } n \in N = \text{natural numbers such that } X > 1/n\}$$

produces a Dedekind cut dividing the reals into two parts, positive and non-positive; in non-standard analysis, the same definition produces a cut of reals into two parts, positive non-infinitesimal on the one hand and non-positive plus positive infinitesimal on the other; in constructive analysis, the same definition produces still a third result, namely a division of reals into absolutely positive, absolutely non-positive, and a third group of "don't know."

Again, in constructive analysis *every* constructible function on [0, 1] is uniformly continuous,[17] while in classical analysis the cardinal number $c^c = 2^c$ of discontinuous functions on [0, 1] is greater than (!) the cardinal number c of continuous functions. It can hardly be denied that, in this area at least, philosophico-religious differences have had their impact!

7. *Mathematical existence*

Does 2 exist? Does ¼ exist? Does $\sqrt{2}$ exist? Does —2 exist? Does $\sqrt{-1}$ exist? Does dx exist? Does the transfinite number aleph-two exist? Does a measurable cardinal exist?

Each of these questions has been debated at some point in the history of mathematics. Part of the problem, of course, is to say what we *mean* by an existence claim. Mathematical entities don't exist in the same way as rocks. But questions of mathematical existence are nevertheless important because they relate to the legitimacy of using certain mathematical symbols in our calculations. If certain mathematical entities don't "exist,"

---

15. Errett Bishop, *Foundations of Constructive Analysis* (New York: McGraw-Hill, 1967).

16. Abraham Robinson, *Nonstandard Analysis* (Amsterdam: North-Holland Publishing Company, 1966).

17. Luitzen E. J. Brouwer, "Consciousness, Philosophy, and Mathematics," in *Philosophy of Mathematics*, p. 79.

presumably they ought not to be used. Because "1/0 doesn't exist," one can't argue

$$0 \cdot 1 = 0 \cdot 2$$
$$(1/0) \cdot 0 \cdot 1 = (1/0) \cdot 0 \cdot 2$$
$$1 \cdot 1 = 1 \cdot 2$$
$$1 = 2.$$

Opinions about mathematical existence are related to religious differences. Consider several examples: the Pythagoreans, for philosophico-religious reasons, did not want to acknowledge the existence of irrationals like $\sqrt{2}$.[18] Leibniz's philosophical convictions about infinity favorably disposed him toward using infinitesimals like dx.[19] From a self-consciously Christian viewpoint, D. H. Th. Vollenhoven and Herman Dooyeweerd rejected the existence of uncountable transfinite numbers, ostensibly because of their antinomic character.[20] (The author does not agree with their decision at this point, but the fact is that their mathematical convictions were religiously motivated.) Such examples show clearly that a question of mathematical existence may not be a religiously neutral affair. More generally, mathematics in the past has not been a religiously neutral science. In short, the neutrality postulate is not borne out by the history of mathematics.

B. *The neutrality postulate internally self-inconsistent*

So far we have focused on the question of whether the neutrality postulate really fits the phenomena of mathematics. We have seen that decisions about mathematical truth are frequently religiously biased. Even apart from these historical facts, however, the neutrality postulate is beset with serious *internal* difficulties:

8. *In its general metaphysical claims*

The neutrality postulate makes the implicit metaphysical claims that (a) mathematical reality is not the result of God's creating activity in any

---

18. *A History of Greek Philosophy*, Vol. I, p. 265.
19. "Toute l'entreprise de Leibniz consiste à créer une logique de l'infini, dont toutes ses doctrines, *mathématiques*, physiques, métaphysiques, *théologiques* et *morales*, ne sont que des aspects divers."—"The whole undertaking of Leibniz consists in creating a logic of infinity, of which all his doctrines, *mathematical*, physical, metaphysical, *theological*, and *moral*, are only diverse aspects" (italics mine). Emile Bréhier, *Histoire de la Philosophie*, Tome II (Paris: Presses Universitaires de France, 1968), p. 210.
20. Vollenhoven, *De Wijsbegeerte der Wiskunde*, p. 188, and Herman Dooyeweerd, *A New Critique of Theoretical Thought*, Vol. II (Philadelphia: Presbyterian and Reformed Publishing Co., 1969), pp. 45, 87, 340. Dooyeweerd's Christian philosophy considers antinomies to be a sure mark of speculative thought which does not recognize the limits of the creature (*ibid.*, p. 38).

essential way (for if it were a result of God's work, we could not imagine it "remaining the same" even though God didn't exist); (b) God's nature and the nature of number are not significantly involved in one another; they are not so related that one could infer properties of one from a study of the other. Otherwise, differing opinions about God might, for all we know, lead to differing opinions about the nature of number.

Claim (a) is already a denial of creation in its Biblical sense, as we shall see (§19); claim (b) involves a denial of the Trinity (see §19). At the moment, however, we are interested, not so much in the fact that these claims contradict orthodox Christian doctrine, as in the fact that they have a far-reaching, astonishingly dogmatic *metaphysical* character. The claim that metaphysics is irrelevant to mathematics turns out to be itself a metaphysical claim about mathematics. The neutrality postulate turns out to be highly "non-neutral." To say the least, this is a paradoxical situation.

9. *In its general epistemological claims*

The neutrality postulate is involved in a similar paradox regarding its implicit *epistemological* claims. This postulate denies, in effect, that God can reveal any truths about mathematics. Suppose He could. Then conceivably He might reveal information not already established by other means. Then those people who believed what He revealed would stand in a different position in mathematics from those who did not. Such differences arising from religious belief would violate the neutrality postulate.

Now the reader may argue that all this is purely speculative, since God has not in fact chosen to record mathematical theorems in Scripture. But note the following. (1) Whether God has given us mathematical information can be determined only by an actual examination of Scripture, not (as the neutrality postulate presumably claims) in an *a priori* fashion. (2) Though the Bible does not contain mathematical theorems in the modern sense, it does contain teachings that instruct us, in certain cases, about what kind of mathematics is legitimate (cf. the examples in §§5-9). (3) God's general (pre-redemptive) revealing activity is involved in *every* kind of mathematical knowledge (see §23). (4) In the light of (1)-(3), the neutrality postulate definitely is concerning itself with religious issues.

In fact, the neutrality postulate claims to know about what the relation of God and numbers can and cannot be, what the relation of theology and mathematics can and cannot be, not only in the past, but (if the postulate is to mean anything substantial) also in the future. Suppose now that we ask how these sweeping claims to knowledge can be backed up. The answer must be: the knowledge comes by revelation—either Christian revelation or some secularized version of revelation. For, in backing up the neutrality postulate, one is involved in explaining how one *comes* to know its supposed truth. This very explaining constitutes a doctrine of revelation. Usually people talk about revelation from some metaphysical ultimate other than God (mind, matter, sense experience, Reason); nevertheless, men require revelation. In short, the neutrality postulate is entangled in the paradoxical net of being able to deny the relevance of (theistic) revelation only on the basis of an underlying doctrine of (secular) revelation. The neutrality postulate is epistemologically non-neutral.

10. *In its general ethical claims*

Third, the neutrality postulate is involved in paradox regarding its implicit *ethical* claims. It makes a statement about what "ought" to be:

Mathematics "ought not" to be influenced by religious belief.

Let us name this statement 'C.' C contradicts Christian ethics, as we shall see (§26). But, once again, let us focus on the *internal* paradox involved in this ethical claim. C: mathematics ought not to be influenced by religious belief. In particular, presumably it ought not to be influenced by the ethical judgments correlated with religious belief. Therefore, mathematics ought not to be influenced by the ethical judgment C that "mathematics ought not to be influenced by religious belief." We are confronted with a self-destructive ethical claim.

The ethical claim C can rescue itself from oblivion only when it is supported by another claim, D.

D: Claim C is not a *religious* (albeit it is an *ethical*) belief.

But most people would agree that general claims like D concerning the relation of the religious to the ethical *are* religious claims. They are closely related to the question whether right and wrong are defined (say) by God's commands or by conscience. Let us therefore agree that D is a religious belief.

But now we are again entangled. First, from C it follows that

E: mathematics ought to be influenced by C.

Also from C, we obtain

F: for any G, if G is a religious belief, mathematics ought not to be influenced by G.

As a special case of F, when C is substituted for G, we get

H: if C is a religious belief, mathematics ought not to be influenced by C.

From E and H it follows

D: C is not a religious belief.

Hence D is a consequence of C. Hence C has, as a consequence, a *religious* belief D. Hence presumably C itself is religious, a contradiction of D.

II. *Antinomies of anti-theistic²¹ mathematics*

11. *Classification of the anti-theist's difficulties*

So far we have concentrated on the difficulties specific to the neutrality postulate. The neutrality postulate, we have seen, is beset by conflict with phenomena in the history of mathematics (§§2-7) and by internal self-inconsistency (§§8-10).

Other difficulties, however, the neutrality postulate shares with all non-Christian, non-theistic world-views (whether or not these views claim for themselves neutrality). To these difficulties common to all non-Christian versions of mathematics we now turn.

Of course, in a sense each particular world-view—materialism, idealism, positivism, Marxism—yes, each individual thinker, has difficulties all his own. A thoroughgoing criticism, from a Christian point of view, would thus have to deal with each thinker separately. In this paper we cannot hope to do more than sketch an outline of the way criticism should proceed. A unified procedure of criticism is to some extent possible because *all* non-Christian systems share similar problems, growing out of their common refusal to honor the true God.

For convenience, we divide the problems into three major areas: metaphysical, epistemological, and ethical. We expect non-Christian philosophy of mathematics (a) to have metaphysical problems because it has abandoned the true Source of being; (b) to have epistemological problems because it has abandoned the true Source of knowledge; (c) to have ethical problems because it has abandoned the true Source of value. We take up these topics in the order (b), (c), (a).

A. *Epistemological problems of anti-theistic mathematics: a priori/ a posteriori*

Mathematicians, like other scientists, have a certain confidence in their convictions. This needs to be justified. How do we come to know that $2 + 2 = 4$? By internal means (*a priori*; independent of experience) or by external means (*a posteriori*; derived from experience)? Do we gain the knowledge by introspection? By reminiscence (Plato)? By logical argument (Russell)? Or do we gain it by repeated experience of two apples

---

21. Here we follow Van Til's practice (e.g., *A Survey of Christian Epistemology*, pp. 210-223) of describing non-Christian world-views, whether "neutral," pantheistic, deistic, or atheistic, by their true colors. The only true theism is the one which worships and serves the *true* God, the Father of Jesus Christ (I John 2:22-24; II John 7-9), acknowledging Him as Lord of all (I Cor. 8:6; Eph. 1:21; Acts 10:36). All else is idolatry (Rom. 1:22-25). We will further explore the importance of a radically Biblical approach in §§19-26.

and two apples (John S. Mill)? Or some combination of these? Or is
'2 + 2 = 4' not real "knowledge" at all, but simply a linguistic convention
about how we use '2' and '4' (A. J. Ayer)?[22]

12. *The a priori answer*

Whichever answer a person on the anti-theistic side chooses, he is
bound to land himself in difficulties. Suppose that one emphasizes the
a priori character of mathematical knowledge. Then '2 + 2 = 4' is some
kind of universal, eternal truth. But why, in that case, should two apples
plus two apples usually, in experience, make four apples? Why should
an admittedly contingent world offer us repeated instances of this truth,
many more instances than we could expect by chance? If the external
world is *purely* a chance matter, if *anything* can happen in the broadest
possible sense, if the sun may not rise tomorrow, if, as a matter of fact,
there may be no sun, or only a sputnik, when tomorrow comes, if there
may be no tomorrow, etc., can there be any assured statement at all about
apples? Why, for instance, don't apples disappear and appear randomly
while we are counting them? If, on the other hand, the external world
has some degree of regularity mixed in with its chance elements, why
expect that regularity to coincide, in even the remotest way, with the
a priori mathematical expectations of human minds? Such questions can
be multiplied without limit. Once one has made the Cartesian separation
of mind and matter, of *a priori* and *a posteriori*, one can never get them
back together again.

A strict a priorist view is also open to more practical objections. If
mathematics is indeed *a priori*, why do paradoxes arise? Such paradoxes
come in the form of actual contradictions (Burali-forti's paradox, Russell's
paradox) and in the form of various counter-intuitive results (the continuous space-filling curves of Peano, everywhere-continuous nowhere-
differentiable functions, the downward Löwenheim-Skolem theorem, etc.).
The paradoxes seem less threatening today, partly because mathematicians
adopt a more conventionist attitude toward them (§14), partly because
we have disposed of them by modifying our axioms (to avoid contradictions) or modifying our intuitions (to square with the theories). Nevertheless, the paradoxes illustrate that, historically considered, supposedly
a priori mathematical convictions are not always reliable.

---

22. "When we say that analytic propositions [among which Ayer includes mathematical propositions] are devoid of factual content; and consequently that they say
nothing, we are not suggesting that they are senseless in the way that metaphysical
utterances are senseless. For, although they give us no information about any empirical situation, they do enlighten us by illustrating the way in which we *use certain
symbols*" (italics mine). Alfred Jules Ayer, "The *A Priori*," in *Philosophy of Mathematics*, p. 295. This same article contains some discussion of Mill's and Russell's
views of mathematical knowledge.

13. *The a posteriori answer*

It is understandable that these difficulties on the *a priori* side have led people to cast about for an *a posteriori* solution. In this case one emphasized the inductive character of mathematical knowledge. One comes to believe that $2 + 2 = 4$ from 'repeated experience (*a posteriori*) of two objects plus two objects making four objects. All right, but no one has repeated experience of 2,123,955 objects plus 644,101 objects making 2,768,056 objects. So why does he believe that $2,123,955 + 644,101 = 2,768,056$? "Ah," so it is said, "he has generalized from his experience with small numbers." Unfortunately, in the word "generalize" is concealed either an infinite regress or the specter of the *a priori*. We may ask, why does a person "generalize" in one way rather than another? Why, after observing that $3 + 2 = 5, 4 + 2 = 6, \ldots 12 + 2 = 14$, does he conclude (generalize?) that $13 + 2 = 15$ rather than $13 + 2 = 14$ or even 13? In terms of a consistently *a posteriori* viewpoint, the answer can only be, because of previous experience with other generalizations. In other words, he has generalized from previous generalizations. Why has he generalized in *this* particular way from those other generalizations? Because he has generalized from previous experience of generalizing from previous generalizations, and so on. Apparently, one can escape this regress only by saying at some point, "Because that's the way the human mind operates." And then one is confronted with an *a priori* knowledge, or at least *a priori* heuristics.

The *a posteriori* solution is also open to more practical, prosaic objections. What about the constantly growing quantity of abstract, nonvisualizable mathematical entities? To claim that transfinite numbers, topological spaces, and abstract algebras are somehow impressed on us from sense experience takes some stretch of imagination.

14. *The conventionalist answer*

A third attempted solution to the epistemological problem deserves mention, if only because of its widespread popularity among mathematicians themselves. This is the view that mathematics is, in some sense, a mere convention of our language, and thus not "knowledge" at all. $2 + 2 = 4$ because we have agreed in our language to use the words "two" and "four" in just that way (Wittgenstein).[23] Or, to put it another way, in saying "$2 + 2 = 4$" we are just saying "A is A" in a roundabout way (A. J. Ayer).[24] Or, "$2 + 2 = 4$ because it follows from our (conventionally determined) postulates" (formalists).

---

23. Ludwig Witt₎ ᷤstein, *Bemerkungen über die Grundlagen der Mathematik*, herausgegeben und bearbeitet von G. H. von Wright, R. Rhees, G. E. M. Anscombe (Oxford: Basil Blackwell, 1967), pp. 4, 6.
24. "The *A Priori*," in *Philosophy of Mathematics*, p. 300.

All these "conventionalist" answers are really so many variations on the *a priori* solution, inasmuch as one can still ask the same unanswerable questions about why mathematics should prove so useful in dealing with the external world. If it is *pure* convention, why should this be? Or if one says that the conventions are chosen *because* they are useful, one moves into the *a posteriori* camp, where he is confronted with the same unanswerable questions about the role of generalization.[25]

The fact that the conventionalist answer can be used either in an *a priori* or an *a posteriori* direction points up another factor: that the conventionalist "answer" may not really be an answer at all, but simply a shifting of the question from the area of mathematics to that of language. The same *a priori/a posteriori* problems reappear when we ask why (mathematical) language functions adequately.

15. *Implications of Gödel's proof*

At this point, we should mention that, in our opinion, certain proof-theoretic results have intensified the *a priori/a posteriori* problem for an antitheistic philosophy of mathematics. We are referring particularly to Gödel's proof of the incompleteness of Whitehead-Russell's axioms for first-order number theory.[26] This proof has been clasped to the bosom of so many philosophers of mathematics that we hesitate to read into it still one more interpretation. Nevertheless, it appears to us that the proof ought to shake confidence in any narrowly *a priori* or conventionalist philosophy of mathematics. For one thing, by showing that no Turing machine can be built to generate all number-theoretic truths and no falsehoods, it has raised question marks over the ability of the human mind itself to know *all* number-theoretic truth. And if we can't know it all, it is certainly not *a priori* for us. Second, by showing that any axiom list will be incomplete, it raises question marks over any conventionalist claim that truth is defined by our choice of axioms. Assuming that number theory is consistent, the machinery of the proof produces a true statement which does *not* follow from the axioms; hence, this truth is not (narrowly speaking) conventionally defined by the choice of axioms.

---

25. Cf., for example, Ernest Nagel: "The choice between alternative systems of regulative principles [in logic and mathematics] will then not be arbitrary and will have an objective basis; the choice will not, however, be grounded on the allegedly greater inherent necessity of one system of logic over another, but on the relatively greater adequacy of one of them as an instrument for achieving a certain systematization of knowledge." "Logic Without Ontology," in *Philosophy of Mathematics*, p. 317.

26. Kurt Gödel, "Über formal unentscheidbare Sätze der Principia mathematica und verwandter Systeme I," *Monatshefte für Mathematik und Physik* 38 (1931): 173-198; "On formally undecidable propositions of Principia mathematica and related systems"; English translation by B. Meltzer (Edinburgh and London: Oliver and Boyd, 1962). Cf. also Carnap's generalization that every formal arithmetic is defective. Rudolf Carnap, *The Logical Syntax of Language* (New York: Harcourt, Brace and Company, 1937), §60d.

On the other hand, Gödel's proof gives little comfort to the *a posteriori* camp. For the crucial true-but-unprovable statement S exhibited in his proof cannot be "experienced" as true or *a posteriori* "seen" as true in any normal sense. The a posteriori camp presumably says that we learn by direct experience (two apples and two apples making four apples) and then later by proofs (the proof procedure itself being a generalization from experience of simple proofs). Yet Gödel's S can be neither directly experienced (it's much too complicated) nor proved. S is the first statement of its kind ever produced (no generalization from previous experience is possible), yet on inspecting the "intuitive" meaning of S, one becomes convinced that S must be true.

Because of the above difficulties, anti-theistic philosophy of mathematics is condemned to oscillate, much as we have done in our argument, between the poles of *a priori* knowledge and *a posteriori* knowledge. Why? It will not acknowledge the true God, wise Creator of *both* the human mind with its mathematical intuition *and* the external world with its mathematical properties. In sections 22-23 we shall see how the Biblical view furnishes us with a real solution to the problem of "knowing" that $2 + 2 = 4$ and knowing that S is true.

B. *Metaphysical problems of anti-theistic mathematics: unity and plurality*

16. *Unity and plurality of truth*

Closely related to the epistemological questions are questions about the metaphysical "status" of '$2 + 2 = 4$' in relation to other truths. What does it *mean* that $2 + 2 = 4$? If we wanted to test whether a child understood '$2 + 2 = 4$,' we would be satisfied only when he not only demonstrated ability to manipulate the symbols properly on paper, but also knew when to use '$2 + 2 = 4$' in word-problems. Such a check is necessary because a child might memorize the visual shapes and manipulations of '2' and '4' without ever understanding what he was doing. Indeed, we might say that to know that $2 + 2 = 4$ *is* knowing how to use those symbols in everyday life. One cannot know '$2 + 2 = 4$' without knowing many other things *in relation to* that one truth. Thus we are inevitably concerned with a great plurality of experiences and truths and the relations among them.

Moreover, as modern linguistic theory in the tagmemic framework has pointed out, no linguistic symbol can be understood without some specification of its contrast, variation, and distribution.[27] In particular, '$2 + 2 = 4$' has meaning (a) only as an identifiable whole, with a certain constancy in time, *contrasting* with certain other possible statements, both

---

27. Kenneth L. Pike, *Language in Relation to a Unified Theory of the Structure of Human Behavior*, 2nd revised edition (The Hague-Paris: Mouton & Co., 1967).

true $(2 + 3 = 5,\ 1 + 2 = 3,\ 1 + 3 = 4,$ etc.) and false $(2 + 2 = 5,$
$2 + 2 = 3,$ etc.); (b) only as a unit with a certain *variational* range,
implying that it can be repeated in varying forms without losing its
identity (two plus two makes four, two plus two equals four, two and two
are four, $II + II = IV,\ (1 + 1) + 2 = 4,$ etc.); (c) only as an item
distributed in larger units of linguistic behavior and general human behavior (proofs using '$2 + 2 = 4$,' word problems referring to it, '$2 + 2 =$
4' used in calculating grocery prices, income tax, and missile trajectories).

The problem here, for any anti-theistic view, is to guarantee any ultimate
unity and stability to the enormous "sea" of truths and experiences in
which '$2 + 2 = 4$' is embedded. How, without knowing everything, can
we really be said to know anything? '$2 + 2 = 4$' is distributed in a larger
context which, if we are to understand it, must be distributed in a still
larger context, ad infinitum. Moreover, how do we know that the next
thing we discover, on the borders of our knowledge, will not upset and
radically overturn what we have hitherto called "knowledge"? Such a
contingency seems not only to be abstractly possible (due to the necessity
of defining knowledge partly in terms of its distribution in larger contexts),
but actually to have occurred in the past in more than one science. Physics
has radically revised its "knowledge" during the Newtonian revolution, the
Einsteinian revolution, and now the quantum revolution. Even mathematics has had to revise itself at times; think of the discovery of irrationals
by the Pythagoreans, of contradictions arising from reasoning with con-
ditionally convergent infinite series, of contradictions like Russell's paradox
arising from reasoning with the naive idea of set. True, each of these three
mathematical "problems" is now considered resolved, but none was resolved without a revision of the standards, yes, and the very concept of
correct mathematical reasoning.

In all this discussion we are really raising, in another form, the old
problem of a source for ultimate metaphysical unity in the world, in this
case the unity of truth. On the Christian basis, we hear a very simple and
clear-cut answer: God knows everything, and His wisdom guarantees that
truth will not be overthrown by the next fact around the corner. He has
made man in His image in such a way that man can know truth ("think
God's thoughts after Him"[28]) without having to know everything. (For
a fuller discussion, see §§22, 24.)

On the other hand, if the anti-theist wants to begin with an ultimate
unity, rather than an ultimate plurality, of truth, he has no way to explain
how plurality arises from this single truth. We have here the problem of
unity and plurality which we confronted already in §2.

---

28. Cornelius Van Til, *A Survey of Christian Epistemology*, pp. 200-201, 94-99,
and *The Defense of the Faith*, 13-14, 41-46.

17. *Unity and plurality of sciences*

The same problem confronts us in still another form if we ask about the relation among different areas of truth or different sciences. How does mathematics relate to physics, to biology, to logic, to linguistics, to economics? How do subdivisions within mathematics, like arithmetic, geometry, calculus, and set theory, relate to one another? Why does any one of these areas have extensive application to others?

Anti-theists usually try to answer using either ultimate plurality or ultimate unity. If, on the one hand, we choose to split up the sciences into an ultimate diversity and *plurality*, we can give no answer beyond "Well, it just happens." But very few people can really live with this. Many scientists have acknowledged that they simply *believe*, they have *faith* that the world is mathematically and physically regular. Einstein puts it this way:

> To this [sphere of religion] there also belongs the faith in the possibility that the regulations valid for the world of existence are rational, that is comprehensible to reason. I cannot conceive of a genuine scientist without that profound faith. The situation may be expressed by an image: science without religion is lame, religion without science is blind.[29]

Yet such postulated gods can never rise above the idols of Isaiah's description: "Tell us what is to come hereafter, that we may know that you are gods; do good, or do harm, that we may be dismayed and terrified. Behold, you are nothing, and your work is nought; an abomination is he who chooses you" (41:23-24; cf. 44:6-11, etc.).

On the other hand, we can make an effort to reduce the sciences to an ultimate *unity* by deriving some from others. The philosophers of mathematics in the past have tried in turn to reduce mathematics (a) to linguistics ("mathematics is the science of formal languages"—the formalists), (b) to psychology ("mathematics is the study of mental mathematical constructions"—the intuitionists), (c) to logic ("mathematics is a branch of logic"—the logicists), (d) to physics ("mathematics is generalized from sense experience"—the empiricists), (e) to sociology ("mathematics is a group of socially useful statements"—the pragmatists). The form of the supposed reduction of mathematics thus gives us a rough and ready catalog of the major schools of philosophy of mathematics.

---

29. *Albert Einstein*, p. 285, quoted from *Science, Philosophy and Religion*, A Symposium (New York: Harper & Row, 1941). Similarly, E. P. Wigner calls this formulability of physical laws in mathematical terms an "article of faith" and a "miracle . . . which we neither understand nor deserve." "The Unreasonable effectiveness of Mathematics in the Natural Sciences," *Communications on Pure and Applied Mathematics*, 13 (1960): 10, 14.

As we might expect, such attempted reductions never really succeed. At some point, they do not do justice to the distinctive character of mathematical truth, as over against physical, linguistic, psychological truth. A detailed discussion of reductionisms is beyond the scope of this work, and we must refer the reader to the extensive foundational work by Dooyeweerd and Vollenhoven, plus particular investigation of mathematics by Strauss.[30] Our suspicions should be aroused, by the very diversity of attempted reductions (to linguistics, to logic, to psychology, etc.), to question whether *any* of these can really be the true story. They each refute the others, by showing up a side of the picture that the others have not sufficiently acknowledged.

C. 18. *Ethical problems of anti-theistic mathematics: motive, standard, and goal*

Finally, we should mention in passing that anti-theistic mathematics has no satisfactory ethical foundations, any more than it has metaphysical or epistemological foundations. No piece of mathematics can be written, no mathematician can ever operate, without some implicit or explicit motive, standard, and goal for the work. A mathematician may be motivated by selfishness, by fear, by altruism, or by the Lord; he may be working for money, for sheer enjoyment, or for the glory of God. But no one ever does mathematics without having this kind of factor in the background. Moreover, his motives, standards, and goals will inevitably affect what kind of problem he chooses to focus on, what relative weight he gives to pure versus applied mathematics, what standards he sets for himself in his teaching and writing, how he divides his time between teaching and research, and so on. The person who regards such factors as "extraneous" to the real business of mathematics has already lost sight of the consistent Biblical focus on the *work* of man as the work of *man* who stands before his Creator: "rendering service with a good will as to the Lord and not to men, knowing that whatever good any one does, he will receive the same again from the Lord, whether he is a slave or free" (Eph. 6:7-8). For further discussion of the Biblical view, see §26.

Since anti-theistic ethical theory is entangled in the same antinomies in the area of mathematics as it is in any other area of life, we need not elaborate here on the excellent discussion of ethics by Van Til.[31]

---

30. Dooyeweerd, *A New Critique*, Vol. II, pp. 47, 91, 103, 106, 385, etc.; Vollenhoven, *De Wijsbegeerte der Wiskunde*, pp. 20-138, 200-402; Vollenhoven, "Problemen en Richtingen in de Wijsbegeerte der Wiskunde," *Philosophia Reformata* 1 (1936): 162-187; D. F. M. Strauss, "Number-Concept and Number-Idea," *Philosophia Reformata* 35 (1970): 156-177 and 36 (1971): 13-42.
31. Cornelius Van Til, *Christian Theistic Ethics*, Vol. III of the series *In Defense of Biblical Christianity* (Philadelphia: den Dulk Christian Foundation, 1971).

III. *A Christian-theistic view of mathematics*

So far our discussion has developed in a predominantly negative direction, because we have occupied ourselves with a criticism of "neutralist" (§§1-10) and anti-theistic (§§11-18) views of mathematics. However, it is hardly possible to appreciate the true poverty of such views without some reflection on what a truly Biblical view of mathematics would look like. To this task we now turn.

In accordance with our earlier critique of anti-theistic metaphysical (§§8, 16, 17), epistemological (§§9, 12-15), and ethical (§§10, 18) foundations, we propose to discuss the Biblical viewpoint also in terms of metaphysics (§§19-21), epistemology (§§22-25), and ethics (§26). Naturally, Biblical foundations in these three areas overlap and complement one another; we take up the topics one by one in order to throw into bolder relief the radical contrasts between theistic and anti-theistic views.

In the following discussion, we are not making an attempt to use mathematics (or other sciences) as some kind of "proof" or support for the Bible. Rather, conversely, we maintain that only on the basis of obediently hearing the Word of God can we find a proper foundation for mathematics. It is God who sustains mathematics, not vice versa.

A. *Christian metaphysics of mathematics, founded in the Being of God*

19. *Ontology*

What is the metaphysical status of numbers and statements about numbers? What is the status of geometry? What is the significance of mathematics in this world? For the Christian committed to Scripture, the most important fact about mathematics must be its relation to the Lord. Since He is Creator and Sovereign over all, everything must find its meaning, yes, its very existence in Him: "in him we live and move and have our being" (Acts 17:28). "Thine, O Lord, is the greatness, and the power, and the glory, and the victory, and the majesty; for all that is in the heavens and in the earth is thine; thine is the kingdom, O Lord, and thou art exalted as head above all" (I Chron. 29:11).

Furthermore, the most basic ontological distinction in Scripture is between God on the one hand and His creatures on the other (cf. Isa. 43: 10-13). Hence Van Til speaks of the Creator-creature distinction as basic to all Christian thinking, and Vollenhoven makes the manner in which philosophies separate God and the universe his most basic criterion for taxonomic classification.[32] If we are confused about who God is, if we

---

32. Cornelius Van Til, *An Introduction to Systematic Theology* (Philadelphia: Westminster Theological Seminary, classroom syllabus, 1966), pp. 11-12; Dirk H. Th. Vollenhoven, *Het Calvinisme en de Reformatie van de Wijsbegeerte* (Amsterdam: H. J. Paris, 1933), pp. 50-51.

identify part of the creation with God or part of God with creation, we are guilty of serious idolatry.

Therefore, the most basic question to ask about mathematical structures and laws is this: are they aspects of creation or of God? Are they, as it were, created things or God, or are they perhaps in some third category? This question is still ambiguous, because its answer depends on what we mean by "mathematics." "Mathematics" may refer to (a) the historically growing science manifested in textbooks, articles, conferences, lectures, etc.; (b) the thoughts of the mathematicians; or (c) mathematical "structure" for the world, somehow existing independently of our thoughts (two apples and two apples making four apples; two distinct points determining a unique line between them; etc.). Mathematics (a) clearly consists in created things and activities of created men; mathematics (b) consists in human thoughts which, as such, never have divine status (Isa. 55:8-9; Ps. 147:5). We shall have more to say about (a) and (b) in §§22, 24.

For the moment, let us concentrate on mathematics (c). Since mathematics (c) concerns properties of *created* things, we might be tempted at first glance to say, "mathematics (c) is created." However, the Bible, while speaking over and over of God's having created things (minerals, plants, animals, men, angels), apparently never speaks of God's having created "structures" or "laws." A little reflection shows us that this is no accident. The Bible never represents the world as being governed by laws as such, independent of the Creator, but rather by the decrees of the King, by God Himself speaking (cf. Gen. 8:22–9:7; Jer. 33:25; Ps. 33:6-11, 18-22; 147:15-20). Because His decrees are in accordance with who He is (Ps. 19:7-9), we expect them to be wise and orderly (Ps. 104:24; Prov. 8:22-31; Rom. 11:33-36).

So it is with mathematics (c). God Himself has a *numerical* nature. He is three in one. It is interesting that Jesus uses the plural pronoun "we" (John 17:21; cf. John 14:23) and plural "are" (*esmen*, John 10:30) in speaking of the Father and the Son. Mathematics (c) is eternal because the Father, Son, and Holy Spirit (3!) are eternal (John 1:1; 17:5; Heb. 9:14). And God's eternal numerical nature is manifested in creation much as His love, wisdom, and justice are manifested.

Following the "pattern" of His own plurality, He creates the world as a plurality: "O Lord, how *manifold* [Heb., many] are thy works! In wisdom hast thou made them all; the earth is full of thy creatures" (Ps. 104:24). This verse traces back the plural nature of God's works to His wisdom. And, in the final analysis, the wisdom of God finds embodiment in Jesus Christ, "in whom are hid all the treasures of wisdom and knowledge" (Col. 2:3), "whom God made our wisdom, our righteousness and sanctification and redemption" (I Cor. 1:30). Jesus gives His invitation in language earlier used, in Ecclesiasticus, by personified wisdom (Matt.

11:25-30; cp. Sir. 24:25 [19]; 51:23-26).[33] Because from the beginning the Son is God's personal wisdom, God has no need to consult anyone else (Isa. 40:13-14). Thus we are justified in saying that the plurality of this world (the works of God) finds its basis in the plurality of the fellowship of the Father and the Son. And Psalms 104:24 also points to an origin for *unity* in this world when it speaks of the wisdom of the *one* Lord. Because there is *one* Lord, there is an inner consistency in everything that He does. Wisdom expresses itself in *orderly* rule, in justice, in proportioned love and hate (Prov. 8:13-17).

In saying "1 + 1 = 2" we are thus stating a truth about the Trinity, a truth about the Wisdom of God, and then, secondarily, a truth about the world that He governs. (Note, however, that since the Trinity and the Wisdom of God are incomprehensible, God's own "mathematics," as it were, is not accessible to us in all its fullness. We cannot assume that our mathematics (b) is necessarily all true or exactly equivalent to God's "mathematics.") How far this is from a "neutralist" view of mathematics, which supposes that mathematics has nothing to do with God!

From this point of view, anti-theistic philosophies of mathematics can be classified as mathematical versions of old heresies. A strict *a priori* view of mathematics (§12), emphasizing that mathematical truth (b) *must* be what it is, is guilty of leveling the distinction between the Divine and human mind. What is *a priori* for God—namely mathematics (c)—is not *a priori* for us. We cannot infallibly reason to mathematical results, because God's mind is different from ours. The leveling process ends by saying that God must conform to our *a priori* mathematics, resulting in Tri-theism.

Next, a strict *a posteriori* view of mathematics (§13), emphasizing the contingent character of mathematical truths (§16), is guilty of ignoring the fixedness of God's numerical nature. This view ends by saying that God is non-mathematical, resulting in mystical monism.

Finally, a conventionalist view of mathematics (§14), emphasizing the role of human postulation in mathematics, is guilty of ignoring the role of God in determining mathematical structure. This view, then, ends in effectively denying God's activity in the world, i.e., practical atheism. Perhaps the disposition of our age toward practical atheism is a major factor

---

33. We do not believe that Jesus, or the great body of his Palestinian contemporaries, in any way thought of Ecclesiasticus, or other so-called apocryphal books, as the Word of God. Nevertheless, these passages are interesting because they show what kind of thinking was in the air on the question of wisdom, and they show the context in which Jews would have understood Jesus' call to "come to him" and to "take his yoke." Even if it could be shown that Jesus is specifically alluding to Ecclesiasticus (rather than merely to the Jewish wisdom tradition of which Sir. is one example), it would prove no more than Paul's allusion to Greek poets in Acts 17:28.

behind the widespread preference for some conventionalist view.[34]

We should also observe that the Biblical view solves, in a clear-cut fashion, the problem of the meaning of '2 + 2 = 4' in relation to other truths (§16). '2 + 2 = 4' finds its ultimate meaning and integration in the unchangeable fullness of the Divine Trinitarian Fellowship. Because God is unchangeable, the truth of '2 + 2 = 4' is not altered by the next human discovery.

20. Modality

What are the characteristic features of mathematical truth, as opposed to other kinds of truth? How is mathematics related to other sciences? In answering such questions we must naturally move further away from the direct testimony of the Bible. Yet the Bible does seem to present us with grounds for a preliminary division of the sciences in Genesis 1:28-30. There God divides His creation into four major groups: mineral, plant, animal, and man; and He instructs Adam about some of the characteristic features and functions of each group. In studying such characteristic features, Adam would make beginnings in the sciences of physics, of biology, of zoology, and of anthropology. See Diagram 1.

In the course of time, we expect that further major divisions would be marked out within these sciences. For a detailed analysis of the major divisions, we refer the reader to the work of the Amsterdam philosophy and the author.[35] For our present purposes, let us confine ourselves to a division of physics. Physical things share with plants, animals, and man not only so-called physical features (force relations, rigidity or non-rigidity, energy, etc.), but also kinematic features (velocity, mobility), spatial features (extension, area or volume, shape), quantitative features (how many?), and aggregative features (being potential members of various aggregates or collections). Thus we obtain Diagram 2. The last four sciences of Diagram 2 jointly comprise mathematics.

---

34. The philosophy of the law-idea, or Amsterdam philosophy, while claiming to take a radically Christian stance, also falls victim to an old heresy—Sabellianism. According to Dooyeweerd, the numerical aspect, subject to mathematical laws, occurs only as one of the diverse aspects of the cosmic order of time. *A New Critique*, Vol. I, pp. 3, 24, 29, fn. 31-32. And cosmic time does not include God, the eternal One. *Ibid.*, fn. p. 31. Hence numerical properties cannot be ascribed to God Himself. $1 + 1 + 1 = 3$, as a theoretical statement, cannot speak about God. "The modal concepts of laws and of subject and object are essentially limited to a special aspect. Unlike the cosmonomic Idea, these modal concepts do not in themselves point beyond the diversity of meaning toward the transcendent origin and totality." *Ibid.*, p. 97. If these strictures are taken at face value, they lead to a decidedly Sabellian (modalistic) view of the Trinity. Cf. the author's paper, "Sabellianism in the Philosophy of the Law-Idea," *Philosophia Reformata* (to appear).

35. J. M. Spier, *An Introduction to Christian Philosophy*, 2nd ed. (Nutley, N. J.: The Craig Press, 1966), pp. 30-130. Spier popularizes the taxonomy of *A New Critique*, Vol. II. Cf. also Vern Poythress, "An Approach to Evangelical Philosophy of Science," Th.M. thesis, Westminster Theological Seminary, 1974.

It is now easy to see that the unity and plurality of the sciences arise

Diagram 1

features or aspects	kingdom	activities in Gen. 1:28-30	science
anthropological	men	dominion (28)	anthropology
zootic	animals	locomotion, breath (30b)	zoology
biotic	plants	green, serving as food (30b)	biology
physical	minerals, physical things	physical support (30a), spatial area (28)	physics

Diagram 2

features or aspects	activity	science
physical	having energy	physics
kinematic	moving	kinematics
spatial	having extension	geometry
quantitative	having number	arithmetic, elementary algebra
aggregative	being distinct	agorology = elementary set theory

from the same basic Source as the unity and plurality within mathematics: from the nature of God and His plan. In particular, the kinematic, spatial, and aggregative properties of this world can be traced back to the nature of God, in a manner similar to what we have already done for the quantitative aspect. As God has a numerical nature (the Trinity), so He has a kinematic, a spatial, and an aggregative nature.

Of course, in using language about God's nature we must exercise caution. God as Creator is ultimately incomprehensible to the creature. No man can understand everything about God. Thus we expect that God's aggregative, quantitative, spatial, and kinematic nature to be, in some way, incomprehensible to us. Created analogies inevitably break down, because they are only *finite* images of the Infinite One. In the case of God's numerical nature, this is obvious. God is Three Persons, yet at the same time *One* God. Jesus can say, "I and the Father *are one*" (John 10:30). No created thing is three and at the same time one in the same sublime way. We shall see also that God's aggregative, spatial, and kinematic nature are not strictly analogous to anything in this created world. That, perhaps, has been one reason why people have (wrongly) tended to deny that God's nature had anything to do with space or kinematics.

First, God has an *aggregative* nature, in the sense that the various Persons of the Godhead, and His attributes, are *distinguished* from one another. This is the eternal foundation for the science of set theory. "Let not your hearts be troubled; believe in God, believe *also* in me" (John 14:1). "And I will pray the Father, and he will give you *another* Counselor, to be with you for ever" (14:16). "He who does not love me does not keep my words; and the word which you hear is *not* mine but the Father's who sent me" (14:24). The personal names Father, Son, and Spirit already imply that there are distinct "aggregates" within the Godhead. The incomprehensibility of God's aggregative nature is expressed by facts such as the mutual indwelling of members of the Trinity, and the inter-penetration of attributes. "Do you not believe that I am in the Father and the Father in me? The words that I say to you I do not speak on my own authority; but the Father who dwells in me does his works. Believe me that I am in the Father and the Father in me; or else believe me for the sake of the works themselves" (John 14:10-11). Somehow we find that all the members of the Trinity participate, in their own ways, in even those works which we associate most distinctly with one particular member of the Trinity. In a certain sense, the members of the Trinity are *not* distinguished, because there is only one Lord (Deut. 6:4-5).

Second, God has a spatial nature. This expresses itself, first, in the teachings about God's filling heaven and earth: "Can a man hide himself in secret places so that I cannot see him: says the Lord. Do I not *fill* heaven and earth? says the Lord" (Jer. 23:24). "*In* him we live and move and have our being" (Acts 17:28). See also I Kings 8:23, 27; Isaiah 66:1-2; Acts 7:46-50; and passages dealing with God's *dwelling* with His people, Deuteronomy 4:7, 39; Isaiah 57:15; 66:2; I Corinthians 6:19; Romans 8:9-11. Note the strong stress on the fact that space offers no resistance or problem to God's rule, but rather that God is Lord of space, doing as He pleases within it.

Still, it might be questioned whether the above expressions of Scripture express only God's *relation* to the created world, without implying anything about what God is in Himself, or was before the world began. A few expressions of Scripture do appear to go beyond the created world into eternity. "Look down from heaven and see, from thy holy and glorious *habitation*" (Isa. 63:15). "For thus says the high and lofty One who inhabits *eternity*, whose name is Holy: 'I dwell in the high and holy place, . . .' " (57:15). These passages say that God was not without a "dwelling place" or "habitation" before the world began.[36] Indeed, the everlasting

---

36. We are not here speaking of heaven in the traditional sense, since heaven is a created place (Acts 4:24; Neh. 9:6). Since God made everything outside of Himself (Col. 1:16), His *eternal* habitation can be nothing else than God Himself. Because, in Trinitarian fellowship, He is Himself a perfect "habitation," He has no

stability of God's own "habitation" forms the foundation for His being the believer's habitation: "Lord, thou has been our dwelling *place* in all *generations*. Before the mountains were brought forth, or ever thou hadst formed the earth and the world, even from *everlasting* to *everlasting* thou art God" (Ps. 90:1-2).

Similarly, some of the passages speaking of the relations of the Trinity speak in distinctively *spatial* terms. There are expressions of indwelling (John 14:10-11; Col. 1:19; 2:9); expressions of face-to-face relationship: "In the beginning was the Word, and the Word was *with* God, and the Word was God" (John 1:1). "No one has ever seen God; the only Son, who is *in the bosom of* the Father, he has made him known" (John 1:18); and expressions of "proceeding": "But when the Counselor comes, whom I shall *send* to you *from* the Father, even the Spirit of truth, who *proceeds from* the Father, he will bear witness to me" (John 15:26). Once again, we meet with incomprehensible intra-Trinitarian relations, since, if the Father and the Son fill all and are in all (Eph. 1:23; 4:6; Jer. 23:24), the Spirit can hardly proceed from the Father in any easily comprehensible sense.

But, instead of requiring God to correspond to our ideas derived from this *created* world, we should rather see that, conversely, the "space" of our mathematics (b) is derived from the impress, on finite things, of God's governing rule. The spatial and physical extent of this world is used in Scripture as one pointer to the original, uncreated immensity of God (Isa. 40:12, 26; Ps. 104:25).

Third, God has a kinematic nature. We mean this in the sense that God's own eternal *activity*, His "motion," if you will, forms the metaphysical basis and origin of created activity and motion. "He [the Son] reflects the glory of God and bears the very stamp of his nature, *upholding* the universe [literally, bearing all things by his word of power]" (Heb. 1:3). "In him, according to the purpose of him who *accomplishes all things* according to the counsel of his will" (Eph. 1:11). The Lord's activity is expressed in a great variety of ways: He lives (Deut. 32:39-42; Isa. 8:19), He rests ("physical" activity?: Gen. 2:1-3), He is moved (emotional activity: Gen. 6:6), He speaks (lingual activity: Ps. 33:9; 147:4; Deut. 4:12-13), He judges (juridical activity: Ps. 75:2-8).

Doubtless most of these descriptions focus on God's relation to this created world, rather than on what "He is in Himself." But the activities within the Trinity cannot be reduced to *merely* activities within the created world, without lapsing into modalism. For example, "God is love" (I John 4:16), and the Father *loved* the Son even before the foundation of the

---

need of creating in order to make for Himself a habitation. Indeed, we might wonder whether the quotation marks should be placed around *our* "habitations," rather than *His*: His Habitation is the Original.

world (John 3:35; Prov. 8:30-31; Col. 1:13-16). Similarly, to use another image from Scripture, the Father has been *speaking* from all eternity, in Trinitarian fellowship (John 1:1-2). God's own eternal activity and "movement" of speaking and loving is what causes the movements, and hence the kinematic character of this world: "He sends forth his *command* to the earth; his *word* runs swiftly. He gives snow like wool; he scatters hoarfrost like ashes. He casts forth his ice like morsels; who can stand before his cold? He sends forth his *word,* and melts them; he makes his wind blow, and the waters flow. He *declares* his *word* to Jacob, his statutes and ordinances to Israel. He has not dealt thus with any other nation; they do not know his ordinances. Praise the Lord!" (Ps. 147: 15-20). Note the connection of His word both with the motions of physical things, and with His love for Israel His son (a love which comes to fulfillment in His love for the only Son).

Once again, as in the case of other aspects of God's nature, God's "kinematic" nature is incomprehensible. At the same time that God is so active, He is also unchanging (Mal. 3:6; Ps. 102:27). His word is *fixed* (Ps. 119:89); it never passes away (Luke 21:33). Thus God Himself forms the foundation, not only for the change in the world (He decrees it out of His own activity), but also for the stability of the world (He and His decrees do not change).

21. *Structurality*

What is the relation among the four major subdivisions of mathematics (Diagram 2)? Between mathematics and the other sciences? Is there, indeed, any constant relation at all (§17)? Such questions must ultimately be answered in the same terms as our earlier questions about unity and plurality (§§16,19). The sciences find their unity in the personal Wisdom of God (Ps. 104:24). "He is before all things, and in him all things hold together" (Col. 1:17). This is why mathematics applies to physics. This is why the fundamental laws of physics have such simple form. We trust that mathematics will continue to find application to physics, not because of blind faith (§17), but out of the conviction that the laws of physics and mathematics are simply two diverse ways in which Christ comprehensively rules the universe.

We can ask similar questions about the major divisions within mathematics. Why should theorems in elementary algebra and set theory apply to geometry and kinematics? Why, for example, should one be able to prove the equality of the base angles of an isosceles triangle *either* by direct, geometrical means, *or* by an *algebraic* calculation in analytic geometry of the cosines of the base angles? Similarly, arithmetical and number-theoretic work can be done *either* in direct, quantitative terms, *or* in set-theoretic terms (starting, say, from axioms of Zermelo-Fraenkel set-theory). The area under curves can be calculated, *either* by direct geometrical approximation, *or* by algebraic calculation of a definite integral, whose definition involves a fundamentally *kinematic* limit process. The reasonings in different parts of mathematics (agorology = elementary set theory, arithmetic, geometry, kinematics [including differential and integral calculus]) agree with one another because of the unity of God. Shifts back and forth between the four major divisions of mathematics constantly exploit the fact that these sciences have their origin in the *one* Wisdom of God.

Because God contains both unity and plurality in Himself, there is no need for us, in the Christian framework, to resort to the futile attempts of reductionism that we discussed in §17. As a matter of fact, the reductionisms of §17 can be seen as a kind of mathematical version of an old heresy: gnosticism. Why should we say that? Well, in exploring mathematics one is exploring the nature of God's rule over the universe, i.e., one is exploring the nature of God Himself. A reductionism thus ultimately amounts to an attempt to derive some aspects$_1$ of God's nature from other aspects$_2$, an attempt to say that the latter aspects$_2$ of God's nature are more fundamental. The aspects$_2$ are then somehow what is "really there," as opposed to the only apparent existence of aspects$_1$. I classify this as a gnostic-type heresy, because gnosticism develops a theory of emanations whereby certain inferior deities derive their being from emanations of the ultimate Deity. This gnostic derivation of being is not so dissimilar to the present-day derivation of aspects.

B. *A Christian epistemology of mathematics, founded in the knowledge of God*

22. *The image of God is a foundation for mathematical a priori*

How do we come to know and discuss mathematics (b), that is, the thoughts and knowledge of human mathematicians? Here, for the first time, we must focus on the Christian view of man. How does man fit into the picture of mathematics? We can have no other starting point than the "definition" of man provided by Scripture: man is the image of God (Gen. 1:26-30; cf. Gen. 2:7; I Cor. 11:7). As such, his talk is to imitate receptively, on a finite level, the works (naming, Gen. 2:19; 1:4; governing, Gen. 1:28; Ps. 22:28; improving, Gen. 2:15; 1:31), and rest (Gen. 2:2; Ex. 20:11) of God. Man's mind is created with the potential, then, of understanding God (though not exhaustively). He has the capability of understanding the aggregative, quantitative, spatial, and kinematic aspects of God's rule, since he himself is a ruler like God. Thus he can generalize with confidence from $2 + 2 = 4$, etc., to $2,123,955 + 644,101 = 2,768,056$.

Here we have the first step in a Christian answer to the epistemological problem of *a priori/a posteriori* (§§12-15). The *a priori* capability of man's created nature really corresponds to the *a posteriori* of what is "out there," because man is in the *image* of the One who ordained what is "out there." At the same time, man's mathematical reasoning is not always right, his intuitive expectations are not always fulfilled (cf. examples in §12), because man is the image of *God* the infinite One. Since God is incomprehensible, His mathematics sometimes baffles us, and it is to be expected that it should. Gödel's proof (§15) perhaps articulates one specific instance of a principial limitation on man's knowledge in comparison to God's

23. *Revelation is a foundation for mathematical a posteriori*

Next, we should ask how a man comes to know mathematical truths that he hasn't known before. This, one might say, is the *a posteriori* side of mathematics. The Bible answers that God reveals to men whatever they know: "He who teaches men knowledge, the Lord, knows the thoughts of man, that they are but a breath. Blessed is the man whom thou dost chasten, O Lord, and whom thou dost teach out of thy law" (Ps. 94: 10b-12). "But it is the spirit in a man, the breath of the Almighty, that makes him understand. It is not the old that are wise, nor the aged that understand what is right" (Job 32:8-9; cf. Prov. 8). The Lord's instruction sometimes comes, of course, by way of "natural" revelation (Ps. 19; Isa. 40:26; 51:6; Prov. 30:24-28). Thus we can do justice to the real novelty that is sometimes found in a new mathematical theorem.

Note that, in the Christian framework, the *a priori* of man's nature and the a posteriori of God's universe and His revelation complement rather than compete with one another.

24. *Excursus on the limitations of human mathematics*

This is perhaps a good point to explore further the relation between human and divine "mathematics." When God reveals Himself, He reveals Himself truly, but not exhaustively. That is one limitation. In the case of mathematics, our knowledge is also limited by the fact that we see the effects of God's decrees and rule on a *finite* world, without having direct access (except in the case of statements of Scripture) to those decrees and that rule itself.

Take the case of geometry. Though God has a spatial nature (§20), it would be blasphemous to say that He has the properties of Euclidean (or non-Euclidean) space. Our own mathematical systems (Euclidean or non-Euclidean) are somehow not identical with His "system." We must say, I think, that Euclidean and non-Euclidean geometries are *both* exhibitions (revelations) of how God might rule the world; for they are both discoveries or constructions of the human mind in the *image* of God.

Presumably God might have created a universe with either a Euclidean or non-Euclidean or some other geometry. Thus the variety of geometries, far from offering an obstacle to the Christian viewpoint, is simply an illustration of the freedom of God.

Is Euclidean geometry (as a system of statements) the Creator or the creature? In some sense both. The above argument shows that in some sense geometry is relative to this world (and thus created). Now, take the statement G that between any two distinct points there is exactly one straight line. (Or, equally, that the sum of angles in a triangle is 180°.) Suppose that G is actually true in our world. Then it is right to say that G expresses one of the laws of God's creation. G is one of those things that God has ordained to be true for this world (Lam. 3:37). After all, we cannot imagine that G could be true for any other reason than because God ordained it. He is Lord! How could we know G in any other way than by reflecting (§22) God's own original knowledge that G? Furthermore, God's decrees, His speech, His Word (Isa. 46:9-12) say who God *is* (John 1:1). G says who God is. Yet G is not in every sense identical with God.

The solution to this paradox presumably should parallel the phenomenon of the Incarnation. Jesus is God, yet God *in the flesh*. The Bible is God speaking *in Hebrew, Aramaic, and Greek*. Is it proper, in parallel fashion, to say that G is a description of God ruling this *finite* spatial world? I think so. G partakes of characteristics of the finite and created (it includes reference to points, lines, and degrees) and of characteristics of the Infinite (it is unchanging). Sometimes (as indeed is the case with the Incarnation) the created and Uncreated cannot be easily distinguished.

25. *The unity of the race and the gift of language are foundations for public science*

The existence of a science of mathematics depends upon the ability of men to communicate with one another, and on the availability of a medium of communication. Both of these factors go back to creation. Men have one racial origin (Acts 17:26), they share a common nature (the image of God, Gen. 1:26-27; 5:1-3), and they have been given the gift of language as part of their equipment to fulfill the cultural mandate (Gen. 2:19-23). This furnishes us adequate grounds for believing today that others understand us, and that our language is adequate to the cultural task that God has given us (cf. §26).

We have also an answer to our earlier question, §1, why science has so much agreement despite religious differences. Men cannot cease to be in the image of God, even if they rebel against Him (Gen. 3:5, 22). They either imitate God in obedience or imitate Him in trying to become their own lord. Neither can they escape the impulse to fulfill, in some fashion, the cultural mandate of Genesis 1:28-30. Thus, in spite of themselves, they acknowledge God in some fashion by "imitating" Him. It is the situation described in Romans 1:18-22; James 2:19.

Hence non-Christians, in the image of God, can and do make significant contributions to mathematics. They can know many mathematical truths. As we have seen in §§19-21, in knowing mathematical truth they know something of God (though not exhaustively, and at places mistakenly). Nevertheless, their "knowledge" is not more beneficial to them than the knowledge of the demons (James 2:19). Hence, Christian and atheist, indeed all kinds of religious people, share mathematical truths, but for all non-Christians it is only *in spite of* their system. It is *because* Christianity *is* true, *because* God is who He is, *because* man is the image of God, the non-Christian knows anything.[37] The supposed "common ground" of shared mathematical truth proves the very opposite of what the neutralist supposes it to prove.

C. 26. *A Christian ethics of mathematics, founded in the righteousness of God*

Finally, we give a brief sketch of how Biblical ethics applies to work in mathematics. A Christian recognizes that he lives under the lordship of God, in the light of God's present commands and God's coming judgment. He sees that, as in the case of Abraham and the nation of Israel, his whole life—marital, political, economic, social, spatial—ought to be structured and determined by his covenantal relation to God. All of life should be a response of service to God (I Cor. 10:31).

Thus, work in mathematics can have relevance to the Christian only insofar as it is motivated by the love of God, commanded by the law of God, and directed to the glory of God and the consummation of His kingdom. These are the motive, the standard, and the goal of work in mathematics[38] (cp. the non-Christian view in §18).

To be more specific, we must take into account the fact that men have a diversity of callings (I Cor. 7:17-24). Not all men are called to be specialists in mathematics. For the one who does so specialize, using the gifts that God has given him (Luke 19:11-26; I Peter 4:10), how does Christian ethics come to bear? How should the Biblical motive, standard, and goal affect him? (a) The mathematician should be motivated by the love of God to understand the mathematical truths which God has ordained for this world (and so understand something of God's mathematical nature, §19); love of neighbor should also motivate him to apply mathematics to physics, economics, etc. (b) The mathematician should

---

37. *The Defense of the Faith*, pp. 154, 159.
38. For an extended discussion of motive, standard, and goal, cf. *Christian Theistic Ethics*.

find his standard in the command of God, the program which God has given man to fulfill: "Be fruitful and multiply, and fill the earth and *subdue* it; and have *dominion* . . ." (Gen. 1:28). Part of this program is that man should understand God's works (Gen. 2:18-23). (c) The mathematician should work for the glory of God. He should praise God for the beauty and usefulness that he finds in mathematics, for the incomprehensible nature of God which it displays, for the human mind which God has enabled to understand mathematics (Ps. 145; 148). And he should endeavor to exhibit ever more fully and clearly to others that "from him and through him and to him are all things. To him be glory for ever. Amen" (Rom. 11:36).

We intend, by the above description, to delineate not only what a mathematician's inward attitudes should be, but also what his work, his words, and his writings should express overtly and covertly. A man's words normally express what he is: "For out of the abundance of the heart the mouth speaks. The good man out of his good treasure brings forth good, and the evil man out of his evil treasure brings forth evil. I tell you, on the day of judgment men will render account for every careless word they utter; for by your *words* you will be justified, and by your *words* you will be condemned" (Matt. 12:34b-37). If a man is working for the glory of God, he won't be a "secret" believer; he will say so as he talks mathematics. How far this is from a "neutralist" stance! The man who ignores God as he does his mathematical task is not neutral, but rebellious and ungrateful toward the Giver of all his knowledge.

Part Three

FOUNDATIONS
FOR
CHRISTIAN
RECONSTRUCTION

Here then are the facts, or some of the main facts, that the Reformed apologist presents to the natural man. There is first the fact of God's self-contained existence. Second, the fact of creation in general and of man as made in God's image in particular. Third, there is the fact of the comprehensive plan and providence of God with respect to all that takes place in the universe. Then there is the fact of the fall of man and his subsequent sin. It is in relation to these facts and only in relation to these facts that the other facts pertaining to the redemptive work of Christ are what they are. They would not be what they are unless the facts just mentioned are what they are. Thus there is one system of reality of which all that exists forms a part. And any individual fact of this system is what it is in this system. It is therefore a contradiction in terms to speak of presenting certain facts to man unless one presents them as parts of this system. The very factness of any individual fact of history is precisely what it is because God is what he is. It is God's counsel that is the principle of individuation for the Christian man. God makes the facts to be what they are. . . .

It is natural that only the supernatural revelation of God can inform man about such a system as that. For this system is of a nature quite different from the systems of which the natural man speaks. For the latter a system is that which man, assumed to be ultimate, has ordered by his original structural activity. The natural man virtually attributes to himself that which a true Christian theology attributes to the self-contained God. The battle is therefore between the absolutely self-contained God of Christianity and the would-be wholly self-contained mind of the natural man. Between them there can be no compromise.

Van Til, The Defense of the Faith
(1963), pp. 147, 148

APOLOGETICS

X

SOCRATES OR CHRIST:
THE REFORMATION OF CHRISTIAN APOLOGETICS

By GREG L. BAHNSEN

It is not difficult to understand the general idea of apologetics. Simply put, apologetics is the study and practice of *defending* the Christian faith against the array of challenges, critical attacks, and scrutinizing questions leveled contrary to it by unbelievers. As Cornelius Van Til expresses the thought in the opening sentence of his apologetics syllabus, "Apologetics is the vindication of the Christian philosophy of life against the various forms of the non-Christian philosophy of life."[1] Consequently, to be an apologist, one simply needs "to join the struggle in defence of the faith, the faith which God entrusted to his people once and for all."[2]

The Unsettled and Complex Character of Apologetics

However, while the general concept of apologetics is uncomplicated, a whole galaxy of issues and questions clusters around the *exercise* of that task. For instance, in his Introduction to *Christian Apologetics*, J. K. S. Reid asks: What does apologetics defend? Can it be faithful to the faith? Against what or whom is the defense conducted? How is the defense to be conducted? What is the relation of apologetics to dogmatics?[3]

The term 'apologetics' was first introduced to denominate a specific theological discipline by Planck in 1794.[4] Yet this label was obviously cognate to the titles of certain second century treatises, like the *Apology* of Artistides, the *First Apology* and *Second Apology* of Justin Martyr, or Tertullian's *Apologeticum*. Whether one studies the church's earliest post-apostolic confrontation with the unbelieving world or the period when apologetics was developed as an academic science, he notes that a complex of material and methodological questions has persisted in generating disputes among various schools of thought, all of which claim to be doing *apologetics*.

Bernard Ramm provides a convenient summary of such key issues in

---

1. Cornelius Van Til, *Apologetics*, class syllabus (Philadelphia: Westminster Theological Seminary, reprinted 1966), p. 1.
2. Jude 3 (N.E.B.).
3. (Grand Rapids: Eerdmans, 1969), pp. 10-14.
4. *Einleitung in die Theol. Wissenschaft.*

Varieties of Christian Apologetics.[5] (1) What is the relation between philosophy and Christian theology? Perhaps philosophy is something for which theology has no need (Tertullian), is inspired (the Alexandrians), is theology's servant (Augustine), is an independent authority (Aquinas), is a completely separate field (Pascal), or at best a merely temporary alliance (Barth). (2) How valuable are the theistic proofs? They have been seen as valid (Thomists), needing to be supplemented with moral conviction (Hodge), invalid (Clark), inconsequential (Calvin), and irreligious (Kierkegaard). (3) What should be our theory of truth? The mark of truth might be probability (Butler), consistency (Clark), consistency and factuality (Carnell), probability and logical precision (Tennant), paradox (Kierkegaard), dialecticism (neo-orthodoxy), personal encounter (Brunner), or an epistemology of the Holy Spirit (Calvin). (4) Are the intellectual effects of sin negligible (Pelagius), slight (Romanism), engulfing (the Reformers), of mollified by common grace (Masselink)? (5) Should special revelation be viewed as completing natural revelation (Romanism), recovering natural revelation (the Reformers), or an event for which Scripture serves as a pointer (neo-orthodoxy)? (6) What is the nature of Christian certainty? It has been found in the church's infallibility (Romanism), scientific probability (Butler, Tennant), inward certitude in the face of ambiguity (Kierkegaard), and genuine epistemic assurance in contrast to mere probability (Van Til). (7) Is common ground created by common grace and general revelation (Carnell), found in existential pre-understanding (Bultmann), or not to be found at all (Barth)? (8) Should faith be seen as the response to a credible authority (Augustine), in contrast to evidentially grounded conviction (Aquinas), a venturesome act of will, a response of the emotions (Kierkegaard), or the correlate to revelation? (9) With respect to the usefulness of evidence, it has been held as *the* means for certifying Christianity (Montgomery), as something which can be appreciated only after the Holy Spirit's work (Calvin), as the complement to the Holy Spirit's work (Warfield), and as immaterial because it is evaluated in terms of one's more basic philosophical perspective (Clark). (10) What is the relation of reason to revelation? Does it prepare the way for revelation, conflict with revelation, or constitute a completely separate domain?

Such questions as these have continually arisen in the history of apologetics. Indeed, well over a century after Christian scholars inaugurated self-conscious attempts to reduce apologetics to a well-defined field of endeavor (a specific discipline), confusion still persisted with respect to the place of apologetics among the theological disciplines, its proper task and divisions, its value, and its relation to faith—as evidenced by B. B. War-

---

5. Baker Book House, 1961, pp. 17-27.

field's 1908 article, "Apologetics," for *The New Schaff-Herzog Encyclopedia of Religious Knowledge*.[6] Some attempted to distinguish apologetics from apology, but they differed among themselves respecting the principle of distinction (Düsterdieck, Kübel). Apologetics was variously classified as an exegetical discipline (Planck), historical theology (Tzschirner), theory of religion (Räbiger), philosophical theology (Schleiermacher), something distinct from polemics (Kuyper), something belonging to several departments (Tholuck, Cave), or something which had no right to exist (Nösselt). H. B. Smith viewed apologetics as historico-philosophical dogmatics which deals with *detail* questions, but Kübel claimed that it properly deals only with the *essence* of Christianity. Schultz went further and said that apologetics is concerned simply to defend a generally *religious* view of the world, but others taught that apologetics should aim to establish *Christianity* as the final religion (Sack, Ebrard, Lechler, Lemme). Still others held that the task of apologetics is to present *evidences* for Christianity, and Warfield claimed that apologetics should seek to establish the presuppositions of theology: namely, the *facts* of God, religious consciousness, revelation, Christianity, and the Bible. Accordingly he divided the discipline into philosophical apologetics, psychological apologetics, revelational apologetics, historical apologetics, and bibliological apologetics. F. R. Beattie more simply divided the field according to philosophical, historical, and practical apologetics. In the tradition of Aquinas, some apologists made it their goal to show Christianity to be worthy of belief for *reasonable* men; yet others, like Brunetière, proclaimed that faith was most powerful as a heartfelt response *apart from* reason.

Therefore we observe that, while the *general* idea of apologetics is easy enough to grasp, it is by no means a simple project to settle upon an incisive *analysis* and decisive *operating method* for the discipline. Amidst a maze of conflicting answers to the fundamental questions rehearsed above, settling upon a course to follow in defending the faith can be very perplexing. Just as the church at large has not settled upon a unified doctrinal perspective, so the many-faceted and theologically oriented issues of apologetics have not been give clear and agreed upon answers. Consequently, when one engages in defending his faith, it is requisite for him to think through complicated questions and make responsible theological judgments, for his apologetic approach will of necessity be selected from a beehive of competitors. And no Christian wishes to be stung with a misguided, incongruous or fault-ridden line of defense.

The Basic Question of Method

How then should the Christian defend his faith? The answer to this

---

6. Ed. S. M. Jackson (New York: Funk and Wagnalls, 1908), I, 232-238.

question will determine the character of one's apologetic. "The serious question in apologetics," says Ramm, "is the question of strategy."[7] The urgency of arriving at the proper answer to this question is underlined by the example of Simon Peter, who solemnly determined and adamantly proclaimed that he would never deny Christ or stumble in his adherence to confessing the Lord.[8] However, though Christ was in need of defense at his trial, Peter stood outside in the courtyard, denying his Lord with increasing vehemence at every confrontation.[9] Nevertheless, the forsaken Messiah later restored Peter and instructed him to feed His sheep.[10] Accordingly, Peter writes in his first epistle that God resurrected and glorified Christ in order that the believer's *hope* might be *in God*; indeed, by the resurrection of Christ the Christian has been born again unto a *living hope*. The Christian can, with a *diligent mind, set his hope without reserve* on the grace brought unto him.[11] Having fed Christ's sheep with the good news about this living hope, and poignantly remembering his own past failure, Peter commands us to set apart Christ as Lord in our hearts and to *be prepared* at all times *to present an apologetic* for that *hope* (assured confidence) which is in us.[12] It may be that developing a responsible and solid apologetic approach takes discernment and diligent thought, but Peter places an obligation for such thought and preparation upon each believer.

The question of apologetic strategy *must* be answered, and answered properly, lest we become unfaithful in defending the faith or even deny it, as did Peter. We are exhorted to hold fast the confession of our hope without wavering,[13] and obedience to that exhortation requires sound preparation with respect to apologetic method—a method which should reflect unwavering *loyalty* to the Lord. As Peter expresses it, the *prerequisite* to apologetics is setting Christ apart *as Lord* in the heart. How then should the Christian defend his faith? How should one's apologetic remain *faithful* to the faith which is defended? How does the apologist stay true to his *Lord*?

The Greek word *apologia* (from which we derive the English word 'apologetics') denotes a speech made in defense, a reply (especially in the legal context of a courtroom) made to an accusation. The word originated in the judicial operations of ancient Athens, but the word occurs several times in the New Testament as well. The difference between the Greek and Christian methods of apologetic can be illustrated by contrasting the *Apology* of Socrates (as Plato records it) with the approach of the apostle Paul, who described himself as "set for the defense (*apologia*)

---

7. Ramm, *op. cit.*, p. 13.
8. Matthew 26:31-35.
9. Matthew 26:69-75.
10. John 21:15-19.

11. I Peter 1:3, 13, 21.
12. I Peter 3:15.
13. Hebrews 10:23.

of the gospel."[14] Despite the *complex* of material and methodological questions which surround the intramural debates over Christian apologetics, in the long run the array of various ways in which believers have defended their faith can be reduced to *two fundamental perspectives*: that of Socrates *or* that of Christ (for whom Paul, as an official representative, or "apostle," spoke with authority). One's understanding of apologetics is ultimately guided by either the paradigm of Socrates' *Apology* or the example of Paul, who was set for the *apologia* of the gospel.

The Socratic Outlook

In Plato's eyes, Socrates was not a mere sage, cosmologist, or Sophist; he was the *philosopher par excellence*.[15] Plato's esteem is manifest in his description of Socrates as "the finest, most intelligent, and moral man of his generation."[16] It was clear even to the ancients that Socrates' influence was sure to be weighty, as evident in the testimony of Epictetus: "Even now, although Socrates is dead, the memory of what he did or said while still alive is just as helpful or even more so to men."[17] And judging from the history of philosophy, Epictetus was correct. Commending his immanentistic motif, Cicero taught that "Socrates was the first to call philosophy down from the heavens."[18] Commending his foreshadowing of the Renaissance spirit, Erasmus placed Socrates among the saints and prayed *"Sancte Socrates, ora pro nobis!"* [Holy Socrates: pray for us!][19] Commending his anticipation of Kant's emphasis upon epistemic subjectivity, Werner Jaeger extolled him as "the greatest teacher in European history."[20] And commending his agreement with the modern spirit of autonomy, Antony Flew presents Socrates' discussion in *Euthyphro* as a paradigm of philosophic argument and progress.[21] Socrates provided a foretaste of *Idealism*'s resolution of the debate between Parmenides (static logic) and Heraclitus (historical flux), and yet by teaching the role of prediction in the notion of knowledge, Socrates looked ahead to *Pragmatism;* his independent spirit and reliance upon an inner voice were a forecast of *Existentialism*, while his method of critical, dialectical questioning anticipated linguistic *Analysis*.[22] Obviously his influence has been pervasive

---

14. Philippians 1:16.
15. *The Encyclopedia of Philosophy*; ed. Paul Edwards (New York: Macmillan, 1967), VI, 216.
16. *Phaedo*, 118.
17. *Discourses*, IV, 1, 169.
18. *Tusculan Disputations*, V, 4, 10.
19. Cited by Werner Jaeger, *Paideia: The Ideals of Greek Culture* (New York: Oxford University Press, 1945), II, book 3.
20. *Ibid.*
21. *An Introduction to Western Philosophy* (London: Thames and Hudson, 1971), p. 28.
22. S. P. Peterfreund and T. C. Denise, *Contemporary Philosophy and Its Origins* (New Jersey: D. Van Nostrand, 1967), pp. 63-69, 123-124, 182-185, 232-239.

even though his apology before the Athenian jury did not carry the day. "Indeed, his real defense, as Plato reports it, was directed to future generations."[23] Throughout those generations Socrates' seminal teaching has gained an extensive hearing among intellectual leaders, and through these implicit disciples Socrates has even exercised sway over the major defenders of the Christian faith.

Notwithstanding the fact that Socrates is popularly remembered *per se* as a philosopher, the comparison between his *method of defense* and that of Paul (or other scriptural writers) is not an uneven one. For Socrates was an intensely *religious* thinker (despite the accusation against him of atheism—which, in Athens, was closely allied to the charge of treason against the democracy).[24] Socrates was religiously motivated and aimed to provide a religious apologetic. He viewed himself as *divinely commissioned* to be "the Athenian gadfly." In the *Apology*, as related through Plato, Socrates recounted how he would preface his critical discussions with men in Athens by asking if they did not care for the perfection of their souls. Then Socrates explained to the jury: "For know that the god commands me to do this, and I believe that no greater good ever came to pass in the city than my service to the god" (30a). His divine mission to teach philosophy so as to perfect men's souls was deadly serious; with words remarkably like those of Peter in Acts 5:29, Socrates declared (29d),

> If you say to me, Socrates, this time . . . you shall be let off, but upon one condition, that you are not to enquire and speculate in this way any more, and that if you are caught doing so again you shall die;—if this was the condition on which you let me go, I shall reply: Men of Athens I honor and love you; but I shall obey God rather than you, and while I have life and strength I shall never cease from the practice and teaching of philosophy. . . .[25]

23. W. T. Jones, *A History of Western Philosophy* (New York: Harcourt, Brace, and World, 1952), I, 96.

24. *Ibid.*, pp. 58, 95-96. The actual indictment, recorded for us by both Xenophon and Diogenes Laertius, read, "Socrates is guilty of refusing to recognize the gods recognized by the state and introducing other, new divinities. He is also guilty of corrupting the youth." Because the state was a religious institution dedicated to Athena, the charge of "irreligion" could apply to any offense against the state. Socrates was a critic of the traditional establishment education (cf. Aristophanes' *T'.e Clouds*) and thereby a corruptor of youth; Socrates saw *this* as the real issue, as evidenced by his conversation in the *Euthyphro* (2c-3d). Zeller states that, while it was not the primary motive, "Socrates, it is true, fell as a sacrifice to the democratic reaction which followed the overthrow of the Thirty. . . . His guilt was sought first of all in the undermining of the morality and religion of his country . . ." (*Die Philosophie der Griechen*, 2. Teil, I. Abteilung, *Sokrates* . . . , 5. Auflage, Leipzig, 1922, p. 217).

25. B. Jowett, trans., *The Dialogues of Plato* (New York: Random House, 1937), I, 412. The reader should note that in the account of Socrates which follows I have not attempted to separate the historical Socrates from Socrates-the-spokesman-for-Plato. Such a delicate and debated task would be tangential to this essay. For present purposes, the view of "Socrates" given herein stems uncritically from the

So dedicated was Socrates to his divine calling that he would not accept his legal option of exile as an alternative to execution (cf. *Apology*, 37; *Crito*); he explained that to leave Athens would be a betrayal of his divine mission as a philosopher. In the *Phaedo* dialogue, Plato recounted the final conversations between Socrates and his friends shortly before the death sentence was executed upon him. Here we gain insight to the high regard Socrates had for philosophy. He says only those souls purified from bodily taint through philosophy (which aims to behold truth with the eye of the soul) can escape the cycle of reincarnation and pass into the company of the gods. Hence philosophy is no mere academic discipline; it is a way of life and the path to salvation. In philosophy, then, Socrates found his own self-established version of "the way, the truth, and the life."

Salvation would be found, held Socrates, through the exercise of one's *rational soul*. For Socrates, the human mind is a spark of the wisdom that is immanent in the universe.[26] Socrates states in the *Alcibiades* (133c), "Can we mention anything more divine about the soul than what is concerned with knowledge and thought? Then this aspect of it resembles God, and it is by looking toward that and understanding all that is divine— God and wisdom—that a man will most fully know himself." Elsewhere he declared, "The soul is most like that which is divine" (*Phaedo*, 80b). The logos was present within man, and as Jaeger rightly observed, "in Socrates' view, the soul is the divine in man." After a detailed examination of Socrates' view of the soul W. K. C. Guthrie wrote,

> To sum up, Socrates believed in a god who was the supreme mind. . . . Men moreover had a special relation with him in that their own minds . . . were, though less perfect than the mind of God, of the same nature, and worked on the same principles. In fact, if one looked only to the *areté* of the human soul and disregarded its shortcomings, the two were identical.[27]

In the Platonic dialogue, *Symposium*, Socrates taught that the supreme life is that of the soul's contemplation of ultimate beauty in its absolute form; hereby a life of intellectual communion paves the way for sharing in the divinity of love. In the inner center of mental contemplation the soul encounters deity and discovers ethical virtue. As Van Til notes:

> He could find no footing for morality except in the soul as somehow participant in the laws of another, a higher world. . . . Socrates sought for a principle of validity by means of his appeal to the logos . . . by means of the idea of man's participation in deity or in an abstract principle of rationality, the logos.[28]

Platonic dialogues; thus "Socrates" tends to become a label for a Platonic-Socratic hybrid. This is adequate for the purposes of *contrast* with the scriptural outlook.

26. Cf. Xenophon, *Memorabilia* I, iv, 8.
27. W. K. C. Guthrie, *Socrates* (Cambridge: University Press, 1971), p. 156.
28. *Christian Theistic Ethics*, In Defense of the Faith, vol. III (Nutley, N. J.: den Dulk Christian Foundation, 1971), p. 183.

Whereas the Council of Chalcedon declared that in *Christ* the eternal and temporal are united without intermixture, Socrates proclaimed that the eternal and temporal are combined in *man* by way of admixture.[29] And so it is that Socrates was the prophet of the religion of immanent reason. He had a divine commission and a message to be proclaimed even upon pain of death—a message of salvation through the incarnate logos, that is, the rational soul within man. All of life and every thought had to be brought under obedience to the lordship of man's reason. Let there be no doubt then, that Socrates was a religious apologist, just as J. T. Forbes recognized:

> By the testimony of his principal disciples, the whole life of Socrates was pervaded by *the thought of God*. . . . It was the sane religion of one who had found a faith that could bear the examination of his mind. . . . As he comes before us, it is as one who has reasoned and wrought his way to a rational creed.[30]

With such a view of man's rational faculty as outlined above, Socrates was quite naturally led to exalt the *intellect*, to commend a *neutral methodology*, and to insist upon *autonomy* as an epistemological standard.

In the *Protagoras*, Socrates established that virtue is not a skill, but is knowledge; consequently, virtue can be taught. The same conclusion was wrought in the *Meno* dialogue, where virtue is identified with knowledge, and knowledge is taken to be a gift of the gods. The result of Socrates' stress upon the intellect and his equation of virtue and knowledge was the doctrine that *no man knowingly does evil*. This point is argued in the *Gorgias*. Socrates said that all men desire to act for the sake of some good, and hence any man who acts wrongly must be acting in ignorance of the evil he does (in which case punishment should aim at *rehabilitation through education*). If "virtue is the knowledge of the good," then an unvirtuous act is one done without knowledge of the good; thus no man deliberately or knowingly does evil. Wrongdoing must be involuntary or ignorant. In this Socrates declared, against the testimony of Paul in Romans 7, that men are not totally depraved—in which case man's reason is not defective due to the domination of sin. Indeed, just the opposite: man's intellect, as the faculty whereby knowledge is gained, must be viewed as virtuous. Socrates exalted the intellect of man as the primary faculty, one which as a charioteer must hold in check the horses of will and passion (*Phaedrus*); all the particulars of human experience must be subordinated under the

---

29. Cf. Cornelius Van Til, *A Survey of Christian Epistemology*, In Defense of the Faith, vol. II (Nutley, N. J.: den Dulk Christian Foundation, 1969), p. 31.

30. J. T. Forbes, *Socrates* (New York: Charles Scribner's Sons, 1905), pp. 212, 213. No less an authority than W. K. C. Guthrie has said with respect to the religious character of Socrates' thought: "Belief in a special, direct relation between himself and divine forces must be accepted in any account of his mentality which lays claim to completeness" (*Socrates*, p. 84).

ordering domination of the reason. Therefore, according to Socratic anthropology, man's reason is not steeped in sin, but man's virtuous intellect
keeps control over his irrational drives. One can and must trust his reason
to guide him toward the good.

There are three notable characteristics of knowledge in the view of
Socrates. *First*, as he argued in the *Meno*, in the course of endless reincarnations, men's souls have become acquainted with the eternal forms
and thus know all things. When man comes to know something in this
life, then, it is not a matter of acquiring some new thing but simply the
recollection of something previously known. Hence knowledge is *innate* in
man. *Secondly*, we find out in the *Theaetetus* that mere sense perception
is inadequate as a source of knowledge. There must be something which
is exempt from the constant, Heraclitean flux of historical particulars that
are perceived by the senses; otherwise there could be no knowledge whatsoever. The world of sense experience is, as recognized by Heraclitus, in
continual movement or alteration. Yet insofar as this world is known, it
must be viewed against an unchanging set of concepts having the character
of the Parmenidean *One*. The principle of unity as well as the principle of
diversity must be incorporated in knowledge. The absolute flux of historical
particulars, all diverse from each other, would be unknowable; however,
the supremely knowable, unifying forms or concepts of reason are purely
abstract and void of content. Therefore, knowledge is a combination of
both the changing and the unchanging. Knowledge combines sense perception with an ordering judgment of the mind. *Sense perception triggers
a recollection of permanent, immutable forms of the non-material realm
above history* (cf. *Phaedo*, 75e). Socrates' characteristic contribution to
the advance of epistemology, said Aristotle, was twofold: (1) induction,
and (2) general definition.[31] Socrates was inductive because he moved
from the many or particulars to the one or universal; yet he aimed at
logical precision by organizing the particulars under general principles.[32]
Induction led to general definition, for a definition consists of a collection
of essential (rather than accidental) attributes which are jointly sufficient
to delineate one class of objects from another. This general definition was
called the form (*eidos*) of the class, its essential nature. In a unique and
forceful way Socrates (as spokesman for Plato) dialectically *combined*
continuity (general principles) and discontinuity (particular facts) in his
epistemological theory. *Thirdly*, according to Socrates (again in the *Meno*)
knowledge requires the ability to give the *grounds* upon which an answer
is established—the *logos* of any *ousia* mentioned. True opinion is insufficient as a criterion of knowledge, for like the statue of Daedalus, unless it

31. *Metaphysics*, 1078b, 27.
32. Francis N. Lee, *A Christian Introduction to the History of Philosophy* (Nutley, N. J.: Craig Press, 1969), p. 83.

is tied down it walks away. Holding an opinion which is in fact correct, but being unable to give a reason for that opinion, does not qualify as knowledge (cf. *Symposium*, 202a). The proper grounding of true opinion is to be found in *recollection* of the truth, a kind of *intuitive* or *direct apprehension* of the absolute idea or form. Hereby true opinion is converted into completely adequate knowledge.

Since Socrates viewed man's reason as normal or untainted by the effects of sin, because he had a rationalized view of knowledge and the inward adequacy of man's mind, he was led to extol *intellectual independence and neutrality* in the search for truth. The philosopher supposedly has learned to avoid the deceptions of sense perception and to refrain from following the untrustworthy leading of emotions; for the philosopher, the soul relies on its own intellectual capability. In the *Phaedo*, Socrates taught that the soul "will calm passion, and follow reason, and dwell in the contemplation of her, beholding the true and divine" (84a). Expanding upon this in the *Crito*, Socrates described the rational man as an independent thinker who is neutral in his approach to truth. The philosopher should be a completely detached, rational thinker who refuses to heed popular opinion in order to follow after the truth wherever it may be. Here we find the self-sufficient, impartial, intellectual. Hear the Socratic exhortation:

> My dear Crito, . . . we must examine the question whether we ought to do this or not; for I am not only now but always a man who follows nothing but the reasoning which on consideration seems to me best. . . . Then, most excellent friend, we must not consider at all what the many will say of us, but what he knows about right and wrong, the one man, and truth herself will say.[33]

It is significant that, having claimed that he *followed nothing but reason* in his intellectual queries, Socrates came to the conclusion of his line of thought and said, "Then, Crito, let be, and let us act in this way, since it is in this way that *God leads us*."[34] Reason's leading is tacitly assumed to be God's leading—in which case the philosopher really is inwardly sufficient, and therefore he is in need of no transcendent revelation in order to carry out the epistemological enterprise. Moreover, nothing could be a more secure method of countenancing and vindicating God's thoughts than utter self-reliance upon one's reasoning ability. To such intellectual independence and self-confidence Socrates was dedicated, advocating that men should follow the critical test of reason alone: "The life not tested by criticism is not worth living," he declared in his *Apology* (38a). Dogmatism is to be forever banished from philosophy in favor of a completely detached,

---

33. H. N. Fowler, tr., *Crito*, in the Loeb Classical Library (Cambridge: Harvard University Press, 1924), at 46b.
34. *Ibid.*, 54e, emphasis my own.

impartial, neutral search for truth and reality. In short, conclude Peterfreund and Denise: "The procedures of analysis themselves must be metaphysically neutral, in the sense that they involve the testing of philosophical proposals by universal standards of reason. . . . This feature of neutrality is well illustrated in the dialogues of Plato."[35]

The motto which Socrates set forth to the world was the Delphic inscription, "Know thyself" (e.g., *Philebus*, 48c), from which it is evident that his challenge to relativistic and agnostic Sophism did *not* include renunciation of the *anthropocentricity* of the Sophists. Socrates countered the scepticism of the Sophists by stressing rational, inward self-sufficiency as the crucial foundation of epistemology. Socrates took the *autonomous man* as his starting point—the man who, as a law unto himself, can adequately arrive at self-knowledge through rational introspection and from that base move out to comprehend the truth beyond him. The Sophist, Protagoras, said, "Man is the measure of all things," meaning that all sense experience is subjective and all laws are mere conventions. That perspective led to scepticism and cynicism. In order to restore objectivity to knowledge, Socrates appealed to reason, but reason which was nevertheless man-centered or autonomous, just as it was for the Sophists.

> Thus, by appealing to reason, that is to the universal aspect in man, Socrates saved the objectivity of both knowledge and ethics. He saved both because saving one is, in effect, saving the other. Saving knowledge is saving virtue, for knowledge is virtue. Thus Socrates was a "restorer of faith." . . . There is only one remedy for the ills of thought, and that is, more thought. If thought, in its first inroads, leads, as it always does, to scepticism and denial, the only course is, not to suppress thought, but to found faith upon it. Socrates agreed with the Sophists that the truth must be my truth, but mine "in my capacity as a rational being."[36]

Socrates did not take an approach fundamentally different from the Sophists; he simply placed *faith* in man's autonomous intellect (as a spark from the wisdom or logos above the material world). Reason is a divine element in man, worthy of religious trust and devotion. The Sophists had not heeded this gospel, this good news which saves the epistemological enterprise. "Socrates was destined to restore order out of chaos because, though with Sophists appealing to the self, he appealed to the self as carrying within itself the universal principle of reason and order."[37] Like the Sophists, Socrates *began with man* and centered his attention on man;[38] unlike the Sophists, he placed supreme *confidence in reason* as something

---

35. Peterfreund and Denise, *op. cit.*, p. 237.
36. Van Til, *Christian Theistic Ethics*, pp. 160, 161.
37. *Ibid.*, p. 159.
38. Lee, p. 81.

within man which participates in the abstract and universal laws of a higher world.[39]

Thus it was appropriate that the Danish irrationalist, Søren Kierkegaard, characterized Socrates as having a "passion of inwardness." While Socrates exalted reason and Kierkegaard deprecated its ultimate usefulness, they both found it necessary to begin their respective philosophies with man's self-sufficient, *inward* experience of *eternity in time*. Man's inward autonomy was crucial to Socratic thinking. Van Til explains that "the Socratic spirit of Inwardness" is "the concentration of all interpretation upon man as the final reference point."[40] Socrates took the knowledge of himself to be so clear that he could use it as the basis for intelligibly interpreting the world outside him. Man's mind supposedly participates in the abstract principle of absolute truth; a knowledge of the forms is innate to man. Consequently, to understand anything at all, man has to look to himself and autonomously interpret his experience in the authoritative light of his own reason.

"Socrates sought to answer the sceptics in his day by thinking of the individual soul as participant in an objective world of intelligence"; however, as entrapped in the prison of the body, man's soul (said Plato) has to be lifted to this world of light by Diotima the inspired.[41] Man in his *individuality*, man as *discontinuous from others* because of his particular body, man in his character as participant in the *irrational flux of history*, is made the sovereign judge of truth by Socrates. But in order to determine the truth for himself, this man must somehow loosen the shackles of the body and philosophically contemplate the *abstract, universal forms* of the *world of pure being*. In the long run, as Antony Flew has observed, knowledge for Socrates ceases to have any connection with the historical world.[42] In the *Phaedo*, Socrates says that the philosopher who seeks knowledge is always pursuing death, seeing that the body hinders the soul's search for knowledge; the attempt to apprehend the forms and thereby find knowledge is an attempt to leave behind the historical world of particulars. Therefore, Van Til rightly parallels Socrates to his Sophist opponents:

> The objectivity for knowledge and ethics . . . which Socrates found by appealing to reason as the universal aspect in man, turns out to be an empty form, and there is no connection of this abstract universal with particulars except in terms of an irrational principle. In other words, Socrates, as well as the Sophists, has finally come back to the

---

39. Cf. Herman Dooyeweerd, *A New Critique of Theoretical Thought*, tr., D. H. Freeman and H. De Jongste (Philadelphia: Presbyterian and Reformed, 1955), I, 51, 355.

40. Cornelius Van Til, *A Christian Theory of Knowledge* (Philadelphia: Presbyterian and Reformed, 1969), p. 144.

41. *Ibid.*, p. 153.

42. Flew, p. 77.

realm of pure contingency. Thus we are back to the Sophistic notion that in practice there is no known validity to any moral law except what man, irrational in his individuality, is willing to approve.[43]

Making man epistemologically autonomous requires the combination of rationality and irrationality. For historical, particular man to *know* anything he would finally have to cease being an *individual* man, and for knowledge to be grasped by *individual man* it would have to cease being *universally* objective truth in some suprahistorical realm. Socrates attempted to make *man* the measure of *truth*, thereby trying to combine oil and water—trying to mix universally rational truth into irrationally particularized (historical) man. The autonomy involved in the Socratic "passion for inwardness" could lead to nothing but a dialectical epistemology.

Regarding Socratic inwardness, Van Til says, "This principle is that the ultimate distinctions between true and false, right and wrong, are to be made by man as ultimate."[44] Perhaps this *anthropocentric, autonomous epistemology* is nowhere more clearly expressed by Socrates than in the *Euthyphro* dialogue. The *Euthyphro* portrays Socrates shortly before his trial in Athens. Socrates, having been charged with corrupting the youth and with religious offenses, happened to meet Euthyphro, who was piously bringing charges against his own father, at the Porch of King Archon. Socrates asked Euthyphro to instruct him in order that he might more adequately defend himself against Meletus in court. Socrates inquired as to the distinction between piety and impiety. When Euthyphro justified the piety of what he was doing to his father by appealing to the fact that Zeus had punished his own father, Cronos, for committing a similar crime, Socrates treated the answer as merely *one more report among many* of what happens in history. There is nothing special about the activity of the gods. What is needed, said Socrates, is not an *example* of piety, but a general statement of the *essential characteristic* of piety. Indeed, general knowledge is crucial for correctly *identifying* the particular cases. Hence Euthyphro offered a definition which is formally more adequate: "What is pleasing to the gods is pious, and what is not pleasing to them is impious." Then the crucial reply of the dialogue was rendered by Socrates: Do the gods love piety because it is pious, or is it pious because the gods love it? Socrates holds that piety has certain characteristics which make it pious in itself—irrespective of what the gods may think about it Thus man should seek a knowledge of piety (or anything else) by self-sufficient, autonomous investigation into the nature of things, not by relying upon the actions, attitudes, or revelation of the gods. At best, the word or *opinion of the gods* is just *one hypothesis among many* to be confirmed

---

43. *Christian Theistic Ethics*, p. 162.
44. *Ibid.*, p. 173.

or discomfirmed by the rational man. Man is the ultimate judge or discerner of goodness, truth, and the like; as such, he can and must critically scrutinize even the opinions of the gods. *By what standard should truth or knowledge be measured? The rational intellect of man,* not the revelation of the gods. To find the truth, man's soul must look to itself; to regard the word of an authority as anything more than incidental information would conflict with the very idea of man's knowledge as sufficient to itself.

Here is illustrated, then, the *Socratic exaltation of the intellect,* the absolute requirement of *impartial or neutral investigation* for the truth, and the *final epistemological standard of sheer autonomy.* Socrates was the prophet of the religion of sovereign, self-sufficient, authoritative reason; to put it as Werner Jaeger does, Socrates was

> the apostle of moral liberty, *bound by no dogma,* fettered by no traditions, *standing free on his own feet, listening only to the inner voice* of conscience—preaching *the new religion of this world,* and a heaven to be found in this life by our own spiritual strength, not through grace but through tireless striving to perfect our own nature.[45]

The *religion of this world* has a definite doctrine of authority; whether in epistemology or any other field, the *voice of authority* must be found in *man himself.* Socrates would not have man relinquish his autonomy at any cost. If man is to follow the gods, it must be on man's own terms—namely, that the gods first be scrutinized and approved by the rational judgment of man. In Athens, the views of deity were expressed through the public opinion of the democracy. Socrates resisted such dogma in favor of a more self-conscious and consistent religion of autonomy—for which he finally stood trial. J. T. Forbes has aptly commented:

> The question of the seat of authority has lasted through the ages, and the Socratic transference of it to the reflective reason, of which his very discussions on piety and justice were the claim, demanded an insight and moral earnestness too great for the mass of his fellows. [Yet] the trend of progress of the human mind was with him.[46]

Socrates was a pioneer and religious apologist for the religion of the world; his martyred blood served as just so much seed for spreading the gospel of man's epistemological self-authority, a dogma which he had brought to purest expression.

With this background to the influence, religion, and epistemology of Socrates, we can now take note of the way in which Socrates carried on his apologetic before the Athenian jury. The *Apology,* along

---

45. Jaeger, *loc cit.,* emphasis mine.
46. Forbes, *op. cit.,* p. 270.

with *Crito* and *Phaedo*, forms a trilogy dealing with the final days of Socrates. The enmity of Socrates' accusers had been generated by his disdain for the democracy and public opinion; Socrates practiced a religious devotion to the pursuit of ultimate truth by following the guidance of independent reason alone. The accusations brought by Meletus had now put Socrates in the position of presenting an apology for his faith. Five strands of defense can be traced in his apologetic strategy.

First, there is the *validation* of the Oracle's statement by *factual testing.* Chaerephon had asked the Oracle at Delphi whether anyone was wiser than Socrates, and he received "No" for his answer. That puzzled Socrates, and so he set out to find a wiser man. Socrates took it to be his religious duty to determine the Oracle's meaning, to prove by factual methods that the god was right. To establish that the Oracle was neither lying nor incorrect, Socrates made it his job to expose the ignorance of supposedly wise men in Athens—thereby corroborating that he was, by recognition of his lack of wisdom, really the wisest of men, just as the Oracle had said.

Secondly, in his apologetic strategy Socrates made use of the *logical test for coherence.* Socrates had been charged with atheism or impiety; as children, his audience had heard (for instance, in Aristophanes' comedy, *The Clouds*) that Socrates pursued *naturalistic* scientific investigations; additionally one of the youths whom Socrates had corrupted, Alcibiades, had been blamed for the *mutilation of the statues of Hermes*—the obscene adornments of every Athenian front doorway—on the night before the military expedition to Sicily. These things might be behind the charge of atheism. However, Socrates rehearsed that Meletus, in the statement of the charges, had accused Socrates "of believing in deities of his own invention *instead of* the gods recognized by the State." As demonstration of his own logical prowess, Socrates pointed out that Meletus had contradicted himself. Socrates was charged simultaneously for believing in no gods, and yet for believing in new deities and supernatural activities (namely, the divine inner voice). Socrates tied other logical knots in the prosecution's case. By questioning Meletus, Socrates got him to say that the best influence on *youth* comes from the *many citizens* of Athens (rather than from the individual, Socrates), but the best training in *other fields* (e.g., raising horses) comes from the one *individual expert* (rather than the incompetent many). Moreover, it is unlikely that he would *intentionally* corrupt the youth, for that would generate a corrupting influence upon himself through his own associates. Thus, if indeed Socrates had corrupted the youth, it must have been unintentional—in which case he has an admonition coming, but not punishment. Logic was a tool in Socrates' arsenal.

Third, Socrates followed the apologetic line that the jury should take into account the *great benefit* which his *divine service* has been to the city. Socrates had urged men to put the welfare of their souls above all else, and Socratic philosophy demonstrated how they should do this. Therefore, if the Athenians executed Socrates, they would actually be inflicting great harm on themselves. They would lose the restraining voice of Socrates, asking "Are you not ashamed that you give your attention to acquiring as much money as possible, and similarly with reputation and honor, and give no attention or thought to truth and understanding and the perfection of your soul?" (29e). Socrates defended himself, then, by appealing to the elevated, noble, and beneficial results of his service and outlook.

Fourth, Socrates took the apologetical approach of asking the jury to examine the *life of the speaker*. Socrates had given loyal service to the military. He had continually sought to follow the path of acting rightly, whatever the personal outcome would be for him. He was not fearful of death. He had given his life in the service of others, being sent as a gadfly by God to Athens in order to keep it from becoming lazy like a large thoroughbred horse. His sincerity is evident from the fact that he lived in poverty, neglecting private affairs so as to fulfill his divine duty. Obviously the religious philosophical outlook of Socrates had transformed him into a praiseworthy individual, good citizen, and public servant. And so he proclaimed in his defense, "You will not easily find another like me, gentlemen, and if you take my advice you will spare my life" (31a).

Finally, after the appeal to fact, logic, beneficial effect, and personal betterment, Socrates came to use in his apology the appeal to *inner guidance*. In answer to why he had not entered political service which would have been consonant with his convictions (if sincerely stated), Socrates claimed that he had been forbidden to carry his convictions to that consistent outcome by a *divine voice* which occasionally came to him. "Plato explicitly represents Socrates turning to an inner voice (daimon)—a voice that is a product neither of social conditioning nor of reason—at crucial moments of decision."[47] "There is no question whatever that he himself regarded it as Heaven sent."[48] Socrates explained this inward, validating, convicting voice in this way: "something divine and spiritual comes to me. . . . I have had this from my childhood; it is a sort of voice that comes to me, and when it comes it always holds me back from what I am thinking of doing" (31d). Socrates even used this subjectivistic apologetic to lend support to his *four other* lines of defense. At the end of the trial, after the guilty verdict had been presented, Socrates said that in nothing he had done or said that day had the inner voice opposed him, even

---

47. Peterfreund and Denise, *op. cit.*, p. 184.
48. J. T. Forbes, *op. cit.*, p. 221. Guthrie says, "he put himself unreservedly in the hands of what he sincerely believed to be an inspiration from heaven" (*op. cit.*, p. 163).

though in the past it sometimes would stop him in the middle of a sentence. Thus his other apologetic devices received subjective validation.

Here we have the five-point apologetic method of Socrates. He was dedicated to the autonomy of man's reason and to neutrality in the search for truth, wherever it should be found. He enthroned man's intellect as the epistemological authority, even over the opinions of deity. He was the rational man, unfettered by dogma and public opinion. Whatever views were to be held had first to pass the scrutiny of his self-sufficient mind. His apologetic strategy was both *rational* (appealing to logical coherence) and *irrational* (appealing to subjectivistic conviction), *factual* (verifying the Oracle's words through experimentation) and *pragmatic* (looking to the beneficial results, both public and personal, of his practice and convictions). As Peterfreund and Denise rightly observe, Socrates' efforts to meet his own criterion of the critically examined life were "characterized by a strange tension."[49] Somehow, he was simultaneously the unique, self-determining, inner-directed adjudicator of all claims to knowledge and the dispassionate, objective observer of that realm of truth which unifies all minds. W. T. Jones says,

> He must have seemed to his fellow citizens more like a Sophist than anything else. But he had a profound, and entirely un-Sophistic, conviction of the reality of goodness, the goodness of reality, and the immortality of the human soul. He combined an intensely realistic and down-to-earth common sense with a passionate mysticism; a cool and dispassionate scepticism about ordinary beliefs and opinions with a deep religious sense.[50]

Socrates could claim in one and the same dialogue (as he did in the *Meno*) that he was both as *ignorant* as his opponents and yet *omniscient* as a result of his preexistent awareness of the forms. He claimed to accept nothing except upon *critical* and *reasonable* scrutiny, and yet he accepted the authority of the *expert* (as in the *Crito*) and followed the leading of a *non-rational* daimon (as evidenced in the *Apology*). He said that *nobody* knows about death, and yet that *he knew* enough not to fear it (cf. *Apology*, 29a). His autonomous apologetic was a strange combination of omnicompetent reason and mysticism, faith in himself alone, yet ready trust in the divine. To protect his autonomy Socrates was forced back and forth between the poles of rationality and irrationality. "What Socrates did was to rationalize the known, and to make the mysterious the divine."[51]

This procedure is virtually identical with the two-step apologetic method of Roman Catholicism and Arminianism (represented by Aquinas and Butler respectively). The field of knowledge is *dichotomized* into truths

---

49. Peterfreund and Denise, *op. cit.*, p. 183.
50. Jones, *op. cit.*, p. 93.
51. Forbes, *op. cit.*, p. 230.

known by reason and truths known by "faith." At the outset, the apologist proceeds with self-sufficient reason to establish *general truths* about God or a probability in favor of them, but after this first level is built, the apologist then completes the edifice by appeals to *faith and revelation*. Supposedly a set area of the known can be rationalized, but the remainder must be relegated to divine mystery. A dialectical dance between rationality and irrationality always results from taking an autonomous, neutral approach to apologetics; such an approach is inherently destructive of the concept of authority in Christianity. Speaking of the Romanist and Arminian notion of authority, Van Til says:

> But such a concept of authority resembles that which Socrates referred to in *The Symposium* when he spoke of Diotima the inspired. When the effort at rational interpretation failed him, Socrates took refuge in mythology as a second best. The "hunch" of the wise is the best that is available to man with respect to that which he cannot reach by the methods of autonomous reason. No "wise man" ought to object to such a conception of the "supernatural." . . . If the Roman Catholic method of apologetic for Christianity is followed then Christianity itself must be so reduced as to make it acceptable to the natural man. . . . The natural man need only to reason consistently along the lines of his starting point and method in order to reduce each of the Christian doctrines that are presented to him to naturalistic proportions.[52]

Socrates transferred the seat of authority to man's autonomous reason; Roman Catholic and Arminian apologetics follow suit, thereby evidencing the justice of J. T. Forbes's earlier comment about the Socratic view of reason and authority: "The trend of progress of the human mind was with him."

The Christian Perspective

A fundamental antithesis exists between the thinking of Socrates and that of the apostle Paul; they radically differ even in the area of philosophical method. The contrast is evident in the following exposition of Paul's apologetic (which thematically corresponds to the exposition of Socrates). As one who had been set apart (sanctified) from the world by God's word of truth,[53] Paul founded his thinking on the solid rock foundation of Christ's words,[54] realizing that no one could improve upon the wisdom of God.[55] Paul had, then, no agreement with the darkness of Socrates' unbelieving approach to knowledge.[56] Along with the other apostles, Paul presupposed the wisdom and veracity of God's word, in contrast to Socrates, who started with the autonomy of man's intellect.

---

52. *The Defense of the Faith* (Philadelphia: Presbyterian and Reformed, 1955), p. 127.
53. John 17:17.
54. Matthew 7:24-25.
55. I Corinthians 2:16.
56. Cf. II Corinthians 6:14-15.

The antithesis could not be greater—the antithesis between truth and error. "They are of the world; therefore they speak of the world and the world hears them. We are of God; the one who knows God hears us, and the one who is not of God does not hear us. By this we know the spirit of truth and the spirit of error."[57]

Paul elaborated upon this stark antithesis between believing and unbelieving philosophy in I Corinthians 1–2. Those who perish see the word of the cross as foolishness, while those who are saved view it as the very power of God.[58] *The gospel is contrary to the presuppositions of unbelieving thought, for it does not cater to rebellious man's demand for factual signs and logical argumentation that will pass the test of autonomous scrutiny.*[59] Infatuation with worldly wisdom was the last thing that would characterize Paul![60] Christian wisdom glories rather in the *Lord*. Socrates was anthropocentric, while Paul was theocentric. Thus, when Paul came to Corinth, he did not rely upon the intellectual tools of the Athenian philosophers; instead, he came with the powerful demonstration of the Spirit in order that faith might *not be in the wisdom of men* but in the power of God.[61] Socrates would have been completely unable to receive this God-centered, presuppositional viewpoint of Paul as anything but foolishness.[62] Their respective epistemological methods were as different as darkness and light.[63]

Paul recognized that he had been divinely commissioned; he had been sent as an apostle, not by men, but by the resurrected Christ.[64] Hence he did not seek to please *men*, for that would have been incongruent with his status as a *servant of Christ*.[65] Paul was not commissioned to be a gadfly who, through dialectical questioning or research, seeks to spur men on to the self-betterment of their souls. As the ambassador for Christ, he beseeched men in Christ's stead, *not* to recognize their inherent *participation* in a higher divine realm of reason, but to be *reconciled* to God.[66] This required the attempt to *persuade* men;[67] yet his persuasion rested not on the self-sufficient reason of man, for Paul walked by *faith* and not by sight.[68] The *gospel* he preached was not based on man,[69] and thus the *weapons of his warfare* were not after the flesh but instead mighty through God for casting down every imagination that exalts itself against the knowledge of God.[70] His aim was *to bring every thought into captivity* to the obedience of Christ. Therefore, in diametric

---

57. I John 4:4-5.
58. I Corinthians 1:18; cf. Romans 1:16.
59. I Corinthians 1:22-23.
60. I Corinthians 1:26-31.
61. I Corinthians 2:1-5.
62. I Corinthians 2:14.
63. Cf. Ephesians 5:6-11.

64. Galatians 1:1.
65. Galatians 1:10.
66. II Corinthians 5:20.
67. II Corinthians 5:11.
68. II Corinthians 5:7.
69. Galatians 1:11.
70. II Corinthians 10:3-5.

contrast to Socrates, Paul had no high regard for autonomous philosophy. He warned that vain, deceitful philosophy which is directed by the traditional presuppositions of the world instead of by Christ will rob man of all the treasures of wisdom and knowledge, which treasures are to be found in Christ.[71] Paul did not oppose the use of persuasion and philosophy, but he absolutely rejected any persuasion and philosophy that were patterned after man's alleged self-sufficient intellectual abilities. True love-of-wisdom (''philosophy'') brings every thought captive to Christ and, thereby, shuns autonomy.

Consequently, rather than preaching salvation through (or dependence upon) the rational soul in man as an incarnate divine logos, Paul stressed the *Creator/creature distinction*[72] and proclaimed that men, suppressing the truth in unrighteousness,[73] are *alienated and enemies in their minds* against God and thus must be *reconciled* through the *cross* of Christ in the *body of His flesh*.[74] It is this Savior who is the eternal yet enfleshed Logos of God, the incarnate word full of grace and truth.[75] Jesus Christ himself is the Truth,[76] the wisdom of God,[77] the reposit of all knowledge,[78] and as such the life-giving light of men.[79] Paul's perspective stands squarely over against that of Socrates. Paul refused to utilize the pseudo-wisdom of the Socratic outlook lest the *cross* of Christ be made of none effect.[80] The rational religion of worldly wisdom knows not God, Paul maintained, for God saves men by the foolishness of preaching the cross of Christ.[81]

With such views as these, Paul certainly did not exalt the intellect of man, commend neutrality in one's thinking, or insist upon autonomy as an epistemological standard.

One of the key reasons why Paul did not exalt and trust the intellect or reason of man is found in his doctrine of *total depravity*. That depravity, held Paul, extends to the intellect of man. "The carnal mind is enmity against God; for it is not subject to the law of God, neither indeed can it be."[82] Because the unbeliever does not base his life and thinking upon the words of Christ, he is nothing less than foolish.[83] To approach the field of knowledge without presupposing the truth of God is to preclude arriving at a proper understanding. The beginning of knowledge is the fear of the Lord,[84] but there is no fear of God before the eyes of the sinner.[85] Hence he needs to have his eyes opened and to

---

71. Colossians 2:8, 3.
72. Romans 1:25.
73. Romans 1:18 .
74. Colossians 1:20-22.
75. John 1:1, 14.
76. John 14:6.
77. I Corinthians 1:24.
78. Colossians 2:3.

79. John 1:4.
80. Cf. I Corinthians 1:17.
81. I Corinthians 1:8, 21.
82. Romans 8:7.
83. Matthew 7:26-27.
84. Proverbs 1:7.
85. Romans 3:18.

turn from darkness to light;[86] in his natural state he has a blinded mind,[87] loving darkness rather than light.[88] Those who are enemies of the cross, noted Paul, are those who mind earthly things;[89] being a child of wrath in his sinful mind,[90] the man of worldly wisdom has vain thoughts.[91] The unbeliever, therefore, has no understanding,[92] cannot receive the Spirit of truth,[93] cannot discern spiritual things,[94] cannot see God's kingdom,[95] and is nothing short of an enemy in his mind against God.[96] *The thinking of the natural man is never a suitable pattern or starting point for Christian apologetics!* Unlike Socrates, Paul did not trust man's reason to guide him naturally toward the good. Man's mind is dominated by sin, and thus knowledge is *not* identical with virtue. Knowing God, all men fail nevertheless to obey Him—resulting in vain thinking and foolish, darkened hearts.[97] The unbeliever's reason is not omnicompetent according to Paul; instead, unbelievers walk in vanity of mind, with darkened understanding, ignorance, and blindness of heart—arriving at nothing but a "knowledge" *falsely* so-called.[98] Therefore, in his apologetic methodology, Paul refrained from exalting man's fallen intellect or building his case for the truth of Christianity upon its misguided standards. The carnal mind was seen for what it is: at enmity with God.

However, this conclusion did not lead Paul to give up the task of apologetics as hopeless. On the one hand, the unbeliever abuses his intellect and cannot avoid foolishness; on the other hand, the sinner yet has a knowledge of God which cannot be eradicated. All men are always accessible to the witness and persuasion of the Christian apologist. This is so because, as Paul teaches in Romans 1:18-21, there is a kind of "innate" knowledge of God which each and every man possesses, even though he mishandles and suppresses that knowledge. Such knowledge is not innate, with Socrates, in the sense that man's mind is in contact with the eternal realm of the forms and recollects them based on endless reincarnations; such innateness as this assumes the *continuity* of man's reason with *divinity*. Paul's doctrine of innate knowledge— a knowledge of God, rather than of Platonic "archetypes" of things in the world of "becoming"—assumes rather the *distinction* between the Creator and creature. It is because God has created man as His image[99] as well as creating everything in the world,[100] that man cannot avoid knowing his Creator. *Man is inescapably confronted with the face of God*

---

86. Acts 26:18.
87. II Corinthians 4:3.
88. John 3:19.
89. Philippians 3:18-19.
90. Ephesians 2:3.
91. I Corinthians 3:20.
92. Romans 3:11.
93. John 14:17.

94. I Corinthians 2:14.
95. John 3:3.
96. Philippians 1:21.
97. Romans 1:21.
98. Ephesians 4:17-18; I Timothy 6:20.
99. Genesis 1:26-27.
100. Colossians 1:16.

within him and the *imprint of God's work all about him;* God's revelation is constantly bearing in upon him, whether he seeks self-knowledge or understanding of the world. God reveals himself through nature unceasingly, universally, and inescapably.[101] The silent communication of God continues to the end of the world, day unto day and night unto night showing forth knowledge. In virtue of *creation*, every man images God; man is the climax of creation, not being made after his own kind (as with the animals), but being made in the likeness of God. In knowing himself, man simultaneously knows his God. Moreover, there is a sense in which Christ enlightens every man.[102] Hence, there is nowhere man can flee in order to escape confrontation with God.[103]

Paul's teaching of these points is plain to see. He asserted that God's invisible nature is clearly perceived and intellectually apprehended by man.[104] God is definitely known both from within man[105] and from the created world.[106] "What can be known about God is plain within them," and therefore man is categorically characterized as "knowing God."[107] It is because of these things that the apologist always has a *point of contact* with the unbeliever. Indeed, because of the unavoidable knowledge of God possessed by all men, the apologist is assured of success in his task of defending the faith. While men suppress the truth in unrighteousness, God nevertheless makes himself so clearly manifest to them that men are without excuse for their rebellion. They are fully responsible. As the Greek original suggests, "they are *without an apologetic.*"[108] The presuppositional apologetic of Paul, then, could never encounter an intellectual fortress which exalts itself against the knowledge of God in an effective manner; by making his apologetic captive to the obedience of Christ, Paul was guaranteed the victory in pulling down such strongholds.[109] He was set for the *apologia* of the gospel against men who had *no apologetic* for their foolish rebellion against the knowledge of God.

In contrast to the dialectical epistemology of Socrates, Paul taught that knowledge for man has to be the *receptive reconstruction of God's thoughts.* In this case, God's revelation is foundational to human knowledge; man's reasoning is *not* self-sufficient,[110] autonomous,[111] or somehow profitable as an independent source of knowledge.[112] As is evident from what was said above, Paul denied the *normative* character of the human mind and its thinking. We should go on to see that Paul also denied the

---

101. Psalm 19:1-4.
102. John 1:9.
103. Psalm 139:8.
104. Romans 1:20.
105. Romans 1:19.
106. Romans 1:20.
107. Romans 1:19, 21.
108. Romans 1:20.

109. II Corinthians 10:4-5.
110. I Corinthians 4:7; II Corinthians 3:5.
111. Colossians 2:4, 8; Job 11:12; Romans 1:21; I Corinthians 1:20.
112. Romans 11:34; I Corinthians 2:16; Isaiah 40:13-14; 41:28.

ultimacy of man's reason as the standard of knowledge and the final category of interpretation. Unlike Socrates, Paul did not seek to determine the nature and possibility of knowledge without reference to God.[113] By making man the final epistemological court of appeal, Socrates was led to a dialectical mixing of continuity and discontinuity, of unity and diversity, of logic and fact, in man's mind. For Paul, it is not man (reflecting on logic and fact) but God and His revelation which constitutes the final reference point of knowledge.[114] Human knowledge can never be comprehensive, but neither does it need to be in order for man to attain to veridical apprehension of reality.[115] Comprehensive knowledge is possessed by God,[116] and since He is the determiner of all things,[117] there is no "realm of possibility" behind Him.[118] Consequently there is no mystery or contingency which can threaten God's knowledge. The temporal realm, with its created unity and diversity, finds its *interpretive* unity in the mind and decree of God.[119] God's self-sufficient, absolutely rational, comprehensive, and coherent *plan* for creation and historical eventuation[120] provides the *integrating category of interpretation* for man's knowledge. God's creation of the world establishes the reality of *particulars*[121] and yet provides a genuine, preinterpreted, *order* to things.[122]

Therefore, we must recognize two levels of knowing,[123] and man must thus think God's thoughts after Him in order to understand God, the world, or himself.[124] That is, God's creative and constructive knowledge[125] is determinative for man's receptive and reconstructive knowledge.[126] What man learns from nature and history must be seen in the context of God's revelation. Even when man is not consciously speaking of God, man must *know* God in order to find intelligibility in *anything* else. Man cannot gain knowledge by looking within himself for the final reference point or interpretative category of experience. *Human knowledge is completely dependent upon the original knowledge of God, and thus God's revelation is foundational for man's epistemological endeavors.* The Psalmist gives

---

113. Colossians 2:3; Isaiah 46:10.
114. Romans 11:36; John 14:6; I Corinthians 1:24; Colossians 2:3.
115. E.g., I Corinthians 2:11-12; 13:11-12; Ephesians 3:19.
116. Romans 11:33; Psalm 147:5.
117. Ephesians 1:11; Psalm 103:19.
118. Isaiah 43:10; 44:6; cf. "Fortune" and "Fate" in Isaiah 65:11 (ASV).
119. Isaiah 40:26; Acts 15:18.
120. Isaiah 40:28; cf. I Corinthians 14:33.
121. Colossians 1:16; Ephesians 3:9; John 1:3.
122. Colossians 1:17; Psalm 104:24; Proverbs 3:19.
123. Isaiah 55:8-9.
124. Proverbs 22:17-21; John 16:13-15; Ephesians 4:20; 8:31-32; I Corinthians 2:
6-13, 16; Colossians 3:10; Ephesians 4:23-24.
125. Proverbs 3:19; 8:1, 12, 22-35 with John 1:1-4.
126. Proverbs 2:1-9; II Corinthians 4:6; 10:5; I Timothy 6:3-4, 20.

succinct expression to this, saying "In Thy light shall we see light."[127] Only God is wise,[128] and it is the Lord who teaches man knowledge.[129] Because Jehovah is a God of knowledge, arrogance must not be expressed by man;[130] instead, "attend unto my wisdom; incline thine ear to my understanding that thou mayest preserve discretion and that thy lips may keep knowledge."[131] The Lord must enlighten man's darkness.[132] Accordingly, it is the entrance of His words which gives light and understanding.[133] Paul would not allow any man to deceive himself: in order to be genuinely wise one must become a fool according to worldly standards[134] (i.e., base his thinking upon the word of the cross rather than the pseudo-wisdom of this world) because all the treasures of wisdom and knowledge are hid in Christ.[135] In His light alone can men see light.

It is quite evident now that the scriptural perspective on knowledge is *theocentric*, in sharp contrast to the anthropocentricity of Socratic epistemology. Only by making God one's starting point for thought and standard of truth can the objectivity of knowledge be preserved. For Paul, God is the final reference point in interpretation. His knowledge has unfathomable depth and wealth; "who hath known the mind of the Lord?"[136] Paul's answer could only be, "we have the mind of Christ."[137] For man to apprehend *any* truth, he must relate his thinking back to God's original knowledge. "For of him and through him, and unto him, are all things."[138] Our thinking requires a theistic orientation: we must see things as Christ does, thinking God's thoughts after Him. Therefore, man's mind needs to be renewed unto genuine knowledge after the image of his Creator,[139] rather than fashioned according to this world.[140] Man must reflect God's thoughts on a creaturely level, making God the measure of all things, instead of being driven ultimately to scepticism by holding man to be the measure. In contrast to the Socratic dictum, "Know thyself," Paul declared that he counted all things to be loss for the excellency of the *knowledge of Christ*; indeed, he reckoned everything as refuse in order that he might *know Him*.[141] While Socrates sought union with the eternal realm by self-knowledge, Christ taught "This is life eternal, that they should *know thee* the only true God, and him whom thou didst send, Jesus Christ."[142]

The scriptural outlook is undaunted in its theocentric epistemology.

127. Psalm 36:9.
128. Romans 16:27.
129. Psalm 94:10.
130. I Samuel 2:3.
131. Proverbs 5:1-2.
132. Psalm 18:28.
133. Psalm 119:130.
134. I Corinthians 3:18.
135. Colossians 2:3.
136. Romans 11:33-34.
137. I Corinthians 2:16.
138. Romans 11:36.
139. Colossians 3:10.
140. Romans 12:2.
141. Philippians 3:8, 10.
142. John 17:3.

By centering his thinking on God's word, man is delivered from sin and its epistemic offspring, scepticism.

> Thy commandments make me wiser than mine enemies, for they are ever with me. I have more understanding than all my teachers, for thy testimonies are my meditation. I understand more than the aged, because I have kept thy precepts. . . . Thou hast taught me. How sweet are thy words unto my taste. . . . Through thy precepts I get understanding; therefore, I hate every false way.[143]

If man applies his heart unto God's knowledge, then he can know the certainty of the words of truth.[144] A knowledge of God's Son prevents one from being tossed about with every passing doctrine,[145] and full assurance of knowledge comes through looking in unwavering faith to the promises of God.[146] One such promise is that of Jesus, "If ye *abide in my word,* then you are truly my disciples, and *you shall know the truth,* and the truth shall make you free."[147] Man in his created individuality has no problem, in the scriptural perspective, with knowing objective truth. Man was created[148] and is now being recreated[149] unto that end.

From the vantage point of the epistemology traced above, it is not surprising to find that Scripture does not extol neutrality as Socrates did. The Lord created all things *for himself,*[150] and He directs every event of history according to His wise plan.[151] He rules over all,[152] and everything in heaven and earth is His possession.[153] Consequently, in *all* things God is to be glorified.[154] Man is commanded to do *everything* he does to God's glory,[155] being consecrated to Him in "all manner of living."[156] This command extends to man's noetic (intellectual) activities. The first and great commandment calls for man to love the Lord with *all his mind;*[157] every word and thought must be under the authority of Christ.[158] Thus, Christ does not allow one to take a detached, open-minded, free-thinking approach to the truth; man's thinking must be committed to the truth and glory of God. Neutrality is impossible. "No man can serve two lords; for either he will hate the one and love the other, or else he will hold to the one and despise the other."[159] One is either submissive to God's word in all his thinking, or he is not; he is deluded to think that an uncommitted spirit characterizes his thought. "He that is not with me is

---

143. Psalm 119:98-104.
144. Proverbs 22:17-21.
145. Ephesians 4:13-14.
146. Romans 4:20-21.
147. John 8:31-32.
148. Genesis 1:28.
149. Ephesians 4:24; II Timothy 2:25.
150. Proverbs 16:4.
151. Ephesians 1:11.
152. Psalm 103:19.

153. I Chronicles 29:11.
154. I Peter 4:11.
155. I Corinthians 10:31.
156. I Peter 1:15.
157. Matthew 22:37.
158. II Corinthians 10:5; Colossians 3:17.
159. Matthew 6:24.

against me."[160] One either has the mind of Christ or the vain mind of the Gentiles,[161] brings every thought captive or is an enemy in his mind against Christ.[162] To be friendly toward the world—even in the area of scholarship or presuppositional commitment—is to be an enemy of God.[163] The lordship of Christ extends to all thinking, thereby precluding any endorsement of neutrality. Instead of a detached following of reason alone, Paul (and the other writers of Scripture) commended a whole hearted commitment to God's revelation. *Dogmatism cannot be banished.* It is simply a question of whether the foundational dogma shall be the automous dictates of reason or the truth of God.

It should be perfectly obvious by this point that everything in the scriptural perspective on truth and knowledge dictates against any attitude which is even remotely similar to that of Socrates in the *Euthyphro* dialogue. Socrates reduced the word of God and the opinion of man to a common environment, subject to the same epistemic conditions and requirements, with a standard of truth or criterion of verification higher than both. God's word is irrelevant to establishing a point or position; the outlook of deity is not crucial to knowledge, but rather endorsed only after *independent* establishment by autonomous man. The revelation of God might or might not *accidentally coincide* with the autonomously discovered truth of man's mind. Socrates said we have to try the spirits, not to see whether they are of God, but whether they agree with self-sufficient evaluations of reason.

Scripture is to another effect. Here we are taught to try the spirits by the absolute standard of God's revealed truth.[164] No one and no consideration is allowed to draw the word of the Lord into question;[165] so God's word cannot be tested by any higher standard or principle of truth. God himself is the absolute, unconditioned, eternal *standard* of truth.[166] His word is infinitely more sure than man's direct, eyewitness experience,[167] which is why faith is not based on sight.[168] God's word is epistemologically foundational or logically *primitive* (i.e., the first priority). It brings all all other worlds into judgment, but it itself is to be judged by no man. There exists *no independent* standard of truth higher than God. Thus, when a question of truth arises, the godly response is "To the law and to the testimony!"[169]

God's word is *never* just "one hypothesis among many others." It *alone* has self-attesting authority. Only the fool will subject God's word to his own autonomous testing, failing to understand the depth of God's

---

160. Matthew 12:30.
161. I Corinthians 2:16 with Ephesians 4:17.
162. II Corinthians 10:5 with Colossians 1:21.
163. James 4:4.
164. I John 4:1ff.

165. Matthew 20:1-16.
166. John 14:6.
167. II Peter 1:19.
168. Hebrews 11:1, 7-8.
169. Isaiah 8:20.

thoughts[170] and that nobody can improve upon His thinking.[171] The word of God has a unique authority, one which does not require it to depend on the endorsement of other experts or authorities.[172] When the word of God is questioned, the proper reply is to call into question the *competence* of the autonomous critic, pointing out that in reality it is this very word which is the standard that draws *him* into judgment.[173] God's sure word is the final criterion of truth, the ultimate authority in the world of thought. Therefore, woe to him who strives with his maker![174] The creature does not have the right to question the Creator. "Shall he that cavilleth contend with the Almighty? He that argueth with God, let *him* answer."[175]

This perspective was foundational in Paul's philosophy. Because God's word is the ultimate, authoritative, standard of knowledge and truth, Paul refused to submit it to the arrogant scrutiny of the sinner in order to have it established and accepted. In a spirit diametrically opposed to that of Socrates in *Euthyphro,* Paul declares "Nay but, O man, who art thou that repliest against God?"[176] Rather than being irrelevant, God's revelation had the *greatest* relevance in establishing the truth for Paul. God's word could never "accidentally coincide" with the truth, for God's word is the necessary presupposition for all true knowledge. Without the word of God, this world would be "sound and fury signifying nothing." Therefore, in *all* of Paul's thinking God's word was taken as his genuine authority. Rather than having God pass the tests of fact, logic, beneficial effect, and subjective satisfaction, Paul realized that logic and fact (along with all the other criteria) would be *senseless without God.* Rather than God's needing such credentials to be admissible to the mind of man, these things themselves *need God* to be meaningful and useful for man's thinking. The *fool* overlooks this, trusting his own heart,[177] uttering his own mind,[178] being right in his own eyes,[179] and taking utmost confidence in himself.[180] Professing self-wisdom, the fool suppresses the truth of God[181] and delights in discovering his own heart's conclusions[182]—returning to his folly like a dog to his vomit.[183] It is impossible to arrive at knowledge in this fashion, and *a fortiori* it is impossible autonomously to verify the word of the God of all knowledge. If one does not *begin* with the truth of God, he cannot conclude his argumentation with *either God or truth.* "The fear of the Lord is the beginning of knowledge, but fools despise wisdom and instruction."[184] By refusing to presuppose the word of the

---

170. Psalm 92:6.
171. Romans 11:34.
172. Matthew 7:29.
173. John 1:15-17; 12:48.
174. Isaiah 45:9.
175. Job 40:2.
176. Romans 9:20.
177. Proverbs 28:26.

178. Proverbs 29:11.
179. Proverbs 12:15.
180. Proverbs 14:16.
181. Romans 1:18, 22.
182. Proverbs 18:2.
183. Proverbs 26:11.
184. Proverbs 1:7.

Lord, the autonomous fool *hates knowledge*.[185] Therefore, Paul would not submit to the presuppositions of worldly philosophy and traditions of men; the elementary principles of learning which do not follow Christ have to be rejected in order to avoid vain deception.[186] Paul's starting point in thought was not autonomous but theonomic; no truth was more basic for him than God's revelation. Consequently, Paul hearkened to the Lord's reaffirmation of the law, "Thou shalt not put the Lord thy God to test."[187] If God's authority needed to be *authorized* by some other consideration, it would cease to be the *final* authority. Hence Paul sought to bring *every thought captive to the obedience of Christ*,[188] not allowing his or any other person's mind to lord it over the word of God. Absolutely nothing would be permitted to question God's authoritative word. And therefore the central thrust of Paul's apologetic was summarized in this bold declaration, "Let God be true, but every man a liar!"[189] He presupposed the truth of God and defended the faith from that sure foundation, challenging the very possibility of truth or knowledge on unbelieving assumptions: "Hath not God made *foolish* the wisdom of the world!"

Paul's Apologetic Method: Acts 17

Some four hundred and fifty years after Socrates stood trial in Athens for subverting the youth and teaching new deities, the apostle Paul was brought before the Areopagus Council in Athens, the most venerable court of its day, in order to determine whether or not he was subverting the public welfare by his teaching of new deities. The dissimilarity between his apologetic and that of Socrates is conspicuous. Paul did not appeal to autonomous reason or stress that he had in common with his audience a lack of wisdom. Paul did not attempt to bolster his contentions with factual demonstrations, logical exhibitions, references to social or personal betterment, or appeals to subjective guidance.

His *hearers* were noticeably aware of the *antithesis* between his outlook and their own: he brought to them new gods, strange things, and new teachings.[190] In his address, *Paul* underscored the *ignorance* of his hearers in their religiosity.[191] On the other hand, he emphasized his *authority*, his prerogative to proclaim the truth about God unto them. "That which you worship openly demonstrating your ignorance *I proclaim* unto you."[192] In accord with his description of the unregenerate mind in Romans 1:23,

---

185. Proverbs 1:22, 29.
186. Colossians 2:8.
187. Matthew 4:7.
188. II Corinthians 10:5.
189. Romans 3:4.
190. Acts 17:18-20.

191. Cf. Ned B. Stonehouse, *Paul Before the Areopagus* (Grand Rapids: Eerdmans, 1957), pp. 18-23.
192. Acts 17:23.

25, Paul characterized the Athenians as very idolatrous.[193] He realized that he could not build the gospel of Christ upon the foundation of pagan natural theology. Paul would not have his declaration of the truth from God *absorbed* into the immanentistic philosophy of heathen speculation, where the resurrection would merely be an oddity springing from the realm of chance. Paul knew that, given their presuppositions, the Athenians were far more ignorant than *they* even thought.[194] Thus, he directly attacked their philosophic assumptions, challenging them with the presuppositions of the Christian faith.

Against the common Greek assumption that all being is at bottom one, Paul clearly declared the doctrine of *creation*.[195] While his hearers gazed upon the Parthenon, Paul asserted that God does *not* dwell in temples made with hands.[196] Paul diametrically opposed the Epicurian notion of ateleological fate, as well as Stoic idolatry and its notion of an exclusive knowledge of divinity for the elite. Instead, he proclaimed God's *providential* control of history and His natural revelation within 'each man.[197] Upon the founding of the court of the Areopagus, Aeschylus had said that Apollo declared, "there is no resurrection." Standing in that same court, Paul diametrically contradicted him, proclaiming the *resurrection of Jesus Christ* as God's assured pledge that Christ shall judge the world in the *eschatological day*[198]—another doctrine which clashed with Greek philosophy: its cyclic view of history. Throughout his address, Paul *undermined* the presuppositions of his hearers and established the foundational doctrines of Christianity, standing forthrightly upon *biblical* ground, making abundant allusions to Old Testament passages instead of arguing from first principles in philosophy.[199] The authority of God, rather than that of autonomous reason, stood behind his preaching of God's demand that the Athenians have a "change of mind"—that is, that those living in ignorance *repent*.[200]

The themes which Paul rehearsed in Athens were the same as those discussed in Romans 1: *creation, providence, man's dependence upon God, future judgment*. Paul knew that he had a *point of contact* with his hearers, and that they had abundant reason to acknowledge the truth of his words. Just as he taught in Romans 1:18-20, Paul explained to the

---

193. Acts 17:16.
194. Cornelius Van Til, *Paul at Athens* (Phillipsburg, N. J.: Lewis J. Grotenhuis, n.d.).
195. Acts 17:24.
196. *Ibid.*
197. Acts 17:25-29.
198. Acts 17:31.
199. Cf. F. F. Bruce, *The Defence of the Gospel* (Grand Rapids: Eerdmans, 1959), pp. 38ff.
200. Acts 17:30; cf. vs. 23.

Athenians that *God was already known* by them through *general revelation,* even though they have *suppressed and misused* that knowledge. God's revelation of himself within and without man left the Athenians fully responsible to the truth. They were very religious by nature and felt a duty to worship.[201] God's providential control of history was calculated to lead them into a knowledge of God.[202] God had so engulfed men with the clear revelation of himself that He is not far from anyone—so much so that even pagan poets, despite their suppression of the truth, cannot help having the revelation of God be reflected at isolated points in their teaching.[203] God has given regular witness of himself to all men, and thus He holds all men under responsibility to repent of their culpable ignorance (i.e., their unrighteous and ineffective suppression of the truth about God).

In his apologetic before the Areopagus, then, Paul appealed to the *truth held down deep within the heart of the unregenerate man,* but insisted that this truth could only be properly apprehended when placed within the proper context of apostolic proclamation. He attacked the religious presuppositions of his hearers with the *voice of authority,* indicting their rebellion against the proper knowledge of God. He stressed ideological antithesis, recognized noetic depravity, made God the reference point of his interpretation of facts and logic, appealed to the revelation of God bearing constantly upon his hearers, avoided both a neutral method and the elevating of man's autonomous standards of piety or truth above God, and reasoned in terms of the ultimate epistemological authority of God. While Socrates' apology was man-centered, piecemeal, and dependent upon certain *autonomous and rootless tests* for truth, the apologetic of Paul was God-centered, presuppositional, and rooted in the *ultimate standard of meaningfulness* and truth: God's authoritative revelation. In the Socratic outlook, God is subject to the self-sufficient testing of man's reason, while in the Christian perspective, God is the necessary presupposition for the use of man's reason and (through His self-attesting revelation) the final criterion of all truth.

An Overview of the History of Apologetics

A detailed history of the way in which men throughout the centuries have attempted to defend the Christian faith is not feasible in the space available here. However, it is possible to get a *general* characterization of apologetical strategies through history, for, as Avery Dulles says in his *History of Apologetics,*[204] "A careful reading of the old masters in the field reveals that the same basic problems continually recur and that it is almost

201. Acts 17:22-23.
202. Acts 17:26-27; cf. Romans 2:4.
203. Acts 17:27-28.
204. Theological Resources Series, ed. J. P. Whalen and J. Pelikan (Philadelphia: Westminster Press, 1971), pp. xvi-xvii.

impossible to say anything substantially new." And the *most characteristic* thing about the apologetic arguments which one encounters in the history of the church is that they were *Socratic* in their outlook: they tended to divide the corpus of dogma into that which can be *rationalized* and that which is *mysterious;* they held that man's mind is *competent* and *authorized* to prove truths in the former category by means of autonomous tests; they subjected God's word to validation by the sinner's (allegedly) *neutral* and *self-sufficient* intellect; and they played down *both* the antithesis between believing and unbelieving epistemology and the sufficiency, clarity, and authority of natural *revelation* (as distinguished from natural theology, of which there has been an overabundance). Like Socrates, historically most apologists have taken the *piecemeal* approach of proving a few items here and there by argumentative appeal to factual evidence, logical coherence, social and individual benefit, and/or inward personal experience. Their attitude (at least in apologetic writings, if not also in theological discourses) has been similar to that of *Euthyphro,* rather than that of Paul's Areopagus address.

During the Patristic Period, up until about A.D. 125, the faith and discipline of the Christian community were the central concerns of the Apostolic Fathers, not the credibility of their message. However, we do find Clement attempting to interpret the resurrection in terms of man's common and natural experience. During the second century, *all the major motifs in apologetical history came to be foreshadowed.* It is a telling commentary upon these apologies that they are modeled after (1) the assaults of the pagan philosophers upon polytheism, and (2) the attempts of Helenistic Jews to show the superiority of Mosaic revelation to pagan philosophy. The recurring themes are illustrated by the following examples. The *Letter to Diognetus* exposed the folly and immorality which are fostered by pagan idolatry, and then it went on to emphasize the moral effects of the gospel on the mind and heart of believers—as does Aristides in his brief *Apology* to the emperor Hadrian. In customary style, Tatian attempted to prove that the Mosaic revelation was more ancient than the Greek writers. In his *Apologies,* Justin Martyr said that the philosophers were enlightened by the divine Logos and thus were Christians without realizing it. Aristides confronted the problem of a plurality of religious options, arguing from comparative studies that Christianity is the least superstitious. Athenagoras argued on philosophical grounds that there cannot be a plurality of gods. In the same vein as Quadratus' stress on the gospel miracles, Athenagoras wrote *On the Resurrection of the Dead.* Justin's *Dialogue with Trypho the Jew* argued for the deity of Christ from the messianic prophecies of the Old Testament. And finally Theophilus appealed in *Ad Autolycum* to the subjective testimony of the heart.

An *epistemological continuity* with the *intellectual perspective* and *in-*

interpretation of experience in unbelieving thought was openly propounded, then, as early as the second century (witness Clement, Athenagoras, and especially Justin). The kinds of arguments which Socrates utilized in his apology were all reflected in the Christian apologetic strategies of the second century (namely, appeals to fact, logic, beneficial effects, and the heart). That is not surprising, seeing that both Socrates and the apologists took a neutralistic, autonomous approach to knowledge. God was in the dock before the bar of human reason and experience. As a result, the apologetic strength of Paul was lacking.

None of the apologists showed Christianity to be the *definitive truth* of God. No argument was forthcoming that the *truth* of the gospel was the necessary condition for the *changed lives* of Christians; indeed, the Christians could have been morally motivated and transformed simply by *believing* that the gospel is true. By arguing that the Greek philosophers had plagiarized Moses and had been inspired by the Logos, the apologists assumed the *veracity* of the philosophers' perspective (yet maintaining that the Jews had the truth *first*). This had certain deleterious effects on the argument for Christianity. If you agree with the philosophers in their *presuppositions*, it appears to be arbitrary selectivity to refrain from agreeing to their *conclusions*. Besides, the educated pagan would say, if you appeal to the philosophers to *validate certain* truths of the faith but *not others*, then this simply shows that the better (validated) teachings of Christianity are *also* taught by the philosophers—thus rendering the Christian revelation *superfluous*. Where Christianity is questionable, the unbeliever *does not want* to follow it; where Christianity agrees with the philosophers, the unbeliever *need not* follow it. Moreover, when the Christian message is placed upon the foundation of pagan thought, it is *naturalized* and distorted; for instance, given the Greek view of fate (where *anything* is said to be possible in history), the resurrection of Christ is a mere oddity of irrational historical eventuation. Appeals to fact are ultimately futile unless the apologist recognizes and avoids the unbeliever's presupposed *philosophy of fact*. For various reasons, the argumentative appeal to fulfilled prophecy and the evaluation of pagan religions as leading to immorality and superstition are mere examples of *begging the question*. From a *non*-biblical perspective, *Christianity* would be immoral and superstitious. And from an *un*believing perspective the arguments from prophecy all appear to rely on *tendentious* readings of the Old Testament. After all, the orthodox Jewish authorities did not interpret the texts in the fanciful and ax-grinding manner of the Christians. Why then should an educated pagan feel *compelled* to believe the Christian apologist? Finally, the fact that a believer has an *inward* indication of the truth of his faith may tell you something about the *believer*, but it says nothing about the *objective truth* of the believer's faith. Thus the second century's Socratic apologies for the faith were just so much grist for the mills of unbelieving thought. The intellectual *challenge* of the gospel was not sounded.

Third-century apologists, especially those of Alexandria, continued to assimilate arguments from Platonic and Stoic philosophers as well as Jewish controversialists. Clement of Alexandria argued that the best aspirations and insights at work throughout *pagan history* (e.g., in the mystery cults and Hellenic philosophy) had been *fulfilled* in their apex, Christianity. Having studied philosophy under the father of neo-Platonism, Origen argued against the criticisms of Celsus by saying that the Bible agrees with *sound philosophy* and that the Christian's inability to prove historical assertions of Scripture is no defect, since the Greeks cannot prove their history either. The *necessity* and *uniqueness* of the Christian message, then, were to a great extent hidden in the apologies of the Alexandrians. The Latin apologists were not much better. In *Octavius*, Marcus Minucius Felix proclaimed that the philosophers of old were unconsciously Christians and that Christians of his day were genuine philosophers. It is only in Tertullian that we begin to see some return from the epistemological "Babylonian captivity" of Christian apologetics. However, along with Tertullian's refusal to integrate Jerusalem with Athens, we also find the counterproductive recommendation of Christian teaching "*because* it is absurd"—rather than *in spite of its apparent* absurdity. The teaching of Athens must be unmasked for *its* presuppositional absurdity and not simply allowed to stand as an (erroneous) option over against the faith. As did the other third-century apologists, Cyprian merely repeated second-century arguments for the faith, adding to the evidences the spectacle of Catholic unity—an argument with *assumptions* which might seem to *disprove* the truth of Christianity with the arrival of the Protestant Reformation.

The fourth and fifth centuries witnessed the attempt by apologists to construct a *new religious synthesis*, a global vision constructed from materials in Stoic and Platonic philosophy, yet reshaped by the gospel. The overriding problem of the previous age had been the relationship between Christianity and classical culture, and now with Christianity seeing amazing success (e.g., the heroic martyrs, advances in doctrinal formulation, the conversion of Constantine), the leading apologists were very open to the solution offered by synthesis. Typical of the era was *The Case Against the Pagans* by Arnobius, who evidently was more familiar with Stoic thought than with Christian theology. Arnobius subscribed to the *tabula rasa* theory of the human mind and argued that, even though all intellectual options are uncertain, we should believe the one which offers more *hope* than the others (thus foreshadowing Pascal, Locke, and Butler). Christianity becomes an eschatological insurance policy. Arnobius admitted that he had no solution to the problem of evil, did not clearly deny the existence of pagan gods, and left us with an apologetic more suited to deism than to Christianity. Lactantius made extensive use of Plato, Cicero, and Lucretius in his apologetic, establishing with the competence of reason the existence and providence of God. From there, he pleaded the *limitations* of philosophy and went on to accept the deity of Christ on the grounds of inspired prophecy.

An instructive contrast can be seen between the attitudes of Ambrose and Eusebius. The former said that, "It is good that faith should go before reason, lest we seem to exact a reason from our Lord God as from a man." For Eusebius, faith undergirded knowledge, and yet knowledge prepared the way for faith (as is evident from his two-part work, *The Preparation of the Gospel*, and *The Proof of the Gospel*). Eusebius was a forerunner to Augustine in two major respects: he pioneered the apologetic of world history (arguing for the truth of Christianity from its *amazing success* in the world), and he platonized the Bible almost as much as he baptized Greek speculation.

The domination of the Socratic outlook in Christian apologetics is further witnessed in Theodoret's work, *The Truth of the Gospels Proved from Greek Philosophy*. Theodoret felt able to incorporate the highest insights of neo-Platonic speculation into his Christian philosophy, yet he argued simultaneously that Christians *alone* live up to the best insights of the pagans. The same problem with *arbitrary selectivity* afflicted the *early* thinking of Augustine, when he felt that unaided human reason is capable of establishing God's existence by indubitable arguments. Augustine was confident that if Socrates and Plato had been alive in his day they would certainly have been Christians. Augustine also argued from the moral miracle and superlative success of the church to the truth of the faith; in *The City of God* he expounded the common argument that the growth of the church and the death of the martyrs are incredible except upon the assumption of the historical resurrection of Christ. Of course, to the extent that Augustine "proved" the existence of God in Platonic fashion—Plato's god, like Plato's static forms, was the *only* god Plato's logic could prove—he testified that God could not come into contact with the temporal realm of history. This God would then be in external dialectical tension with His creation, as in all Greek speculation. On the other hand, when Augustine turned from this a-historical, rationalistic god to the evidential apologetic of world history, he encountered difficulties again. With Eusebius he had found evidence for the truth of Christianity in the beneficial effects it brought the empire as well as in the church's success. But now that the course of history and the conditions in state and church had been attributed to God (in order that they could serve as evidence for Him) Augustine was compelled to turn around and argue in *The City of God* that the state of affairs was *not the* responsibility of the Christians; he felt compelled to vindicate the Christian faith and its God from culpability for the sack of Rome by Alaric in 410. Augustine had wanted to prove the truth of Christianity from the hard evidence of history, and to the hard facts his opponents now forced him to go—landing him right in the midst of the problem of *theodicy*. (Later, Salvian completed the turning of the apologetic of world history on its head, arguing that the course of events evidences the *judgment* of God rather than His beneficence. It is clear that, from Eusebius to Salvian, it was *not* the *simple facts* of history that could be taken to prove the truth of Christianity, for facts of a conflicting character—facts of both weal and woe—were appealed to in order to prove the *same* conclusion. Obviously, a presuppositional commitment to the Christian faith was brought to bear in an interpretative way upon the facts, rather than the brute facts leading to Christian commitment.) As for Augustine's argument for the credibility of Christ's resurrection, his considerations merely showed that the martyrs either *believed* a false tale or that they were *willing to sacrifice* their lives, not for a specific story, but for a *broad ideal* which (for the sake of winning popular attention) incorporated elements of historical exaggeration. The *presuppositions* brought by unbelievers to the facts would determine whether one of *these* interpretations with respect to Christ's resurrection should be preferred over the believer's interpretation—just as *Augustine's* presuppositions determined what interpretation he should give the facts of *world history* (allowing them to evidence *both* God's beneficence and God's judgment).

In the later writings of Augustine, however, we do recognize a movement toward a clearer understanding that *by faith alone* does the Christian accept the existence of the triune God, that the Bible is accepted on its own terms, and that all of history and life must be interpreted in the light of God's revelation in order to be intelligible. Augustine moved away from the dialectical epistemology of Greek thinking and toward an epistemology consonant with the doctrine of salvation by grace alone (which he urged against Pelagius). In his *Retractions* Augustine expressed the conviction that "there is no teacher who teaches man knowledge except God.' In a manner parallel to that of Ambrose, Augustine came to appreciate more accurately that one must *believe in order to understand*. Such a non-Socratic perspective would not be propounded with force again until the time of John Calvin.

In the period intervening between Augustine and Calvin, the key apologists were Qurrah, Anselm, Peter the Venerable, Abelard, Thomas Aquinas, Martini, Lull, Duns Scotus, Henry of Oytha, Sabundus, Denis the Carthusian, Nicholas of Cusa, and Ficino. The most significant light was of course that of Thomas, but all contributed toward turning the tide of apologetical argument into more *mystical* and *metaphysical* channels. Qurrah's famous allegory emphasized the necessity for man to compare the competing world religions and make a decision between them based on his own autonomous standards of plausibility. Christianity was simply one hypothesis among many which had to be judged by the sinner's anticipatory ideas of divinity. Characteristically for such autonomous apologetics, Qurrah failed to give any adequate resolution or basis for choice between competing anticipations! In Anselm, we find the beginning of very sophisticated reflections upon the relationship between faith and reason. Anselm understood the necessity of spiritual renewal and held that man needs faith in order to have understanding. However, he was not consistent with this Augustinian perspective, for he did agree to write in such a way "that *nothing* from Scripture should be urged on the authority of Scripture itself, but that whatever the conclusion of *independent* investigation should be to declare to be true" (*Monologion*). Anselm did not completely divorce himself from the pitfalls of autonomy. Peter the Venerable was the most eminent apologist of the twelfth century, appealing in his arguments against Jews and Moslems to the objectivity of philosophical study as a model for the *impartiality* he thought should characterize apologetics. Abelard complemented this theme by holding that *human reason*, making use of evidences, could pave the way for an *initial* faith, which in turn prepared for the *supernatural* act of faith elicited under divine grace. Abelard assigned *reason* the jurisdiction to select which authority to follow, and he maintained that the divine Logos had illumined not only the Old Testament prophets but also the *Greek philosophers*—both of which prepared for the revelation of Christ. Socrates could not have .been more satisfied. *His* autonomous reason could then have dealt with the prophets as just *one more* tradition among many.

In the conflict between Anselm and Abelard, Thomas Aquinas agreed with Abelard that it is possible to prove from *reason* the basic truths of theism, especially with the help of Aristotelian philosophy. However, in order to guarantee that there is some need for *faith* (which must be sharply distinguished from knowledge, with its rational foundations) Thomas went on to argue, in agreement with the Jewish theologian Maimonides, that there is a *higher level of religious truth* that is impenetrable except by means of revelation from God. Reason builds the lower story of religious truth, and revelation completes the superstructure. Yet even in the *upper* story, reason can show the *credibility* and *probability* of the truths believed on faith. In the lower preamble to faith, Thomas used his famous Five Ways to prove God's existence; in the upper story dealing with the mysteries of the faith Thomas utilized arguments which we have seen propounded many times previously. Subsequently, however, Thomas stopped penning his *Summa Theologica* after undergoing a mystical experience which he felt dwarfed his previous argumentation. And thus all the elements of the Socratic apology finally came to expression in the approach of Thomas Aquinas: neutrality, autonomy, dialectical epistemology, subjecting God to test, dichotomizing the field of knowledge, assuming the natural ability of human reason, and locating the seat of authority in man's thinking process. Aquinas would have been warmly *welcomed* at the Areopagus, without the mockery Paul received. He would have appealed to *facts, logic, beneficial effects,* and *mystical experience* in a way which would have been congenial to the philosophers of Athens; Thomas would have helped them to absorb totally the Christian message into an alien philosophy and thereby *transform* and *naturalize* it.

Martini and Lull expounded the position of Aquinas with missionary fervor, both giving *primacy* to *reason* over faith. Martini propounded the Thomistic apologetic to Saracens and Jews, and Lull devised a set of diagrams (with concentric circles and revolving figures) that he claimed could, when used properly, answer the most difficult theological questions to the satisfaction of Averroists, Saracens, Jews, and Christians alike. Like Richard of St. Victor, Lull even contended that all the *mysteries of the faith* could be supported by *necessary reasons.* The Thomistic lower story of autonomous reason began to *engulf* the upper story of authoritative revelation. John Duns Scotus held a similar position, holding that *faith* could be objectively *justified* before the bar of autonomous reason; he produced a list of ten extrinsic reasons which he felt demonstrated the credibility of the Bible. His medieval list represents the non-presuppositional apologetic arguments which are in vogue even *today!* Henry of Oytha distinguished between intrinsic evidence (internal, rational demonstration) and extrinsic evidence (external reasons which point to the probability of something), maintaining that "any man of reasonable and uncorrupted judgment" (where we are to find such men was not indicated) must rightly conclude that the combination of intrinsic and extrinsic evidence undoubtedly *proves* the Bible to be divine revelation. Catalan Raimundus Sabundus composed the *Book of Creatures,* which aimed to lead the mind to rise through the various stages of the chain of being to a contemplation of God. Like all "chain of being" schemes, this one effectively denied the *Creator-creature distinction.* Sabundus held that human reason had the power to *prove* most *everything* in the Christian faith *without* reliance upon the authority of revelation. Contrary to Isaiah 55: 8-9, God's thoughts really are quite like man's thoughts, apparently. He saw *both* his *Book of Creatures and* the Bible as authoritative and infallible; thus they were held to be concordant—with the *Book of Creatures* having *priority* as the necessary road to accepting the trustworthiness of Scripture! Here it becomes quite clear that *autonomy* in apologetics leads to the undermining of Scripture's self-attesting *authority;* if Sabundus were correct in his estimates of reason's capability, there would be little if any *need* for supernatural revelation. The progress of post-Augustinian, intellectual self-sufficiency in apologetics resulted finally in the disintegration of the *faith defended!*

In the fifteenth century, the scholastic apologetical method was best supported by Denis the Carthusian, who is known for his *Dialogue Concerning the Catholic Faith*—wherein he explained that faith cannot proceed from self-evident principles, since it is not a form of worldly wisdom, *and yet* historical arguments can *verify* the miracle stories. He is also remembered for a chapter-by-chapter refutation of the Koran based upon *historical validation* of the Bible, *Against the Perfidy of Mohammed.* Denis wrote this work at the urging of Nicholas of Cusa, who himself wrote on the same subject in his *Sifting the Koran*. Nicholas held that the Koran could be sifted and used as an *introduction* to the gospel; indeed, principles in the Koran, he imagined, lead one naturally to accept the Trinity, incarnation, and resurrection. In harmony with this spirit, Nicholas also composed a *synthesis* of the major religions of the world, outlining their *lowest common denominator* in *On Peace and Concord in the Faith.* Marsilio Ficino, whose principal work was entitled *Platonic Theology,* thought of the philosophers of the ancient world as *precursors* to Christianity and attempted to use Platonic reason to support Christian faith (in contrast to the prevailing Aristotelianism of his day). However, after an initial commitment has been made to a positive use of the world religions or Greek philosophers in apologetics, the Christian faith is eventually distorted and modified. Once you have said "yes" to the principles of apostate philosophy, it is too late to say "but" when you subsequently want to disagree with its conclusions. And thus Ficino was led to believe that, since Plato was only "Moses speaking the Attic language," the variety of religions found in the world are permitted by God in order to give the creation luster; Christianity is simply the most perfect among the various religions. It is just one more testimony among many, albeit the "best" one.

In the history of apologetics up to the Reformation, then, Christians wedded themselves for the most part to a Socratic approach, which in turn undermined the definitiveness of Christianity, the significance of miracles, the self-attesting strength of Scripture, the necessity of special revelation, the clarity of general revelation, the prerequisite of faith for understanding, the necessity of faith at all, and even the uniqueness of the Christian message. What emerged was the exaltation of the intellect, the natural integrity of reason, the delusion of neutrality and autonomy, and the dominating authority of Greek philosophy. By beginning with Socrates, apologetics could not conclude with Christ.

While there is a multitude of apologetical works which could be rehearsed between the sixteenth and eighteenth centuries, there is little need for our purposes to consider them. No *new* grand syntheses or new metaphysical inroads were attempted in any noteworthy fashion. Instead, initiative was profitably assumed by Christianity's *adversaries* in these centuries; since the presuppositions of unbelieving thought were being *shared*, instead of being challenged, by Christian apologists, critics were able to make the faith's defenders rush to answer detail-objection after detail-objection. Especially during the eighteenth century was this the case, as blatant, positivistic attacks upon Christianity became stylish for Enlightenment thinkers. The emphasis in apologetics steadily shifted toward the "shotgun" method of adducing a variety of particular evidences for the credibility of Christianity. That is, Christian apologists undertook to answer their positivistic critics in kind. However, the highly destructive philosophy of David Hume vanquished the evidential approach. Hume effectively illustrated that, given the assumptions of autonomous thinking, *induction* could not lead to anything better than *psychologically* persuasive conclusions. Hume's nominalism, representationalism, and undermining of the uniformity of nature guaranteed that the "brute facts" of experience would be *mute* facts, incapable of demonstrating anything—either conclusively *or* probabilistically. Hume's consistent empiricism was the definitive death blow to the empiricistic apologetic schemes that were in vogue (e.g., Butler's *Analogy of Religion, Natural and Revealed, to the Constitution and Course of Nature*, 1736). Men like Toland and Tindal converted the case for *natural* evidences into *deism*, and men like Lessing and Reimarus effectively countered the autonomous case from *historical* evidences, the former with respect to *principle* and the latter with respect to *fact*.

In terms of general approach, the apologetics of the sixteenth to eighteenth centuries produced nothing remarkably new. Christianity was defended by appeals to pagan philosophers (Steucho), moral effects (Suarez), prophecy (Gonet), common religious notions (Herbert), historical indications (Bosseut, Lardner), inductive proofs (Houtteville), natural teleology (Bentley, Ray), and natural theology (Clarke). The diversity of defensive stances was remarkable. Pascal defended Christianity from the subjective reasons of the heart. Others like Elizalde, Huet, and Wolff strove to produce quasimathematical proofs for the faith. Appeals were made to the inevitability of general scepticism in order to justify blind faith for the Christian (Montaigne, Charron), while others argued in favor of the presumption and probability of Christianity's veracity (Banez, Gregory of Valencia, Butler, Paley). Evidence was culled from natural facts (Locke, Butler, Paley, Nieuwentijdt, Bonnet), the strength of miracles (Juan de Lugo, Boyle), especially the resurrection (Sherlock, Euler, Less). And because none of these approaches was convincing in its own right, appeal was also made to the *convergence* of many signs in favor of Christianity (Hurtado).

However, despite all of this variety, apologists were still bound to the crucial defects of the Socratic approach taken by their predecessors. There was no conscious and consistent attempt to distinguish the Socratic outlook from the Christian perspective and to argue in terms of the latter. The reformation of theology effected in the sixteenth century had made no noticeable modification of apologetic strategy, for apologists continued to view their reasoning as *independent* of their theological commitments. Indeed, the ideal seemed to be that apologetics would *autonomously* establish the basic truths of theology. The deeper mysteries of the faith were to be erected upon the self-sufficient foundation of reason and evidential probability.

The volume and complexity of apologetical treatises in the nineteenth century prevent any convenient detailing or cataloguing, but the trends simply remained constant. This was the century in which attempts were made to reduce apologetics to a special science—without achieving, however, any unity in the field (as discussed earlier in this article). For the most part, Schleiermacher's call for apologetics to establish the prolegomenon to theology was heeded. This project was initiated by both the Romanists (Drey) and the Protestants (Sack); it was worked out to its consistent end by Thomists (Perrone) and Reformed thinkers (Warfield) alike. In the wake of Kantian criticism and Hegelian idealism, many apologists assigned matters of science, history, and reason to one domain, while setting religious faith apart as a distinct mode of knowing—thereby surrendering completely the transcendental necessity of God and His revelation for intelligible reasoning, which is the inevitable outcome of divorcing faith from knowledge and granting autonomy to human reason. The outcome—blind faith—was *fideism* in apologetics (Kierkegaard, Maurice, Herrmann, Bautain), and apologetical appeals to the *heart* (Schleiermacher, Tholuck, Chateaubriand, Ventura), *intuition* (Gratry), and *religious pragmatism* (Hermes, Ritschl, Kaftan). Some apologists resorted to arguing that Christianity fosters social order, welfare, and progress as a reason for accepting it (Cortès, Newman, Brownson, Hecker, Luthardt, Weiss). Since apologists had surrendered the battle at the *presuppositional* level already, it is no surprise that we find them accommodating to the *methods* of idealistic philosophy (Orr), higher criticism (Lightfoot, Harnack, A. B. Bruce), and Darwinian science (Mivart, Drummond).[205] The same arguments which appeared throughout the history of the church were again rehashed, with all of the ensuing defects of the Socratic outlook thwarting their success.

By taking as its starting point an agreement with apostate thought and presuppositions, Christian apologetics has throughout its history ended up

---

205. The foregoing abridged history of apologetics is indebted to the works of Dulles, Ramm, and Reid cited previously; their works can be profitably consulted for an expansion and filling out of the history. See also Van Til's three-volume syllabus, "Christianity in Conflict."

in captivity behind enemy lines. Having said "yes" to unbelieving episte-mology or interpretation at the *outset*, the *later* attempt to say "but" and correct the conclusions of non-Christian thinking has been manifestly un-successful. In this we see again the justice of J. T. Forbes's comment to the effect that the progress of the human mind has been with Socrates. A striking illustration of the dreadful outcome fostered by taking a Socratic approach to apologetics is afforded by Alec R. Vidler in his book, *Twentieth Century Defenders of the Faith.*[206] The seed of autonomous (Socratic) thinking was planted within Christian apologetics in the second century; it is finally harvested in the twentieth century in the fact that *not one* of the "apologists" discussed by Vidler holds to the faith once for all delivered to the saints! Vidler takes as the key defenders of the faith in this century: Harnack, Reville, R. J. Campbell, Loisy, Tyrrell, Le Roy, Figgis, Quick, Spens, Rawlinson, Barth, Brunner, Hoskyns, Niebuhr, Davies, Robinson, and Van Buren—that is, the proponents of liberalism, modernism, neo-orthodoxy, and radicalism.

While Socratic apologists will not be impressed by the following fact (given their Socratic presuppositions), consistently biblical apologists should remind themselves from time to time that Socrates *lost* his case before his own Athenian peers. If the logical armor of Socrates resulted in a belly full of hemlock tea, it would seem reasonable for Christians to put on a different kind of armor—specifically the "whole armor of God" (Eph. 6:13-17). Socrates came to his own, and his own received him not. The same is the general experience of autonomous apologists in speaking to autonomous unbelievers. When the commitment of "Athenians" is tested, they will be found to *tolerate* the presence of Socrates only because they prefer Socrates to Jesus Christ. In hell, there are no Socratic dialogues. And in their hearts all Athenians know this to be true; the whole of their lives is spent in a systematic attempt to suppress this truth. The sinner will use any means at his disposal to evade the claims of Christ, and the autonomy of Socratic apologetics is just one such means.

The principial implication and ultimate outcome of a Socratic apologetic for Christianity is a grotesque transformation of the orthodox faith and a failure to challenge the unbeliever to renounce his autonomy for the gospel of Christ. Nevertheless, the influence of Socrates continues to be influential in Christian apologetics. It is seen in the non-evangelical, Richard Kroner, who held that Socrates demonstrated the ability of the human mind by its own effort to approach the truth revealed in the Bible.[207] And it is seen in

206. (New York: Seabury Press, 1965).
207. *Speculation in Pre-Christian Philosophy*; cited by Van Til, *Christian Theistic Ethics*, p. 218.

the popular evangelical, C. S. Lewis, who wrote in "The Founding of the Oxford Socratic Club": "Socrates had exhorted men to 'follow the argument wherever it led them': the club came into existence to apply his principle to one particular subject-matter—the *pros* and *cons* of the Christian religion."[208] The proper evaluation of such an autonomous and neutralistic approach was expressed in the title of Willard L. Sperry's critique of compromising defenses of the faith: *'Yes, But—' The Bankruptcy of Apologetics*.[209]

The Reformation of Apologetics

It is highly fitting that just one year after the appearance of the acknowledgment of apologetics' bankruptcy, the first extensive work of Cornelius Van Til should appear, for it is in the approach which Van Til takes to the defense of the faith that apologetics is called back from its Socratic bondage and restored to solvency and full wealth. Van Til fully realizes that an irradicable, principial antithesis exists between the outlook of Socrates and the perspective of Christ, and thus he seeks to set his apologetic self-consciously over against the autonomous and neutralistic methodology of Socrates and correspondingly to align his apologetic strategy with that of Scripture.

> If Socrates be regarded as the highest product of the Greek spirit, this only points up the striking character of Paul's words: "Where is the wise? where is the scribe? where is the disputer of this world? hath not God made foolish the wisdom of the world? For seeing that in the ' wisdom of God the world through its wisdom knew not God, it was God's good pleasure through the foolishness of preaching to save them that believe" (I Cor. 1:20, 21). . . . The ideal or perfect man of Greece is the perfect covenant-breaker; the ideal man of Scripture is the perfect covenant-keeper.[210]

Van Til is conscious of the fact that the failure to bring every thought into captivity to Christ, *even in the area of apologetic argumentation*, is itself a violation of the *covenantal obligations* under which all men live as the creatures of God. Thus while so many schools of apologetics are more than willing to assume the philosophic perspective of Socrates in order to gain men to Christ, Van Til declares that the *principle* of Socrates (an honorary saint of the Enlightenment spirit) stands *antithetically* over against every principle of the Christian position.[211]

The attitude assumed in the *Euthyphro* epitomizes for Van Til man's intellectual rebellion against God; it is the same attitude that was assumed

---

208. *God in the Dock*, ed. Walter Hooper (Grand Rapids: Eerdmans, 1970), p. 126.
209. (New York, 1931).
210. *Christian Theistic Ethics*, p. 219.
211. *Ibid.*, p. 184; cf. *Christian Theory of Knowledge*, p. 144.

by Adam and Eve in the garden. If revealed truth is to be accepted by man's mind, then it is to be accepted, not because it is authoritatively revealed from God, but because man can *independently* satisfy himself that it passes *his* tests for truth. This *subordinc'·s* revelation to speculation. To the contrary effect Van Til teaches that we must adopt

> . . . the presupposition that revelation is primary and that human speculation is, when properly conducted, the attempt of covenant-redeemed man, man in Christ, to submit his every thought, his every conceptual thought, captive to the obedience of his Lord. If this approach is not taken from the outset, the subordination of revelation to speculation is a foregone conclusion. And with this subordination goes the destruction of human speculation.[212]

The "perfect man" (the perfect covenant-breaker) in the Socratic perspective is the autonomous intellectual, unfettered by the authority of his Creator; yet Van Til is aware that such a thinker brings about the ironic effect of destroying *that very rationality* in which he prides himself. In suppressing the truth of God, he professes to be wise, but in reality becomes a fool.

The bankruptcy of apologetics stems from an overlooking of this fact. By allowing even a small measure of autonomy into his thinking at the outset, the traditional apologist cannot prevent his system from sharing the crucial defects, rootlessness, and dialectical tensions of unbelieving thought. A little leaven leavens the whole lump.

> The Christian revelation is imperious in its nature. Christ wants to be Lord of the conceptual thoughts of men as well as of every other aspect of their personality. And the autonomous intellect and moral consciousness of man is equally imperious. It seeks to withdraw the realm of conceptual thought from the Lordship of Christ by claiming the honor of its origination in man instead of in God.[213]

The Christian apologist must not halt between two opinions; because the Lord is God, the apologist must serve *Him*—with his *whole* heart, strength, *and mind*. His argumentation must reflect the crown rights of Jesus Christ, not the usurping claims of autonomous reason. For no man (not even the apologist) can serve two masters. Van Til is acutely conscious that for apologetics the choice is clear: Socrates *or* Christ. The two cannot be synthesized, as traditional apologetics had vainly attempted to do.

> When Socrates assumes the autonomy of the moral consciousness and when in modern times Kant does likewise, they are finding their absolute, their absolute ideal, their absolute criterion and their self-sufficient motive power in man as autonomous. Neither the Socratic nor the Kantian position can ever be harmonized with the Christian position, no more in ethics than in the field of knowledge.[214]

It is because of the clarity of this insight that Van Til has been able

---

212. *Ibid.*, p. 209.   213. *Ibid.*, p. 210.   214. *Ibid.*, p. 209.

to activate a momentous *reformation* in the field of apologetics. The incisive and decisive analysis of apologetics which was lacking in Warfield's day was being supplied a generation later by a young scholar who realized that he was standing on the shoulders of his Reformed fathers: Calvin, Hodge, Warfield, Kuyper, Bavinck. From that vantage point, he could more clearly see the fundamental need for a Reformed apologetic—that is, an apologetic true to the fundamental insights of Reformed theology. The absolute sovereignty of God in epistemology, as in every other order, led Van Til to repudiate the influence of Socrates (as well as his historical and implicit disciples) in the defense of the Christian faith. The methods of Socrates could not be harmonized with the teachings of Christ.

Van Til answered the basic question of *methodology* in apologetics by propounding a *presuppositional* defense of the faith. The foundation of Christian scholarship was taken to be the presupposed truth of God's inspired word. This presupposition stands over against the autonomous effort of the unbeliever. "In the last analysis we shall have to choose between two theories of knowledge. According to one theory God is the final court of appeal; according to the other theory man is the final court of appeal."[215] The former approach holds that there are two levels of thought, the absolute and derivative, and thus that man must think God's thoughts after Him in a receptively reconstructive manner; the latter approach holds to the ultimacy and normative quality of man's mind, and thus that he should seek to be creatively constructive in his interpretation of reality.[216] "The essence of the non-Christian position is that man is assumed to be ultimate or autonomous. Man is thought of as the final reference point in predication."[217] In contrast,

> The Protestant doctrine of God requires that it be made foundational to everything else as a principle of explanation. If God is self-sufficient, he alone is self-explanatory. And if he alone is self-explanatory, then he must be the final reference point in all human predication. He is then like the sun from which all lights on earth derive their power of illumination.[218]

The presuppositionalist must challenge the would-be autonomous man with the fact that *only* upon the presupposition of God and His revelation can *intelligibility* be preserved in his effort to understand and interpret the world. Christian truth is the *transcendental* necessity of man's epistemological efforts.

> Now the only argument for an absolute God that holds water is a transcendental argument. . . . Thus the transcendental argument seeks

---

215. *The Defense of the Faith*, p. 51.
216. *Ibid.*, pp. 64-66.
217. *Christian Theory of Knowledge*, pp. 12-13.
218. *Ibid.*, p. 12.

to discover what sort of foundations the house of human knowledge must have, in order to be what it is. . . . A truly transcendent God and a transcendental method go hand in hand.[219]

Van Til's presuppositional defense of the faith allows him to start with *any fact whatsoever* and challenge his opponent to give an intelligible interpretation of it; the presuppositionalist seeks to show the unbeliever that his epistemology reduces to absurdity. Nothing less will do. Standing firmly within the circle of Christianity's presupposed truth, "We reason *from the impossibility of the contrary.*"[220] This is the most fundamental and effective way to defend the faith.

> How then, we ask, is the Christian to challenge this non-Christian approach to the interpretation of human experience? He can do so only if he shows that man *must* presuppose God as the final reference point in predication. Otherwise, he would destroy experience itself. He can do so only if he shows the non-Christian that even in his virtual negation of God, he is still really presupposing God. He can do so only if he shows the non-Christian that he cannot deny God unless he first affirms him, and that his own approach throughout its history has been shown to be destructive of human experience itself.[221]

Van Til's Reformed, presuppositional defense of the faith requires us to repudiate the assumed *normative* character of the unbeliever's thinking as well as his supposed *neutrality*. In this Van Til is simply applying the scriptural perspective of Paul, as examined earlier.

> To argue by presupposition is to indicate what are the epistemological and metaphysical principles that underlie and control one's method. The Reformed apologist will frankly admit that his own methodology presupposes the truth of Christian theism. . . . In spite of this claim to neutrality on the part of the non-Christian, the Reformed apologist must point out that *every* method, the supposedly neutral one no less than any other, presupposes either the truth or the falsity of Christian theism.
>
> The method of reasoning by presupposition may be said to be indirect rather than direct. The issue between believers and non-believers in Christian theism cannot be settled by a direct appeal to "facts" or "laws" whose nature and significance is already agreed upon by both parties to the debate. The question is rather as to what is the final reference-point required to make the "facts" and "laws" intelligible.[222]

It is only within the theological school of Reformed interpretation of Scripture that the strength of presuppositional apologetics could develop. By their compromising stands on man's depravity and God's total sovereignty, Romanism and Arminianism are hindered from issuing the transcendental challenge of presuppositionalism.

---

219. *A Survey of Christian Epistemology*, p. 11.
220. *Ibid.*, pp. 204, 205.
221. *Christian Theory of Knowledge*, p. 13.
222. *The Defense of the Faith*, pp. 116-117.

Roman Catholics and Arminians, appealing to the "reason" of the natural man as the natural man himself interprets his reason, namely as autonomous, are bound to use the direct method of approach to the natural man, the method that assumes the essential correctness of a non-Christian and non-theistic conception of reality. The Reformed apologist, on the other hand, appealing to that knowledge of the true God in the natural man which the natural man suppresses by means of his assumption of ultimacy, will also appeal to the knowledge of the true method which the natural man knows *but suppresses.* . . . He suppresses his knowledge of himself as he truly is. He is a man with an iron mask. A true method of apologetics must seek to tear off that iron mask. The Roman Catholic and the Arminian make no attempt to do so. They even flatter its wearer about his fine appearance. In the introductions of their books on apologetics Arminian as well as Roman Catholic apologists frequently seek to set their "opponents" at ease by assuring them that their method, in its field, is all that any Christian could desire. In contradistinction from this, the Reformed apologist will point out again and again that the only method that will lead to the truth in any field is that method which recognizes the fact that man is a creature of God, and that he must therefore seek to think God's thoughts after him.[223]

A *covenantal* theology of *sovereign grace* absolutely requires this kind of *presuppositional* method; no measure of human autonomy can be permitted, since man, as a covenantal creature, has been created to glorify God and subdue all of creation under the direction of his Creator, and also since man's restoration from the effects of his fall into sin can be accomplished and applied solely by the work of Christ and the Spirit.

Underlying this covenantal theology of sovereign grace is the presupposed *authority* of God's inspired, infallible word. For Van Til, Scripture is our most basic authority, which means that there is nothing higher by which it could be proven.

We have felt compelled to take our notions with respect to the nature of reality from the Bible. . . . We have taken the final standard of truth to be the Bible itself. It is needless to say that this procedure will appear suicidal to most men who study philosophy. . . . To accept an interpretation of life upon authority is permissible only if we have looked into the foundations of the authority we accept. But if we must determine the foundations of the authority, we no longer accept authority on authority.[224]

At the end of every line of argumentation there must be a self-evident or *self-attesting* truth, or else we are committed to either *an infinite regress* or *question-begging.* The basic authority for the Christian must be God's word. In the very nature of the case, then, this word must be self-attesting; it must be accepted on *its own* authority.

223. *Ibid.*, pp. 118-119.
224. *Ibid.*, p. 49.

It is impossible to attain to the idea of such a God by speculation independently of Scripture. It has never been done and is inherently impossible. Such a God *must* identify himself. . . . Such a view of God and of human history is both presupposed by, and in turn presupposes, the idea of the infallible Bible. . . . It thus appears afresh that a specifically biblical or Reformed philosophy of history both presupposes and is presupposed by the idea of the Bible as testifying to itself and as being the source of its own identification. . . . *It was against such a specific self-identification that man sinned.* . . . Thus the Christ as testifying to the Word and the Word as testifying to the Christ are involved in one another. . . . It is of the utmost apologetical importance. It is precisely because God is the kind of God he is, that his revelation is, in the nature of the case, self-attesting. In particular, it should be noted that such a God as the Scripture speaks of is everywhere self-attesting. . . . Objectively the Scriptures have on their face the appearance of divinity while yet none will accept its self-attestation unless the Holy Spirit, himself divine, witness to the Word which he has inspired the prophets and apostles to write.[225]

According to Van Til *only Christ* can *testify* to himself and *interpret* His acts and words. This avoids the dual problem of spiritual *subjectivism* (irrationalism) and intellectual *autonomy* (rationalism); one does not approach divine truth through the Spirit *apart from* the word, nor does one first interpret himself and his world, only then to *add* Christ's word to his own (as though his problem were merely a lack of information). Fact, logic, and personality must be interpreted by Christ, not *vice versa*, or else Christ's testimony would be subordinated and absorbed into man's self-testimony and self-sufficient interpretation. Consequently, the word of Christ must be its own authority; it must be *self*-attesting. One cannot reason up to the authority and truth of Christ's word from a point outside of that position.

Complementing this understanding of the authority of God's word is Van Til's insistence on the necessity, sufficiency, and clarity of God's revelation, both general and special.[226] The sinner has no excuse for rebelling against the truth. He recognizes the voice of his Lord speaking in *Scripture*, and that which may be known about God is continually being manifested unto him by God through the *created* order.

Whatever may happen, whatever sin may bring about, whatever havoc it may occasion, it cannot destroy man's knowledge of God and his sense of responsibility to God. Sin would not be sin except for this ineradicable knowledge of God. . . . This knowledge is that which all men have *in common*.[227]

However, sin *does* explain man's refusal to *acknowledge* his Creator,

---

225. *Christian Theory of Knowledge*, pp. 28, 30, 31, 32.
226. *Ibid.*, pp. 52-71; cf. "Nature and Scripture," *The Infallible Word*, ed. Paul Woolley (Philadelphia: Presbyterian and Reformed, reprinted 1967), pp. 263-301.
227. *The Defense of the Faith*, p. 173.

his *suppression* of the revelation of God within and without him, and his *rejection* of the salvation found in God's Son. Thus, Van Til is aware that *the success of apologetics finally depends upon the work of God's sovereign Spirit in the hearts and minds of men.* In addition to the *transcendental necessity* of presupposing the existence of the *Creator* God, the *self-attesting authority* of Christ the *Son* speaking in Scripture, and the concrete biblical understanding of *man* as both *possessing yet suppressing* the knowledge of God, Van Til should be known for his apologetical dependence upon the powerful work of *God's Spirit* in bringing men to renounce their would-be autonomy (which is in principle destructive of all experience and intelligible understanding) and bow before Christ as He commands them to in His inspired word.

> As for the question whether the natural man will accept the truth of such an argument, we answer that he will if God pleases by his Spirit to take the scales from his eyes and the mask from his face. It is upon the power of the Holy Spirit that the Reformed preacher relies when he tells men that they are lost in sin and in need of a Savior. The Reformed preacher does not tone down his message in order that it may find acceptance with the natural man. He does not say that his message is less certainly true because of its non-acceptance by the natural man. The natural man is, by virtue of his creation in the image of God, always accessible to the truth; accessible to the penetration of the truth by the Spirit of God. Apologetics, like systematics, is valuable to the precise extent that it presses the truth upon the attention of the natural man.[228]

By refusing to follow a presuppositional approach to defending the faith, apologists throughout history have seen their witness absorbed into the autonomous schemes of unbelief; indeed, the very position of those who profess to defend the faith has been both compromised by, and transformed into, the perspective of unbelief. If one's theology is not to be made over into the image of autonomous man, then *his theology must ground his apologetic* and inform its argumentation with respect to *starting point, method,* and epistemological *standard.* In contrast to Warfield (as well as the rest of traditional apologists), who held that apologetics must establish the presuppositions of theology, Van Til has reformed the field of apologetics by unashamedly holding that *theology must supply the presuppositions of apologetics.* The biblical truth of Reformed theology requires a *specific approach* to defending the faith; just as Reformed theology alone *proclaims* good news which fully and actually saves men, so a Reformed apologetic alone can remain faithful to the faith and be successful in *defending* the good news before Christianity's cultured despisers.

> If there is not a distinctively Reformed method for the defense of every article of the Christian faith, then there is no way of clearly telling

228. *Ibid.,* pp. 121-122.

an unbeliever just how Christianity differs from his own position and why he should accept the Lord Jesus Christ as his personal Savior.[229]

The faith is best defended by that method of argumentation which does not entail an alteration of the faith defended. By allowing his Reformed theology to guide his presuppositional apologetic, Van Til has signalized the crucial difference between the Socratic outlook and that of Christ. He has done for apologetics what Calvin did for theology. By aiming to bring every thought into captivity to the obedience of Christ, Van Til's presuppositional apologetic has triggered the reformation of Christian apologetics. The foundation of Christian scholarship is to be found in the rigorously biblical epistemology to which Van Til adheres in his defense of the faith.

Although he undoubtedly intended it as a compliment, C. F. H. Henry inaccurately designated Cornelius Van Til as one of three "men of Athens" in his dedication of *Remaking the Modern Mind*. We may be thankful that this has not been the case. The Lord has given Dr. Van Til a love and dedication for that city which *has foundations,* whose builder and maker is God. Van Til's citizenship as a Christian apologist belongs, not to Athens, but to the New Jerusalem. He has been a loyal follower of Christ rather than Socrates; in his extensive writings, his unceasing personal evangelism, and his loving counsel, he has continually demonstrated that "unless the Lord build the house, they labor in vain who build it." May God grant that his presuppositional apologetic will indeed signalize the *remaking* of the modern mind.

---

229. *Ibid.*, p. 335.

In fact the 'free man' of modern non-Christian thought is Janus-faced. He turns one way and would seem to be nothing but an irrationalist. He talks about the 'fact' of freedom. He even makes a pretence of being hotly opposed to the rationalist. With Kierkegaard he will boldly assert that what cannot happen according to logic has happened in fact. Then he turns the other way and would seem to be nothing but a rationalist. Surely, he says, the 'rational man' will accept nothing but what has intelligible meaning for him in accord with the law of contradiction. There must be coherence in experience. It is meaningless to talk about the 'entirely single thing.' But both in his irrationalist and in his rationalist features, the would-be autonomous man is seeking to defend his ultimacy against the claims of the Christian religion. If he is right as an irrationalist then he is not a creature of God. If he were a creature of God, he would be subject to the law of God. He would thus be 'rationally related' to God. He would know that he was a creature of God and that he should obey the law of God. If he is right as a rationalist, then too he is not a creature of God. The law that he then thinks of as above him, he also thinks of as above God; God and he are, for him, subject to a common law. If he were a creature of God, he would grant that what God has determined, and only that, is possible. He would then subject his logical manipulation of 'reality' to the revelation of God.

It is this Janus-faced covenant-breaker, then, who must be won for the gospel. It is he who walks the streets of New York and London. And no one but he does. All men are sinners; all are interested in suppressing the fact of their creaturehood. The irrationalist and rationalist have become friends in the face of their common foe. And this common foe is historic Christianity.

The implication of all this for Christian apologetics is plain. There can be no appeasement between those who presuppose in all their thought the sovereign God and those who presuppose in all their thought the would-be sovereign man. There can be no other point of contact between them than that of head-on collision. The root of both irrationalism and rationalism is the idea of the ultimacy of man. If this root is not taken out, it will do little good to trim off some of the wildest offshoots of irrationalism with the help of rationalism, or to trim off some of the wildest offshoots of rationalism with the help of irrationalism.

Van Til, *The Intellectual Challenge of the Gospel*
([1950] 1953), pp. 18-19.

PHILOSOPHY

XI

PRAGMATISM, PREJUDICE, AND PRESUPPOSITIONALISM

By GREG BAHNSEN

This essay cannot attempt to do justice to the multiple avenues traversed by twentieth-century philosophers; they constitute a maze of both overlapping and divergent lines of thought: idealism, realism, phenomenology, process philosophy, existentialism, positivism, pragmatism, and linguistic analysis. Each has a claim on the Christian scholar's attention. However, we must narrow the field. It is reasonably accurate to distinguish the emphasis on phenomenology and existentialism on the Continent from the dominance of pragmatism and analysis in England and America. Since the present study is being done in the context of Anglo-American scholarship, we shall focus our attention on the schools of pragmatism and linguistic analysis—all the while recognizing the affinities which can be seen between them and aspects of European thought. Three prominent philosophers in these traditions who have had distinctive proposals in the theory of knowledge are John Dewey, Ludwig Wittgenstein, and John L. Austin; as will be later exhibited, common elements in their approaches bind them together in various ways.

The present essay will aim to demonstrate that the central motivating inquiry of epistemology—the search for *certainty*—has not and cannot be satisfied by Dewey, Wittgenstein, and Austin. Fundamental issues in the theory of knowledge cannot be toned down or evaded, and yet due to certain shared problems—notably, arbitrariness, phenomenalism, and dialecticism—these three philosophers have supplied no adequate answers. At this point we shall observe the relevance of Christianity, for as the writings of Cornelius Van Til have shown, presuppositional epistemology avoids the pitfalls of pragmatism and prejudice, finding a solid basis for epistemic certainty in God's self-attesting revelation.

Epistemology and Certainty

Bertrand Russell, perhaps the most prolific of the significant twentieth-century philosophers, opened his treatment of *The Problems of Philosophy* (which has been continually reprinted since 1912) with these words:

Is there any knowledge in the world which is so certain that no reasonable man could doubt it? This question, which at first sight might not seem difficult, is really one of the most difficult that can be asked. When we have realized the obstacles in the way of a straightforward and confident answer, we shall be well launched on the study of philosophy—for philosophy is merely the attempt to answer such ultimate questions. . . .[1]

The theory of knowledge, *epistemology*, is a critical issue in philosophy; the philosophical scholar not only discusses what reality is and what moral obligations we have, but he must ask "*how* do we *know* that these things are so?" One could no more avoid the questions of epistemology in studying philosophy than a marine biologist could avoid the ocean. While it is certainly not the whole of philosophy, epistemology has, for better or worse, dominated philosophy since the seventeenth century, and its crucial questions retain their intellectual challenge today.

Is there any knowledge in the world which is certain? Can anything be known for sure? Is there an answer to the skeptic? Such questions as these have been a key motivation in the development of epistemology. The guiding spirit of the Vienna circle and a founder of modern analytic philosophy, Moritz Schlick, wrote in his 1934 article, "The Foundation of Knowledge":

> All important attempts at establishing a theory of knowledge grow out of the problem concerning the certainity of human knowledge. And this problem in turn originates in the wish for absolute certainty.
>
> The insight that the statements of daily life and science can at best be only probable . . . has again and again stimulated philosophers . . . since ancient times to search for an unshakeable, indubitable foundation, a firm basis on which the uncertain structure of our knowledge could rest.[2]

The problem of epistemic certainty looms large in the theory of knowledge and, thereby, has determinative significance for all of philosophy. As Hamlyn says in his recent text: "The search for indubitable and infallible truths is therefore a common feature of traditional epistemology."[3]

Of what can one be certain? What justification is there for claims to knowledge? Every philosopher, indeed every person, faces these disquieting questions, for everyone distinguishes between sense and nonsense, adjudicates conflicting claims as to the truth, and acts upon fundamental convictions. Evaluations and decisions such as these are guided by some

---

1. Bertrand Russell, *The Problems of Philosophy* (New York: Oxford University Press, reprinted 1973), p. 7.
2. "Uber das Fundament der Erkenntnis," *Erkenntnis* IV (1934); reprinted in *Logical Positivism*, ed. A. J. Ayer, trans. David Rynin (New York: Free Press, Macmillan, 1959), p. 209.
3. D. W. Hamlyn, *The Theory of Knowledge* (New York: Anchor Books, Doubleday and Co., 1970), p. 14.

implicit theory of knowledge. One does not decide *whether* to form some epistemological viewpoint and theoretical basis for certainty or not; he simply chooses whether he shall do it self-consciously and well. Epistemological concerns then are unavoidable, and *in particular* we cannot escape asking after the basis for *certainty* in knowledge.

Dewey and Pragmatism

However, the fact that the search for epistemic certainty has been pervasive in the history of philosophy and has critically influenced the issues of epistemological theory does not mean that the various positions which have been set forth have all been positive and constructive. In particular, the impact of evolutionary naturalism and scientific positivism has created a negative response to the search for certainty in the area of knowledge. For many, the mind has come to be viewed as a completely natural phenomenon, a mode of bodily behavior subject solely to the causal factors of one's brain organism, and important only in virtue of the historical struggle for survival. Moreover, early in this century the positivism of the Vienna circle (e.g., Schlick, Carnap, Feigl, Gödel, Neurath) and empiricalistic bias of English-speaking philosophers like Russell and Wittgenstein generated strong anti-metaphysical sentiments and the rejection of unperceived entities and forces; this, of course, radically altered the conception of man, the objects of knowledge, and the knowing process. Speaking of such doctrines as the essential rationality of the universe, Russell declared:

> There can be no doubt that the hope of finding reason to believe such theses as these has been the chief inspiration of many life-long students of philosophy. This hope, I believe, is vain. It would seem that knowledge concerning the universe as a whole is not to be obtained by metaphysics. . . .[4]

Consequently, Russell was led to adopt a decidedly negative attitude toward the search for certainty in epistemology. In the Introduction to his *Human Knowledge: Its Scope and Limits* he wrote:

> That scientific inference requires, for its validity, principles which experience cannot render even probable is, I believe, an inescapable conclusion from the logic of probability. . . . "Knowledge," in my opinion, is a much less precise concept than is generally thought, and has its roots more deeply embedded in unverbalized animal behavior than most philosophers have been willing to admit. . . . To ask, therefore, whether we "know" the postulates of scientific inference is not so definite a question as it seems. . . . In the sense in which "no" is the right answer we know nothing whatever, and "knowledge" in this sense is a delusive vision. The perplexities of philosophers are due, in a large measure, to their unwillingness to awaken from this blissful dream.[5]

---

4. *The Problems of Philosophy*, p. 141.
5. Bertrand Russell, *Human Knowledge: Its Scopes and Limits* (New York: Clarion Books, Simon and Schuster, 1948), pp. xv-xvi.

One must give up the vain delusion of finding a theoretically adequate grounding for knowledge claims; *certainty*, as traditionally understood, is not to be found.

An extension of such a naturalistic and disparaging approach to epistemological issues was elaborated and popularized by the American school of philosophy known as *pragmatism*. Its foremost spokesman, John Dewey (1859–1952), called for a complete "Reconstruction in Philosophy."[6] The effect of this naturalistic reconstruction on the theory of knowledge was most clearly revealed by Dewey in his book *The Quest for Certainty*.[7] Dewey insisted that knowledge should no longer be understood in terms of *theoretical justification*, but rather in the context of man's *active struggle* to adapt to his environment and survive in the face of whatever threatens his life.

> Man who lives in a world of hazards is compelled to seek for security. . . . The quest for certainty is a quest for a peace which is assured, an object which is unqualified by risk and the shadow of fear which action casts. . . . If one looks at the history of knowledge, it is plain that at the beginning men tried to know because they had to do so in order to live. In the absence of that organic guidance given by their structure to other animals, man had to find out what he was about, and he could find out only by studying the environment which constituted the means, obstacles and results of his behavior. The desire for intellectual or cognitive understanding had no meaning except as a means of obtaining greater security as to the issues of action.[8]

Knowledge should be viewed as practical, according to Dewey, but because practical activity is inherently uncertain and precarious, men have exalted pure intellect above practical affairs in their quest for a certainty which is absolute and unshakeable.[9] Therefore, "thought has been alleged to be a purely inner activity, intrinsic to mind alone."[10] But this is misguided, Dewey thought; knowledge and intelligence are not determined by abstract thinking or mental justification for one's beliefs, but rather by problem-solving and methods of active control. " 'Thought' is not a property of something termed intellect or reason apart from nature. It is a mode of directed overt action."[11]

No longer would scholars be pressed for an intellectually adequate

---

6. See Dewey's book by the same name (New York: Mentor Books, New American Library, originally published 1921). It should be noted that Dewey's reconstruction was not met with complete approval by Russell: cf. his "Dewey's Logic" in *The Philosophy of John Dewey*, ed. P. A. Schilpp (Chicago: Northwestern University Press, 1939; 2nd edition 1951). However, in broad perspective, it is clear that this was simply an internal family squabble within humanistic naturalism.

7. John Dewey, *The Quest for Certainty: A Study of the Relation of Knowledge and Action* (Gifford Lectures 1929), (New York: Capricorn Books, G. P. Putnam's Sons, reprinted 1960).

8. *Ibid.*, pp. 1, 8, 38.
9. *Ibid.*, pp. 6, 33.
10. *Ibid.*, p. 7.
11. *Ibid.*, p. 166.

account of their theory of knowledge and for a ratiocinative justification of their knowledge claims; theoretical considerations would become irrelevant. Dewey summarized his pragmatic position as

> the theory that the processes and materials of knowledge are determined by practical or purposive considerations—that there is no such thing as knowledge determined by exclusively theoretical speculative, or abstract intellectual considerations.[12]

The quest for certainty should now take on a new character, unhampered by the epistemological problematics of the past with its theoretical preoccupation.

> Henceforth the quest for certainty becomes the search for methods of control; that is, regulation of conditions of change with respect to their consequences. Theoretical certitude is assimilated to practical certainty; to *security*, trustworthiness of instrumental operations. . . . Knowing is, for philosophical theory, a case of specially directed activity instead of something isolated from practice. The quest for certainty by means of exact possession in mind of immutable reality is exchanged for search for security by means of active control of the changing course of events. Intelligence in operation, another name for method, becomes the thing most worth winning.[13]

What really counts is not that one's thinking corresponds to reality, but *practical success* in *adjusting to one's environment* and *responding to its problems*—security via control over future change.

"The first step in knowing is to locate the problems which need solution." Given this practical orientation, Dewey's directive is as follows:

> Drop the conception that knowledge is knowledge only when it is a disclosure and definition of the properties of fixed and antecedent reality; interpret the aim and test of knowing by what happens in the actual procedures of scientific inquiry. . . .[14]

Dewey's reconstruction of philosophy would thus have the dual attraction of being scientific as well as practical, avoiding the abstract and dead-end questions of past thinkers. "The question of truth is not as to whether Being or Non-Being, Reality or mere Appearance, is experienced, but as to the *worth* of a certain concretely experienced thing.[15] Science is problem-solving and useful, thereby *creating* the objects of "knowledge":

> All experimentation involves *overt* doing, the making of definite changes in the environment or in our relation to it. . . . Experiment is not a random activity but is directed by ideas which have to meet the con-

---

12. *The Century Dictionary Supplement*, Vol. II (New York: Appleton-Century-Crofts, 1909), p. 1050.
13. *The Quest for Certainty*, pp. 128, 204.
14. *Ibid.*, p. 103; cf. p. 131.
15. *The Influence of Darwin on Philosophy and Other Essays in Contemporary Thought* (New York: Peter Smith, 1951), p. 235.

ditions set by the need of the problem inducing the active inquiry. . . .
The outcome of the directed activity is the construction of a new empirical situation in which objects are differently related to one another,
and such that the *consequences* of directed operations form the objects
that have the property of being *known*.[16]

Thus the value of a mental operation is not tested by its accurate reflection
of reality, but by its *practical consequences,* the *active controls* it affords
us, and the *successful prediction* of future change (verification).

Basically, for Dewey, ideas are plans for action, provisional hypotheses
for solving a concrete problem, and as such tested in experience:

> Ideas are anticipatory plans and designs which take effect in concrete
> *reconstructions of antecedent conditions of existence. . . . Ideas that are
> plans of operations to be performed are integral factors in actions which
> change the face of the world.[17]

> The idea, or anticipation of *possible* outcome, must, in order to satisfy
> the requirements of controlled inquiry, be such as to indicate an op-
> eration to be *existentially* performed, or it is a means (called *pro-
> cedural*) of effecting the existential transformation without which a
> problematic situation can not be resolved.[18]

> Ideas have to have their worth tested experimentally . . . in them-
> selves they are tentative and provisional.[19]

The meaning of ideas is determined by the practical consequences they have
in experience. If a judgment's truth or falsity makes no difference in one's
experience, then it is meaningless (the parallel here to analytic philosophy
is conspicuous). A belief (judgment, idea) *predicts* certain future consequences and *generates a particular course of action* which aims to solve
the problem which initially provoked inquiry. As Dewey's fellow pragmatist, William James, said: "The ultimate test for us of what a truth means
is . . . the conduct it dictates or inspires. But it inspires that conduct because it first foretells some particular turn to our experience which shall
call forth just that conduct from us."[20]

From this, the pragmatic theory of truth becomes evident. If a meaningful idea is useful in adjusting to a practical situation, if it helps to
predict events and thus control what happens to us, it is deemed "true."

> According to experimental inquiry, the validity of the object of
> thought depends upon the *consequences* of the operations which define
> the object of thought. . . . The conceptions are valid in the degree

16. *The Quest for Certainty*, pp. 86-87.
17. *Ibid.*, pp. 166-167, 138.
18. "Inquiry and Indeterminateness of Situations," *Journal of Philosophy* XXXIX
(May 21, 1942), p. 293.
19. *Democracy and Education* (New York: Macmillan Co., 1961), p. 189.
20. William James, *Collected Essays and Reviews* (New York: David McKay Co.,
1920), p. 412.

in which . . . we can predict future events. . . . The test of the validity of any particular intellectual conception, measurement or enumeration is functional, its use in making possible the institution of interactions which yield results in control of actual experiences of observed objects.[21]

An idea or belief is true if it is *verified* (with respect to the prediction it makes about the future turn of events) or *useful* (with respect to solving the initial problem which one faces). "This is the meaning of truth: processes of change so directed that they achieve an intended consummation."[22] A problem confronts a person, leading him to formulate a certain belief, the meaning of which is the practical action it calls for on his part; the belief thus predicts a certain turn of events and thereby a useful way to resolve the initial difficulty. *If the predicted consequences are realized, the hypothesis* (idea, belief) *is verified*—which is to say, true. "Verification and truth are two names for the same thing."[23]

> It is therefore in submitting conceptions to the control of experience, in the process of verifying them, that one finds examples of what is called truth. . . . Truth "means" verification. . . . Verification, either actual or possible, is the definition of truth.[24]

A belief proposes a plan of action which shall resolve a problem; if the belief is verified, the proposed plan was useful. Thus the true is the useful. "The effective working of an idea and its truth are one and the same thing—this working being neither the cause nor the evidence of truth but its nature."[25]

However, one must be cautious and fair to Dewey here, for he does not mean useful in the sense of personally advantageous. The satisfaction required of a true belief is not just a personal one, but the "satisfaction of the conditions prescribed by the problem."[26] One should recall that "ideas are always working hypotheses concerning attaining particular empirical results, and are tentative programs (or sketches of method) for attaining them." In light of this, the usefulness relevant to establishing a truth is determined by the *kind of problem* engendering the belief which is tested:

> I have never identified any satisfaction with the truth of an idea, save *that* satisfaction which arises when the idea as working hypothesis or tentative method is applied to prior existences in such a way as to fulfill what it intends.[27]

21. *The Quest for Certainty*, p. 129.
22. *Experience and Nature* (Chicago: Open Court, 1929), p. 161.
23. *The Influence of Darwin on Philosophy*, p. 139.
24. *Philosophy and Civilization* (New York: Capricorn Books, 1963), p. 23.
25. *The Influence of Darwin on Philosophy*, p. 143.
26. "Experience, Knowledge, and Value: A Rejoinder," *The Philosophy of John Dewey*, p. 572.
27. "What Does Pragmatism Mean by Practical?," *Journal of Philosophy* V (1908), pp. 85-99.

With this in mind, then, we can summarize by saying that the criterion of truth for a belief (idea, judgment) is the degree to which it and the action based upon it are *useful* (practical) in *resolving the problem which elicited it*. A sentence is considered true when everyone who checked matters out would be satisfied with the sentence, that is, when it is validated, corroborated, or verified.

Therefore, according to Dewey, because the state of affairs *antecedent* to inquiry is *not* the object of knowledge,[28] one's judgments should no longer be taken as attempted copies of reality, but rather as *foresights toward future adjustment* to some environment (physical, psychological, social, etc.). Dewey's reconstructed theory of knowledge sees true judgments as generating behavior which brings predicted, useful results in adjusting to environment and its problems. Through scientific experimentation, we can gain control over the environment, thereby *producing* the objects of "knowledge."

> The sum and substance of the present arguments is that if we frame our conception of knowledge on the experimental model, we find that it is a way of operating upon and with the things of ordinary experience so that we can frame our ideas of them in terms of their interactions with one another, instead of in terms of the qualities they directly present, and that thereby our control of them, our ability to change them and direct their changes as we desire, is indefinitely increased. Knowing is itself a mode of practical action and is *the* way of interaction by which other natural interactions become subject to direction.[29]

When a particular idea (plan for action) gains for us greater *control* in the environment, then it is warranted. "Knowledge is warranted assertion." "When there is possibility of control, knowledge is the sole agency of its realization."[30] Dewey's new objects of "knowledge" have a practical and future orientation: "Knowledge is always a matter of the use that is made of experienced natural events, . . . as indications of what will be experienced under different conditions."[31] He utterly disdained what he called "the spectator approach" to knowledge, with its theoretical headaches and misguided desire for intellectual certainty. Dewey aptly summarized his revolutionary approach to epistemology in *The Quest for Certainty* by saying "knowledge is the fruit of the undertakings that transform a problematic situation into a resolved one."[32] As traditionally understood, *certainty is not to be found*. But so what?

---

28. *Experience and Nature*, p. 156; cf. *The Quest for Certainty*, p. 71.
29. *The Quest for Certainty*, pp. 106-107, and "Propositions, Warranted Assertibility, and Truth," *Journal of Philosophy* XXXVIII (March 27, 1941), p. 173.
30. *Experience and Nature*, p. 22.
31. *John Dewey on Experience, Nature, and Freedom*, ed. R. J. Bernstein (New York: Liberal Arts Press, 1960), p. 53.
32. *The Quest for Certainty*, pp. 242-243.

However, in response to Dewey's pragmatism, we can observe that one is not so easily absolved from the rigorous demands of epistemology; the key questions in the theory of knowledge have a recalcitrance which is not overcome by Dewey. The following line of critique will hopefully point this out.

It is to be noticed, first, that pragmatism places a peculiar strain on our use of language. On the one hand, the pragmatist uses language in a perplexingly extraordinary way, and on the other hand, in a deceptively vague manner. An understandably common reply to the proposal of pragmatism is this: even if a belief or idea does have a useful function (works well), is this not because it is first *true?* Just here it is evident that pragmatism is at variance with the way we use language, for Dewey took "effective working" to be, not the evidence of truth, but the very nature of truth. Yet there are many things which are ordinarily taken as true which are so taken *irrespective* of any pragmatic justification (e.g., that of those who died last year, some had brown eyes), and this is because we ordinarily take truth to be related to something *objective*, rather than as the valuable functioning of a belief. It seems as though the pragmatist wants us to adopt a very specialized use of key epistemic words, reserving them for those ideas which have the privileged status of being relevant, important, or practical. Such a programmatic reformation of our linguistic habits, however, is of little philosophic value, since traditional epistemic questions can still be asked—although with a new vocabulary; we still wonder whether certain statements or beliefs are "true" in the old sense, and linguistic renovation will not of itself prevent us from asking.

Moreover, when it is reported that such and such a solution to a problem is more useful ("true," new sense) than another proposal, one would be especially interested in asking whether this report is *true* (old sense). In response, the pragmatist will either be right back into the thick of it respecting traditional epistemological issues, or he will prohibit the question (or just ignore it) as being pointless and impractical. But such a reply would be clearly ridiculous, because here we are not asking whether some *proposal* (e.g., "Quinine is a specific treatment for malaria") is true or useful, but rather whether a certain *conclusion* (e.g., "Quinine is more useful than salt tablets for treating malaria") is veridical. Certainly it is *not* pointless to ask after the *accuracy* of the pragmatist's judgments about what works and what does not.

The ever-latent problem with schemes which require a sharp deviation from the ordinary use of words is that they covertly exclude perfectly legitimate and meaningful questions, such as the one asked above. But pragmatism's tendency to be a Procrustean bed is not its only difficulty. It also lacks requisite *clarity.* The emphasis upon a belief's usefulness or ability to work is very vague and ambiguous. Just what does it mean for a belief or idea to "work"? We readily understand the working of a machine or an employee, but the notion is odd when applied to a thought to which we give assent. Dewey's reply would be to treat beliefs as plans for action, and we do know what it is like for a plan to be successful. Yes, but then what comes of the *propositional attitude* traditionally called "belief"? Has it simply been obliterated from nature?[33] More to the point, though, is a specific question about the meaning of 'useful' in Dewey's instrumentalism. Just what is the nature of the *end* served by the usefulness of "true" be- liefs? And how does one go about assessing usefulness? The pragmatists have been not at all unified in their answers to such questions. Their own respective leading interests (Peirce: math and science; James: psychology; Dewey: social reform) significantly colored and diversified their replies. Indeed, already in 1908 Arthur O. Lovejoy could distinguish thirteen dif- ferent forms of pragmatism![34] Such ambiguity can be removed, and in- evitable relativism obviated, only by engaging in the questions associated with traditional disputes about objective truth. Failing this, pragmatism is an imprecise and unclear point of view.

A final observation should be made about the use of the words 'useful' and 'true' in pragmatism. Dewey sought to avoid the obviously defective view that truth is useful in the narrow sense of private expediency. This he did by correlating usefulness to the problem which raised a question for inquiry initially. When one examines, then, the way in which Dewey recommended that we verify the usefulness of judgments in relation to the questions which prompted them, it turns out that the *useful* is coextensive with that which meets the *empirical and coherence tests*, just as is de- manded by common scientific procedure. That is, in order to salvage the credibility of pragmatism, Dewey had to trivialize its key notion, usefulness, in such a way that it amounted to what is commonly meant by 'true' (old sense) anyway. It appears, then, that Dewey's use of epistemic vocabulary is, first, contrary to ordinary and meaningful usage; second, it is far from precise and clear. But finally, in Dewey's novel approach to truth, its alleged equivalent ('useful' in the sense of 'confirmed') is deprived of any distinctive meaning in comparison to the way scientific secularism goes about determining truth and what it picks out as such.

In the long run, the novelty of Dewey's view of truth was not *how* it decided (or how it assessed) *what* is true; rather, it was Dewey's com- mentary on the *nature of truth*. Being content with well-established scien- tific procedure, he went on to speculate that truth does not exist antecedent to, or separate from, inquiry. Instead it is a property which is *acquired*

---

33. Like a city under nuclear attack? No, if anything, more like a viewpoint sub- jected to brain-washing.

34. Arthur O. Lovejoy, "The Thirteen Pragmatisms," *Journal of Philosophy* V (1908), pp. 29-39.

by an idea when investigation confirms it; when an idea becomes a warranted assertion through our experimentation, we have *made it true.* This is plainly false. The word 'true' is *not* functionally equivalent to the word 'confirmed'. The law of excluded middle leads us to agree that "Either p is true, or not-p is true." When 'confirmed' is substituted for 'true' we get: "Either p is confirmed, or not-p is confirmed"—and this is patently absurd (e.g., science has not confirmed the assertion "There were 17 billion ants in the world in 459 B.C.," but *neither* has it confirmed that there were not!). The fact is that 'confirmed' is a *time-conditioned* word, whereas 'true' is not. That is why one does not usually hear the expression *"Today* it was true that Washington once crossed the Delaware,"[35] but we might have occasion to say "Today it was confirmed that Washington once crossed the Delaware." Again, if this has just now been *confirmed,* nevertheless five years ago it was just as *true* that Washington did it. Furthermore, it is hardly credible that we *make* a sentence true (e.g., "The wind is blowing southwesterly") unless, as G. E. Moore observed, we have control over what it describes! It thus appears that Dewey's novel approach to truth is in some respects trivial and in other respects false.

Beyond its linguistic difficulties, pragmatism comes to futility in the working out of its view of knowledge. We have been told that the sentences which are true (and hence knowable) are those whose predicted consequences are verified. Knowledge depends upon this confirmation. But this program for determining what *counts* as known and unknown already *presupposes* a *knowledge* of what results we can *expect* from the true sentences. Therefore, pragmatism requires that we *first know* the truth *in order to* indicate how we can know which sentences are true! This method is precariously circular. How can one *know in advance* what should count as verified consequences for a sentence? This question is especially telling for pragmatism, since according to it one cannot *know* anything but the objects *created* as the *result* of experimentation. And yet if one does *not* know in advance, then he will be unable *after* experimentation to separate out the true sentences from the false ones (since Dewey identified truth with verification). Thus, pragmatism can know nothing at all.

However, overlooking this defect, even when the pragmatist knows what conditions must be met in order to accept a belief as true, he still has no protection from error and wishful thinking. One need only *believe* that the satisfying conditions are met in order to be satisfied with a sentence or belief and thus take it as true. For instance, one believes that he is in Australia, and he wants to confirm it. He establishes this verification condition: if one is in Australia, then he can find kangaroos running wild. He then goes outside, and being in the Rocky Mountains, he comes across

---

35. Although it might have been stated on some day many years ago.

bears roaming wild. However, he *believes* that they are kangaroos. Thus, the verification condition is (albeit erroneously!) satisfied. What this indicates is that Dewey's pragmatism does not escape the traditional epistemological question known as the ego-centric predicament.[36]

We must further observe that Dewey fell far short of satisfying his own requirements of practicality and warranted assertion; his pragmatism, by attempting to suppress the standard-problems of epistemological theory, failed to be useful or verified. *First*, it shortsightedly selected *which problems* to concentrate upon and *what standard* to use in assessing the usefulness of certain answers. For instance, it is perfectly conceivable that some belief might work well for the present, but in the long run not really be useful ("true"). "Eat, drink, and be merry, for tomorrow we die" might conceivably work well for someone; it might help him adjust to his secular social environment, ease his psychological frustrations, and be more efficient in attaining the securities and comforts of life. And scientific investigation has verified that everyone does die. A sophisticated case for this "plan of action," then, might very well pass the pragmatist's test. Hence, he could accept it as "true" and ignore the "irrelevant, abstract, and (here-and-now) inconsequential" theories of the eschatological religions. Yet should the threat of an after-life, where men's deeds are judged, accurately describe the real situation, "eat, drink, and be merry" would quite obviously be *impractical*. Dewey's quest for *security instead of certainty*, then, cannot be satisfied until one first arrives at *certainty*— for instance, as to the question of men's destinies. Since the problem of an after-life is not subject to the trial-and-error method of scientific experimentation, it must needs be resolved on somewhat other grounds, which means that Dewey would be forced to confront the difficult philosophic issues traditionally associated with epistemology just as his scholarly predecessors did. Pragmatism is extremely impractical and insecure if it abandons, as it does, the quest for intellectual certainty.

Secondly, even with respect to the more mundane problems of the present life, pragmatism turns out to be *impractical*. Dewey said that the first step in knowing is to locate the problems which need solution; this is eminently practical. However, he has also insisted that ideas are anticipatory plans for some *future* operation, tentative programs of action, foresights for adjustment. Hence, one *cannot* have an idea or knowledge of the *pre-existing* problem which must be the *starting point* for inquiry and knowledge! Since ideas are forward-looking, how can one know what a problem is, that a situation has certain features, or that these features are problematic? We need veridical ideas about the *present* before we can devise

---

36. Pragmatism is surely not *practical* if it fails to answer this question, for otherwise it would not make us secure against such things as man-eating wallabies!

successful plans for the future. This again will bring us up against the necessity of answering standard epistemological problems, for the attempt to produce an accurate description of a real situation (and thereby know it as a problem to be resolved) assumes an adequate answer to various skeptical challenges. Dewey's theory, then, would make his own starting point unknowable and thereby preclude solving problems.

Thirdly, pragmatism is impractical for the reason that *standard intellectual problems* in the theory of knowledge are among those which we encounter in our environment and trouble us, and yet pragmatism arbitrarily relegates them to the classification of impertinence. But why should social reform be worth inquiry, but overcoming skepticism's nagging difficulties ignored? Intellectual problems are just as real problems as other kinds. Therefore, we can ask just how well Dewey's viewpoint "works" if it fails to give us a *coherent and unified conceptual mastery over the data of experience.* On this score, pragmatism must be rated quite low, for the coherence of Dewey's philosophy can be seriously questioned. Obviously, there is the problem mentioned in the previous paragraph.

It is clear that Dewey has overstated his case for a *consequentialist* approach to knowledge; ideas cannot be solely future oriented, and the objects of knowledge cannot be exclusively created as the outcome of experimentation. Not surprisingly, then, we find that Dewey attempted to salvage the common-sense conviction that objects of knowledge are not completely subjective, that existents have antecedent reality, and that what we experience is somewhat independent of our thinking about it. And yet he simultaneously wished to avoid the idea of "the total transcendence of knowledge."

> Any experienced subject-matter whatever may *become* an object of reflection and cognitive inspection. . . . The emphasis is upon "become"; the cognitive never *is* all-inclusive: that is, when the material of a prior non-cognitive experience is the object of knowledge, it and the act of knowing are themselves included within a new and wider non-cognitive experience—and *this* situation can never be transcended.[37]

But we must ask whether Dewey, in his attempt to avoid the pitfall of idealism, has not smuggled into his account elements which he elsewhere explicitly denies. Although he wants to assert that we experience things *as* being antecedent to our experience of them, nevertheless he viewed "experience" as a *reconstruction* of situations in such a way that it make the world different from what it would have been *without* human operational thinking. What, then, are existents *in themselves* when not the object of cognitive reflection? The status of objects when they are not being thought

---

37. *Experience and Nature,* p. 24.

upon is a real problem for pragmatism. It seems to make the "given"—that aspect of reality which is antecedent to the operation of human thought upon it—into a mysterious thing-in-itself. Likewise, the objects of human cognition are unavoidably altered in character from those external objects which exist independent of our experience of them.[38] This leads us right back into the irradicable subjectivism of Kantian idealism with its noumenal/phenomenal dichotomy.[39] Dewey was hopelessly caught in a *dialectical tension:* objects of knowledge are *created* by rational inquiry (the real is the rational), and yet the intended objects of experience exist *independently* of cognitive control and reconstruction (the cognitive is never all-inclusive). This reflects the rational-irrational antinomy of all secular thought.[40]

Such an antinomy is also illustrated in the *necessity-contingency* syndrome of Dewey's thought. *On the one hand,* Dewey spoke as though logic and science have certain *autonomous* norms characterized by universal necessity and invariance, norms which reflect the permanent structure of real existence. Hence, intellect demands that "contradictions" (i.e., unresolved problems) be overcome in accordance with the useful instruments of logic and scientific method.[41] If we are to arrive at warranted assertions, certain conditions *must* be satisfied. Knowing must be a "regulated course" of interaction with nature,[42] and inquiry must be subject to the *requirement* of logical forms.[43] "Logical forms are invariants. . . . 'Invariants' are necessary for the conduct of inquiry."[44] The sole way of *control* was through *scientific knowledge,* and science was foremost "controlled inference,"[45] "regular methods of controlling,"[46] Inquiry is the "controlled and directed transformation of an indeterminate situation."[47] Thus, there are *universal*

---

38. Note: "Knowing . . . marks a transitional redirection and rearrangement of the real." *The Quest for Certainty,* p. 295.

39. It is certainly not without significance here that Dewey's doctoral dissertation at Johns Hopkins in 1884 was written on the psychology of Kant.

40. The antinomy takes various expressions in connection with different problems: the object of knowledge (reconstructed by thought/independent of thought), the subject of knowledge (must be omniscient/can know nothing with certainty), the standards of knowledge (there are universal norms/contingency precludes all criteria), nature of the external world (completely determined/thoroughly contingent), nature of values (there are objective guidelines/everything is relative to person judging).

41. "The function of reflective thought is, therefore, to transform a situation in which there is experienced obscurity, doubt, conflict, disturbance of some sort, into a situation that is clear, coherent, settled, harmonious." *How We Think* (Boston: D. C. Heath and Co., 1933), pp. 100-101.

42. *The Quest for Certainty,* p. 295.

43. *Logic: The Theory of Inquiry* (New York: Henry Holt and Co., 1938), p. 5.

44. *Ibid.,* p. 390.

45. *Essays in Experimental Logic* (New York: Dover Publications, 1953), p. 435.

46. *Philosophy of Education* (New Jersey: Littlefield, Adams, and Co., 1958), p. 211.

47. *Logic,* p. 104.

prescriptions which regulate our judgments about experience.[48] There are set controls on intelligent method. Moreover, Dewey could speak of *necessary conditions* of experience[49] and testing,[50] of laws (or relations) as "the constancy among variations,"[51] and of development according to "the structures of the world."[52] Indeed, *continuity and permanence* are studied by science as *imbedded in the conditions of nature:* "Constant relations among changes are the subject-matter of scientific thought,"[53] and "Nature and life manifest not flux but continuity, and continuity involves forces and structures that endure through change."[54] Hence, such things as mathematical relations "are derived from natural conditions" and *not* "fictions . . . called into being by that particular act of mind in which they are used."[55] Therefore, one cannot miss a commitment to necessary criteria, laws, and constant relations of nature (or permanent structures) in Dewey's writings.

And yet, *on the other hand,* Dewey's evolutionary naturalism *precludes* permanently fixed orders or norms, since all existence and experience are held to be radically *contingent.* He insisted that "Experience is *of* as well as *in* nature"[56] and that the human mind has *developed* in the context of a world of change.[57] It was his conviction "that reality *is* process, and that laws as well as things develop in the processes of unceasing change."[58] The future is always marked by contingency.[59] Thus "from the standpoint of existence, independently of its subjection to inquiry there is no criterion."[60] There are *no* objective necessities or norms, and what we take as invariants are, due to the contingency of reality, mere matters of cognition. *Prior* to the knowing activity of man, the world is *not* "intellectually coherent," but rather the knowing process *gives* relations to the world, just as it *gives* form to experienced objects, which the world of objects did not itself have.[61] In light of this, Dewey taught that "all logical forms . . .

---

48. Hence, e.g., "Logical Conditions of a Scientific Treatment of Morality," *Philosophy of Education*, pp. 211-249.

49. *Art as Experience* (New York: Capricorn Books, G. P. Putnam's Sons, 1958), p. 212.

50. *Logic*, p. iv.

51. *Experience and Nature*, p. 146.

52. *Ibid.*, p. 277.

53. *The Quest for Certainty*, p. 248.

54. *Art as Experience*, p. 323.

55. *Essays in Experimental Logic*, pp. 56-57. Dewey went so far as to say that concrete things dictate what is necessary for an intellectual grasp of themselves: *The Influence of Darwin on Philosophy*, pp. 107, 235.

56. *Experience and Nature*, p. iii.

57. *Ibid.*, p. 277.

58. *John Dewey on Experience, Nature, and Freedom*, p. 229.

59. *Human Nature and Conduct* (New York: The Modern Library, 1939), p. 208.

60. *Logic*, p. 268.

61. *The Quest for Certainty*, p. 295.

arise within the operation of inquiry."[62] They are not ultimate invariants to which inquiry must conform;[63] thus no logical principles are absolute or immune from revision. Every law of logic is a result of inquiry, developed within contingent nature, and as such subject to change when human habits change.[64] *Logical rules* are a matter of *convention*, comparable to civil law.[65] As a matter of experience, we see that meeting certain conditions leads to valid conclusions, so that *experience* regulates the norms of inquiry and validates the standards of science. Logical operations have no autonomous status, but are defined by existential conditions and consequences—never *vice-versa*.[66] That is, logic is "relative to consequences rather than to antecedents," and its rules "like other tools . . . must be modified when they are applied to new conditions and new results have to be achieved."[67] *There simply can be no necessary relations or permanent laws in a world of constant change:* "That conditions are never completely fixed means that they are in process—that, in any case, they are moving toward the production of a state of affairs which is going to be different in *some* respect."[68] *Contingency precludes necessity:* "The necessary is always necessary for, not necessary in and of itself; it is conditioned by the contingent."[69] Thus, results of inquiry never attain the status of an "inherent *logical* necessity" but must always remain "a brute fact."[70]

If the previous two paragraphs read like night and day, it is because Dewey has throughout his writings tried unsuccessfully to combine irreconcilable attitudes. He wants to hold onto both criteria *and* contingency. He wants science to control inquiry into experience, *and yet* he wants experience to determine the controls of scientific inquiry. He wants a basically *incoherent* world to be amenable to the demands of *rational reflection*. He aims to make logic both autonomous from *and* dependent upon temporal process. He teaches that existence is both radically contingent *and yet* subject to the conditions laid down by developed logic. In short, Dewey has suppressed the theoretical issues of epistemology only to wind up being forced back and forth between rationalism and irrationalism, and hence his viewpoint is undeniably inadequate to satisfy or resolve the problems of intellect. As suggested above, this is further proof that pragmatism is thoroughly *impractical*. Epistemological futility is anything but useful.

---

62. *Logic*, pp. 3-4.
63. *Ibid.*, p. 11.
64. *Ibid.*, pp. 13-14, 82, 156-157, 328-329, 372, 374.
65. *Ibid.*, pp. 16-17, 102, 120, 372ff.
66. *Ibid.*, p. 15.
67. *Philosophy and Civilization*, pp. 138-139.
68. *Logic*, p. 500.
69. *Experience and Nature*, p. 65.
70. *Logic*, p. 279.

Not only did Dewey's pragmatism fail to satisfy its own demand for practicality (at least in the three ways mentioned above), but finally it must be observed that Dewey never did in fact subject his pragmatic theory to the required test of consequences and prediction. That is, his viewpoint never was *verified* in the way it required every other claim to be. Indeed, he firmly *accepted* the pragmatic outlook admittedly prior to the ability to verify it.[71] Dewey simply did *not* put aside every putative authority and refuse to admit anything which could not first be validated. For instance, Dewey's naturalistic view of the world was assumed, not proven.[72] Again, his whole outlook stems from an evolutionary presupposition, but if the history of scholarship demonstrates anything about the theory of evolution, it is that this is an unscientific, speculatively preconceived *gestalt*—a philosophically rooted commitment which is immune to factual scrutiny.[73] Further, the philosophic and scientific challenges to behaviorism—another basic assumption of Dewey's pragmatism—are notorious even today; the debate over this theory continues unabated at present, more than two decades after Dewey's death. Thus, it can hardly be said that Dewey had confirmed his most elementary theses: naturalism, evolution, and behaviorism.

Moreover, Dewey's writings are permeated with a commitment to certain *values*. He taught that human experience discovers values in *nature*, just as it discovers other facts. However, he also had to admit the distinction between something being *valued* and something being valuable. What *is* desired may not be *desirable*, and Dewey never did demonstrate that his own values should be favorably evaluated by us. There have been plenty of values which have endured longer than his own, and they continue to be cherished today. Dewey aimed to produce a "better" social order, but not everyone is convinced that his order *is* better. For him merely to presume that there is a broad consensus on values would be unjustifiable. Thus, he could not legitimately escape the central epistemological question, *how* do you *know* that such is the case?, as this is applied in the area of axiology. In the the absence of any well-argued basis for the choice of values, Dewey's thought must be seen as the expression of an arbitrary preference.

It is not at all clear what *rules* Dewey followed in adopting or rejecting truths, values, criteria, or operating methods. Therefore, his disdain for theoretical epistemology left his adoptions and rejections *arbitrary*. His

---

71. "The Problem of Truth," *Old Penn* IX (Feb. 11, 18, and March 4, 1911), pp. 522-528, 556-563, 620-625.
72. That supranaturalistic views were not instrumental in resolving social problems (*even if* true) would *not* verify naturalism.
73. See my article, "On Worshipping the Creature Rather Than the Creator," *Journal of Christian Reconstruction* I (Summer, 1974).

standards and procedures were unjustified; they failed to pass Dewey's own self-proclaimed requirement of verification. The inescapable conclusion is that instrumentalism is not the result of a scholarly analysis but rests on a personal choice. It buys practical relevance and popularity at the expense of a thorough explication, examination, and justification of the foundations of its teachings. Like so many programs which are impatient with the exacting and hard issues of traditional epistemology, pragmatism, under the guise of down-to-earth practicality and progress, promotes a thoughtless dogma. Dewey was not doing philosophy; he was writing a creed. But upon reflection this should not surprise us. At the beginning, we noted that pragmatism set forth the view that truth is that which "works." At that point, we could have asked whether the pragmatic theory claims to be *true* in the older sense of a correct description of what is the case. If it does not (and it could not, given Dewey's disdain for a spectator approach to truth), then what could *pragmatism* be? It could only be a *recommendation*. And as such (prescriptive, rather than descriptive), we are free to reject it.

Consequently, we conclude that Dewey's pragmatism has not eliminated the need to confront the issues of epistemological theory. At best it is a trivial linguistic reform, and at worst it is a mere recommendation. Furthermore, between these two extremes, we have observed that it is unclear, circular, subject to self-delusion, shortsighted, self-defeating as to its practical interests, and incoherently dialectical. Dewey's position has been the most sophisticated attempt to escape the difficulties posed by the theory of knowledge and the traditional search for certainty, but it is clearly a dead-end. Epistemology has an incredible, and often unappreciated, recalcitrance. Dewey's philosophy was not adequate to its demands. Therefore, even though Dewey may have given philosophy a refreshing return to practical matters in contrast to curious and dubious soaring of absolute idealism, he had no successful answer to the skeptic.

Wittgenstein and Language-games

It is widely recognized that the most influential philosopher in recent years (and perhaps the most significant in this century) has been Ludwig Wittgenstein (1889–1951). In 1939 he succeeded G. E. Moore in the chair of philosophy at Cambridge University.[74] Along with Russell,

---

74. It is of passing interest to note the various social relations of many eminent men of the past century. John Stuart Mill served as an informal godfather to Bertrand Russell, who became an atheist after reading Mill's *Autobiography*. Russell was converted to Hegelianism by McTaggart and Bradley, and subsequently to a modified platonism by G. E. Moore. He co-authored *Principia Mathematica* with Alfred North Whitehead. When a court order cancelled Russell's appointment to the City College of New York in 1940, John Dewey was among those who wrote in his defense (as did Ducasse, Beard, Becker, Lovejoy, Perry, Brightman, Einstein, and so on). Rus-

Wittgenstein saw language as *the key* to unlocking basic philosophic problems. His earliest work, *Tractatus Logico-Philosophicus*,[75] pursued the "perfect language" of Russell's *logical atomism*, according to which each sentence should picture a fact in the world (taken to be comprised simply of things, properties, and relations) and each word should denote an element thereof. Thus, language would be made to mirror reality, and logic would determine the limits of meaningful expression—that is, circumscribe the boundaries of the "sayable." The *Tractatus* understandably had a noteworthy influence on the Vienna Circle with its emphasis on the logical analysis of language (especially the language of the hard sciences) and the necessity for empirical verification of all cognitive propositions.

However, Wittgenstein later came to disagree with his early thinking about language. In the *Tractatus* the connection between language and reality depended upon a correlation between thought-elements and simple atoms of the experienced world. In the 1940's Wittgenstein composed observations which were published under the title *Philosophical Investigations*,[76] a work in which he recognizes "grave mistakes" in his previous book and sets out a contrasting position. Here he argued that the notion of atoms which are absolutely simple is incoherent, and that a private correlation between items in reality and elements of thought is impossible. Whereas the ultimate data of the *Tractatus* are the atoms comprising reality or the world, the ultimate data of the *Investigations* came to be the "forms of life" in which language-games are embedded. Whereas Russell's logical atomism had formerly been the authority for determining meaningfulness, now the limits of the sayable would be determined by ordinary linguistic use. Everything which has a real use or performs an important task in language counts as sayable and meaningful.

From this vantage point Wittgenstein approached philosophy with an attitude very similar to Dewey's in many respects. Toward the end of his life Wittgenstein reflected: "In other words I want to say something that sounds like pragmatism." Dewey had been an instrumentalist who revolted

---

sell carried on extensive correspondence with D. H. Lawrence. Wittgenstein, whose family numbered Johannes Brahms among its friends, was advised by Gottlob Frege to study under Russell at Cambridge. Wittgenstein often thought upon suicide (something which three of his four brothers actualized) but identified coming to study with Russell as his "salvation." While in a prison camp during the First World War, he passed a completed manuscript to Russell through the good offices of their mutual friend, John Maynard Keynes. This was later given an introduction by Russell and published as the *Tractatus*. For it, in addition to an oral exam given by Moore and Russell, Wittgenstein was given the Ph.D. He was consulted by Moritz Schlick, Friedrich Waismann, and Frank Ramsey (all influential scholars in their own right). Subsequently he apostatized from Russell's salvation to head up his own philosophical cult.

75. Translated by D. F. Pears and B. F. McGuinness (London: Routledge & Kegan Paul, 1921, reprinted 1971).

76. Third ed., trans. G. E. M. Anscombe (New York: Macmillan Co., 1953).

against the traditional philosophical preoccupation with essences (rather than functions). Wittgenstein held that "*Essence* is expressed by grammar," and "Grammar . . . only describes and in no way explains the *use* of signs."[77] Accordingly, he took an *instrumentalist approach to language*. The thesis of the *Investigations* is well summarized in this directive: "Look at the sentence as an instrument, and at its sense as its employment."[78] Also like Dewey, Wittgenstein viewed the aim of philosophy as the *solving of problems* rather than the discovery of esoteric facts; one should never pursue philosophy for its own sake, but only in order to dissolve problems which have arisen through a misuse of ordinary language. "What is your aim in philosophy?—To shew the fly the way out of the fly-bottle"; "the results of philosophy are the uncovering of one or another piece of plain nonsense and of bumps that the understanding has got by running its head up against the limits of language."[79] Furthermore, as Dewey's pragmatism was behavior-oriented, so also Wittgenstein insisted that personal behavior, one's situation and resonses, the full context of human living must be taken into account when analyzing meaning and solving the problems of philosophy via an examination of linguistic usage. The speaker's form of life is crucial: "the term 'language-*game*' is meant to bring into prominence the fact that the *speaking* of language is part of an activity, or of a form of life." Indeed, "to imagine a language means to imagine a form of life."[80] One must not forget the *social* nature of language.

In Wittgenstein's later way of looking at things, the meaning of words is not to be identified with their referents or mental images, but rather "for a *large* class of cases—though not for all—in which we employ 'meaning' it can be defined thus: the meaning of a word is its use in the language."[81] And when we examine the various uses to which a word is put we see that it is not bound by strict criteria or rules; rather, a kind of "family resemblance" holds between the diverse functions (a complicated network of overlapping similarities instead of one underlying common feature).[82] The philosopher must recognize the *inherent ambiguities of ordinary language* and the *multiple functions* which language serves; thereby he will resist the lure of an allegedly perfect language and the temptation to resolve problems through linguistic refinement or artificial usage. "What *we* do is to bring words back from their metaphysical to their everyday use" (s. 116); "we

---

77. *Ibid.*, sections 371, 496.
78. *Ibid.*, s. 421; cf. "Language is an instrument. Its concepts are instruments" (s. 596); see also the illustration of a tool-box (s. 11).
79. *Ibid.*, s. 309, 119; cf. s. 38, "Philosophical problems arise when language *goes on holiday*" or is not *doing work* (s. 132).
80. *Ibid.*, s. 23, 19. "I shall also call the whole, consisting of language and the actions into which it is woven, the 'language-game' " (s. 7); cf. s. 489.
81. *Ibid.*, s. 43.
82. *Ibid.*, s. 65-69.

remain unconscious of the prodigious diversity of all the everyday language games" (p. 224e). Complexity and vagueness in the use of language cannot always be reduced to simplicity and precision. Language is too varied, fluid, messy for that.

However, this does not open the door to the possibility of completely *private,* individually unique, languages; languages follow a rough grammar, and *grammar* is always something *public.* One's definitions may be chosen according to his interests or purpose,[83] but all definitions are governed by *custom and function* within a *form of life* which determines the language-games utilized.[84] "Interpretations by themselves do not determine meaning."[85] This is akin to the fact that a sign-post is in itself dead and does not indicate which way the arrow is supposed to point you;[86] only a regular use of it—a custom—gives it life. "Following a rule is analogus to obeying an order. We are *trained* to do so; we react to an order *in a particular way.*"[87] Hence *language-games* are *publicly determined,* are part of a common way of acting and responding. "To obey a rule, to make a report, to give an order . . . are *customs* (uses, institutions). To understand a sentence means to understand a language. To understand a language means to be master of a technique."[88] Obeying a rule is a *practice*—which explains why someone cannot be said to obey a rule privately or only once in his life.[89] The reasons why we follow a rule in a certain manner (or use language the way we do) eventually give out, and we simply have a *convention*: "This is simply what I do."[90] Regular public practice determines the meaning of words; it requires common behavior and agreed-upon results —that is, the *sharing of a form of life.* "If language is to be a means of communication there must be agreement not only in definitions but also (queer as this may sound) in judgments. . . . They agree in the *language* they use. That is not agreement in opinion but in form of life."[91] And this form of life is the bedrock for all explanations, the place where all justifications give out. "When I obey a rule, I do not choose. I obey the rule *blindly.*"[92]

It is within one's language-game, i.e., his form of public life, that thinking and understanding are defined. Hence *knowledge* is taken as one's *ability to use the language-game,* and what counts as justification for propositions is *internally determined* by the language-game itself: "The chain of reasons has an end. . . . Is our confidence justified?—What people accept as

---

83. *Ibid.,* s. 560-570; cf. 17, 132, 499.
84. *Ibid.,* e.g., s. 257, 344; p. 18e.
85. *Ibid.,* s. 198.
86. *Ibid.,* s. 432.
87. *Ibid.,* s. 206.
88. *Ibid.,* s. 199.
89. *Ibid.,* s. 199, 202.

90. *Ibid.,* s. 211, 217.
91. *Ibid.,* s. 242, 241.
92. *Ibid.,* s. 217, 219.

justification—is shewn by how they think and live."[93] Thus different standards or norms will be used in different systems, different situations, or different language-games. The *criteria for certainty* will be *internal* and a *matter of practice* or *form of life*. Without the context provided by the language-game there would be no sense to doubting, testing, concluding, etc. There are points where doubt is completely lacking, for "doubting has an end."[94] This should be identified as the place where reasons and justifications have an end as well: the paradigms which guide the grammar of our language, our language-games.

. Toward the end of his life, while in New York during 1949, Wittgenstein was stimulated to reflect further on the subject of certainty by rereading G. E. Moore's "Defence of Common Sense" and "Proof of an External World." He wrote extensive notes about certainty up until two days before his death.[95] While elsewhere in the book differing with Moore, in *On Certainty* Wittgenstein agreed with him *against* Descartes' procedure of methodological doubt. Wittgenstein exhibited the unintelligibility of the procedure which calls for us to *doubt everything* in order to arrive at certainty; unintentionally he also showed the impossibility of skirting the traditional questions of epistemology.

Wittgenstein insightfully noted that *doubt presupposes the mastery of a language, its procedures, and rules.* Doubt cannot be so radical that it calls into question the very meanings of the words used to express it; to doubt a sentence, you need first to understand what is meant by the sentence.[96] Thus "if you are not certain of any fact, you cannot be certain of the meaning of your words either."[97] So also, a *reasonable* suspicion about some assertion requires *specific*—not just imaginable—*grounds*.[98] One could always imagine that what is described in some indicative sentence, p, is actually the contrary, not-p; yet doubting p would be idle unless a concrete reason against p could be offered. Therefore, the very activity of doubting requires a context of accepted beliefs; one can doubt only if he first has learned to handle a language and to use some judgments to call other judgments into question. *Learning precedes doubt,* and *learning precludes doubting everything;* to get on with learning, the student must not doubt certain things.[99] "For how can a child immediately doubt what it is

---

93. *Ibid.*, s. 326, 325; cf. 353, 486; 143-242; 316-341, 75.
94. *Ibid.*, II.v (p. 180e).
95. Subsequently they were organized and edited by G. E. M. Anscombe and G. H. von Wright, being published as: Ludwig Wittgenstein, *On Certainty*, trans. D. Paul and G. E. M. Anscombe (New York: Harper Torchbooks, Harper and Row, 1969).
96. *Ibid.*, sections 306, 369, 456.
97. *Ibid.*, s. 114.
98. *Ibid.*, s. 120, 247, 323, 458; e.g., s. 4.
99. *Ibid.*, s. 329, 310-315. "Learning is based on believing," s. 170.

taught? That could mean only that he was incapable of learning certain language games."[100]

These observations have important epistemological consequences. "The child learns by believing the adult. Doubt comes *after* belief."[101] Also "doubt itself rests only on what is beyond doubt."[102] Thus, "a doubt that doubted everything would not be a doubt."[103] In short, Wittgenstein has shown universal doubt to be impossible. Doubt requires the testing of assertions,[104] but testing comes to and end and thus assumes something which is not tested;[105] therefore, "the *questions* that we raise and our *doubts* depend on the fact that some propositions are exempt from doubt, are as it were like hinges on which those turn."[106] Wittgenstein's conclusion on this point is surely one with which we should agree: "If you tried to doubt everything you would not get as far as doubting anything. *The game of doubting itself presupposes certainty*."[107]

Wittgenstein wanted to distinguish between *madness* and making a *mistake*.[108] Being mistaken requires that there are a modicum of judgments on which you agree with the rest of mankind,[109] but when you cannot imagine what it would be like to convince the skeptic of p, or to correct his mistake about p, or what other propositions should be any more trustworthy than p, then what we have is madness.[110] When doubts can never be corrected, no sense can be attached to them.[111] Now, what Wittgenstein wanted to hold is that you can doubt each sentence one by one, but you can never doubt them all.[112] To doubt *everything* is not a mistake; it is madness.[113] Furthermore, there are particular places where doubt is simply senseless; there are propositions which are, for us, indubitable—that is, which stand fast for us and are regarded as absolutely solid.[114] With respect to such indubitable beliefs, it maks no sense to doubt them; we are not ready to let anything count as disproof of them, and their contradictories cannot be seriously considered.[115] Wittgenstein offered many examples of such indubitable propositions which might lead the uncritical

---

100. *Ibid.*, s. 283.
101. *Ibid.*, s. 160.
102. *Ibid.*, s. 519.
103. *Ibid.*, s. 450.
104. *Ibid.*, s. 125.
105. *Ibid.*, s. 163-164, 337.
106. *Ibid.*, s. 341.
107. *Ibid.*, s. 115, emphasis mine.
108. *Ibid.*, e.g., s. 71, 75, 155, 196.
109. *Ibid.*, s. 156.
110. *Ibid.*, s. 300-304; e.g., s. 257, 420.
111. *Ibid.*, s. 383, 642, 676.
112. *Ibid.*, s. 232.
113. *Ibid.*, s. 217.
114. *Ibid.*, s. 112, 116, 151.
115. *Ibid.*, s. 2, 93, 245, 226, 657.

reader toward agreement with him.[116] To doubt, e.g., that I had great grandparents might indeed be brushed off as madness.

We are ready to agree that there *are*, and must be, *indubitable propositions;* and *universal* doubt is, true enough, senseless. However, we must demur when Wittgenstein starts talking about the *madness* of those who fail to recognize *his* indubitables. Here we have a damaging pointer to how Wittgenstein settled upon his most basic commitments. Before exposing it, though, one needs to recognize Wittgenstein's *proper* assessment of the *role* which each person's indubitable beliefs play for him.

Wittgenstein was correct in holding that the system of propositions one accepts as certain are the unmoving foundation, the essential presuppositions, of his language games—the basis for his actions and thoughts.[117] These indubitables comprise one's world-picture, his way of looking at the world, his *Weltanschauung.*[118] As such, they are not taken one by one as indubitable, but rather as a connected *system:* "A *totality* of judgments is is made plausible to us. When we first begin to *believe* anything, what we believe is not a single proposition, it is a whole system of propositions. . . . It is not single axioms that strike me as obvious, it is a system in which consequences and premises give one another mutual support."[119] The grounds for adopting some world-picture are not experience or outstanding success;[120] our indubitable propositions have a "peculiar logical role in the system" *bordering* on being logical (methodoligical) *and* empirical (i.e., within a method),[121] rather than arrived at as the result of investigation.[122] Instead, these *indubitable propositions* themselves "form the foundation of all operating with thoughts,"[123] "the matter-of-course foundation for research,"[124] and "the substratum of all enquiring and asserting."[125] Therefore, they are the hinge on which disputes turn,[126] providing *rules for testing* and the *foundation for all judging.*[127] "All testing, all confirmation and disconfirmation of a hypothesis takes place already within a system. And this system is . . . the element in which arguments have their life."[128] One's indubitable propositions, his world-picture, thus function as *the rules of a game.*[129] When the rules change, so does the (language-) game or system. Hence, about the statements which one accepts as certain Wittgen-

---

116. *Ibid.*, e.g., every human being has a brain (s. 4, 159, 281); I have here two hands (s. 3, 125); the earth has existed for the past hundred years (s. 138) and is round (s. 299); the sun is not a hole in the vault of heaven (s. 104); motor cars do not grow out of the earth (s. 279); $12 \times 12 = 144$ (s. 651); water boils at 100°C (s. 599); I had great grandparents (s. 159).

117. *Ibid.*, s. 403, 411, 524, 558.

118. *Ibid.*, s. 92, 422.

119. *Ibid.*, s. 140-142.

120. *Ibid.*, s. 131.

121. *Ibid.*, s. 136, 318-319.

122. *Ibid.*, s. 138.

123. *Ibid.*, s. 401.

124. *Ibid.*, s. 167; cf. s. 87.

125. *Ibid.*, s. 162; cf. s. 88.

126. *Ibid.*, s. 655.

127. *Ibid.*, s. 96, 98, 614.

128. *Ibid.*, s. 105.

129. *Ibid.*, s. 95.

stein says, "if I speak of a possible mistake here, this changes the role of 'mistake' and 'truth' in our lives";[130] consequently, anyone who doubts these presuppositions "does not accept our whole sysetm of verification."[131]

Therefore, we see that one cannot doubt everything, for doubting assumes certainty, and we all hold to *some* system of propositions taken as certain. They form a *worldview* which functions as the *presuppositional starting point* for inquiry and determines our *standards of verification*. These were Wittgenstein's incisive observations and merit our agreement.[132] However, Wittgenstein did not do so well by them, for he was led by them to arbitrariness at best, and to prejudice at worst. Above, it was noted that Wittgenstein wanted to settle the rigorous questions of epistemology by saying that, with respect to one's indubitable beliefs, doubts entertained about them can be brushed off as madness. One's presuppositions are correlated with what he personally deems madness.[133] This tips us off to the fact that Wittgenstein would, in the long run, hold that there are no *absolutely correct* presuppositional certainties; there are only *deep convictions* which some society ingrains in us as the indubitable propositions for sane and reasonable men. There is no way to settle *disagreements* at the most basic presuppositional level; one cannot know for sure that his certainties are the correct ones to hold, but can only resort to name-calling with his opponent. "Where two principles really do meet which cannot be reconciled with one another, then each man declares the other a fool and heretic."[134] Reasoning ends and *persuasion* takes over.[135] One who is skeptical about what you take as certain cannot be *answered;* he can only be *silenced.*

Wittgenstein may have seen the necessity and function of presuppositional certainties, but he was wrongly led to think that epistemological reasoning had to be abandoned at this point between differing philosophers. Where did he go wrong? I propose that it was with a confusion here: "I did not get my picture of the world by satisfying myself of its correctness."[136] This observation is true—for Wittgenstein and many others. But it does not properly imply either that one *should not*, or that one *cannot*, be satisfied (intellectually, not merely emotionally) with the correctness of his presupposition (or worldview) in the face of skepticism or a competing system.

---

130. *Ibid.*, s. 138.
131. *Ibid.*, s. 279.
132. Of course, long before the later Wittgenstein was forced to these conclusions by an observation of ordinary language, Professor Cornelius Van Til had expounded to Christian scholars the critical importance of one's own presuppositions for all his subsequent thought, questioning, verification, standards, conclusions, and behavior. When Van Til was beginning to teach Christian apologetics from this decisive standpoint, Wittgenstein was submitting the *Tractatus* for his Ph.D. at Cambridge.
133. *Op. cit.*, s. 420.
134. *Ibid.*, s. 611.
135. *Ibid.*, s. 612.
136. *Ibid.*, s. 94.

That one does *not* verify or prove his presuppositions in any *ordinary manner* (i.e., like hypotheses to be experimentally and logically tested—which would be deceptively circular since the presuppositions themselves set the standards and starting point for verification) does *not* mean that some cannot be seen to be wrong and others right; it simply indicates that philosophical argumentation here must take a different, yet legitimate, tack—namely, examining *which* presuppositions provide the *necessary preconditions* for *any* intelligent reasoning and which presuppositions *scuttle* man's epistemic endeavors. Wittgenstein (and others) may not have satisfied himself about the correctness of his presuppositions precisely because they *were not* correct. In that case, he could avoid reforming his thinking and admitting error by placing everyone in the same (sinking) ship of presuppositional arbitrariness, that is, by teaching that one's certainties were not a matter of truth and intellectual grounding but sociological conditioning.

"What we believe depends on what we learn."[137] As a matter of training, men can be led to hold, what to others appears to be, strange positions (e.g., that men can make rain); they may be *induced* to change them, but *not* on the grounds of correctness.[138] This is all relative to the society in which one learns to do his judging. What one takes as certain is *not learned*, said Wittgenstein, but *implicitly* swallowed *along with* what is learned.[139] Presuppositions are smuggled in with our learned beliefs and not argued for or against. Thus, one's system of indubitable propositions is "acquired"—but not "learned"—by instruction;[140] that is, they are simply "inherited background."[141] One's presuppositions, then, are not known as true; they are merely voluntaristically acted upon. Argumentation comes to an end at one's language game or worldview, "but the end is not certain propositions' striking us as immediately true, i.e., it is not a kind of *seeing* on our part; it is our *acting*, which lies at the bottom of the language-game"[142]—"an *ungrounded* way of acting."[143] Therefore, one can sum up by saying that the concept of knowing is coupled with that of the language game (embodying a presuppositional worldview),[144] and "you must bear in mind that the language game is so to say something unpredictable. I mean: it is not based on grounds. It is not reasonable (or unreasonable). It is there—like our life."[145] The epistemological quest for certainty is eventually washed away in the flood of intellectual arbitrariness and radi-

---

137. *Ibid.*, s. 286.
138. *Ibid.*, s. 92, 132. Wittgenstein said that one can be "converted" (in a special sense) to a changed way of looking at things, but this new perspective is not *proved*: s. 92, 279. That is, it cannot be shown to be true over against the former perspective.
139. *Ibid.*, s. 152, 476.
140. *Ibid.*, s. 279.
141. *Ibid.*, s. 94.
142. *Ibid.*, s. 204.
143. *Ibid.*, s. 110, emphasis mine.
144. *Ibid.*, s. 560.
145. *Ibid.*, s. 559.

cal skepticism *at* the presuppositional level. The following note by Wittgenstein tells the whole story: "The difficulty is to realize the groundlessness of our believing."[146]

The procedure described by Wittgenstein above may very well be an accurate reflection of what actually happens as one *initially* forms his presuppositions. However, it does *not* lay down what *should* happen when men philosophically reflect upon serious questions about knowledge or certainty—when there is a conflict over foundational certainties. To leave matters where Wittgenstein did is not to finish the task of the philosopher, but to descend to the sociology of prejudice. Wittgenstein too quickly abandoned epistemological theorizing and capitulated to a skeptical relativism which chooses to follow those teachings bolstered by some group's esteem for them. He should have pressed on and considered the question: Which propositions *should* be most trusted, obvious, and indubitable to us (not merely which propositions *are* most indubitable in this society)? As we have seen previously, epistemology has a recalcitrance that is not appreciated.

The *necessity* for Wittgenstein to keep on asking deep questions about certainty and not stop short epistemologically is clearly revealed in considering one of his illustrations of a bed-rock position to be accepted as certain. Remembering that Wittgenstein's only defense for his indubitable beliefs was finally to declare that anyone who doubted them was mad (in terms of commonly accepted linguistic practice and world-picture), we need to note that he asserted that "our whole system of physics forbids us to believe" that someone could ever go to the moon![147] We believe this, he said, on the grounds of what we learn;[148] it is instilled in us, and no reasonable man doubts it. Those who think contrary are to be, in terms of the thinking of our system, straighforwardly dismissed as mistaken.

> We believe that it isn't possible to get to the moon; but there might be people who believe that that is possible and that it sometimes happens. We say: these people do not know a lot that we know. And, let them be never so sure of their belief—they are wrong and we know it. If we compare our system of knowledge with theirs then theirs is evidently the poorer one by far.[149]

Surely this is embarrassing today, but our point is not to shame what Wittgenstein thought. Rather, this infelicitous example is adduced in order to demonstrate that epistemology *cannot end* with the recognition that we all have, and operate upon, presuppositions accepted as certain—even when one enjoys the social support of the current intelligentsia. Skepticism's challenge is not thereby met, even though important points about the impossibility of universal skepticism and the critical function of pre-

---

146. *Ibid.*, s. 166.
147. *Ibid.*, s. 108.

148. *Ibid.*, s. 171.
149. *Ibid.*, s. 286.

supposed worldviews in epistemological disputes have been made. Wittgenstein has insisted that one cannot avoid entertaining *some* propositions as certain, but he did not go on to show *which* propositions they must be. How should one distinguish the genuinely indubitable propositions from the others? In light of the above illustration, Wittgenstein cannot dismiss this crucial question. Having not answered it, Wittgenstein has not even *silenced* the skeptic, much less satisfied the quest for certainty by answering him. The traditional problems of epistemology must still be entertained.

This arbitrariness which we have discerned in Wittgenstein's philosophy as expressed in *On Certainty* was reflected in the *Philosophical Investigations* as well. There he pointed out that reasons, justifications, and explanations (not to say doubts) must end somewhere. But where? Contrary to what he thought, we do *not* find an ultimate epistemological bed-rock, a final resting place which needs no explanation, in our form of life or behavior. One must press on and ask, what justifies these practices and purposes? "That's just the way we live" offers no adequate response to those who prefer to live differently.

In reply to philosophical perplexities, Wittgenstein recommended that we seek to get words back into their own everyday language-games, proposed that we thereby engage the clearest or best uses of language, and insisted that philosophy not let its language go on holiday or simply idle like an engine. However, he failed to follow through with his program, for he could not specify *which norms* should govern the proper use of terms. *Which are* the best uses? *When is* language on holiday? *What counts* as a word operating in an alien language-game? *Whose* ordinary language is superior? Are some language-games being *arbitrarily* cut off? Such critical questions leave Wittgenstein very much in the same condition as Dewey: namely, recommending an arbitrary personal choice to us. In this light, we can uncover new significance in Wittgenstein's statement that there is no single philosophic method, just different *therapies*.[150] He likened his work to persuasion and propaganda: "I am in a sense making propaganda for one style of thinking as opposed to another. I am honestly disgusted with the other. . . . Much of what I am doing is persuading people to change their style of thinking."[151] However, philosophy is deeper than a recommendation about forms of life; it pursues not merely the sociology of knowledge but the justification of knowledge. Otherwise it becomes concealed prejudice.

Also like Dewey, Wittgenstein said things which suggest strong parallels to Kantian idealism.[152] One's language-games are determined and regu-

---

150. *Philosophical Investigations*, s. 133.
151. *Lecture and Conversations on Aesthetics, Psychology, and Religious Belief*, ed. Cyril Barrett (Berkeley: University of California Press, 1966), p. 28.
152. Cf. the parallels drawn between Kant and Wittgenstein in modern commen-

lated by his form of life; we must get outside of language to determine and define it (while staying within the world), that is, get to the bed-rock of a form of life, which is itself not explained. Thus *reality is finally inexpressible.*[153] No less than with the *Tractatus* Wittgenstein could conclude that "There are, indeed, things that are inexpressible. They *show* themselves. They are what is mystical."[154] Wittgenstein saw his investigation as directed toward the *possibilities of phenomena.*[155] The limits of my world of experience are the limits of language.[156] *What is possible is bounded by what is sayable;* thus understandable phenomena are what one's structure of language (for Kant, thought) allow them to be. Hence the notion of an ideal of clarity and truth to be found in reality "is like a pair of glasses on our nose through which we see whatever we look at."[157] However, try as we may, *our understanding is limited by our language;* the substratum of an experience, the context in which it is possible, is the mastery of some technique, some language-game.[158] And these language-games are set by our forms of life which are brute, unexplained, givens: "What has to be accepted, the given, is—so on could say—*forms of life.*"[159] There is no way to get outside, to achieve an objective perspective on, our language-games: "Man has the urge to thrust against the limits of language. . . . This running against the walls of our cage is perfectly, absolutely hopeless."[160]

Finally we must observe that Wittgenstein, again like Dewey, was caught in a rational-irrational dialectical tension. On the one hand Wittgenstein had a revolutionary outlook: "The spirit of this book is a different one from that of the mainstream of European and American civilization, in which we all stand."[161] A certain therapy was required in philosophy, the fly needed to be let out of the bottle, language had to be called back from its holiday and useless idling, men needed to be shown that their intellectual bumps are due to violating the boundaries of sense. According to him, philosophers put false interpretations on expressions and then draw the queerest conclusions from them;[162] thus he taught that philosophy must become "a battle against the bewitchment of our intelligence by means of

---

tators: e.g., S. Morris Engel, "Wittgenstein and Kant," *Philosophy and Phenomenological Research* 30 (1970), pp. 483-513.

153. Cf. *Zettel*, ed. G. E. M. Anscombe and G. H. von Wright, trans. G. E. M. Anscombe (Berkeley: University of California Press, 1967), s. 144: "How words are understood is not told by words alone."

154. *Tractatus*, s. 6.522.

155. *Investigations*, s. 90.

156. *Ibid.*, e.g., s. 119.

157. *Ibid.*, s. 130

158. *Ibid.*, pp. 208-209e.

159. *Ibid.*, p. 226e.

160. *Philosophical Revew* 74, no. 1 (1965), pp. 13, 11-12.

161. Foreword to *Philosophische Bemerkungen*, ed. R. Rhees (Oxford: Basil Blackwell, 1965).

162. *Investigations*, s. 194.

language."[163] Wittgenstein aimed to achieve *complete clarity* in order that philosophical problems would *completely* disappear.[164] To do this he sought to draw the boundaries between sense and nonsense,[165] to appy a pragmatic criterion of meaning in order to judge the sensibility of philosophical utterances,[166] and spoke strongly against metaphysical statements.[167] Therefore, we cannot avoid concluding that Wittgenstein held that there are norms or standards for use and misuse of language; he aimed to purify illegitimate usages and to decree what is legitimate and what is not. *Linguistic use* would guide him to the limits of the sayable.

However, on the other hand, Wittgenstein took a very *non*-revolutionary attitude toward his philosophizing. He determined to leave language just as it is,[168] for ordinary language leaves nothing to explain, already possesses perfect order, and is adequate for our needs.[169] Hence *he definitely renounced the goal of reforming language*.[170] Moreover, such reform would be impossible, since linguistic situations are not completly bounded by rules,[171] and with the countless different kinds of use of language and their fluidity[172] no universal norms could be found. Thus *there is no specific standard for linguistic use,* and everyone is left to follow his own language-games—blindly.[173] Therefore, we cannot avoid concluding the Wittgenstein denied any definite guide for the limits of the sayable.

In light of the two previous paragraphs we can understand the failure of Wittgenstein's philosophy; it has created its own antinomy or self-vitiation. Wittgenstein was simultaneously being a rationalist and an irrationalist, an absolutist and relativist; he set out to do prescription, *but* limited himself to description. Linguistic use was to be guided by rules in order to achieve clarity; *yet* usage was completely open-ended and immune to permanent standards. He promoted a new method for philosophy, *but* denied that philosophy had any one method; his position led him both to castigate previous philosophies *and* to endorse them as one practice or custom among many. This dialectic in his thought, along with his inherent (post-Kantian, idealistic) skepticism, and in the long run the arbitrariness with which his epistemology ends up, all point out his failure to lay the disquieting questions of the theory of knowledge to rest.

Wittgenstein has not set forth a well-argued theory; he has composed

163. *Ibid.,* s. 109.
164. *Ibid.,* s. 133.
165. *Ibid.,* e.g., s. 499.
166. *Ibid.,* s. 268.
167. *Ibid.,* e.g., s. 116, 216, 271; *Zettel,* s. 458.
168. *Ibid.,* s. 124.
169. *Ibid.,* s. 126, 98, 120.
170. *Ibid.,* s. 132.
171. *Ibid.,* s. 84.
172. *Ibid.,* s. 23.
173 *Ibid.,* s. 219.

what can best be likened to religious *confessions*.[174] Dewey had his creed, Wittgenstein his confessions. However, unlike Augustine, Wittgenstein (as all his biographers testify) could never say that his heart had found rest. "The real discovery is the one that makes me capable of stopping doing philosophy when I want to.—The one that gives philosophy peace, so that it is no longer tormented by questions which bring *itself* in question."[175] Because of the difficulties we have explored above, Wittgenstein's thought could never find this peace; he had no escape from eventual skepticism, and his philosophy was never released from the torment of calling itself into question. He did not press to, and did not find, the self-attesting starting point, the certain presuppositions, of knowledge. He wanted to have a beneficial and healing influence on philosophy: not long before he died, Wittgenstein quoted Bach's inscription on his *Little Organ Book,* "To the glory of the most high God, and that my neighbor may be benefited thereby." Pointing to his own pile of manuscripts he said, "That is what I would have like to have been able to say about my own work."[176] He never achieved the helpful *end* for which he hoped, for he never *started* with the presuppositions which alone can successfully complete the quest for certainty.

Austin and Performative Utterances

G. J. Warnock has said that no recent philosopher "has been more influential or more original" than J. L. Austin (1911–1960); he has been designated an "extremely influential pioneer" (Peterfreund and Denise), the "most brilliant member of the Oxford group" (William P. Alston), and "the archetypal linguistic philosopher" (Antony Flew). Austin's approach to epistemology is particularly worth investigation as a contemporary and unique outlook on traditional problems.

Like Dewey, Austin viewed the traditional problems associated with the debates between rationalism and empiricism, monism and dualism, realism and idealism, representationalism, or phenomenalism as artificial. Both men aimed to make such problems disappear through an examination and rejection of certain key presuppositions of the debate; these assumptions, held Dewey and Austin, generate unresolvable difficulties due to misconceptions (said Dewey) or confused conceptions (said Austin). Austin thus

---

174. K. T. Fann has convincingly exhibited the likeness between the *Philosophical Investigations* and religious confessions like Augustine's in *Wittgenstein's Conception of Philosophy* (Berkeley: University of California Press, 1971), pp. 105-107. He also indicates parallels with the Zen Buddhist procedure for achieving enlightenment, pp. 104, 110.

175. *Investigations*, s. 133.

176. M. Drury, "Wittgenstein: A Symposium," *Wittgenstein, The Man and His Philosophy, an Anthology,* ed. K. T. Fann (New York: Dell, Delta Books, 1967), p. 71.

complemented Dewey in calling for a quite different approach to epistemology and challenging the mistaken foundations of traditional theorizing.
Where Dewey thought that philosophy was sidetracked by the illusory goal
of conceptual stability and the misguided view of experience as intrinsically
private, Austin felt philosophers had been misled by the conceptual confusions which arise through the abuse of everyday or ordinary language.
However, Dewey and Austin were both agreed in their negative attitude
toward the fundamental error of epistemologists.

Dewey rejected the misconceived quest for certainty; similarly, Austin
rejected the confused pursuit of the incorrigible. Philosophers have asked
the wrong questions and bypassed their proper roles because they set out to
establish basic items of knowledge as absolutely certain—truths which will
serve as the secure foundation for every other knowledge claim. The task
of discerning such basic certainties is too general, tangled in confusion,
and ultimately unprofitable.

> The general doctrine about knowledge which I have sketched . . . is
> *radically* and *in principle* misconceived. For even if we were to make
> the very risky and gratuitous assumption that what some particular
> person knows at some particular place and time could systematically be
> sorted out into an arrangement of foundations and super-structure, it
> would be a mistake in principle to suppose that the same thing could be
> done for knowledge *in general*. And this is because there *could* be no
> *general* answer to the questions: what is evidence for what, what is cer-
> tain, what is doubtful, what needs or does not need evidence, can
> or can't be verified. If the Theory of Knowledge consists in finding
> grounds for such an answer, there is no such thing.[177]

The full-scale and serious attack which had earlier in this century been
brought against *metaphysics* has now been extended to a similar charge
against general *epistemology*. Austin proposed to undermine skepticism by
challenging its assumption that knowledge requires that absolute certainty
(the elimination of all possible error) be found in some realm, object,
source, method, or basic premise of knowledge.

The parallels with Dewey which we have noted should have added to
them certain obvious parallels between Austin and Wittgenstein. Both
were renowned for taking ordinary language analysis as crucial to philosophic method. Both saw common philosophical perplexities as arising from
abuses of everyday language, muddled uses of words outside of their natural
environment, and quixotic philosophical technicalities or causes. Failing to
give careful attention to the correct uses of language, philosophers have
created insoluble pseudo-problems that linguistic analysis must now dissolve
by exposing artificiality and elucidating the best uses of ordinary language.

---

177. *Sense and Sensibilia*, ed. G. J. Warnock (London: Oxford University Press,
1962), pp. 123-124.

Thus philosophy should become *therapeutic*, agreed Austin and Wittgenstein. However, Austin wished to proceed beyond Wittgenstein's singular attention to particular difficulties in philosophy; Wittgenstein thought that analysis only had a point when an actual problem had arisen for it to treat. Everyday linguistic use was studied only as a means toward correcting pre-existing philosophic prejudice and perplexity. But Austin saw positive merit in examining ordinary language as an end in itself. He pressed *linguistic analysis* beyond a therapeutic function into *constructive service*. Its positive role was to reveal the *basic concepts embedded in ordinary speech;* there is not only something to be *dissolved by* ordinary language analysis, there is definitely something to be *learned from* it. Hence Austin's efforts were more systematic and attuned to fine detail than were Wittgenstein's, in order that by it he could gain insight into the well-established facts and distinctions which have made everyday use what it is. He hoped to break open the *inner structure of words* having related meanings and thereby contribute something positive toward philosophical field-work and toward traditional philosophic inquiries. He was not merely trouble-shooting.

> When we examine what we should say when, what words we should use in what situations, we are looking again not *merely* at words . . . but also at the realities we use the words to talk about: we are using a sharpened awareness of words to sharpen our perception of, though not as the final arbiter of, the phenomena. For this reason I think it might be better to use, for this way of doing philosophy . . . 'linguistic phenomenology'. . . .[178]

Language sets traps for us and can be like blinkers as we look at the world; thus "words are our tools, and, as a minimum, we should use clean tools: we should know what we mean and what we do not."[179] Attention to linguistic analysis will aid us in using clean tools; moreover,

> our common stock of words embodies all the distinctions men have found worth drawing, and the connexions they have found worth marking, in the lifetimes of many generations: these surely are likely to be . . . more sound since they have stood up to the long test of the survival of the fittest, and more subtle, at least in all ordinary and reasonably practical matters, than any that you or I are likely to think up in our arm-chairs of an afternoon—the most favoured alternative method.[180]

This disdain for speculative (spectator) philosophy, this instrumentalist outlook, and this emphasis upon the survival of the fittest in the adaptations necessary for living, all bring Dewey's creed back to mind. Further, Austin joined in Wittgenstein's confession by making ordinary language analysis

---

178. "A Plea for Excuses," reprinted in *Philosophical Papers*, ed. J. O. Urmson and G. J. Warnock (London: Oxford University Press, 1961), p. 130.
179. *Ibid.*, p. 129.
180. *Ibid.*, p. 130.

the indispensable prerequisite for philosophy: "Certainly, then, ordinary language is *not* the last word: in principle it can everywhere be supplemented and improved upon and superseded. Only remember, it *is* the *first* word.[181]

As a philosopher, Austin is perhaps best remembered for drawing attention to the distinctively *performative function* of many utterances. There are some utterances in ordinary usage which are perfectly legitimate, but which do *not* purport to *describe* some state of affairs; such utterances are used to *do* something in speaking, to *perform* an action; for example, when the groom says "I do" at the wedding, he is not describing anything, but rather performing a vow. Here *the saying is the doing;* as a speech-action it is no more susceptible to being true or false than any other action (e.g., running). Austin applied his theory of performative utterances to knowledge, thereby setting forth an extremely novel thesis, in his well-known article "Other Minds."[182] This is one of the most highly regarded pieces in the genre of linguistic analysis and deserves our attention as a unique approach to a central issue in epistemology. When all is said and done, however, it will be apparent that Austin no more avoids the traditional questions in the theory of knowledge than did Dewey or Wittgenstein. The challenge of skepticism will remain unmitigated.

First, Austin contends that *knowledge* is to be distinguished from *belief*. When someone makes a statement of fact, he can be challenged in two ways: '*How* do you *know* that p?' or '*Why* do you *believe* that p?' These interrogatives are never interchanged; that is, the person is not asked *why* he *knows* or *how* he *believes*. There is a further difference to be found in the way we respond to someone whose claim is that p cannot be adequately supported. We conclude that he *did not know* after all, or that he really *ought not to have believed;* again, these judgments (just like the previous interrogatives) are never reversed. The crucial difference is that "The 'existence' of your alleged belief is not challenged, but the 'existence' of your alleged knowledge *is* challenged."[183] Therefore, says Austin, in ordinary language 'I believe' functions differently from 'I know'.[184]

Now the fact that inadequate grounds can jeopardize the existence of one's knowledge might suggest that we should view knowledge as some kind of *certitude*. Hence Austin shifts his concern and proceeds to eliminate the supposed *incorrigibility of knowledge* in its various forms. When someone is asked 'How do you know?', he does not improperly use the word 'know' if he answers by citing some authority, for knowledge at second hand is one of the main points of talking with others. Since (cautiously

---

181. *Ibid.*, p. 133.
182. Reprinted in *Philosophical Papers*, pp. 44-84.
183. *Ibid.*, p. 46.
184. *Ibid.*, p. 47.

accepted) authoritative testimony is a source of knowledge, Austin dismisses the view that knowledge is a variety of *immediate experience* (direct apprehension) of the stated fact.[185] Moreover, it is often the case that we know something quite well without being able to state the precise grounds for our knowledge-claim; for instance, you may know that a particular car is a given model and year without being able to put your finger on just which feature of the car is your evidence. Because one's vagueness in answering the question 'How do you know?' does not disqualify his knowledge, we must *not* identify knowledge with the *provability* of the claim.[186]

Furthermore, Austin dismisses the skeptic's taunt that what *appears* to be so may not actually be so *in reality*. According to Austin, such doubts about reality must have a particular and specifiable basis. Despite our general fallibility or the possibility of outrages in nature (e.g., the future being radically different from the past), *there are recognized procedures* appropriate to various types of cases for allaying these doubts; indeed, the doubts are meaningful only in correlation with the accepted ways of answering them in ordinary language. If standard procedures have been observed, fallibility does not prevent us from speaking of people 'knowing' what appears to be the case.[187]

Still further, Austin disagrees with the view that one can only claim to know that of which he is completely sure (e.g., his own sense-statements). There are obvious and normal instances where someone is hesitant or baffled by his sensations and wishes to avoid misnaming them (discriminating and identifying them improperly). Thus one can even doubt his own sense-statements. If certainty were required in order to make knowledge-claims legitimate, there would be few if any instances of knowledge at all.[188] Therefore, *knowledge is not to be identified with the certitude of immediacy, provability, or incorrigibility*. The traditional view of knowledge has held that it is *true justified belief*. Austin has, however, indicated that knowledge is *not a* variety of *belief* at all, much less *justified* belief.

Moreover, and most surprisingly, Austin does not even think that the third element (namely, truth) of the traditional view of knowledge is requisite. He disagrees with the statment 'If I know, then I cannot be wrong'. "We are often right to say we *know* even cases where we turn out subsequently to have been mistaken. . . ."[189] Here Austin's clear divergence from the ordinary philosophic use of 'knowledge' is most pronounced, for if anything is nearly universally held as a condition for 'X knows that p', it is p be *true*. Most philosophers would say that, after all, we *know* only *truths*. From Austin's perspective, this maxim is confused.

---

185. *Ibid.*, pp. 50-51.
186. *Ibid.*, pp. 51-53.
187. *Ibid.*, pp. 54-57.

188. *Ibid.*, pp. 58-65.
189. *Ibid.*, p. 66.

P. F. Strawson wrote that the utterance 'is true' is logically superfluous; it does not ascribe a property or relation to p, but instead it is used to express personal assent to p. Austin strongly disagreed, holding that 'is true' is a non-superfluous predicate of statements which indicates that they *correspond to the facts* in a *linguistically conventional manner*.[190] Austin maintained that to say 'p is true' is to *assess* p in a particular way,[191] and this assessment is concerned with both a state of affairs and a verbal description.[192]

However, the case is completely otherwise when one says 'I know that p'. Here he does not mean to describe two things as corresponding to each other; indeed, according to Austin, 'I know' does *not describe* anything at all. Thus he denies the necessity for knowledge to be free from error and allows that *we can "know" statements which are mistaken.* Hereby Austin hoped to salvage the ordinary use of the verb 'to know' in the face of the intellect's ability to err: "It is futile to embark on a 'theory of knowledge' which denies this liability; such theories constantly end up admitting the liability after all, and denying the existence of 'knowledge'."[193] Using 'to know' must be *compatible with error.*

The common error lying behind traditional epistemologies is the assumption that 'I know' *describes* something, states something which corresponds to a fact in the world, or that can be assessed as true or false. "To suppose that 'I know' is a descriptive phrase, is only one example of the *descriptive fallacy*, so common in philosophy."[194]

> Not merely is it jejune to suppose that all a statement aims to be is 'true', but it may further be questioned whether every 'statement' does aim to be true at all. The principle of Logic, that 'Every proposition must be true or false', has too long operated as the simplest, most persuasive and most pervasive form of the descriptive fallacy. . . . Recently it has come to be realized that many utterances which have been taken to be statements . . . are not in fact descriptive, nor susceptible of being true or false. . . . It is simply not the business of such utterances to 'correspond to the facts'.[195]

Some utterances do not describe an activity being performed; they *constitute* the *actual performance* of that activity (e.g., naming, swearing, apologizing, inviting, promising, guaranteeing, etc.). These "performative utterances"

---

190. "Truth," *Philosophical Papers*, esp. pp. 89-90; see also Austin's reply to Strawson's rejoinder (namely, that Austin wrongly treats facts as pseudo-objects) in *How to Do Things with Words*, ed. J. O. Urmson (New York: Oxford University Press, 1962), pp. 144, 148.

191. Cf. J. L. Austin, *How to Do Things with Words*, ed. J. O. Urmson (New York: Oxford University Press, 1962), pp. 144, 148.

192. "Truth," p. 92n.: "It takes two to make a truth."

193. "Other Minds," *loc. cit.*

194. *Ibid.*, p. 71.

195. "Truth," pp. 98-99.

do something as opposed to *reporting* something truly or falsely. For example, 'I name you X' is not the description of a naming process; it is the actual naming.

Throughout his scholarly career, Austin developed and refined the notion of performatives.[196] It was most thoroughly discussed in his *How to Do Things with Words*, the William James Lectures at Harvard University for 1955.[197] Therein Austin gradually gave up some former distinctions (e.g., between constative and performative) as well as former criteria for picking out performative utterances (e.g., grammatical criteria); he developed instead a theory of illocutionary and perlocutionary speech-acts. However, despite the extensive modification, Austin still retained the classification of *explicit* performatives.[198] In their case there is no ambiguity as to whether the designated act was performed simply by means of speaking or not.[199] Austin proposed four criteriological characteristics of explicit performatives:[200]

(1) When the performative is uttered under appropriate (felicitous) circumstances, it makes no sense to ask 'But did he (do you) *really?*' (i.e., 'Couldn't he (you) be mistaken?').
(2) The utterance is essential to the action performed.
(3) The action performed by the utterance must be able to be done willingly or deliberately.
(4) Although I may be insincere, it cannot literally be false that I Xed if I said 'I X'.

That is, a verb is a performative if it follows that I *have performed* the designated act simply by *saying* that I do.

Now then, we have seen above that the descriptive fallacy leads people to think that 'I know' is incompatible with error. Austin proposes, instead, that the reason we are prohibited from saying 'I know that p, but p is false' is not because knowledge entails truth, but because the statement is parallel to 'I promise to q, but I might fail to q'. In *particular* cases where *we are aware of specific reasons* why we might be mistaken or unable to do something, we *ought not* to say 'I know' or 'I promise'. This explains our bewitching feeling that knowledge must be incorrigible. 'To know' functions like 'to promise'.

Consequently, in "Other Minds" Austin held that the first-person, present

---

196. It was first introduced in "Other Minds"; subsequently Austin described the features of this class of utterances and the rules for their use in "Performative Utterances" (reprinted in *Philosophical Papers*). The distinction between these utterances and those which are considered true or false can be pursued in "Performative-Constative" in *The Philosophy of Language*, ed. J. R. Searle (London: Oxford University Press, 1971), pp. 13-22.
197. *Op cit., passim.*
198. *Ibid.,* p. 149.
199. *Ibid.,* pp. 32-33, 57, 69-70, 91, 130-131.
200. *Ibid.,* pp. 83-84.

active indicative, 'I know that p' has a nondescriptive function, the function of *guaranteeing* or *authorizing the acceptance* of p. Like 'I promise . . . ,' the utterance 'I know that p' performs the task of giving my word so that another person might rely upon it. I do not give information about p, but assure you or authorize you to accept p. When someone says 'I promise' or 'I know', "a new plunge is taken. . . . I have bound myself to others, and staked my reputation in a new way."[201] Austin goes through a number of putative parallels between the verbs 'to promise' and 'to know'.[202] This then is Austin's performative theory of knowledge. It rests on two main considerations: (1) 'I know' functions in parallel fashion to the performative 'I promise', and (2) analysis shows that 'I know' means 'I give my authority (or assurance)', which is an action performed in speaking.

Austin's thesis is thoughtful and provocative, but it must finally be evaluated as defective. In significant respects the verb 'to know' does *not* function in parallel fashion with 'to promise'. For instance, 'to promise' has a normal (albeit rare) continuous present tense (e.g., interrupted with the question "What are you doing now?", someone might say "I am promising [to come more often, to practice my lessons, etc.]"), whereas 'to know' does not (i.e., 'I am knowing that the book is blue' is a locutionary abnormality). More importantly, we must observe that insincere promises are *still* considered promises (i.e., when you have said 'I promise' we always report that 'You promised'), but a groundless knowledge-claim is *not* viewed as an instance of knowing (i.e., we do not say 'You knew but were wrong', but rather 'You *said that* you knew but were wrong'). These examples show us that saying 'I promise' is sufficient to promise, but saying 'I know' is insufficient to know. A truth-claim is at stake in the latter case which is not in the former. A consideration of correspondence with the facts might be used to bolster or challenge the statement 'I know', but correspondence with the facts is not used to challenge a promise. We *reproach* someone who breaks his *promise*, but we *refute* someone who mistakenly claims to *know* something. Therefore, these two verbs differ significantly in their grammar, logic, and effects of use.

Let it be noted that the similarities between 'I know' and 'I promise' would outweigh the dissimilarities between them *only if* in fact 'I know' *is* a performative utterance. However, according to *Austin's own criteria*, 'I know' should *not* be classified as one.[203] (1) Certainly we *can* (and often do) ask 'Do you really? Couldn't you be mistaken?' when someone claims 'I know that p'. (2) It makes perfect sense to hold that someone

---

201. "Other Minds," p. 67.
202. See *ibid.*, pp. 66-71.
203. The following observations follow the order of Austin's criteria as listed above; cf. footnote 200.

knows his address even when he has never had occasion to utter it out-loud; utterance is not essential to knowledge. (3) While someone might say 'I hereby (willingly, deliberately) promise to q', it does not make good sense to say 'I hereby (willingly, deliberately) know that p'. Knowledge is a matter of truth, not volition. Finally, (4) It cannot strictly be false that 'you promised' if you said 'I promise'; however, it most certainly is strictly false that 'you knew' if (when p is false) you said 'I know that p'. Furthermore, it should be noted that 'know' cannot be substituted for X in the formula: to say 'I X' is to X (Austin's simple test for an explicit per-formative). It is plainly false that to *say* 'I know' is *to know!* The action is no more performed by simply stating it than jumping is performed by saying 'I jump'.

Austin might reply to these observations by pointing out that they all derive their force from the presupposition that 'I know that p' entails that p is true; hence we have *begged* the entire question. For Austin 'I know' means 'I assure you', and the *latter* expression clearly passes the test for an explicit performative. However, ironic as it may seem in the case of Austin, his claim that 'I know that p' is a performative utterance is *inaccurate as an analysis of ordinary language.* Many examples come to mind where the utterance 'I know' is not used to guarantee, assure, or give one's word for something (e.g., the child impresses his father, saying "I know that Sacra-mento is in California"; clearly this is not giving authorization for the father to believe the statement). *If* people ordinarily understood your statement 'I know that p' as the performing of an assurance to them, then they would *not* say 'You did not know that p' when it turned out you were wrong about p—because even in that case you still *would* have given your assuring word to them. Consider also that 'I promised but did not come through' is a legitimate statement in ordinary usage, but there simply is no normal occurrence of 'I knew but was wrong'; this exhibits the fact that people ordinarily assume that being correct is essential to an acceptable knowledge-claim.

Therefore, we cannot but conclude that Austin's performative theory embodies an unacceptable epistemology. There are notable differences be-tween the grounds called for in saying 'I know that p' and saying 'I give my assurance that p'. The latter can be said just in case you are prepared to take responsibility for error or misleading your hearers, but the former statement requires that you be *in a position* to know that p (e.g., have certain evidence, etc.). Conversely, if something (say, p) is within one's cognizance, then he knows p whether he ever assures someone of it or not. One cannot silently promise something to someone (that is, prom-ising requires words, written or spoken), but there are many things that everybody knows in silence (indeed, some of their deepest secrets). Know-ing is not a performative because it is *not an action* at all, much less a speech-action. One does not decide to perform a feat of knowledge, but he can decide to give assurance to someone.

This is not to say that 'I know' is never used with a performatory element in it (e.g., the doctor says to the distraught wife, 'I know that your husband shall live' after the husband has undergone surgery). However, just as Austin observed that Strawson (who thought that 'is true' does nothing except confirming or granting a point) improperly confined himself to the performatory aspect of a phrase which also functions to describe something,[204] we must conclude that Austin himself wrongly confined his attention to the performatory aspect of the phrase 'I know' even though it commonly functions to describe as well. A wedge can be driven between knowledge-claims and knowledge which cannot be driven between explicit performatives (e.g., 'I promise') and their designated actions (e.g., promising). Thus it has not been demonstrated that traditional epistemological theories commit a descriptive fallacy. The fact that 'I know' can be either true or false, that it corresponds to the facts or does not, that it is a descriptive phrase is sufficiently shown by the fact that it functions perfectly well in syllogistic arguments (e.g., If I know that Jones is guilty of the crime, my life is in danger. I know that Jones is guilty. Therefore my life is in danger). *Actions* like promising and running, however, *cannot* operate within a standard logical proof. 'I know' is not an action but a straightforward descriptive phrase, a report, a claim which can be true or false. 'I know', therefore, is not an explicit performative utterance, and the charge of descriptive fallacy must be withdrawn.

The preceding critique of Austin's analysis demonstrates that he cannot simply dismiss traditional epistemological issues on the ground that they rest on muddled assumptions. He has failed to show this to be the case. No escape from skepticism, therefore, has been uncovered by Austin. The search for certainty—for a firm, indubitable foundation or source of knowledge—is still a necessity in order to salvage knowledge and avert relativism. Basic certainties must be found, not haphazarly assumed, but Austin offered no answer as to how we could be certain of our ultimate convictions. Austin's response to the possibility of ultimate disagreements between people (reflected in their linguistic usage) is noteworthy for exhibiting the weakness of his philosophy:

> Nevertheless, *sometimes* we do ultimately disagree: sometimes we must allow a usage to be, though appalling, yet actual. . . . But why should this daunt us? . . . If our usages disagree . . . your conceptual system is different from mine, though very likely it is at least equally consistent and serviceable. . . . A disagreement as to what we should say is not to be shied off, but to be pounced upon: for the explanation of it can hardly fail to be illuminating. If we light on an electron that rotates

204. "Truth," p. 101.

the wrong way, that is a discovery, a portent to be followed up, not a reason for chucking physics: and by the same token, a genuinely loose or eccentric talker is a rare specimen to be prized.[205]

This approach results either in *relativism* (our conceptual systems are equally serviceable) or *prejudice* (like Wittgenstein, Austin suggests treating someone whose linguistic usage differs from his own as an eccentric specimen, thus merely presuming that this *other* speaker—rather than Austin—is "loose" or "wrong"). Either way, *objectivity* is lost in epistemology. The skeptic can continue to challenge and question the claims made by Austin, then, and rightly so; Austin could not know for sure that he was correct in what he thought, but only that he harmonized with the usage of some *subsection* of the linguistic community.

It turns out that, in the name of ordinary language analysis, Austin's outlook on knowledge actually *reforms* everyday linguistic usage—and mistakenly at that. Moreover, reducing 'I know' to a performative utterance would still not cancel the need to answer traditional epistemological questions. When does a person have the *right* to *claim truth* for his assertions? He may go about assuring us that p, but when can he rightly say that p is true? That is, we still want to ask whether Austin *knew* (old sense) his conclusions to be true. If he did *not*, then what could those conclusions, those assertions he made, have been? Indeed, they would be mere *personal recommendations*, one which were prejudicial against the pervasive, deep, and general questions of the theory of knowledge. Like Dewey, Austin gave no good reason to abandon the quest for certainty; he simply decreed it. Like Wittgenstein, Austin's position was rooted in a sociological preference for his own linguistic community.

Arbitrariness of his position shows up in a number of other ways which can be briefly mentioned. First, on what *grounds* could Austin establish his philosophic method as the *necessary preliminary* to *all* other kinds of philosophic investigation? Did ordinary language analysis establish *its own* foundational character? Second, Austin offered no argument for the isomorphism between the form of ordinary language and external reality. Does grammar get us to reality? Or, perhaps, is it rather that common linguistic usage reflects only a pervasive *way of looking* at (or interpreting) reality? Third, Austin personally trusted the time-tested distinctions which he said were embedded in ordinary language. But why should he? *Disputes* over distinctions, inferences, evaluations, etc., *also* carry down through history in the vehicle of language; thus one cannot directly appeal to linguistic use but must first actually *resolve* the conflicts between ultimately different language-games (to use Wittgenstein's phrase). Fourth, why did Austin recommend that we concentrate our analysis on *ordinary*

---

205. "A Plea for Excuses," p. 132.

language and exclude the linguistic usage of the *philosophers?* After all, philosophical discussion is also a time-honored tradition and has stood the long test of the survival of the fittest (men have from ancient times searched for answers to the "big questions" of axiology, ontology, and epistemology). Finally, we should indicate that, while there is some benefit in Austin's point that a skeptic must offer *specific* reasons for questioning our assertions (rather than throwing out the general question, "how do you know that what you have identified is *'real'*?"), nevertheless such specific questions only arise *within* systems of thought and linguistic usage. A general question addressed from someone in *one* system to another person in a *different* system must not be arbitrarily ruled out; there is no good reason (at least offered by Austin) why scholarly questioning must be restricted to the lower level issues peculiar to one philosophic position and not rise to the higher and more general questions concerning *competing* systems.

To this point we have seen that Austin shares fundamental defects with Dewey and Wittgenstein (namely, an inadequate epistemology, an unwise abandonment of objective certainty, a failure to resolve ultimate disagreements, and personal arbitrariness). In concluding our critique of him it must be pointed out that the dialectical tension in which Dewey and Wittgenstein were caught was a pitfall for Austin as well. This is evident in three illustrations. First, there is an antinomy which has the shadow of Kant cast over it. On one hand Austin portrayed ordinary language as something which imposes a particular order on experience, thus operating as a "phenomenal filter" which stands between us and the world. "Ordinary language *blinkers* the already feeble imagination"; indeed, the imagination "is enslaved by words."[206] Hence "there may be extraordinary facts, even about our everyday experience, which plain men and plain language overlook."[207] Language can keep us from apprehending the noumenal realm it seems. The attempt to compare our ordinary usage with the world itself will only shift the problem to the *other language* used now to describe the world (and then compare to ordinary language); we cannot get beyond language-conditioned experience in order to stand outside and test that language itself. Yet on the other hand, Austin also treated ordinary language as the road to revelation. Words show us the realities beyond them.[208] Analysis of ordinary language must be used to discover facts and thereby remove confusions;[209] it can unveil the inner kernel of truth which has been ingrained through time in our language. For instance, because it is not consistent with what we ordinarily say, determinism can be dis-

---

206. "The Meaning of a Word," *Philosophical Papers*, pp. 36, 35; cf. "A Plea for Excuses," p. 130.
207. *Ibid.*, p. 37.
208. "A Plea for Excuses," p. 130.
209. "Ifs and Cans," *Philosophical Papers*, p. 179.

puted[210]—which assumes that ordinary language is a source and standard for truth. Therefore, Austin treated ordinary language as *both* a screen from and an unveiling of reality.

A second illustration of dialectical tension in Austin's thought is related to his "survival of the fittest" test for linguistic use. On the one hand Austin assumes *continuity* because, as seen previously, ordinary language allegedly gives us truths that have passed the test of time. That is, there are distinctions which have been firmly embeded in language and continued there through the passing years. Yet on the other hand, Austin holds that grammar is "in a state of flux"[211]—an obvious indication that he worked on the assumption of *discontinuity*. In fact, this presupposition was strong enough that Austin in effect undermined the survival test altogether: "Superstition and error and fantasy of all kinds do become incorporated in ordinary language and even sometimes stand up in the survival test."[212] Therefore, Austin simultaneously affirmed the normative value of the test of time and recognized its untrustworthy character. It was a standard which was also no standard.

Finally, another way in which we can express the antinomy of Austin's epistemology is through his attitude toward ordinary language. According to him ordinary language analysis was the greatest and most salutary revolution in history, one which maintained that it was wrong to attempt to escape philosophical tangles by invoking new linguistic uses.[213] Logical grammar should ultimately not be different than ordinary grammar.[214] The mistakes in philosophy, then, were to be cleared up through ordinary language analysis,[215] for ordinary language embodies uses and distinctions which are more sound than those of armchair speculation.[216] Because there was genuine value buried in it, ordinary language must become our *guide*[217]—showing us how to reach agreement with respect to scholarly discoveries.[218] For all these reasons, then, ordinary language analysis was absolutely necessary at the outset of all philosophizing.[219]

Here Austin was saying that correct usage was to be discovered through ordinary language analysis; he suggested that ordinary language should be left as it is because ordinary language was assumed to be a necessary guide for philosophers. Yet Austin was just as bold to maintain, on just the opposite hand, that ordinary language is *not* authoritative, and that there are *no* final standards. Ordinary language does not have the last word, for there is *no such thing*.[220] Ordinary language is in fact inadequate and

210. *Ibid.*
211. *Ibid.*
212. "A Plea for Excuses," p. 133.
213. "Performative Utterances," pp. 221-222.
214. "Ifs and Cans," p. 180.
215. "Performative Utterances," p. 239.
216. "A Plea for Excuses," p. 130.

217. *Ibid.*, p. 129.
218. *Ibid.*, p. 131.
219. *Ibid.*, p. 133.
220. *Ibid.*

arbitrary,[221] in need of being straightened out.[222] (At this point we want to ask, straightened out *by what?*) The confusions in it must be removed.[223] Quite bluntly, ordinary language *fails us*,[224] shows us our need for a better language,[225] must be overridden,[226] superseded and improved.[227] Ordinary language cannot be a standard for our philosophy because it is infected with error, superstition, the jargon of extinct theories, and our own prejudices.[228] So then, Austin has again confronted us with a self-vitiating attitude: ordinary language is our guide to resolving philosophic problems (it is a standard more sound than speculation), and yet the philosopher must correct the failing, infected, error-infested usage of ordinary discourse. In the long run there is no last word. Therefore, just like Dewey and Wittgenstein, Austin attempted to be both a rationalist and an irrationalist, an absolutist and relativist, assuming continuity along with flux, teaching the categorizing (enslaving) and yet revelatory nature of ordinary language.

Austin hoped to dissolve the general questions of epistemology which had been inspired by skeptical challenges, but his performative theory of knowledge was not adequate to the task. He promoted ordinary language analysis as the method for philosophy, but it has turned out to be prejudicial and arbitrary at best and dialectically incoherent at worst. *Twentieth-century epistemology, under the direction of pragmatism and linguistic analysis, has undergone a silent but sure demise.*

Van Til and Revelation

Four basic issues can be distilled from the preceding discussion of Dewey, Wittgenstein, and Austin with respect to epistemology. First, there is the question of the *necessity of facing up to standard epistemological* problems. We have seen that the quest for certainty cannot be arbitrarily dismissed. General questions about the theory of knowledge are still legitimate philosophic fare, for knowledge cannot be treated as anything less than descriptive of the truth; moreover, one cannot capitulate to doubt because even that presupposes certainty. Thus, philosophers and indeed all men need to have dependable norms and must seek infallible or indubitable truths. All important and self-conscious attempts to establish a theory of knowledge must seek a defense against skepticism and must ask what our certainties should be. What is the unshakeable foundation, the knowledge which is so certain that no reasonable man should doubt it?

---

221. *Ibid.*, p. 130.
222. "How to Talk," *Philosophical Papers*, p. 181.
223. "Ifs and Cans," p. 179.
224. "The Meaning of a Word," p. 36.
225. *Ibid.*, p. 37.
226. "A Plea for Excuses," p. 134.
227. *Ibid.*, p. 133.
228. *Ibid.*, pp. 130, 133.

This brings us, secondly, to the major epistemological question of *verification*. The justification for knowledge-claims is a critical issue. We have observed, though, that verification procedures and standards of testing function within a system of thought or discourse—that is, they are *internal to a worldview*. Justifications come to an end; procedures for testing are rooted in the indubitable presuppositions which undergird the system or worldview in which they operate. What one accepts is an interrelated system of truths (rather than adopting each proposition one by one), a system which is interwoven with a form of life or pattern of behavior. Thus, circularity in support of specific truths and actions (in relation to other specific truths and actions) will be inevitable.

What this raises, thirdly, is the question of the *objectivity of truth*. The problem of subjectivity, prejudice, or arbitrariness with respect to one's presuppositional worldview now looms large over the epistemic enterprise. How can one be certain of his foundational assumptions or avoid self-delusion? Is there any way to settle conflicts between competing systems with their respective circular patterns of thought and forms of life? Is epistemology doomed to prejudice, so that truth becomes what works for you or what is adopted by some particular linguistic community? The critical issue, then, becomes the attainment of correspondence with objective facts in order to avert skeptical relativism.

Finally, then, if certainty in epistemology will be a matter of one's worldview or presuppositions, there is the question of a *self-attesting worldview*. Is there a philosophical position which can finally gain peace for the philosopher, which escapes the damaging need to call itself into question eventually? Such an ultimate grounding for objective epistemology will need to: (a) avoid the ego-centric predicament and phenomenalism, (b) prevent self-vitiating dialectical tension or incoherence, and (c) have practical relevance or instrumental value in solving concrete problems in philosophy and other areas, thus being beneficial to our neighbor who struggles with intellectual tangles and practical difficulties.

The theory of knowledge, and thereby all philosophy in some respect, eventually comes down to this point. And at this point we can turn our attention to the teaching of Cornelius Van Til in the area of epistemology. The only worldview which salvages epistemology, the objectivity of truth, and genuine certainty is that which *presupposes the revelation of God*, according to Van Til. Systems of thought which refuse to begin with God and His revealed truth make nonsense out of human experience, succumb to skepticism or prejudice, and in the final analysis have to promote human reason to the place of God as expounded in Christian theology. Only within the biblical worldview where man is to think God's thoughts after Him can infallible truths and norms be found and can arbitrariness be avoided at the presuppositional level. Van Til has done a great service to philosophical scholarship by pointing out how to meet the deepset needs in an adequate theory of knowledge; the quest for certainty must end with God and His self-attesting, infallible word. Here we find the foundations not only of *Christian* scolarship but of *any* genuine scholarship whatsoever.

In the Introduction to *A Christian Theory of Knowledge* Van Til said, "The present work seeks specifically to show the relevance of Christianity to modern thought. Its main contention is that Christianity has the answer that modern thought seeks in vain." Van Til's writings have persistently argued that the quest for certainty must begin and end with God's revelation. In his Preface to *A Survey of Christian Epistemology* Van Til says that when the syllabus was written (1932) he recognized the drift toward positivism in the new day, and

> The answer is that then, as now, I was convinced that only if one begins with the self-identifying Christ of Reformation theology, can one bring the "facts" of the space-time world into intelligible relation to the "laws" of this world. Science, philosophy and theology find their intelligible contact only on the presupposition of the self-revelation of God in Christ—through Scripture understood properly by the regeneration of the Holy Spirit.[229]

Van Til's *Survey* is recommended to the reader for a more detailed account of the position which we can only summarize here.

Van Til indicates that "the core of our system of philosophy is our belief in the triune God of Scripture, and in what he has revealed concerning himself and his purposes for man and his world."[230] This means that the Christian has a *revelational epistemology:* God has revealed Himself both in the created realm and in the mind of man; when man's reasoning is carried on in this atmosphere it expresses the truth as established by God. The *impress of God's plan* is upon both the "facts" and man's mind and thus they are adapted to each other. "True human knowledge corresponds to the knowledge which God has of himself and his world." What is all-important in epistemology is the *completely self-conscious God,* one who is surrounded by no ignorance or mystery at all; thus "God is the ultimate subject of knowledge."[231] Accordingly, as Van Til said in the *Defense of the Faith,* "the only method that will lead to the truth in any field is that method which recognizes the fact that man is a creature of God, that he must therefore seek to think God's thoughts after him."[232] Knowing must *begin with God* who self-sufficiently determines and hence knows all reality and history; God's knowledge is revealed in the created realm and appre-

---

229. Cornelius Van Til, *A Survey of Christian Epistemology* (Ripon, Calif.: den Dulk Christian Foundation, 1969), p. iii.

230. *Ibid.,* p. xiii.

231. *Ibid.,* pp. 1, 133.

232. Cornelius Van Til, *The Defense of the Faith,* 1st ed. (Philadelphia: Presbyterian and Reformed Publishing Co., 1955), p. 119.

hended by man's mind which itself operates in terms of God's revelation of Himself. God, as the *original subject of knowledge,* must be the *final reference point* for man's knowledge, which is accordingly a receptive reconstruction of God's thinking. "Human knowledge of anything presupposes God's ultimate self-consciousness as the point of reference for man's knowledge of anything."[233] This goes to indicate the fundamental difference between Christian and non-Christian epistemologies: "according to the Christian position, the basis of human investigation is in God, while for the antitheistic position the basis of human investigation is in man."[234] The Christian recognizes that all explanation must end somewhere and that only if it ends in the self-sufficient Creator of all things whose revelation is expressed through the facts as well as man's mind can genuine knowledge be attained.

> The Protestant doctrine of God requires that it be made foundational to everything else as a principle of explanation. If God is self-sufficient, he alone is self-explanatory. And if he alone is self-explanatory, then he must be the final reference point in all human predication. He is then like the sun from which all lights on earth derive their power of illumination.[235]

In his *Survey of Christian Epistemology,* Van Til argues that in the theory of knowledge all options reduce down to a choice between a Christian and non-Christian epistemology; each position finally understands different things by the standard epistemological vocabulary. The *most significant contrast* between them lies in how each conceives of the *relation of the human mind to the divine mind.* The key question in epistemology can be variously put as: *can the human mind or consciousness function independently of God,* or *is the mind in itself able to interpret reality intelligently?* The options which the philosopher faces are these: he can attempt to interpret reality in terms of (1) the sense world, (2) an ideal world, (3) a mixture of these two, or (4) instead in terms of the mind (revelation) of God. Van Til exposes the deficiencies of the first three positions, showing that throughout, the antitheist has taken for granted what he is supposed to prove. According to the Christian philosopher, the objects of knowledge exist and derive their meaning from the presupposed absolute self-consciousness of God (His all-encompassing, self-sufficient understanding of reality and sovereign direction over historical eventuation). The secondary subject of knowledge, man, does *not* have a mind which is independent, ultimate, or self-sufficient; he must take God's revealed word as his starting point and standard for knowledge.

---

233. *Survey of Christian Epistemology* (hereafter *SCE*), p. 109.
234. *Ibid.,* p. 9.
235. Cornelius Van Til, *A Christian Theory of Knowledge* (Nutley, N. J.: Presbyterian and Reformed Publishing Co., 1969), p. 12.

The foregoing has been a very brief and general outline of the epistemological position taught by Van Til. Becoming more specific, we can
observe how Van Til's revelational epistemology replies to the four basic
questions which the discussion of pragmatism and linguistic analysis has
left to be answered. Van Til notes that "every man educated or not educated has an epistemology implied in his practice."[236] It is this which each
man must give an account of. "Every system of philosophy must tell us
whether it thinks true knowledge to be possible. Or if a system of philosophy thinks it impossible . . . it must give good reasons for thinking
so."[237] Because "the very possibility of error presupposes the existence of
truth,"[238] no philosopher (not even the critic or skeptic) will be able to
ignore the necessity of answering basic epistemological questions—in
particular, how do you account for knowledge (its nature, possibility,
assumptions, and validation)? As we have noted previously, there is no
escape from confrontation with such a major question, whether through
Dewey's pragmatism, general skepticism, or Austin's novel linguistic analysis. An indubitable foundation for knowledge must be found.

Van Til has been bold to recognize from the outset of his career that,
contrary to the impression given by pragmatism, when it comes to verifying
one's knowledge-claims or giving an account of his conclusions, the starting
point, method, and conclusions will all *mutually require* each other; they
go hand in hand. Consequently, what one takes as the proper test, origin,
or result of knowledge will be internally dictated by his overall worldview or
his general presuppositions.[239] Because one's conclusion and starting point
require each other, "every system of thought necessarily has a certain
method of its own," one which corresponds to its idea of knowledge.[240]
Hence *circularity* will be operative in every man's thinking, creating a
fundamental philosophy of life which is contrary to any system having
different presuppositions.[241] The most basic doctrines of a system are
interdependent and color each other, thus giving a distinctive method to
the system.[242] This in turn means that *neutrality is an impossible illusion;*
every thinker will in the nature of the case begin with a certain bias.[243]

However, unlike other philosophers in this century who have come to
recognize this truth, Van Til has refused to capitulate to relativism. "We
cannot choose epistemologies as we choose hats. Such would be the case
if it had been once for all established that the whole thing is but a matter

---

236. *SCE,* p. 15.
237. *Ibid.,* p. xiii.
238. *Ibid.,* p. 23.
239. *The Defense of the Faith* (hereafter *DF*), p. 118.
240. *SCE,* pp. 4-5, 6.
241. *Ibid.,* pp. 7, 12.
242. *A Christian Theory of Knowledge* (hereafter *CTK*), p. 11.
243. *SCE,* pp. 5-6, 19.

of taste. . . . That is exactly the point in dispute."[244] On the same page, Van Til notes that the attitude which allows for epistemological or presuppositional relativity rests on the conviction that man can have no knowledge of ultimate things; however, this conviction must be made reasonable, which due to its very content is going to be impossible. When two systems which have fundamentally antithetic presuppositions come into conflict, says Van Til, the opponents *can* and *must reason* with each other;[245] the worldview which is contrary to your own "ought to be refuted by a reasoned argument, instead of by ridicule and assumption."[246] Here it is evident that Van Til will not allow himself to slip into the damaging arbitrariness and prejudice of Wittgenstein. Van Til has consistently taught that the ultimate question in the last analysis concerns one's most basic assumptions or presuppositions, and these *must not be left unchallenged* when systems disagree.[247] Instead, the two opponents must seek to determine which presuppositions are necessary for the intelligibility of the objects of knowledge, the intelligibilty of facts and laws, the interpretation of experience, the foundations of logic, the task of predication, or the consciousness of self, objects, or time.[248] To put if briefly, *what are the necessary preconditions of knowledge?* To settle this question is to see which worldview corresponds to the facts, which is of necessity true, which gives an adequate answer to the perennial quest for certainty.

The fundamental question in epistemology turns out to be this: can reality be intelligibly interpreted in exclusively immanent or temporal categories? That is, the pivotal question is this: *which mind, man or God's, is to be taken as original and epistemologically ultimate?*[249] "There can be no more fundamental question in epistemology than the question whether or not facts can be known without reference to God . . . whether or not God exists."[250] Because Christianity forces us to face such questions, and because Christianity has an adequate answer to them, Christian epistemology need not degenerate into unreasoning presuppositional arbitrariness. "If the Christian position with respect to creation, that is, with respect to the idea of the origin of both the subject and the object of knowledge is true, there is and must be objective knowledge."[251] "Only the Christian theist has real objectivity, while the others are introducing false prejudices or subjectivity."[252] This last comment has been abundantly

---

244. *Ibid.*, p. xiv.
245. *Ibid.*, chap. XIV.
246. *Ibid.*, p. 23.
247. *DF*, pp. 94, 110.
248. *SCE*, pp. 189, 201, 204, 206; *DF*, pp. 94, 110, 117.
249. *SCE*, pp. 15, 107, 133.
250. *Ibid.*, p. 4.
251. *DF*, p. 60.
252. *SCE*, p. 201; cf. p. 103.

illustrated in our discussions above of Dewey, Wittgenstein, and Austin. *Objectivity* becomes possible only with *revealed presuppositions*. Hence the objectivity of an epistemological position is a matter of whether it places things in relation to the *absolutely self-conscious God;* "we must call any system of thought subjective if it sets up human thought or the human consciousness as the ultimate standard of truth."[253]

Therefore, in the last two chapters of *A Survey of Christian Epistemology*, Van Til teaches that Christians, in order to be consistent with their position, must reason by thinking God's thoughts after Him, taking His revelation as their most basic certainty, and reducing all other positions to absurdity—indeed, showing that even antitheism must presuppose theism in order to reason against it! The Christian method in epistemology should be the "transcendental" method of "implication", seeking to bring every fact which is investigated into the illuminating context of God's revealed truth and plan.[254] This method takes any *fact* and recognizes the presuppositions which are necessary for it to be what it is. When worldviews collide, the Christian transcendental epistemology calls for us to ask what foundations knowledge must have in order for man intelligibly to understand the facts at all. Van Til calls this *"spiral reasoning"* because "we are not reasoning about and seeking to explain facts by assuming the existence and meaning of certain other facts on the same level of being with the facts we are investigating, and then explaining these facts in turn by the facts with which we began. We are presupposing *God*, not merely another fact of the universe."[255] This is not circular; it is transcendental. Nor is it autonomous, seeking to establish the groundwork of knowledge by means of a scholarly investigation which is carried on independently of God's revealed word. The Christian begins with an interrelated system, a revealed worldview, and from *that vantage point* examines all facts, competing systems, and the transcendentals of knowledge. Therefore, we can say that Christian epistemology is *revelationally transcendental* in character.

According to Van Til, then, epistemology is not abandoned to skeptical relativism in the end. Instead, there is a self-attesting worldview which supplies an objective foundation for epistemic certainty. That Wittgenstein so much wanted, but could not find on his own, has been provided by God's revelation. Peace can finally come to the philosopher when he realizes that Christianity is the presupposition without which predication would be unintelligible, for nothing can be known of any fact except by way of one's fundamental knowledge of God; nothing can be known unless the Creator and Redeemer is first known, thereby enabling successful rational inquiry based on His revelation, in terms of which reason and

---

253. *Ibid.*, pp. 4, 134.
254. *Ibid.*, pp. 7, 10, 11, 201.
255. *Ibid.*, p. 201; cf. p. 12.

fact are intelligible or meaningful.[256] "If it be said to such opponents of Christianity that, unless there were an absolute God their own questions and doubts would have no meaning at all, there is no arguement in return. There lie the issues."[257] This must count, according to Wittgenstein, as the *real discovery* because it establishes a philosophy that is no longer tormented by questions which bring *itself* into question or jeopardy.

When one refuses to presuppose this self-attesting revelation of God in his overt or conscious reasoning, he must eventually exalt man's mind to a functional equivalence with God. What God does in terms of the Christian's system, autonomous man must claim the prerogative to do in his own system.[258] But of course he is unable to do this in any adequate fashion. Therefore, observes Van Til, modern philosophy is afflicted with *phenomenalism* wherein *all systems of interpretations become relative to the mind of man;* what the autonomous thinker takes to be true is simply *his own imposition of order* on a chaotic or irrational realm of factuality.[259] Because Christianity begins with the revelation of the living God who created all things and knows them completely, it alone does not end up legislating for reality.[260] Because the autonomous epistemologist must make his mind determinative for reality while simultaneously admitting that reality is beyond his rational control and characterized by brute, uninterpreted, chance eventuation, the non-Christian is unavoidably led into *dialectical tensions* between rationalism and irrationalism.

> It was thus that man, in rejecting the covenantal requirement of God became at one and the same time both irrationalist and rationalist. These two are not, except formally, contradictory of one another. They rather imply one another. Man had to be both to be either. . . . In ancient philosophy the rationalistic motif seemed to dominate the scene; in modern times the irrationalistic motif seems to be largely in control. But the one never lives altogether independently of the other.[261]

Abundant evidence of antinomy in secular thought was found in our discussion of pragmatism and linguistic analysis above; a rational-irrational dialectic was firmly embedded in the positions of Dewey, Wittgenstein, and Austin. None was immune, and thus each of their respective epistemological positions was unsatisfactory. This tension in non-Christian theories of knowledge is inevitable given their assumed autonomy or independence from God's revelation: "we would maintain that all of the antinomies of

---

256. *Ibid.*, pp. 5, 116, 117, 123, 183; *CTK*, pp. 18, 41, 45.
257. *SCE*, p. 11.
258. *CTK*, p. 15.
259. *DF*, p. 144.
260. *CTK*, p. 51.
261. *Ibid.*, pp. 49, 50; cf. *DF*, pp. 133, 142.

antitheistic reasoning are due to a false separation of man from God."[262]
The attitude of autonomy must finally posit the ultimacy of mystery and
thereby capitulate to skepticism in the long run.[263] Autonomy is inherently
destructive of human experience, for it makes impossible demands of the
finite and dependent human intellect.[264]

In sharp contrast to the fate of twentieth-century pragmatism and
linguistic analysis, Christian presuppositionalism in epistemology faces up
to standard problems in the theory of knowledge, recognizes the critical
function of presuppositions in one's worldview with its interrelated starting
point, method, and conclusions, and yet fully holds to the objectivity of
truth and the need for conflicting systems to reason with each other, seeking
the self-attesting and transcendental groundwork for epistemology—an
intelligible position which untangles philosophical problems, does not
crumble under dialectical tensions, and averts the skepticism of phenomenalism. As Van Til has so beneficially expounded, "Christianity
can be shown to be, not 'just as good as' or even 'better than' the non-
Christian position, but the *only* position that does not make nonsense of
human experience."[265] In God's word, we find the indubitable and infallible truths which have been sought throughout the history of epistemological theorizing; in His revelation, the philosopher finds that knowledge
which is so certain that no reasonable man should doubt it. Modern epistemology points up the continued necessity for philosophy to find all the
treasures of wisdom and knowledge in Christ (Col. 2:3), for aside from
Him and His self-attesting word man can produce nothing but the vain
opposition of "knowledge falsely-so-called" (I Tim. 6:20). Therefore,
we conclude that the quest for certainty can be successful only as one takes
the fear of the Lord as the beginning of knowledge (Prov. 1:7). *Presuppositionalism secures knowledge while eschewing the errors of both
pragmatism and prejudice.*

Harry Frankfurt once wrote, "The claim that a basis for doubt is inconceivable is justified whenever a denial of the claim would violate the conditions or presuppositions of rational inquiry."[266] What Van Til has contributed to the theory of knowledge is an acute awareness that a reasonable
basis for doubt is inconceivable with respect to God's revelation, and apart
from *this* sure foundation all other ground is sinking sand (Matt. 7:24-27;
Prov. 1:29).

---

262. *SCE*, p. 109.
263. *CTK*, p. 50; see also *The Reformed Pastor and Modern Thought* (Nutley,
N. J.: Presbyterian and Reformed Publishing Co., 1971), e.g., p. 89.
264. *CTK*, pp. 12-13.
265. *Ibid.*, p. 19.
266. "Doubt," *The Encyclopedia of Philosophia*, ed. Paul Edwards (New York:
Macmillan Co., The Free Press, 1967), II, p. 414.

The doctrine that God controls whatsoever comes to pass is simply the historical doctrine of providence as expressed in the Reformed Confessions. It is the concomitant of the doctrine of creation out of nothing. And both are concomitant to the idea that God is self-determinate, self-contained, that is, independent of the world he has created. All forms of heresy, those of the early church and those of modern times, spring from this confusion of God with the world. All of them, in some manner and to some extent, substitute the idea of man's participation in God for that of his creation by God. This is the case with Romanism, with its concept of analogy of being, borrowed from the Greek philosopher, Aristotle. It is no less the case with Barth. His entire idea of atonement, which for him is, he says, identical with election, is in effect that man participates in the very aseity of God.

The nature of grace is that it is sovereign grace, and this is the position of Calvin, Dort, and the adherents both of supralapsarianism and infralapsarianism, as well as those who hold and those who deny common grace. The sovereignty of this God is not naked sovereignty. The power of this God is not absolute, that is, arbitrary power. The fact that as creatures made in the image of God we have to do with his revealed will and are not to search behind it or pass it by in seeking for the definition of grace, and, therefore, for the hope and comfort of salvation, does not mean that this will is not expressive of his self-determinate and therefore holy nature. Calvin's theology is not nominalism and irrationalism, nor is it realism and rationalism; neither is it a combination of these two. It is not a system of theology in accordance with a logical methodology borrowed from Aristotle or from Kant. On the other hand, it is not chaos. Biblical truth is systematic, that is, it is orderly. Its various doctrines are not deductions from a common central theological principle, but they stand in orderly relation to one another. The one is meaningless without the other. They supplement one another. Together, they form what may properly be called a system of truth; that is, the content of Scripture is an analogical system of truth.

Van Til, *The Theology of James Daane*
(1969), pp. 122-23.

THEOLOGY

XII

THE PROBLEM OF THEOLOGICAL PARADOX

By JOHN M. FRAME

In 1961, Cornelius Van Til reviewed a book by R. H. Bremmer called *Herman Bavinck als Dogmaticus* (*Herman Bavinck the Theologian*).[1] Having run across this review in a recent perusal of the Van Til corpus, I asked myself whether someday there might be a book called *Cornelius Van Til als Dogmaticus.*

Perhaps one's first instinct would be to say no. Van Til, after all, is an apologist, not a dogmatician. He did indeed teach courses in systematic theology for many years, but those courses (if some of his former students are to be believed) were essentially apologetics courses in disguise. Where Van Til does discuss theological issues, furthermore, he includes little exegesis (in the traditional sense of that term). What exegesis he does present is usually borrowed from other sources. His dogmatic formulations, too, are often simple repetitions or paraphrases of the creeds and of the great Reformed theologians from Calvin onward. Even when Van Til's theology sounds most strange to American ears (for example, his strong emphasis upon the ethical/metaphysical distinction), he is very often paraphrasing ideas from the Dutch tradition. (In the case of the ethical/metaphysical distinction, the source is Bavinck.)

If, however, from the above considerations we conclude that Van Til's theology is uninteresting and/or unimportant, we will merely expose ourselves as shallow thinkers and cut ourselves off from one whose contribution to theology is of virtually Copernican dimensions. If Van Til had done nothing more than to introduce some of the best insights of the Dutch theologians to the American public, even then his work would have been of substantial importance. But when one considers the uniqueness of his apologetic position and then further considers the implications of that apologetic for theology, one searches for superlatives to describe the significance of Van Til's overall approach.

Van Til's apologetics may well be described as a group of original applications of some familiar Reformed doctrines. In Van Til's view, apologetics and theology (particularly systematic theology) are very closely

---

1. C. Van Til, "Bavinck the Theologian, A Review Article," *Westminster Theological Journal* XXIV, 1 (November, 1961), 1-17. Incidentally, this article is important in that, so far as I can tell, it is Van Til's first serious written criticism of Herman Dooyeweerd.

related: ". . . defense and positive statement go hand in hand."[2] There can be no adequate positive statement without defense against error, and *vice versa*. In fact, "Systematic Theology is more closely related to apologetics than are any of the other disciplines. In it we have the system of truth that we are to defend."[3] Thus Van Til begins the exposition of his apologetic with an outline of Reformed systematic theology.[4] It is clear from the outset that one of Van Til's basic concerns is to present an apologetic which is true to Scripture and Reformed doctrine. His major complaints against competing apologetic methods are theological complaints, that is, that they compromise the incomprehensibility of God, total depravity, the clarity of natural revelation, God's comprehensive control over creation, and so on. His appeal to the non-Christian contains much exposition of Reformed doctrine, in order that the unbeliever might know *what sort of* God is being argued for.[5] Thus, Gordon R. Lewis[6] and John W. Montgomery[7] charge that Van Til *confuses* apologetics with systematic theology. This criticism is mistaken, for it suggests that Van Til would merely proclaim doctrine to a non-Christian without evidence or argument. Even though "defense and positive statement go hand in hand," Van Til is quite capable of distinguishing between them, and he is self-consciously concerned to supplement the one with the other.[8] Yet the Lewis-Montgomery criticism shows a real insight into the structure of Van Til's thought, for in one sense it is indeed difficult to distinguish apologetics from systematic theology in Van Til's position. Though Van Til does clearly distinguish "positive statement" from "defense," and though in general he aligns the first with theology and the second with apologetics, he does insist that, because each is indispensable to the other, theology must have an apologetic thrust, and apologetics must expound theology. The difference between the two in practice, then, becomes a *difference in emphasis* rather than of subject matter.

This practical identification of the two disciplines makes Van Til's apologetics highly responsive to the demands of Reformed doctrine. But

---

2. Van Til, *Apologetics* (Syllabus, 1959), 3.

3. *Ibid.*, 4.

4. *Ibid.*, 4ff; cf. Van Til, *The Defense of the Faith* (Philadelphia: Presbyterian and Reformed, 1955), 23ff.

5. Note, for example, the treatment of creation, providence, prophecy, and miracle in Van Til's pamphlet, *Why I Believe in God* (Philadelphia: Orthodox Presbyterian Church, n.d.), 13-15.

6. In E. Geehan, ed., *Jerusalem and Athens* (Nutley, N. J.: Presbyterian and Reformed, 1971), 349.

7. In *ibid.*, 391f.

8. Van Til, *Apologetics*, 3f.; *Why I Believe in God*, 16. The idea that Van Til's apologetic substitutes proclamation for argument is frequently denied in Van Til's writings, but is nevertheless one of the most prevalent misunderstandings of his position.

the converse is also true: the traditional doctrines take on, in many cases, a very new appearance when put to Van Til's apologetic use. Unoriginal as his doctrinal formulations may be, his *use* of those formulations—his *application* of them—is often quite remarkable. The sovereignty of God becomes an epistemological, as well as a religious and metaphysical principle. The Trinity becomes the answer to the philosophical problem of the one and the many. Common grace becomes the key to a Christian philosophy of history.[9] These new applications of familiar doctrines inevitably increase our understanding of the doctrines themselves, for we come thereby to a new appreciation of what these doctrines demand of us. Sometimes these new understandings are of quite a radical sort— radical enough to require new formulations, or at least supplementary formulations, of the doctrines themselves. Van Til, as we have observed, rarely provides such revised formulations, though he does at some significant points, as we shall see. But there is much in Van Til that will require future orthodox Reformed dogmaticians to rethink much of the traditional language and thus to go beyond Van Til himself. Not that the traditional language is wrong (generally speaking); it is just that through reading Van Til we often become painfully aware of how much more needs to be said.

Thus, Van Til's theology, conventional and traditional as it may seem at first glance, is just as significant in its own way as is his apologetics. If Van Til has given a new epistemological self-consciousness to apologetics, then he has done the same for theology and all other types of Christian thought. If (as may well be said) Van Til has done for Christian thought what Kant accomplished for non-Christian thought, giving it a revolutionary awareness of the uniqueness and comprehensiveness of its distinctive principles, then as with Kant the "Copernican" radicalism of his contribution must be appreciated in all areas of human thought and life.

This paper attempts to set forth the contributions of Van Til to theology, both the "explicit" and the "implicit" ones. As suggested above, the importance of Van Til's contribution does not always lie on the surface. At times the logic of his position requires us to go beyond his explicit teachings, to say more than he himself says. I intend to suggest some areas where such is the case and also to suggest clarifications and corrections in Van Til's formulations where the genius of his own thought demands them.[10]

---

9. For references and further discussion on these matters, see below.

10. Here let me say a word on behalf of the need for *constructive critical analysis* of Van Til. Van Til, like any human thinker, is fallible. Those who love and honor him can pay him no higher service than to help him see his own weaknesses and thereby to increase the effectiveness of his future efforts. We must therefore be

Where shall we begin? In this sort of paper, one is often torn between focusing upon a thinker's *basic concerns* and focusing on his *distinctive teachings*. The two are not always the same. Van Til's concern is to be faithful to the biblical gospel: the sovereignty of God, the authority of Scripture, the reality of Christ's redemptive work in history, etc. But these concerns are also the concerns of many others—Augustine, Calvin, Kuyper, Warfield, many more. If we portray Van Til as, say, a "theologian of divine sovereignty," then how do we distinguish him from Calvin? Is it that Van Til is *more* concerned for divine sovereignty than was Calvin? Doubtful. Is it that Van Til *does more justice* to divine sovereignty than does Calvin? Well, perhaps. But if so, how does he do it? What we want to know is not so much what Van Til's concerns are, for these are obvious to anyone who reads Van Til, and are in any case the common property of the whole Christian church. We want to know, rather, how Van Til is able uniquely to implement these concerns in certain areas of controversy. What is it that is *distinctive* to Van Til? What does he do that Calvin, say, does not? Therefore, this paper will focus, not on Van Til's "basic concerns," but on his "distinctive teachings." The reader should be warned, however, that such a focus may distort the

---

greatly saddened by the fact that there has been *almost no* quality critical work done on Van Til's writings from sources sympathetic to his position. (a) Most critical work on Van Til has come from sources deeply *un*sympathetic to him—from "debunkers." Note in this connection James Daane, *A Theology of Grace* (Grand Rapids: Eerdmans, 1954), the contributions of Montgomery and Pinnock in *Jerusalem and Athens*, and many more. (b) Most *sympathetic* responses to Van Til have been utterly uncritical and generally non-analytical. They simply laud Van Til's positions and castigate his opponents without any serious wrestling with the issues Van Til raises. Such writers mean to do him tribute, yet meek acquiescence is hardly an adequate response, certainly no compliment, to a thinker who means to challenge us at the most profound intellectual and spiritual level. As an example of this tendency, note D. Vickers' review of *Jerusalem and Athens*, in *Westminster Theological Journal* XXXIV, 2 (May, 1972), 174-179. (c) A third group, the cosmonomic idea thinkers, has taken a middle ground, mingling appreciation of Van Til with criticism. Yet their critique of Van Til rests on a rather bizarre misinterpretation of his teaching—a misinterpretation resulting from their attempt to squeeze Van Til's thought into the rigid categories of their philosophical scheme. Cf. the contributions of Dooyeweerd and Knudsen in *Jerusalem and Athens*. (d) The best material on Van Til comes from the Chalcedon group— R. J. Rushdoony, Gary North, Gregory Bahnsen, and a few others such as Vern Poythress, a recent graduate of Westminster Seminary. These alone have made a truly creative use of Van Til's work, building on what he has done, applying it to areas which Van Til himself has not considered. We expect much of this in the present volume. Such *applications* of Van Til are most useful in themselves and provide implicitly an analytical perspective, thus distinguishing themselves from those treatments noted under (b). But this last group, like group (b), has generally refrained from criticism. Perhaps these men feel that they are better equipped to "apply" than to "critically analyze." But *someone* ought to get busy on the latter job. *Semper reformanda!* Great as Van Til's achievement is, the mind boggles at how much greater it might have been if Van Til had been surrounded by loving, appreciative, yet critically perceptive, fellow apologists.

shape of Van Til's system in a certain way. It may seem from this treatment that Van Til's thought is preoccupied with abstractions—unity and diversity, paradox and logic, analogy, epistemology, etc. Such, however, would be a false impression. These "abstract" concerns are fairly high on the list of Van Tillian "distinctives," but fairly low on a list of his "basic concerns." Van Til pursues such philosophical questions only in order to be faithful in his witness to Jesus Christ. *Far from being "preoccupied" with such abstractions, Van Til brings them up with reluctance, and only as a means of showing the implications of the gospel of God's saving grace.*

As I have hinted in the above caveat, I find Van Til's major distinctiveness in the area of theological introduction or "meta-theology"—the theology of theology, the study of theological method and structure. This area is sometimes called "theological prolegomena," a term which designates those things which must be "said before" theology may be done. Sometimes "prolegomena" is conceived of as not properly belonging to a theological system. Louis Berkhof and others fail to include the doctrine of Scripture in their major dogmatic works, relegating that doctrine to supplementary or "introductory" volumes, since they feel, apparently, that the doctrine of Scripture belongs to "prolegomena" and not to theology. Whatever may be said on behalf of this procedure, a "Van Tillian theologian" will wish to guard strongly against any implication that "prolegomena" is some kind of autonomous rational activity which *precedes* the believer's submission of his mind to God's Word. "Prolegomena" must be just as subject to Scripture as any area of theology—especially so, since prolegomena so greatly influences *every* phase of theological thinking. *All* our thoughts, "introductory" and otherwise, must be captive to the obedience of Christ (II Cor. 10:5). Thus I insist that in *one* sense, perhaps the most important sense, "prolegomena" is a properly theological discipline.

Yet prolegomena, or theological introduction,[11] deals with many matters which are more often associated with philosophy than with theology: questions of epistemology, of logic, of analogy, and so on. Distinctive to Van Til's thought in this area is a generalized reflection upon the *relation of unity to diversity* in the theological organism. In my view, Van Til is the first orthodox Christian thinker to have studied this question in a distinctively theological way. This is what I take to be *Van Til's most distinctive contribution to theology.* Only a man with his philosophical background could have attacked such a problem, but only a man with

---

11. I prefer the second designation for reasons discussed in the previous paragraph. So does Van Til, although, so far as I know, he has never explicitly stated the argument I have presented.

his profoundly biblical commitment could have adopted his distinctive approach.

In the rest of this paper, I shall discuss Van Til's concept of the Christian "system of truth." The analysis will focus on the various sorts of "unities" and "diversities" to be found among the various Christian doctrines. In particular, I shall ask in what ways the various doctrines are "interdependent"—in what ways they "require one another"—and, on the other hand, in what sense these doctrines are "paradoxically" related. In the course of the discussion, I concern myself not merely with these methodological questions. I will explore many of Van Til's specific doctrinal teachings, some in passing, others at length.

Is there a "system" of Christian truth? Surely that is an important "introductory" consideration to theology, especially systematic theology! It has been a controversial question: Kierkegaard and Barth have condemned the very idea of a doctrinal "system" as an affront to God, as a human attempt to master and manipulate God's revelation. On the other hand, E. J. Carnell set forth something called "systematic consistency" as the final test of religious truth.[12] What does Van Til say? Typically, his answer carries with it a demand for further analysis: it all depends on what you mean by "system." In one sense, yes, there is such a system; in another sense, no. Thus, at times Van Til appears unequivocally to endorse the idea of "system," while at other times he seems to attack it.

I. Pro-System

Van Til's endorsement of "system" begins with the consideration that God himself is "exhaustively comprehensible to himself."[13] God's self-knowledge is in no way defective; it is in perfect order. And to say this is to say, in one sense, that God's knowledge is "systematic": ". . . there must be in God an absolute system of knowledge."[14] This knowledge includes knowledge not only of God himself but also of His works. Since God has planned and controls all things, "All created reality therefore actually displays this plan. It is, in consequence, inherently rational."[18] *God, therefore, has a "systematic" knowledge of himself and of the world, since He knows His own plan exhaustively and since the world perfectly conforms to that plan.*

---

12. E. J. Carnell, *An Introduction to Christian Apologetics* (Grand Rapids: Eerdmans, 1948), 56ff.

13. Van Til, "Nature and Scripture," in N. Stonehouse and P. Woolley, ed., *The Infallible Word* (Philadelphia: Presbyterian and Reformed, 3rd revised printing, 1967), 277.

14. Van Til, *The Defense of the Faith*, 61. Cf. "God is absolute rationality. He was and is the only self-contained whole, the system of absolute truth," *An Introduction to Systematic Theology* (Syllabus, 1961), 10.

Because of this absolute divine system of truth, *true knowledge is available to men.* God has created the world and us, adapting each to the other according to His rational plan. "We see then that our knowledge of the universe must be true since we are creatures of God who has made both us and the universe."[14] God's rationality vindicates human knowledge: "We say that if there is to be any true knowledge at all there must be in God an absolute system of knowledge."[14] This human knowledge is not "exhaustive" or "comprehensive"; only God has that sort of knowledge. But it is, or is capable of being, genuinely true.[15] Even more: with regard to "the existence of God and the truth of Christian theism," there is "absolutely certain proof."[16] Not only do we have *true* knowledge of God, but *certain* knowledge as well. God is *clearly* revealed, so that His existence and the truth of His word is not just "possible" or "probable," but certain.[17] There *is* a cogent "theistic proof."[18]

This knowledge of God available to man is "systematic" in two related senses. In the first place, it is "systematic" in the sense of being *internally coherent:*

> But I do, of course, confess that what Scripture teaches may properly be spoken of as a system of truth. God identifies the Scriptures as his Word. And he himself, as he tells us, exists as an internally self-coherent being. His revelation of himself to man cannot be anything but internally coherent. When therefore the Bible teaches that God controls by his plan, whatever comes to pass, it does not also teach that God does not control whatever comes to pass. If such were the case, God's promises and threats would be meaningless.[19]

There is no "real contradiction" in God's revelation. It cannot be the case that "the same ultimate will of God wills, and yet wills not, the salvation of sinners."[20] There can be no "contradiction between the secret and revealed wills of God."[21] Note also:

---

15. Van Til, *An Introduction to Systematic Theology,* 24, 164; *The Defense of the Faith,* 60; "Nature and Scripture," 277.

16. Van Til, *The Defense of the Faith,* 120; *Apologetics,* 64.

17. Van Til, *An Introduction to Systematic Theology,* 114f.; *Apologetics,* 13; "Nature and Scripture," 278f.

18. Van Til, *An Introduction to Systematic Theology,* 102ff., 196; *The Defense of the Faith,* 196; *A Christian Theory of Knowledge* (Nutley, N. J.: Presbyterian and Reformed, 1969), 292; *Common Grace and the Gospel* (Nutley, N. J.: Presbyterian and Reformed, 1972), 179ff., 190ff. In this note I have indulged in a bit of referential overkill, because this point is often missed. Van Til is not simply opposed to the theistic proofs as students often imagine. On the contrary, he gives them strong endorsement. But he insists that they be formulated in a distinctively Christian way, rejecting any "proof" based on a non-Christian epistemology.

19. Van Til, *The Defense of the Faith,* 205. Cf. *A Christian Theory of Knowledge,* 38f.

20. Van Til, *Common Grace and the Gospel,* 76.

21. Van Til, *An Introduction to Systematic Theology,* 251.

God can reveal only that which is consistent with his nature as a self-identified being. The law of identity in human logic must be seen to be resting upon the character of God and therefore upon the authoritative revelation of God. But to say that God is both omnipotent and not omnipotent, because conditioned by the ultimate determinations of his creatures, is to remove the very foundation of the law of identity. This is irrationalism. It allows the legitimacy of the non-Christian principle of individuation, namely chance.[22]

Related to this internal coherence of God's revelation is a slightly different sense in which the revelation may be said to be "systematic": there are *relations of dependence* among biblical doctrines. Some may be said to be "fundamental" to others. Some, in fact, are "fundamental" to the whole system.

> Naturally, in the system of theology and in apologetics the *doctrine of God* is of fundamental importance. *In apologetics it must always be the final if not the first point of attack.* In theology the main questions deal with the existence and the nature of God.[23]
> Fundamental to everything orthodox is the presupposition of the antecedent self-existence of God and of his infallible revelation of himself to man in the Bible.[24]
> First and foremost among the attributes, we therefore mention the independence or self-existence of God. . . .[25]

Another "central" doctrine is the historical fall of Adam: only if we take the fall as historical can a sound theology be maintained.[26] "Temporal creation" is another doctrine with which "Christianity stands or falls."[27] Furthermore, predestination, as Warfield says, is the "central doctrine of the Reformation."[28] And the Trinity is the "heart of Christianity."[29]

More specifically, there are doctrines which Van Til sets forth as necessitating other doctrines:

> . . . the Christian-theistic conception of an absolute God and an absolute Christ and an absolute Scripture go hand in hand. We cannot accept one without accepting the others.[30]

Self-contained God implies self-attesting revelation.[31] The doctrine of

---

22. Van Til, *A Christian Theory of Knowledge*, 202, cf. 38f.
23. Van Til, *Apologetics*, 4 (emphasis his). Cf. *A Christian Theory of Knowledge*, 12, *The Defense of the Faith*, 59.
24. Van Til, *An Introduction to Systematic Theology*, 1.
25. *Ibid.*, 206.
26. Van Til, *An Introduction to Systematic Theology*, 29.
27. Van Til, *The Defense of the Faith*, 229.
28. Van Til, *The Theology of James Daane* (Philadelphia: Presbyterian and Reformed, 1959), 76.
29. Van Til, *The Defense of the Faith*, 28.
30. Van Til, *Christian-Theistic Ethics* (n.p.: den Dulk Foundation, 1971), 28.
31. Van Til, *The Defense of the Faith*, 203; cf. *An Introduction to Systematic Theology*, 62, "Introduction," to B. B. Warfield, *The Inspiration and Authority of the Bible* (Philadelphia: Presbyterian and Reformed, 1948), 36f., *A Christian Theory of Knowledge*, 70.

analogical knowledge is a "corollary" from the doctrine of the Trinity.[32] Man's knowledge is true "because," not in spite of, the fact that it is "analogical."[32] Man's being and action are genuinely his own "because of" (again, not "in spite of") "the more ultimate being and activity on the part of the will of God."[33] The *personality of God* (and hence the ultimately *personal character of man's environment*) becomes the key to avoiding determinist and indeterminist conceptions[34]—a somewhat surprising idea at first glance, but worked out cogently by Van Til. For one thing, denial of the self-sufficient holiness of God entails denial also of temporal creation and historical Fall.[35] For another, "God is free not in spite of but because of the necessity of his nature."[36] Therefore, "deny the doctrine of creation and you have denied the Christian concept of God."[37] The creation of man in God's image is at the same time a "presupposition of revelation" and a "corollary from the notion of an absolutely self-conscious God."[38]

Van Til's stress on the interdependence of biblical doctrines can be seen from the following examples of his reasoning. The providential involvement of God in all created things and events, His all-foreordaining direction of the world (so characteristic of Reformed theology), requires a distinctively Reformed view of Scripture.[39] To deny biblical authority is to assert one's autonomy or independence of God's control.[40] The differences between Calvinism and Arminianism require a difference in apologetic method.[41] Christian ethics presupposes double predestination.[42] To deny the historicity of the fall is to deny the directness of revelation in history.[43] Modernism, Barthianism,[44] and Arminianism, because of their distinctive teachings, cannot do justice to the biblical

32. Van Til, *A Survey of Christian Epistemology* (n.p.: den Dulk Foundation, 1969), 48; cf. 97.

33. Van Til, *Apologetics*, 11.

34. Van Til, *A Survey of Christian Epistemology*, 67f.; *Christian-Theistic Ethics*, 35, 48. Note also the account of the centrality of God's absolute personality in *The Defense of the Faith*, 29, 59.

35. Van Til, *An Introduction to Systematic Theology*, 244.

36. *Ibid.*, 177.

37. Van Til, *The Defense of the Faith*, 231.

38. Van Til, *An Introduction to Systematic Theology*, 63.

39. Van Til, *The Doctrine of Scripture* (den Dulk Foundation, 1967), 37; *The Defense of the Faith*, 202; *The Sovereignty of Grace* (Nutley, N. J.: Presbyterian and Reformed, 1969), 63.

40. Van Til, *An Introduction to Systematic Theology*, 139.

41. Van Til, *The Defense of the Faith*, 35.

42. Van Til, *The Theology of James Daane*, 118f.

43. Van Til, *A Christian Theory of Knowledge*, 47.

44. Van Til, *Christianity and Barthianism; The New Modernism*.

doctrine of grace.[45] Secondary causes in the universe have genuine significance "not in spite of, but just because of the fact that they act in accord with the one ultimate *Cause* or plan of God."[46] To summarize and generalize:

> A truly Protestant method of reasoning involves a stress upon the fact that the meaning of every aspect or part of Christian theism depends upon Christian theism as a unit . . . the whole claim of Christian theism is in question in any debate about any fact.[47]

> The starting point, the method, and the conclusion are always involved in one another.[48]

No other American theological writer gives his readers such a profound sense of the *unity* of Christian truth. Again and again we learn that to affirm one doctrine is to affirm another and to affirm the whole; to deny one doctrine is to deny another and to deny the whole. All doctrines are interdependent; the parts depend on the whole; the whole depends on the parts. In this emphasis, Van Til has given Reformed theology much to think about. Any one of the relationships listed above might be made the subject of a theological treatise. Why is it that the self-contained nature of God implies that His revelation be self-attesting? A theologian could spend a great number of pages arguing that point. Van Til himself rarely argues for any of these relationships at any great length. To him they are virtually self-evident. Yet fuller explorations of these matters could bring much edification to the church. How is it, for example, that denial of creation involves denial of God? An answer to that question could help us see the importance of creation in a new way.

Further, the formula "not in spite of, but because of," which recurs so often in Van Til's thought, places a substantial challenge before theologians as they deal with apparent contradictions in biblical teaching. Have we too often been content merely to point out the *consistency* of biblical doctrines when the Bible itself would have us do more? Have we been content merely to show that human responsibility is *compatible with* divine foreordination, rather than showing that human responsibility *depends upon* divine foreordination and is inconceivable without it? If we are going to do the latter, some hard thinking may be necessary. We will certainly have to go beyond the elliptical, highly summarized arguments of Van Til's own writings. Yet the rewards will be great.

---

45. Van Til, *An Introduction to Systematic Theology*, 239; *The Theology of James Daane*, 122.

46. Van Til, *The Defense of the Faith*, 207; cf. 267ff., *Common Grace and the Gospel*, 73, cf. 65ff. As should be evident by now, the formula "not in spite of, but because of" is one of the *leitmotifs* of Van Til's thought.

47. Van Til, *Apologetics*, 73.

48. *Ibid.*, 62.

Van Til's approach here also has another interesting ramification. To-day there is much concern in theology as to the "central focus" of the Christian revelation. Many theologies have arisen attempting to persuade us of the "centrality" of something or other in the Christian faith: theologies of the Word, of "crisis," of personal encounter, of divine acts, of history, of hope, of self-understanding, of celebration, of covenant law, of doxology, and so on. Van Til's emphasis reminds us, however, that *there are many "central" doctrines of the faith*, not just one single one. And further, any scheme which would dismiss *any* teaching of Scripture as unimportant or false must be rejected. *In Christianity, the "central" doctrines do not become central by cancelling out other scriptural teachings; rather, they undergird and support and necessitate those other doctrines.* Though Van Til himself does not say this, his thought suggests the desirability of an orthodox Christian "perspectival" approach to theology: *each major doctrine provides a "perspective" in terms of which the whole of Christianity can be viewed.* The atonement, for example, presupposes certain attributes of God, a certain doctrine of sin, a definite conception of redemptive history; and it in turn generates a further history of redemptive application. The seventh commandment, to use another example, pro-vides a "perspective" upon *all* sin; for idolatry is a form of adultery in Scripture, and idolatry is the essence of sin in general. Thus, all sin is adultery of a sort; and all sin is theft (theft of what is due to God); and all sin is false witness (exchanging the truth of God for a lie). Each of the ten commandments presents a characterization which applies to *all* sin and which therefore defines *all* righteousness. Thus, in Chris-tianity, each major doctrine[49] provides a certain "perspective" upon the *whole* of Christian truth. Each one can be "central." The use of *various* centers at various times can enrich our understanding of Scripture.

II.   Anti-System

Thus far, I have been intentionally vague as to the precise logical re-lations among Christian doctrines. Van Til's language is not the precise language of a modern logician. One doctrine can "require" or "necessi-tate" another in various ways. To say that one doctrine is true "because" of another is to speak with some ambiguity: even Aristotle recognized four senses of "because." And even when Van Til uses more technical logical terms like "corollary" and "entail," it is not clear that he is using them in their technical senses.

---

49. Even for Van Til, I assume, not all doctrines are "major." "Abraham lived in Ur of the Chaldees" is not as "central" as the doctrine of the Trinity. Yet the line between "major" and "minor" is not sharp, and even "minor" doctrines are systematically related to major ones. Specifically, they presuppose the reliability of Scripture, which in turn presupposes the whole Christian worldview.

One might conclude from what was said above that Van Til regards Christianity as a deductive system in which each doctrine, taken by itself, *logically* implies all the others. Van Til, however, explicitly *denies* this notion. There is no "master concept" from which the whole of Christian doctrine may be logically deduced.[50] But then in what sense is the self-contained character of God "central" to Christianity? In what sense does this doctrine "require" a certain doctrine of Scripture, of Christ, etc.?

Even more perplexing is Van Til's attitude toward the logical consistency of Christian doctrines. We have seen earlier that Van Til affirms the "internal coherence" of the Christian system and attacks positions which introduce contradictions into that system. The natural assumption is that this coherence is a logical coherence. Doesn't he say that "The rules of formal logic must be followed in all our attempts at systematic exposition of God's revelation, whether general or special"?[51] And yet at the same time Van Til teaches that the Christian system is full of "apparent contradictions":

> Now since God is not fully comprehensible to us we are bound to come into what seems to be contradiction in all our knowledge. Our knowledge is analogical and therefore must be paradoxical.[52]

> . . . while we shun as poison the idea of the really contradictory we embrace with passion the idea of the *apparently* contradictory.[53]

> All teaching of Scripture is apparently contradictory.[54]

Let us look at some specific examples. With regard to the doctrine of the Trinity, Van Til denies that the paradox of the three and one can be resolved by the formula "one in essence and three in person." Rather, "We do assert that God, that is, the whole Godhead, is one person."[55] Van Til's doctrine, then, can be expressed "One person, three persons"— an apparent contradiction. This is a very bold theological move. Theologians are generally most reluctant to express the paradoxicality of this doctrine so blatantly. Why does Van Til insist on making things so difficult? In the context, he says he adopts this formula to "avoid the specter of brute fact." (Brute fact, in Van Til's terminology, is uninterpreted being.) The argument here is somewhat elliptical, but if we fill in some missing premises, it seems to go like this: If we deny that God is one person,

50. Van Til, *The Defense of the Faith*, 205; cf. 227, *A Christian Theory of Knowledge*, 38.
51. Van Til, *Common Grace and the Gospel*, 28. On p. 143 he refers approvingly to Kuyper's view that "all men have to think according to the rules of logic according to which alone the human mind can function." Cf. also references in notes 19-22, above.
52. Van Til, *The Defense of the Faith*, 61.
53. Van Til, *Common Grace and the Gospel*, 9.
54. *Ibid.*, 142.
55. Van Til, *An Introduction to Systematic Theology*, 229.

then the unity among Father, Son, and Holy Spirit becomes an *impersonal* unity. The diversities among the three in that case would not be functions of personal planning and interpretation; rather these diversities would "just happen" to exist. Such a view would in effect place an impersonal "chance" or impersonal "fate" behind and above the persons of the Godhead. Somehow, then, the three persons must function in such *intimate interdependence* that it may be truly said that *the three are one person.*[56] Bold as it may seem, this view not only conforms to the metaphysical teachings implicit in Scripture but also to the simple language by which Scripture refers to God. Scripture, after all, *does* refer to God as one person. It distinguishes among Father, Son, and Holy Spirit; yet very often it speaks of God as a person without mentioning those distinctions. It is true, as the traditional formulae suggest, that God is one in one respect, three in another respect. Such language is necessary to guard against the possibility of a "real contradiction," a chaos, in the Godhead. Yet Scripture does not clearly specify the "respect" in which God is three as over against the "respect" in which God is one. In other words, Scripture leaves us with an "apparent contradiction" here. God is one, and God is three. And Van Til's view gives us an important warning not to go beyond Scripture in this matter.

Van Til treats the relation between God's nature and His attributes in the same way as he treats the trinitarian question: ". . . the unity and the diversity in God are equally basic and mutually dependent upon one another."[57] *God is one and God is many*—that, it seems, is the best we can do. The apparent contradiction might be resolved if we could specify in what respects, precisely, God is one and many, but to do so would be to go beyond Scripture and to raise again "the specter of brute fact." Cosmic impersonalism would again be a threat.

The necessity and freedom of God's will are also paradoxically related according to Van Til. If God's will is directed by His intelligence, then His free acts (creating the world, for example) become necessary: God *had* to create. If, on the other hand, God's free acts are truly free, then it would seem that they must be unconnected with His intelligence and therefore random: God *just happened* to create. Neither alternative is

---

56. The term "person" has a rather different meaning in its modern use from any meaning attached to it (Greek: *hypostasis*) at the time of the Nicene creedal formulation. Van Til's use is more like the modern than like the ancient. Still, it is important to ask about God's "personality" in the modern sense. Scripture does describe God as what *we* would call a "person"—one who thinks, plans, loves, creates, judges, speaks, etc. It is important, then, to ask as Van Til does how "personality" in *this* sense is related to the doctrine of the Trinity. And I believe that Van Til's conclusion is not different from the one we would have to draw with regard to the ancient usage of *hypostasis*.

57. Van Til, *The Defense of the Faith*, 26; cf. *An Introduction to Systematic Theology*, 229.

biblical; nevertheless, Scripture requires us to affirm the intelligence *and* freedom of God's acts. Van Til does suggest that we need to distinguish between two kinds of necessity—the necessity of God's nature and that necessity by which His free acts come about. But, he adds, "this is as far as our finite minds can reach."[58] There is no definitive and final solution for finite thought. Again, the apparent contradiction could be resolved if we could specify the precise differences between the two "necessities," but God has not revealed those differences.

Van Til's paradigm case of the concept of "apparent contradiction" is what he calls the "full-bucket difficulty." *God is self-sufficient;* He needs nothing outside himself; He cannot become greater than He is, in knowledge, love, power, glory, for a greater than God is inconceivable. Nevertheless, *He creates a world for His own glory*—to obtain more glory, to enter into significant knowledge; love- and power-relationships which He would not have entered otherwise. In other words, on the one hand, God's knowledge, love, power, and glory *preclude* addition; on the other hand they *demand* addition.[59] The course of history is somehow significant and important for God, even though that whole course is completely known to God before it begins.[60] Secondary causes are significant and important (again, for God!—God is the determiner of significance), even though God's primary causality controls all that comes to pass.[61] Again, if we could determine more precisely *what sort of* significance world history has for God, then the "contradiction" would drop away. Evidently, there is one sense in which secondary causes *are* "significant" and another sense in which they are *not.* Yet God has not chosen to give us information by which these difficulties might be resolved.

Does God's plan "include" evil? Yes and no. God brings evil to pass, but He is not therefore to be blamed for it. God foreordains sin, but man is not forced to sin. God ordains the damnation of the reprobates, but that gives them no excuse.[62] Apparent contradictions again. But we should note that here, as in the previous cases, Van Til also approves a non-contradictory formulation:

> Thus all Reformed Confessions and all Reformed always reject the *eodem modo* idea. It is abhorrent to any true believer to make God the author of sin, to say that God is as much interested in the

---

58. Van Til, *An Introduction to Systematic Theology,* 249f., cf. 176ff. Note also the reference in note 36 above, where Van Til says that God's will is free *because* it is necessary. Van Til can state that two concepts are "apparently contradictory" while at the same time making the one logically dependent upon the other.

59. Van Til, *Common Grace and the Gospel,* 10; *The Defense of the Faith,* 61f.

60. Van Til, *Common Grace and the Gospel,* 28.

61. *Ibid.,* 73ff., 141f.; *The Defense of the Faith,* 207ff., 245, 267ff., 269ff.

62. Van Til, *An Introduction to Systematic Theology,* 248; "Nature and Scripture," 271; *Christian-Theistic Ethics,* 36, 139.

death of the sinner as in the blessedness of the saved. God's decree is not *in the same manner* back of reprobation as of election. The counsel of God is *primarily* concerned with the establishment of God's kingdom through Christ. There must be no equal ultimacy of election and reprobation that forgets this fact.[63]

God does not ordain damnation (or, by implication, any other evil) *in the same way* as He ordains good. Somehow the word "ordain" does not designate quite the same sort of divine act in the two cases. Somehow God's plan does not both "include" evil and "exclude" it in the same respect. Yet divine revelation does not tell us precisely in what respect God's plan includes evil and in what respect it excludes it. Thus, a paradox remains for us, though by faith we are confident that there is no paradox for God. Faith is basic to the salvation of our knowledge as well as the salvation of our souls.

In other doctrinal areas also, Van Til formulates his positions in strikingly paradoxical ways. The traditional distinction between the image of God in the "wider" sense (man's personality, moral agency) and the image in the "narrower" sense (knowledge of God, righteousness, holiness) Van Til accepts as only "relatively satisfactory."[64] If pressed, he argues, this distinction would imply that man's personality as created by God has no ethical character—historically a Roman Catholic position rejected by the Reformation.[65] Is it possible, he asks, for the image in the "narrower" sense to be wholly lost in the Fall while the image in the "wider" sense is left entirely intact? Though Van Til does not spell out an alternative view in any precise way, he seems to move in the direction of saying: The image is lost (in some sense) and also remains (in some sense). Since the precise senses are not specified, we are left with a paradoxical formulation. Yet to call such a formulation "contradictory" would be to ignore the fact that specification of the senses is possible in principle, and God is surely capable of specifying them.

Note also: (1) Van Til's view of mankind existing and yet not existing in Adam as its representative;[66] (2) his view that apart from common grace, sin would and would not have destroyed the creative work of God;[67] (3) his view that the unregenerate man is both able and unable to know the truth;[68] (4) his view that the significance of human actions is both guaranteed by, and rendered logically problematic by, the all-controlling

---

63. Van Til, *The Theology of James Daane*, 90.
64. Van Til, *Christian-Theistic Ethics*, 46; cf. *The Defense of the Faith*, 29.
65. Van Til, *Common Grace and the Gospel*, 202ff.
66. Van Til, *The Defense of the Faith*, 249ff.
67. Van Til, *Common Grace and the Gospel*, 199f.
68. Van Til, *An Introduction to Systematic Theology*, 26, 112f.

plan of God;[69] (5) his view of Chalcedon as an acceptance of and formulation of apparently contradictory biblical teaching.[70] In all of these matters, Van Til appears to deny that any fully satisfactory non-paradoxical formulation is possible. Still, in each of these cases (as in the ones discussed more fully in the preceding paragraphs), the "apparent contradiction" appears to arise from our ignorance concerning the precise senses of certain key terms.[71] So construing the problem, it is not difficult for us to assume that the paradoxes are resolvable for one who has more complete or exhaustive knowledge of the truth. Surely we must assume that they are resolvable in God's own thought, and thus not "really" contradictory.

Yet for us men, with the revelation now available to us (which in Van Til's view is sufficient and will not be increased before the return of Christ), the necessity of formulating doctrines in "apparently contradictory" ways certainly increases the difficulty of developing a "system of doctrine," especially a system such as Van Til himself advocates, wherein all doctrines are profoundly interdependent, wherein one doctrine is frequently said to "require" another. How may it be shown that one doctrine "requires" another, when our paradoxical formulations fail even to show how the two are compatible? His stress on apparent contradiction, though it does not render Christianity irrational or illogical, does seem at least to make very difficult if not impossible the task of the systematic theologian. Does this emphasis amount to an anti-system polemic which in effect contradicts his pro-system theme?

III. The Analogical System

Van Til reconciles his pro-system statements with his view of "apparent contradiction" by means of his doctrine of analogical reasoning. Only one kind of "system" is possible if we are to be true to God's revelation: an "analogical" system.[72] What does Van Til mean by "analogical system" and "analogical reasoning"?

On first hearing these phrases, we might suppose that Van Til here is advocating a doctrine about Christian religious language—that such language is "analogical," figurative, as opposed to being "literal." The term "analogical" is often used this way in theological and philosophical litera-

---

69. Van Til, The Theology of James Daane, 64f.; cf. references in note 46 above. By "logically problematic" I mean that for Van Til the relation of human responsibility to God's plan must invariably be formulated in an "apparently contradictory" fashion.

70. Van Til, The Defense of the Faith, 205.

71. Van Til does not himself suggest that the paradoxes turn on such ambiguities; yet all his examples of "apparent contradiction" may be analyzed in such a way.

72. Van Til, The Doctrine of Scripture, 123; A Christian Theory of Knowledge, 38; Jerusalem and Athens, 126.

ture, especially when contrasted with "univocal," as it is in Van Til. It is evident, however, that Van Til's concept of analogy is a doctrine about human reasoning (even human life!) in general, not about religious language in particular. He rarely if ever discusses the religious language question, and he never discusses it in contexts where the concept of "analogy" is prominent. There are two passages in his writings where analogous reasoning is said to legitimize certain "anthropomorphic" expressions.[73] However, in view of Van Til's usual accounts of "analogy" (see below), I would hold that in those two passages, the term "anthropomorphic" means "from a human perspective" in a broad sense, and not the more narrow formulation, "utilizing figures comparing God to man." Van Til may well hold (though he never says so) that since revelation presents God to us "from a human perspective," it often presents God in figurative terms. Yet he has never taught that *all* language about God is figurative, and there is nothing in his thought that demands such a conclusion.

Rather than such a doctrine about language, Van Til's view of analogy is essentially this: analogous reasoning is reasoning which presupposes as its ultimate basis the reality of the biblical God and the authority of His revelation. We shall analyze this concept under three headings: analogy and God, analogy and revelation, analogy and logic.

A. *Analogy and God*

> The necessity of reasoning analogically is always implied in the theistic conception of God. If God is to be thought of at all as necessary for man's interpretation of the facts or objects of knowledge, he must be thought of as being determinative of the objects of knowledge. In other words, he must then be thought of as the only ultimate interpreter, and man must be thought of as a finite reinterpreter. Since, then, the absolute self-consciousness of God is the final interpreter of all facts, man's knowledge is analogical of God's knowledge. Since all the finite facts exist by virtue of the interpretation of God, man's interpretation of the finite facts is ultimately dependent upon God's interpretation of the facts. Man cannot, except to his own hurt, look at the facts without looking at God's interpretation of the facts. Man's knowledge of the facts is then a reinterpretation of God's interpretation. It is this that is meant by saying that man's knowledge is analogical of God's knowledge.[74]

Analogical reasoning begins with the assumption that God is both the ultimate *source* of all facts and the ultimate *interpreter* of all facts. Man, therefore, can be "creative" and "interpretative" only in a secondary way. He may create and interpret only that which has *already* been created

---

73. Van Til, *Common Grace and the Gospel*, 73; *A Christian Theory of Knowledge*, 37.
74. Van Til, *A Survey of Christian Epistemology*, 203f.

and interpreted by God. Man does not ultimately determine the nature and meaning of the world; rather, he is born into a world which God has already structured, and he must, willingly or not, live with that God-ordained structure.

Therefore, "God's knowledge is archetypal and ours ectypal."[75] God's thought is "creatively constructive" while ours is "receptively reconstructive."[76] God "interprets absolutely" while man is the "re-interpreter of God's interpretation."[77]

This distinction is both a fact and a norm. It is a *fact*, because human thought *in the nature of the case* can be nothing else than "reinterpretation." It may be a faithful or faithless reinterpretation; it may be a true or false reinterpretation; it may be admittedly reinterpretative or allegedly autonomous; but it cannot help but be reinterpretation, for that is what God made it to be. The distinction is also a *norm:* if our thinking is to be sound and true and right, then it *ought to acknowledge* its character as reinterpretation; it ought to take its actual status as reinterpretation into account; it ought to presuppose that status in all its work. Thus, the fact of our created status entails our obligation to "think as creatures,"[78] to think in a way appropriate to our creaturely status. Analogical reasoning, then, for Van Til, is human thought which is not only reinterpretative (as *all* human thought must be), but which acknowledges its character as reinterpretation and seeks to think in a way appropriate to creatures.

Analogical reasoning, then, is not only dependent upon God, but *self-consciously dependent.* God is not only its creator and sustainer, but also its "ultimate reference point of predication."[79] Analogical reasoning recognizes God as the final authority, the ultimate criterion of truth and falsehood, right and wrong, possibility and impossibility. Our interpretation must be submissive to the authoritative interpretation of God.[80]

This view implies both a continuity and a discontinuity between God's thoughts and those of human analogical reasoning. There is *continuity* because the very nature of analogical reasoning is to agree with God, to conform to God's own thought. But there is also *discontinuity,* for human thought, even analogical human thought, can never be divine. Human thought can never be the ultimate interpretation, the ultimate reference point. Analogical thought, again by its very nature, confesses its creatureli-

---

75. Van Til, *An Introduction to Systematic Theology*, 203. The terminology is from Kuyper's *Encyclopedia.*

76. *Ibid.*, 126.

77. Van Til, *The Defense of the Faith*, 64.

78. Van Til, *Common Grace and the Gospel*, 205.

79. Van Til, *An Introduction to Systematic Theology*, 101.

80. Van Til, *The Doctrine of Scripture*, 15.

ness, its non-divinity. The slogan "thinking God's thoughts after him"[81] reflects both the continuity and the discontinuity: we think God's thoughts (continuity) *after* Him (discontinuity).

Thus, just as it is important for us to *agree* with God, so it is equally important to *distinguish* our thoughts from His. God reveals himself to us, not exhaustively, but "according to man's ability to receive his revelation."[82] We do not know God the same way He knows himself. Without such discontinuity, the continuities mentioned earlier would be meaningless, for if we cannot clearly distinguish between our thoughts and God's, how can we regard the latter as authoritative for the former? Van Til, therefore, even acknowledges a sense in which man himself is a kind of "starting-point" for thought: he is a "proximate" starting-point, while God is the "ultimate" starting-point.[83] God is our final authority; but for that very reason we must be content to think as human beings.

So far, Van Til's position is generally straightforward, and it is hard to see how it could offend any Bible-believing Christian. However, Van Til's view of the continuity and discontinuity between human and divine thought (sketched above) precipitated within Bible-believing Christian circles one of the most heated controversies in Van Til's controversial career—the debate over the "incomprehensibility of God," otherwise known as the "Clark case."[84] In that controversy, the argument focused on Van Til's statement that there is no "identity of content between what God has in his mind and what man has in his mind."[85] As I understand it, this statement is merely another way of asserting the "discontinuity" between divine and human thought which we have discussed above. It sets forth the *same* discontinuity we have already noted, and not some further discontinuity in addition to that one. To deny "identity of content" between God's thought and man's is, for Van Til, simply to assert the Creator-creature distinction in the area of thought. God's concept of a rose, let us say, is different "in content" from man's, because God's concept is the original and ours is derivative; His is self-justifying, while ours must be justified by reference to His. So far as I can see, this is *all* Van Til means to say in denying "identity of content."

I would argue, however (with the benefit of hindsight), that in making

---

81. Van Til uses this slogan: cf. *A Christian Theory of Knowledge*, 16, "Nature and Scripture," 271.

82. Van Til, *A Christian Theory of Knowledge*, 37.

83. Van Til, *An Introduction to Systematic Theology*, 203; cf. *The Doctrine of Scripture*, 14. Cf. also the opening section of Calvin's *Institutes*.

84. The protagonists in the controversy were Van Til and Gordon H. Clark, a well-known Christian apologist and philosopher. I shall not discuss Clark's position, since my purpose is rather to analyze Van Til's.

85. Van Til, *An Introduction to Systematic Theology*, 165; cf. 171ff. Cf. also Van Til, "Introduction" in B. B. Warfield, *The Inspiration and Authority of the Bible*, 33.

such a statement Van Til was somewhat unwise in his choice of terminology. "Content" is an exceedingly ambiguous term when applied to thought. The "content" of my thought may mean (1) my mental images, (2) my beliefs, (3) the things I am thinking of, (4) the epistemological processes by which knowledge is acquired (including the roles of sense-experience, intuition reason, etc.), (5) the meaning of my language, conceived in abstraction from the linguistic forms used to state that meaning, (6) anything at all to which the physical metaphor "contained in the mind" may conceivably apply. In senses (2) and (3), there seems to be no reason to assert any necessary "difference in content" between divine and human thought. Surely God and man may have the same beliefs and may think about the same things. As for (1) and (4), Scripture tells us very little about the processes of divine thought—how He knows what He knows, whether He has mental images or not, if so what they are like, etc. Doubtless there are continuities and discontinuities in these areas, but the whole question borders on the speculative. As for (5), surely there is an *identity of meaning* between God's words and ours at least on those occasions when God uses human language. Van Til himself, I think, has sense (6) in mind when he denies "identity of content" between divine and human thought. And with that meaning Van Til's assertion is obviously true. There is "in" God's mind what can never be "in" any man's mind, namely, *ultimate authority* and *creative power*. Man can never know fully what it is like to think with such self-validating autonomy. Epistemological lordship attaches to *every* thought God has, and to *no* thought any man ever has. Thus there is, with regard to any item of knowledge, always something "in" God's mind different from anything "in" man's. Yet the preposition "in" here is rather metaphorical, as is the term "content" in sense (6); it is further a rather vague metaphor, one which does not specify with any precision the *sort of* discontinuity Van Til wishes to assert. Still further, it tends to obscure the *continuities* upon which Van Til himself has placed such emphasis—that we must have the *same* opinions God has, that we must think about the *same* matters that God speaks of in His revelation, that we must attach the *same* meanings to God's words that He does, that our thinking must have the same "reference point" God's thinking has (namely, divine authority).[86] To assert without further definition a difference in "content" between divine and human thought obscures the senses in which divine and human thought ought to have the *same* content.[87]

---

86. Van Til, *An Introduction to Systematic Theology*, 165—above the previously cited passage.

87. I might point out another terminological problem which may also have hindered communication during the "Clark case." In my view, it was unfortunate that this controversy was ever described as a controversy over the "incomprehensi-

Whatever we may think about the "content" terminology, however, we cannot deny the basic points Van Til is making here about analogical reasoning: (1) our thought must *conform* to God's, His thought being the ultimate standard of truth; and (2) we must *not confuse* our thought with God's, for ours is *not* ultimate, *not* self-validating.

B. *Analogy and Revelation*

If analogous reasoning means bringing our creaturely thoughts into accord with (but not into identity with) God's divine thoughts, how is this to be done? Certainly not by direct inspection of the divine thought-processes, as if I could distinguish an apple from a tomato by comparing them with duplicates in God's mind.[88] That sort of Platonism is far from Van Til's position. Van Til rather affirms with all Reformed thought that we can have *no* knowledge of God unless He *voluntarily* reveals himself. Our only access to God's mind is through His voluntary self-revelation—His word. Thus, Van Til is able to define analogical reasoning as reasoning which is fully subject to God's authoritative word.[89] This revelation is not exhaustive, and therefore *analogical reasoning may not attain to exhaustive knowledge.*[90]

Van Til's doctrine of revelation is for the most part standard, familiar, Reformed theology. *General revelation* in his view is revelation given by God to all men through nature and through human constitution, declaring the reality and nature of God, and revealing enough of God's will for man as to leave sinners without excuse (Ps. 19:1ff.; Rom. 1–2). *Special revelation* consists in the words spoken by God to and through prophets, apostles, the incarnate Christ, and the written Scripture, not only once again to display His nature and utter His commands, but particularly to set forth His provision for the forgiveness of sin in the work of Christ.

What is unusual about Van Til's teaching in this area, however, is (a) his emphasis on the correlativity between general and special reve-

---

bility of God." The term "incomprehensibility" generally denotes a relation between human knowledge and the *being* of God, not a relation between human knowledge and divine knowledge. To say that God is incomprehensible is generally to say that we lack exhaustive knowledge of God's *being*, of what he *is* (and does). In the Clark controversy, however, the term was often used, as we have seen, to denote various sorts of discontinuities between our *knowledge* (of anything) and God's *knowledge* (of anything), or between our thoughts and his thoughts. Doubtless the two problems are closely related. The discrepancies between human and divine thoughts certainly account at least in part for the limitations in our knowledge of God's being. Yet in my view the two problems should have been more clearly distinguished than such use of "incomprehensible" permits them to be.

88. Cf. Van Til, *The Defense of the Faith*, 300f.

89. Van Til, *Common Grace and the Gospel*, 206; *An Introduction to Systematic Theology*, 256-60; *Jerusalem and Athens*, 126; cf. "Introduction," 49.

90. Van Til, *A Christian Theory of Knowledge*, 16.

lation and (b) the delicate balance he strikes between this correlativity and the primacy of Scripture.

(1) *The Correlativity of General and Special Revelation:* Van Til likes to emphasize that general and special revelation are related to one another in "organic, supplemental fashion."[91] By this he means, *first,* that neither has ever existed apart from the other. Even before the Fall, from the first moment of man's existence, he was confronted *both* with God's spoken word (Gen. 1:28f.; 2:16f.) *and* with God's revelation in creation. *Second,* neither was ever intended to function apart from the other. Fact-revelation and word-revelation "require each other."[92] The fact always "needed to be explained by God himself,"[93] and the word always explains *facts* about God, man, nature, and redemptive history. Either without the other would be unintelligible, would communicate nothing. Adam needed to hear a word of God to know his duty with respect to the trees of the garden, but this verbal command presupposes Adam's knowledge of the "situation": "The supernatural could not be recognized for what it was unless the natural were also recognized for what it was."[94] *Third,* both general revelation and special revelation are "necessary, authoritative, clear and sufficient." Those four adjectives apply to general revelation in view of its distinctive purpose. To *render sinners without excuse* and to *provide the factual referent* for special revelation, general revelation is necessary, speaks with authority, speaks clearly, and contains sufficient content to accomplish its work.[95]

This sort of emphasis is unusual in American theology, though it has precedents in the Dutch literature. I find it refreshing and exciting; its implications for theological work are innumerable. For one thing, it means that we need not be embarrassed about using *extra-scriptural information* to interpret Scripture. If indeed the creation were somehow autonomous, then we might fear that the use of such data might to some extent hide the full truth of God's revelation. But creation is not independent of God.[96] God controls it and speaks through all of it. And He has chosen to reveal himself, not by nature or Scripture alone, but always by the two together in organic union. Thus, we can use such data fearlessly and thankfully.

---

91. Van Til, *The Doctrine of Scripture,* 65.
92. Van Til, "Introduction," 32.
93. Van Til, *An Introduction to Systematic Theology,* 133.
94. Van Til, *Apologetics,* 30.
95. Van Til, "Nature and Scripture," 269ff.; *Apologetics,* 30ff.
96. Notice that Van Til's doctrine of Scripture is distinctively *Calvinistic.* It presupposes an uncompromising view of God's sovereignty. Van Til is fond of speaking about the "isolation of the Reformed view of Scripture" (cf. *The Doctrine of Scripture,* 37). The division between Calvinism and Arminianism is not only over soteriology and providence, but it cuts across the whole range of Christian doctrine, in Van Til's view.

For another thing, Van Til's emphasis frees us to see a very important principle: Scripture is seen for what it is *only* when it is properly related to the world into which it has come. God never intended otherwise. This means not only that Scripture must be interpreted in the light of its original cultural environment, but also that it must be *applied* to our own lives and culture—to the environment in which it *now* speaks. We do not know what Scripture says until we know how it relates to our world. *The question of interpretation and the question of application are the same.* To ask what Scripture says, or what it means, is always to ask a question about application. A question about the meaning of Scripture always arises out of a personal problem—an inability to relate the words of Scripture to our lives, to our language, our thought-forms, our culture, our fears and hopes.

This principle, in turn, helps us attain greater clarity on the question of what theology is all about. *Theology is simply the application of Scripture to all areas of human life.* On this matter, Reformed writers have often been unhelpful. They have talked about theology as a study of God or Scripture, as an ordering of biblical data, as a process of theory construction from the facts of the Bible, etc. But they have not seriously asked the question, "Why do we need theology if Scripture is sufficient?" Often they have talked as if theology is necessary for us to obtain the truth about God, forgetting for the moment that God has *already* told us the truth about himself in Scripture. Sometimes they have suggested that the scriptural account of the truth is somehow defective—in form if not in content—and that theology is needed to remedy that defect, to put the Scripture into proper form, perhaps. Such options are not open to a follower of Van Til. *Scripture is not lacking in truth, order, rationality.* It is not a brute fact which stands only as data for human interpretation. It *is* interpretation—divine interpretation. We need theology not because of any defect in Scripture, but because of *defects in us,* because of our inability to *relate* the clear revelation of Scripture to our own lives. We need theology—not to restructure or improve upon Scripture, but to *apply* Scripture to our lives.[97]

If theology is "application," then theology necessarily must make use of general as well as special revelation. To know how Scripture *applies,* we must know something about ourselves and our world. If we are to know how Scripture applies to abortions and ecology and energy crises and nuclear war, we must have at our disposal more than the text of

---

97. Van Til himself has not defined theology as "application" as we have in this paragraph. His own definitions of theology are of a more traditional sort. But this is one of those areas where we must go beyond Van Til in order to be fully true to his distinctive insights. The concept of theology as "application" has a firm basis in the thought of Van Til, though it is not found among his explicit doctrines.

Scripture; we must have information about all these matters as well. But if Van Til is right, we may use such information without embarrassment.

(2) *The Primacy of Scripture:* But what has happened to the sufficiency of Scripture in all of this? If theology may and must use general revelation "without embarrassment," and if general revelation is needed for us to understand (= apply) Scripture, then in what sense does Scripture have primacy? If our knowledge of Scripture is dependent to some extent upon our "natural knowledge," can we have any more confidence in Scripture than we can have in our natural knowledge? Does Scripture itself, on this view, merely become another form of general revelation?

We have already observed that for Van Til nature and Scripture are related in "organic, supplemental fashion."[91] *Scripture is unintelligible without those facts which it interprets, but the facts also are unintelligible apart from God's spoken and written interpretation of them.* Even before the Fall, therefore, there is a sense in which God's spoken words had a "priority" over His revelation in nature. Man was to accept God's spoken words as ultimately authoritative interpretation, as that interpretation by which all other interpretation must be judged. Eve sinned in accepting the serpent's words (and eventually her own) as having this ultimate authority. It was not that God's spoken words were more true or more authoritative than His revelation in nature. Rather, God's spoken words were more authoritative than any human (or Satanic) *interpretation* of natural revelation. Thus, Adam and Eve were under obligation to make God's *spoken* words the "starting point" of their thought, to accept them as the criterion for all sound interpretation of God's world.

After the Fall, the spoken and written words of God take on an even more crucial role, since man's normal activity of interpreting the universe has been distorted by sin.[98] After the Fall, it becomes even more important to point to these spoken and written words as the only ultimately authoritative sentences known to man. Therefore, "the revelation in Scripture must be made our starting-point. It is only in the light of the Protestant doctrine of Scripture that one can obtain also Protestant doctrine of the revelation of God in nature."[99] "But since the entrance of sin it is necessary to begin even the study of the works of God through the Word of God."[100]

The point is that natural revelation must indeed be used in the interpretation (= application) of Scripture, but once that interpretation is ascer-

---

98. Van Til, *A Christian Theory of Knowledge*, 163f.; "Introduction," 33; *An Introduction to Systematic Theology*, 110f.

99. Van Til, *Apologetics*, 27.

100. Van Til, *The Doctrine of Scripture*, 120; cf. "Nature and Scripture," 265; *Christian-Theistic Ethics*, 133, 139f.

tained, it must take precedence over hypotheses derived from *any* other source. "Theology as application" presupposes a finished, complete, authoritative Scripture (see above discussion). Theology is the application of *Scripture* and Scripture alone.[101] Even when we use extra-scriptural information (as we must) to understand Scripture, we must hold *loosely* to this information—loosely enough to allow Scripture to call it in question. It is only when our methods of Scripture interpretation are themselves purified by Scripture that real progress can be made in theology.

In Van Til's view, the primacy of Scripture is comprehensive—it covers all areas of life. He clearly rejects the view that the Bible contains only "truths of faith" or "religious teaching" as over against, say, teaching about the physical universe.[102] The philosopher, too, is "directly subject to the Bible. . . ."[103] Directly or indirectly, there is no matter about which the Bible is silent.[104]

It has been asked that if Scripture has such primacy for Van Til, why is his method not more "exegetical"? G. C. Berkouwer has chastened Van Til on this score, and Van Til himself has admitted guilt in this regard.[105] Van Til rarely exegetes specific biblical passages; his terminology is often abstract and philosophical. There is some truth in this criticism, but there is also much to be said in favor of Van Til's approach. *First,* many critics are unaware of the extent to which Van Til's mind is steeped in the content of Scripture. His sermons and class lectures are full of biblical references, allusions, illustrations. For some reason, this emphasis has not been prominent in his published works; yet his published works grow out of this Bible-saturated mentality. *Second,* many critics are unaware of the fact that Van Til's favorite professor at Princeton was Geerhardus Vos, the brilliant biblical theologian. The influence of Vos upon Van Til is profound, though rarely seen on the surface of Van Til's writings. There are places in Van Til's works, however, where the influence of Vos

---

101. Nothing could be further from Van Til's view than the idea that nature-study reveals divine commandments beyond Scripture and equal to Scripture in authority. Van Til's *sola scriptura* stands in sharp contrast to the views of Dooyeweerd and his followers. See my article, "Toronto, Reformed Orthodoxy and the Word of God," *Vanguard* (Jan.–Feb., 1975) and my pamphlet (with L. J. Coppes), *The Amsterdam Philosophy* (Phillipsburg, N. J.: Harmony Press, 1972).

102. Van Til, "Bavinck the Theologian," 10; *Apologetics*, 2; *The Defense of the Faith*, 24; cf. *The Doctrine of Scripture*, 89ff. Compare this with the assertion of Dooyeweerd that Scripture is a "book of faith" and therefore may not speak, e.g., of the chronology of creation: Dooyeweerd, *In the Twilight of Western Thought* (Nutley, N. J.: Craig Press, 1968), 149ff.

103. Van Til, *Apologetics*, 37. Cf. the discussion in *Jerusalem and Athens*, 81, in which Dooyeweerd takes issue with Van Til's position on this point.

104. Van Til, *Apologetics*, 2, *The Defense of the Faith*, 24.

105. Van Til, *Jerusalem and Athens*, 203f.; cf. *Toward a Reformed Apologetics* (no publication data), 27.

is unmistakable to anyone who reflects on the matter.[106] *Third,* Van Til has had the advantage of teaching at an institution where there has been a remarkable unity of mind among the faculty. Unlike some theologians, Van Til has felt that he could *trust* his colleagues in the exegetical disciplines and build upon their exegetical work. Van Til's trust in his colleagues has given him the freedom to concentrate his work in areas most suited to his own gifts, which are more philosophical than philological. Thus in reply to Berkhouwer's criticism, he simply refers to the exegetical work of John Murray as expressing his own view. *Finally,* we must rethink, in my view, our common concept of what "exegesis" is. If, as we have argued earlier, *interpretation and application of Scripture are the same thing,* then we ought to conclude that *"exegesis" is a broader discipline* than it is often conceived to be. Is Van Til not doing "exegesis" when he translates the biblical concepts into philosophical language?[107] What is the difference, really, between translating biblical concepts into philosophic terms and translating Greek words into English? The two activities require different sorts of skills, but is it really fair to describe the one activity as "exegetical" and to deny such a description to the other? Is Van Til not doing "exegesis" when he applies biblical teachings to problems of philosophy and apologetics? What is the difference, really, between applications of that sort and applications to problems of achieving syntactical equivalence? Perhaps when all is said and done it will be seen that Van Til's work is indeed "exegetical" in a very significant sense. This is not to reject the need or importance of those grammatical and historical studies which are commonly called "exegesis." These considerations do suggest, however, that the *whole* work of exegesis cannot be done by any one man, by any one method, by any one set of gifts.

C. *Analogy and Logic*

But I seem to have forgotten the problem which led me to consider Van Til's concept of "analogical reasoning" in the first place. How do we reconcile Van Til's emphasis on "system" with his zest for "paradox"? How is it that the doctrines of Christianity are both *dependent* on one another and somehow in *tension* with one another? Our earlier discussion of analogical reasoning is not irrelevant to this point. We have learned that analogical reasoning is the first kind of "thinking God's thoughts after him"—a type of thinking which seeks *conformity to God's thoughts* while

---

106. Note particularly the emphasis on "taking history seriously" in *Common Grace and the Gospel (passim)*, the discussion of the kingdom of God in *Christian-Theistic Ethics*, the frequent references to the "Adamic consciousness," etc., as in *An Introduction to Systematic Theology*, 25ff., and the discussion of modern trends in terms of God's covenants with Adam, Noah, Abraham, etc., in *The Great Debate Today* (Nutley, N. J.: Presbyterian and Reformed, 1971).

107. Cf. Van Til, *The Defense of the Faith*, 40n.

simultaneously acknowledging its own *creatureliness*. We have learned that analogical reasoning, therefore, is reasoning which is subject to God's revelation in general and which tests all ideas by the criterion of Scripture. As such, this reasoning attains truth, but not all the truth. It is true as far as it goes, but not exhaustive. It is true insofar as it actually conforms to God's mind, but the *amount of truth obtainable is limited* by (a) the creaturely status of the reasoner, and (b) the sovereign decision of God concerning what is to be revealed and what kept secret.

Insofar as we attain truth, we attain a sense of the *interconnectedness of the creation*. God's plan is a wise one. He has not planned any one thing in creation without taking everything else into account. All elements of His plan "dovetail" with one another. Scripture often reflects upon these interconnections: faith establishes the law (Rom. 3:31); the glorification of the elect necessitated the sufferings of Christ (Heb. 2:10); true faith always issues in good works (James 2:18); to control the tongue is to control the whole body (James 3:2); to disobey one point of the law is to be guilty of all (James 2:10). A truly biblical theology will reflect upon these interconnections, for they are part of God's truth.

Since, however, *our knowledge is limited* both by our created status and by God's sovereign limitation of revelation, we can expect to find paradox also in Scripture. If we do not know *all* the truth, then we do not know *all* the interconnections between the truths. And *paradox,* as we have earlier presented it, is simply *the result of our ignorance about interconnections.* In many doctrinal areas, we do not know fully *how* various elements of God's plan are related to one another. We do not know precisely *how* they "dovetail," *how* they take account of one another. We know that they *do* dovetail, for we know that God's plan is wise and exhaustive, and usually we know how they fit together to some degree, but the gaps in our knowledge often demand that we rest content with a paradoxical formulation.

God is good, yet He foreordains evil deeds. We know that these truths are compatible, for Scripture teaches both and God does not deny himself. We know, further, that the denial of any one may lead to the denial of the other, and in that sense the two truths are "interdependent." God can foreordain evil only if He is himself good, for in Scripture "evil" is "evil" only by contrast with the goodness of God. God is truly good only if the evil in the world is foreordained by Him, for only if evil is fully controlled by God can we be confident that there is a good purpose in it, and only if there is a good purpose in it can we trust the overall good purpose of God. Scripture, then, teaches us that these two truths are interdependent; they "require" each other. Yet at the same time there is paradox here. Indeed, in this case we know not only *that* there is interdependence, but we also know, to some extent, *how* there is interdependence. But we do not have the *full* knowledge of the "how." There is still something strange about this, something we cannot quite reconcile. How *can* a good God foreordain evil? Thus, we are in a strange state of affairs: we have two propositions ("God is good" and "God foreordains evil") which we can show to be *logically interdependent* in one sense; yet we *cannot* show them to be *logically compatible* except by an appeal to faith! Strange indeed; yet this is where we must stand if we are to do justice both to the truth of God's revelation and to the limitations of our creaturely knowledge, if we are to "reason analogically." This *balance of interdependence and paradox* is in the interest of thinking in submission to Scripture. Scripture must be followed both in its assertions of interdependence and in its refusal to reconcile all doctrines to our satisfaction.

But to what extent, then, may we use *logic* in the derivation of "good and necessary consequences" from Scripture? Are we to deduce doctrines from one another only when Scripture itself does that explicitly? Or may we go beyond what Scripture teaches explicitly to unfold its *implicit* message? Surely Van Til thinks we can. But to what extent? How?

Van Til's general teaching on logic is along the following lines:[108] The *validity of the laws of logic* derives from the *character of God*.[109] God is not subject to some source of (logical or other) possibility more ultimate than himself.[110] Rather, He *himself alone determines ultimately what is possible*.[111] It is God, therefore, who both vindicates and limits the competence of human logic. First, He *vindicates* it. His revelation contains no logical contradiction—no "real" contradiction. There are *apparent* contradictions in Scripture, but *only* apparent ones.[112] Apparent to whom? They appear ultimately irreconcilable to unbelievers because unbelievers have a false view of the foundation of logic.[113] But the "ap-

---

108. Van Til's idealist philosophical training creates some problems in assessing his view of logic. It is not always clear when he is using the term "logic" to mean *formal logic* and when he is using it (as in idealism) to refer to the *methodology of thought in general*. In my discussion, formal logic is in view throughout, and I have tried to set forth Van Til's views on that narrow subject. I may not always have been successful, but rather often the distinction is not important, since Van Til's views on formal logic often parallel closely his views of intellectual methodology in general.

109. Van Til, *A Christian Theory of Knowledge*, 202; *An Introduction to Systematic Theology*, 11, 37, 256; *The Doctrine of Scripture*, 72, *Common Grace and the Gospel*, 28.

110. Van Til, *A Christian Theory of Knowledge*, 202; *An Introduction to Systematic Theology*, 11.

111. Van Til, *The Doctrine of Scripture*, 131.

112. Van Til, *The Defense of the Faith*, 61f.; *A Christian Theory of Knowledge*, 38.

113. Van Til, *Common Grace and the Gospel*, 28; *The Defense of the Faith*, 253; *An Introduction to Systematic Theology*, 171, 230. Van Til grants that unbeliever and believer may observe the same laws of formal logic: *An Introduction to Systematic Theology*, 37, 254; *The Defense of the Faith*, 296ff.; *Common Grace and the Gospel*, 27. The difference is that believer and unbeliever disagree on the

parent contradictions" also are apparent to all men, believers and unbelievers alike, because of their *finitude*.[114] Still, from God's point of view, there is no contradiction; and thus the believer knows that whatever may seem to be the case, God's revelation is fully consistent with itself. Logic applied to God's revelation, therefore, will not lead us astray, if it is *used* rightly. Logic itself, properly used, will discover no real contradiction in Scripture.

Second, "proper use" involves certain *limitations* in the process of logical reasoning. We cannot reason any way we want to. We must reason in full awareness of the fact that God is the foundation of logic.[115] Logic itself does not determine what is possible or probable; only God does that.[116] Logic does not give to man exhaustive knowledge; only God has that.[117] Thus, we cannot assume that all biblical doctrines can be *shown* to be fully consistent in terms of our present understanding.[118] Van Til says, therefore, that the "system" of Christian theology is not a "deductive" system, and that we must not use "deductive" exegesis.[119] What does Van Til mean by "deductive" here? He does not actually define the term anywhere, perhaps assuming (I think wrongly) that it needs no explanation. Judging from his overall position, however, I would say that in opposing "deductivism" he means to say (1) that theology ought not to make deductions from one or several doctrines, the conclusions of which contradict other scriptural teachings;[120] (2) that theology ought not to assume that it can demonstrate the formal logical consistency of all its doctrines (see above discussion); and (3) that there-

---

basis of logic and that they hold different "premises" about ultimate origins and authority. Cf. *Apologetics*, 50; *A Survey of Christian Epistemology*, 213f.

114. Van Til, *The Defense of the Faith*, 228. Van Til leaves open (as he must, to avoid speculation) the question of *how* God resolves these apparent contradictions, whether by a better-than-human logic, by fuller knowledge of the facts, or by somehow transcending the whole logic/fact problematic.

115. Van Til, *An Introduction to Systematic Theology*, 11; *Common Grace and the Gospel*, 28. Van Til criticizes Hodge, not for using logical reasoning to evaluate Scripture, but rather for failing adequately to distinguish Christian from non-Christian *ways* of doing so: *An Introduction to Systematic Theology*, 31ff.; *Apologetics*, 47ff.

116. Van Til, *An Introduction to Systematic Theology*, 256; *Jerusalem and Athens*, 19; *Common Grace and the Gospel*, 28.

117. Van Til, *A Christian Theory of Knowledge*, 37f.; *The Defense of the Faith*, 228.

118. Van Til, *An Introduction to Systematic Theology*, 169ff.; *Common Grace and the Gospel*, 10. In the latter passage he suggests that the contradiction appears only at "first sight." Elsewhere, he seems to argue that it is irresolvable by any created intellect.

119. Van Til, *A Christian Theory of Knowledge*, 38; *The Defense of the Faith*, 204f., 227; *The Doctrine of Scripture*, 123; *An Introduction to Systematic Theology*, 257; *Common Grace and the Gospel*, 202.

120. Above references (previous note). Also cf. Van Til, *An Introduction to Systematic Theology*, 256; *Jerusalem and Athens*, 126.

fore the *characteristic method of theology* is not deduction (as in Euclid's geometry) but rather a *putting together of all the biblical data on a particular subject,* adopting paradoxical formulations when these are warranted by the biblical teaching. In this way we should understand the more obscure formulations of Van Til's method, for example, that "we seek to *implicate* ourselves more deeply into a comprehension of God's plan,"[121] and that "it is reasoning in a spiral fashion rather than in a linear fashion."[122]

For all of this it must be admitted that there remains some unclarity in Van Til's teaching about logic, for he does not always explain adequately why he uses deductions in some cases and rejects them in others. For instance, Van Til admits that there *is* a proper use for logical deduction in theology, despite the above-mentioned limitations.[123] As over against the Lutheran, Pieper, Van Til insists that "God can reveal only that which is consistent with his nature as a self-contained being."[124] He argues that it is irrationalism to say that "God is both omnipotent and not omnipotent."[124] He denies that "the Bible can teach both that God elects men to salvation and at the same time that they have the power to reject the grace of God."[125] In these cases, he is deducing (logically! how else?) from one scriptural truth the negation of its opposite. He is saying that since Scripture teaches a particular truth, it cannot (logically) teach the opposite of that truth. On the other hand, he forbids us to "start with the idea of the sovereign control of God over all things and deduce from it the idea that there is no human responsibility."[125] In the one case, logical deduction is permitted, even demanded. In the other case, it is forbidden. Yet in this context, Van Til does not state clearly how the cases differ. Is it that the one sort of deduction is formally valid and the other one is not? Is it that one deduction takes account of all scriptural data while the other does not? Van Til does not say.

Further: to say that God is both omnipotent and not omnipotent is indeed to say something "apparently contradictory." It may be "really contradictory." But, of course, if "omnipotent" and "not omnipotent" employ different senses of "omnipotent," then this apparent contradiction is biblically resolvable. Yet Van Til's argument suggests that in *this* case (though not in others) we *know* that the contradiction is a real one (not merely "apparent"), and therefore we must reject it. But *how* do we know that *this* contradiction is "real" while others are only "apparent"? *How*

---

121. Van Til, *A Survey of Christian Epistemology,* 7.
122. *Ibid.,* 201. Van Til sometimes uses the phrase "circular reasoning," but "spiral reasoning" is far closer to the concept he seeks to convey.
123. *Ibid.,* 7.
124. Van Til, *A Christian Theory of Knowledge,* 202.
125. *Ibid.,* 38. Cf. references above, notes 19-22.

do we know that one contradiction is irresolvable while another is resolvable, when we cannot ourselves resolve either one?

Van Til does explain why we must sometimes be satisfied with apparently contradictory formulations. He does not explain why in *some* cases we must rest content with such paradox while in *other* cases (as in the Pieper example) we must press for an explicit logical consistency. I suspect, however, that if Van Til were to address this problem, he would do it somewhat as follows: Since we believe that there is no "real" contradiction in Scripture, our exegesis should strive to achieve, as much as is humanly possible, a logically consistent interpretation of biblical teaching. Yet this goal is not the primary goal. *The primary goal of exegesis is not logical consistency but faithfulness to the text.* And sometimes in trying to formulate one doctrine with logical consistency, we may find ourselves compromising another doctrine of Scripture. When that happens, something is wrong. *We must not simply push our logic relentlessly to the point where we ignore or deny a genuine biblical teaching.* Rather, we must rethink our whole procedure—our exegesis, our reasoning, the extra-biblical knowledge we bring to bear on the matter, etc. *If no explicit logical consistency can be obtained without conflict with other biblical teaching, then we must remain satisfied with paradox.* In the omnipotence example, explicit logical consistency is possible without any compromise of biblical teaching. Scripture teaches that God is omnipotent. It does not teach the opposite. Logically consistent affirmation of God's omnipotence does not put us in conflict with any other biblical teaching. Therefore we affirm it and insist upon logical consistency. In the example of God's sovereignty and human responsibility, the case is somewhat different. Here there is (in Van Til's mind) an "apparent contradiction." Yet to remove that contradiction would be to compromise either God's sovereignty or man's responsibility. That may not be done, since both doctrines are clearly taught in Scripture. The general principle: we may (and ought to) use logical deduction freely except where such deduction puts us in conflict with the explicit teachings of Scripture.

But if this is the proper analysis of Van Til's position, what are we to make of his statement that "All teaching of Scripture is apparently contradictory"?[126] This statement is rather strange since, as we have seen above, Van Til sometimes *refuses* to accept "apparently contradictory" formulations of scriptural teaching. The omnipotence of God, for Van Til, is *not* (it would seem) an "apparently contradictory" doctrine. It is *wrong*, in his estimation, to say that God both is and is not omnipotent. Furthermore, as we have seen earlier, Van Til does approve other formulations which are not in any sense "apparently contradictory." When he

126. Van Til, *Common Grace and the Gospel*, 142.

says, then, that "all teaching of Scripture is apparently contradictory," we are tempted to think that here (as elsewhere; see above, note 108) Van Til has something other than formal logic in mind. Indeed, the paragraph which explains this statement makes no mention of formal contradiction or even of formal logic in general. It simply presents the sovereignty and authority of God over our thought. Is "apparent contradiction" here just a metaphor for the general subordination of man's thought to God's?

A metaphor, perhaps, but not "just" a metaphor. At this point it is important for us to note Van Til's view of Christian doctrines as "limiting" "supplementative" concepts. This principle is the connecting link, in a sense, between Van Til's general view of analogical reasoning and his specific view of formal logic. In saying that *theological concepts are "limiting concepts,"* Van Til is drawing out an *implication of man's creaturely status.* Since man is finite, none of his concepts exhausts the "essence of the thing it seeks to express."[127] Our concept of a tree may be accurate as far as it goes, but it can never *exhaustively* describe the tree. The same holds true for our concepts of God, sin, salvation, etc. Even the concepts of Scripture, presented as they are in human language and adapted therefore to human understanding, do not *exhaustively* describe the realities to which they refer. Scripture tells us what we need to know, but it does not tell us everything. Our concepts, therefore, are "approximations" to the truth in a certain sense.[128] Caution is needed here. Van Til is not saying, for example, that the doctrine of justification by faith is only "approximately true" in the sense of being partly false. Rather, this and other biblical doctrines are completely and dependably true, yet they do not tell us everything God knows about the matters in question. The fact that all doctrines are "non-exhaustive" in this sense implies that various doctrines should be seen as "supplementary" to one another.[129] Scripture clearly

---

127. *Ibid.*, 201. Cf. Van Til, *An Introduction to Systematic Theology*, 256. The term "limiting concept" comes from the philosophy of Immanuel Kant. Kant argued that the "noumenal world," the world as it really is, could not be known by man, but that the *idea* of a noumenal world could be entertained and used for a certain purpose: "The concept of a noumenon is thus a merely *limiting concept,* the function of which is to curb the pretensions of sensibility; and it is therefore only of negative employment." Kant, *Critique of Pure Reason,* tr. Norman Kemp Smith (New York: St. Martin's Press, 1929), 272. In Kant's thought, a "limiting concept" has no positive content. For Kant, "God" is a limiting concept, and this means, not that God actually exists, but only that the term "God" may properly be used in describing the limitedness of our experience. To say that "God exists," for Kant, means only that our experience is limited *as if* by God. Van Til, however, uses the term very differently. In his thought, limiting concepts *do* have positive significance. God really *does* exist, though our concept of God is a "limiting concept." To say that the concept of God is a "limiting concept" in Van Til's thought is merely to say that our knowledge of who God is, though true, is non-exhaustive.

128. *Ibid.*, 11.
129. Van Til, *An Introduction to Systematic Theology,* 255ff.

teaches that God is sovereign, but it does not tell us in complete (exhaustive) detail how His sovereignty operates. The theological concept "divine sovereignty" does not suffice to comprehend and exhaust all of God's actual relations to the world. Thus, we ought not to derive our view of human responsibility exclusively from our concept of divine sovereignty, while ignoring what Scripture explicitly says about human responsibility. We should rather allow the two concepts to supplement one another: the biblical teaching on human responsibility will deepen our understanding of divine sovereignty, and vice versa. If putting the two together produces an "apparent contradiction," then so be it. But even the recognition of logical tension helps the believer to see the deeper logical unity of the two doctrines. For the sovereignty of God cannot be seen for what it is—that is, in its full paradoxicality!—except in its relationship to human responsibility. It is in this sort of way that Van Til can describe the two doctrines as "requiring one another" while at the same time insisting that their relationship is "apparently contradictory."

But remember that *all* teachings of Scripture are "limiting concepts." *All* concepts of Scripture are "mutually supplementative" in the above sense. The doctrine of justification by faith also supplements, and is supplemented by, the doctrine of divine sovereignty. The doctrine of divine sovereignty tells us what sort of God is justifying us. Thus, the doctrine of justification by faith incorporates the paradox of divine sovereignty. The doctrine of justification by faith—when fully explained in its relations to the rest of scriptural truth—is just as paradoxical as divine sovereignty. Even the omnipotence of God, then, shares with other doctrines a paradoxical element. That paradoxical element is not properly (scripturally) formulated by the phrase "God is and is not omnipotent." We reject, on scriptural authority, *that* paradox. Yet there is another sort of paradox which applies to the divine omnipotence. The omnipotence of God is "limited" in a sense. God cannot do "everything" if that "everything" includes things contrary to His nature or contrary to His promises, or contrary to His eternal purpose. God's "omnipotence" will not rob man of his responsibility, nor will it eliminate the significance of human action as a secondary cause.

"Apparent contradiction," then, results from the "limiting" nature of biblical concepts. And since these "limiting concepts" are "supplementative," the paradoxes which attach to one attach to all, while at the same time each concept is seen to "require" all the rest. This does not mean that *every* paradox is to be accepted simply because it is a paradox. The paradoxes must be exegetically formulated. Nor does it mean that every doctrine must always be stated in paradoxical terminology. Yet the paradoxes found in Scripture must be fearlessly stated in any complete theological work, and the relations of these paradoxes to each biblical doctrine must be traced. There is a sense, then, in which "all teaching of Scripture is apparently contradictory": (a) all teachings of Scripture are "limiting concepts"; (b) limiting concepts generate apparent contradictions; (c) since limiting concepts are supplementative, an apparent contradiction in one doctrine generates apparent contradictions in all doctrines.

Does this doctrine render Scripture unintelligible? If all doctrines are apparently contradictory, do they have any meaning at all? It is not enough to reply that the contradictions are "apparent" though not "real." An "apparent contradiction," before it is resolved, poses the same problems of intelligibility as a "real contradiction," it would seem. Or does it? Let us go back to our earlier remarks about "theology as application." If interpretation and application are the same, then *the question of intelligibility becomes the question of whether a consistent pattern of application is possible*. A sentence may be intelligible, even though it does not conform to logical canons, if it unambiguously dictates a particular response on the part of the reader or hearer. In a sense, logical laws themselves are secondary to "intelligibility" in this broad sense. Logic aims (fallibly) to describe the conditions under which such application is possible. But as many contemporary logicians have observed, no present logical system describes *all* such conditions of intelligibility. Logic has made only small steps in this task, describing the conditions of intelligibility for a few key terms like "all," "if-then," "some," "none," etc. It has succeeded in analyzing these key terms only in certain narrowly defined contexts of their occurrence. Now, since scriptural doctrines are not "really" contradictory, they are intelligible, but their intelligibility is not demonstrable by the limited canons of current human logic. For example, according to Van Til, man has (in one sense) and has not (in another) lost the image of God as a result of the Fall. Since the senses are not clearly specifiable, we have apparent contradiction, but since God knows what the senses are, there is no real contradiction. Is this doctrine intelligible? Yes, for as taught in Scripture it has a clear application. We are to treat men as made in the image of God, even though they are fallen (Gen. 9:6; James 3:9). We have no right to despise our fellow men on the ground that they have lost the image of God. Though the supposed right to despise our fellow men might seem to follow from part of the doctrine taken in isolation, it is a conclusion uniformly—consistently!—rejected by Scripture. The "loss" of the image *does* have a legitimate application, but not an application contrary to that of the "continuance" of the image. The "loss" of the image motivates us to recognize our own need for renewal, the need to "put on the new man" (Eph. 4:24; Col. 3:10). There is no inconsistency, then, in the overall application of these two apparently contradictory principles. There is no contradiction between loving fallen human beings and recognizing our own need of renewal.

We should now be able to see the peculiar structure of Van Til's "analogical system." *All doctrines are interdependent,* in that none can be adequately understood except in the light of the others. All doctrines are "apparently contradictory," in that *none exhausts the fullness of the truth,* and their non-exhaustive character limits our ability to demonstrate formal logical consistency. Yet *all doctrines are true as far as they go,* are not "really" contradictory, and are intelligible in that even though they may be unassimilable to the forms of our logic, nevertheless provide clear guidance for God's people. This account of the nature of the Christian "system" is a theological accomplishment of immense magnitude.[130]

Epilogue

In my view, Van Til's concept of a "theological system" is his most important contribution to theology, as well as the most difficult one for most of us to understand. I trust that what I have written has clarified this concept, at least for some. I have also mentioned quite a number of Van Til's distinctive formulations of specific doctrines, each of which is important in its own right. I have discussed (in the context of our broader concern) Van Til's view of general and special revelation, his concept of the "incomprehensibility of God," and his many interesting formulations of the various kinds of "interdependence" and "paradox" found at many doctrinal loci. In these discussions, I have provided an outline of Van Til's distinctive theological positions, as well as an account of his general view of the nature and method of theology.

There is much more that could be said, however. Van Til's concept of "common grace" as "earlier" grace is highly significant and merits much close analysis.[131] His non-intellectualistic view of man's nature,[132] his view of sin as "ethical,"[133] his view of the Chalcedon Christology as a function of the Creator-creature distinction,[134] his immensely fertile account of the goal, motive, and standard of ethics:[135] all of these and others deserve close examination, analysis, proclamation. Further, a really complete account of Van Til's theology could not ignore his critiques of non-Reformed thought—critiques both interesting in themselves and useful in

---

130. See if the above account does justice to the difficult passage in *The Defense of the Faith,* 231f., where Van Til argues that temporal creation is "implied in" but not a "logical derivative from" the doctrine of God. I think myself that Van Til's concept of "implication" here is a *sort* of "logical derivation"; yet it is different enough from other types of derivation, perhaps, to merit a different name in Van Til's estimation.
131. Van Til, *Common Grace and the Gospel.*
132. Van Til, *An Introduction to Systematic Theology,* 32.
133. *Ibid.,* 24f., 253ff., elsewhere.
134. Van Til, *The Defense of the Faith,* 32ff.
135. Van Til, *Christian-Theistic Ethics.*

helping us better to formulate the doctrines in question. Van Til's critique of Barth's universalism, for instance, is instructive not only in warning us against Barth, but also in showing us the ways in which alien philosophical motifs may lead to compromise in the doctrine of definite atonement. Hopefully, other studies will be produced dealing with these matters in detail. The present study, having already exceeded the editor's length requirement, is nearly at an end. I do feel, however, that this paper demonstrates something of the immense significance of Van Til's work for the theologian, and something of the difficulty involved in understanding and appropriating it. If I am right, then I have furnished herein the best and only justification for further research into this extremely important thinker. Surely one day there will have to be a *Cornelius Van Til als Dogmaticus!*

EPILOGUE

THE PLACE OF PUBLICATION
IN CHRISTIAN RECONSTRUCTION

By Gary North

Christianity is preeminently a religion of verbal, written revelation. Historically, only Judaism and, to a lesser extent, Islam rival Christianity as religions of the Book. No other faith places more importance on the power of words to reshape the world. Man, made in the image of the Creator, is to think God's thoughts after Him, subduing the earth to the glory of God, but only in terms of God's word revelation to man.

"In the beginning was the Word, and the Word was with God, and the Word was God" (John 1:1). The centrality of the concept of the word could not be made more explicit. God created the universe by the power of His sovereign word—"And God said, Let there be light: and there was light" (Genesis 1:3)—and we are told that by His Word, Jesus Christ, all things were made and are now sustained (Colossians 1:13-19). The foundation of Christian faith is in terms of God's revealed word: "God, who at sundry times and in divers manners spake in time past unto the fathers by the prophets, hath in these last days spoken unto us by his Son, whom he hath appointed heir of all things, by whom also he made the worlds" (Hebrews 1:1-2). It is Christ who is presently "upholding all things by the word of his power" (Hebrews 1:3). God's power and God's word: the two are inescapably linked.

It is not surprising to find in paganism a perverse imitation of this centrality of words: magical incantations, formulas, prayers, and even prayer wheels (spinning out prayers more efficiently). The satanic rebellion of men at the Tower of Babel involved the illegitimate attempt of men to deify themselves by giving themselves a name—by defining themselves apart from God (Genesis 11:4). God's response was in like measure: He scattered them and confounded their language. Men live or die in terms of words. As we read in the longest of all the Psalms, Psalm 119: "Thy word have I hid in mine heart, that I might not sin against thee" (vs. 11). Psalm 119 and Proverbs 1-9 are calls to commitment to the words of God, the only foundation of true wisdom. "Wisdom is the principal thing; therefore get wisdom: and with all thy getting get understanding" (Proverbs 4:7).

Christians should understand the power of the written word more than any other people; it is the foundation of their faith. But in the twentieth century, they have abandoned the world of scholarship to the secularists. They confine their writing to simple tracts, sentimental biographies, pietistic devotional literature, and, at best, to antiquarian theological studies. With the exception of the Wycliff translators—significantly, a labor of language—Christians have made little impact on the world of ideas and scholarship. This failure has led to cultural irrelevance, pietistic retreat, and pessimism concerning the possibility of Christian reconstruction (unlike the optimism of the prophet Isaiah, chapters 2, 65, and 66). So complete has this intellectual retreat been, that few Christians, even those holding advanced educational degrees, see the need for a thorough rewriting of all the academic fields in terms of God's written revelation. They have been content to baptize the secular textbooks and secular methodologies in all but a few pietistic particulars.

Ideas have consequences. The Marxists have grasped this fact, and they have tried to reconstruct every academic discipline in terms of Marxian presuppositions. The evolutionists have tried to reconstruct the thought of modern man along evolutionary lines. The Fabians virtually wrote England into socialism. John Maynard Keynes, the most influential economist of the twentieth century, ended his *General Theory* (1936) with the statement that "the ideas of economists and political philosophers, both when they are right and when they are wrong, are more powerful than is commonly understood. Indeed the world is ruled by little else. Practical men, who believe themselves to be quite exempt from any intellectual influences, are usually the slaves of some defunct economist." The triumph of Keynesianism is a living testimony to the truth of Keynes's theory of ideas: even wrong ideas are enormously powerful. Christians, however, have been content to sit on the academic sidelines, waiting for the end.

Christ died to heal his people from the effects of sin. Adam fell in his whole being when he rebelled against God's word; Christ restores the whole man. By focusing almost exclusively on the personal salvation of individual souls, modern Christianity has returned to the ancient heresy of neoplatonism: the soul, and not the whole man, is the key to the future. But Christ was a whole man, incarnate in flesh. We dare not forget this.

The test of Chalcedon's ministry is its commitment to a program of publication. It stands or falls in terms of this vision. The battle for the souls of men cannot be won apart from the battle for their minds. Victory is in terms of God's word.

LIST OF CONTRIBUTORS

GREG BAHNSEN: Ph.D., philosophy, University of Southern California. Th.M., Westminster Theological Seminary, Philadelphia. Author of *Theonomy in Christian Ethics* (1977) and *Homosexuality: A Biblical Perspective* (1978). Minister in Orthodox Presbyterian Church. He is editor of a newsletter, *Biblical Ethics*.

WILLIAM BLAKE: Ph.D., education, University of Alberta, Canada.

JOHN FRAME: Ph.D. candidate, religious studies, Yale University. Associate professor of apologetics and systematic philosophy, Westminster Theological Seminary. Co-author of *The Amsterdam Philosophy* (1972).

GARY NORTH: Ph.D., history, University of California, Riverside. President of the Institute for Christian Economics. Author of *Marx's Religion of Revolution* (1968), *An Introduction to Christian Economics* (1973), *Puritan Economic Experiments* (1975), *None Dare Call It Witchcraft* (1976), and *How You Can Profit from the Coming Price Controls* (1977). He is the editor of *The Journal of Christian Reconstruction*, in addition to four newsletters. His articles and reviews have appeared in over 30 periodicals, including *The Wall Street Journal, National Review*, etc.

VERN POYTHRESS: Ph.D., mathematics, Harvard University. Th.M., Westminster Theological Seminary. He is assistant professor of New Testament at Westminster Theological Seminary. He has served as an instructor at Wycliffe's Summer Institute of Languages. He is the author of *Philosophy, Science, and the Sovereignty of God* (1976).

LAWRENCE PRATT: B.A., political science, American University. Executive director, Gun Owners of America. Formerly the executive director of the American Conservative Union.

ROUSAS J. RUSHDOONY: M.A., education, University of California, Berkeley. B.D., Pacific School of Religion. President, Chalcedon Foundation. He is the author of over twenty books, including *The Messianic Character of American Education* (1963), *Foundations of Social Order* (1968), *The One and the Many* (1971), *Institutes of Biblical Law* (1973), and *Revolt Against Maturity* (1977).

C. GREGG SINGER: Ph.D., history, University of Pennsylvania. Prior to his retirement he served as chairman of the History Department, Catawba College, Salisbury, North Carolina. He is the author of *A Theological Interpretation of American History* (1964) and *The Unholy Alliance* (1975), a study of the history of the National Council of Churches.

INDEX OF SUBJECTS

322f 324ff, 328
Control, 244ff. *See also* Antinomy:
  nature/freedom
Conventionalism, 170f, 178
Corinth, 209
Corporations, 154n
Courts, 11
Covenant, 29, 43, 65, 69f, 232f, 240
Covenant-breaker, 29, 43f, 65, 240
Covenant-creature, 74
Creation, x, 2, 10, 28ff, 34, 38, 43, 64,
  69, 85, 107, 111, 158, 166, 186, 190,
  212f, 215, 219, 224, 237, 289, 300ff,
  307, 321
Creator/creature distinction, 30, 108,
  111, 113, 176, 210, 294, 321
Creature, 26, 29
Creeds, 24, 78, 100
Crime, 11
Cross, 209ff
Cronos, 203
Cultural mandate, 10, 24, 64, 114. *See
  also Scripture Index:* Gen. 1:26-28
Culture, x, 10, 28, 30, 104, 115f, 129f,
  157, 317
"Cure of souls," 42
Cycles, 28f, 62, 83

Daedalus, 199f
Death, 44, 138
Death of God, 20, 46
Decentralization, 156
Decree, 28, 32, 43, 177, 185, 309
Dedekind cut, 164
Deductivism, 87ff, 294, 306, 323f. *See
  also A priorism*
Definitions (economics), 75, 78
Democracy, 12, 14, 18, 60f, 63. 72f, 135f,
  142, 154, 204f
Democracy of emptiness, 35
Demons, 187
Dependence, 32, 43f, 219
Depravity, 210, 220, 296
Development, 5, 127, 136, 147, 153
Deviance, 11
Devil, viii, xi, 44, 90, 118
Dialectics, 29f, 120, 134ff, 136n, 145,
  227, 233, 254, 270, 285, 291. *See
  also* Antinomy; Dualism
Discontinuity. *See* Antinomy: continuity/
  discontinuity.
Disenchantment of world, 135
Division of labor, 24
Doctrines, 294, 302, 310, 320, 326, 329
Dogma, 4f, 106, 204, 207, 216
Dominion, 24, 113, 115, 132
Doubt, 262f, 275, 291
Dualism, ix, 30, 55, 79, 91, 95, 126,
  129ff
  of man, 29, 47. *See also* Antinomy

Economics
  antinomies, 75

autonomy, 78
calculation, 136, 143ff, 146, 148f
capitalism, 136f, 142f, 146
centralization, 157
choice, 79f
Classical, 85f
competition, 147
deductivism, 87ff
definitions of, 75, 78
determinism/indeterminism, 95f
ends-means, 79f
exhaustive knowledge, 96
experience, 91, 93, 96
faith of, 83
free will, 95ff
freedom, 95
God and, 78, 94f
good life, 93f
human action, 89
humanism, 88
history and, 89f
imagination, 98
inductivism, 81ff
input-output analysis, 86
intuition, 83f, 92, 97f
judgment, 82f
mathematics and, 82
methodology, 75f
mind, 88f
mind/matter, 83, 91ff, 96f
models, 82
mysticism, 92f
nature/freedom, 79, 86, 92, 96
neutrality, 78ff, 85f, 93f
normative, 86
objectivity, 82
order, 83, 88
planning, 17n, 86, 95, 112, 136, 142
power and, 86, 92
pragmatism, 88
predictions, 81, 86, 97
rationality, 80
real world, 76, 82f
rent, 149
scarcity, 97
socialism, 101, 124, 131, 136, 143f
specialization, 76
stationary economy, 149
theory/facts, 81f, 84f, 87ff, 93, 97f
verification, 81, 91f, 93
will and, 91, 95f
Education
  certainty of knowledge and, 105
  Christian culture, 104
  drift, 103, 116
  independent, 115f
  methodology, 112f
  public, 5, 103, 124
  practical, 114
  progress and, 104, 107
  reconstruction, 103, 111, 116
  rehabilitation and, 198
  salvation by, 44

one/many, 172ff
plurality, 161
religion and, 160, 165
revelation and, 185ff
solutions, 184ff
structurality, 183f
Trinity and, 180ff
Turing machine, 163, 171
two plus two, 160ff, 168ff
Maturity, 50
Meaning, x, 5, 31, 34, 36, 52, 55f, 58, 63ff, 68f, 89, 114, 138, 259f, 270
Memory, 59f
Metaphysics, 26, 29, 42f, 94, 166, 243, 270, 272
Methods (academic), 7f
Methodology
economics, 75f, 79
educational, 112f
scientific, 89
Middle Ages, 41, 129f
Mind
autonomous, 44, 66, 109, 231
change of, 219
dependent, 286f
finite, 308
Gentiles', 216
God's, 162, 214
immanentism and, 197
late-medieval dualism, 130f
man's = God's, 118, 121, 291
man's ≠ God's, 286, 314
mathematical, 171f, 188
"Other," 274
sin's effects on, 69
Thomistic dualism, ix, 29
Miracles, 228
Mistake, 263, 265
Modality, 179ff
Modalism, 182
Models, 82, 110
Modernism, 3, 231, 313
Monism, 161, 178
Moon, 24, 267
Morality, 31, 119. See also Ethics
Motive, 175
Multiverse, 28, 45f
Munich syndrome, 12
Mystery, 134ff, 213, 269
Mystery cults, 223
Mysticism, 23, 78, 139, 207, 225f

Natural law, 55, 129
Natural man, 28, 31f, 65, 86, 99f, 102, 111, 134, 190, 208, 236, 238
Natural revelation, 296, 315
Natural theology, 2, 221, 229
Naturalism, 257
Nature/freedom. See Antinomy
Navajo shamanism, 20
Neo-isolationism, 13f
Neo-orthodoxy, 231. See also Barth; Barthianism

Neo-platonism, 223
Neutrality, viii, 13, 32, 36, 43, 69f, 76, 78ff, 80, 86f, 93f, 98f, 102, 118f, 121f, 129, 159f, 165ff, 175, 198, 201, 204, 207, 215f, 220ff, 227f, 235, 288
New Deal, 12ff, 72
New Frontier, 20f
New Left, 8f
New morality, 119
Newark College of Engineering, 20
Newtonian revolution, 132
Nihilism, 5, 105
Nominalism, 130, 294
Novelty, 185
Number (God and), 182

Objectivity, 9, 36, 56f, 60, 63, 90, 105ff, 201, 215, 249, 281, 285, 289f
Occultism, 19f
One/many dualism
education and, 111
God and, 47, 306f
human personality, 47
mathematics and, 161, 172ff, 180ff, 183f
sociology, 156
Socrates, 199
Trinity, 108, 110, 297, 307
Ontology (math), 176f
Operationalism, 163
Optimism, x, 7, 60, 104, 157
Oracle at Delphi, 205
Order, 28, 111, 116, 127, 178, 201

Paradigms. See Presuppositions; Kuhn
Paradoxes, 169, 325, 327
Parents, 116
Passivity, 112f
Paul, 195f, 198
apologetic method, 208-20
suppressed truth, 30, 35. See also Romans 1:18ff
Pedagogy, 111f
Pensacola Christian School, 113n
Pensée, 18f
Pentagon, 9, 22
Performatives, 274, 276, 287
Personalism, 306f
Personality, 40, 47, 237, 309
Personality (ideal of), 8, 96, 136n, 145
Persuasion, 210, 265
Pessimism, 7, 60, 127
Philosophy
apostate, 228
first principles, 219
of history, 64f
limitations of, 224
problems of, 241
salvation, 197
St. Paul's, 209f
Pietism, ix, xi, 100

INDEX OF NAMES

faith, 201, 207
God = reason, 200
grace, 204
history, 199, 202
humanism, 201ff, 213
idealism, 195
induction, 199
intellect, 198f
intuition, 200
inwardness, 202f
Lewis, C. S., and, 232
logic, 205
mysticism, 207
neutrality, 198, 201, 204, 207
objectivity, 201
opinion, 199f, 203f
Oracle at Delphi, 205
philosopher, 195f
piety, 203
pragmatism, 195, 206
reason, 198, 207
recollection, 199
reincarnation, 197
religious calling of, 196f, 200, 205
revelation, 204, 206
salvation, 197
sense perception, 199f
skepticism, 201
soul (rational), 197, 200, 204, 206
standards, 204
verification, 220
virtue = knowledge, 198
voice (*daimon*), 206
Somerset, Duke of, 43
Spengler, Oswald, 61
Spens, 231
Sperry, Willard, 232
Spier, J. M., 179n
Stent, Gunther, 34f, 138n, 157
Stigler, George, 80
Steucho, 229
Strawson, P. F., 276, 280
Stuart, Lyle, 19
Suarez, 229
Siegfried, John, 76n

Tansill, Charles, 13f
Tatian, 221
Teilhard de Chardin, 21
Tertulian, 192, 223
Theodoret, 224
Theophilus, 221
Thoburn, Robert, 112n
Tholuck, 193, 230
Tindal, 229
Toland, 229
Towle, Katherine, 6
Trombley, William, 6
Troost, A., 101n
Tyrrell, 231
Tzschirner, 193

Vacca, Roberto, 156

Van Buren, 231
Van Til, Cornelius
  abnormal psychology, 49f
  abstract concerns, 299
  activism (psych.), 48
  Adam, 114, 302, 309
  alienation (God-man), 26, 44
  analogical personality, 49
  analogical reasoning, 34, 40, 64f, 74,
    110, 232, 236, 286, 294, 303, 320ff
  analogical system, 310ff
  analogy of being, 294
  anthropomorphisms, 311
  anti-system, 305ff
  antinomy. See *Subject Index*
  antitheism, 37, 102, 118
  apologetic method, 26, 30, 33, 49, 191,
    232ff
  apostate man, 99
  application-interpretation (theology),
    317f
  Aristotle, 294
  Arminianism, 49, 208, 236
  atonement (Barth), 294
  authority, 106, 208, 236, 303, 312
  autonomy, 30, 40, 66, 99, 126, 233,
    240, 292
  basic concerns, 294, 298f
  Barth, 140, 294
  Bible, 30, 36f, 236f, 302, 318, 324ff
  borrowed capital, 30, 34
  brute fact, 30, 33f, 306. See also facts
  Calvin, 84, 294
  central doctrine (none), 305
  certainty, 289
  Chalcedon, 310, 329
  chance, viii, 48, 109, 126, 291. See also
    contingency
  change, 84, 126
  child psychology, 47, 50
  Christianity, 34, 240
  circular reasoning, 33f, 37, 288. See
    also spiral reasoning
  Collingwood, R. G., 66f
  colored glasses analogy, vi
  common grace, 2, 294, 297, 309, 329
  conscience, 31
  consciousness, vi, 31f, 43f, 49
  contingency, 118, 126, 202f
  continuity/discontinuity, 312ff
  contradictions (apparent), 324ff
  covenant, 65
  covenant-breaker, 240. See also
    natural man
  creation, 2, 30, 34, 64, 69, 111, 115,
    158, 190, 289, 294, 300ff, 321
  Creator/creature distinction, 30, 113,
    294, 321
  crown rights, 51
  decree, 309
  deductivism, 294, 323ff
  deductions, 306, 324
  depravity, 296

INDEX OF SCRIPTURES

OLD TESTAMENT

NEW TESTAMENT

CPSIA information can be obtained
at www.ICGtesting.com
Printed in the USA
FSOW01n0424191017
39897FS

9 781879 998254